INTERNATIONAL LAW

FOURTH EDITION

By

REBECCA M.M. WALLACE, M.A., LL.B., Ph.D.

Professor of Law

LONDON · SWEET & MAXWELL · 2002

First Edition 1986
Second Impression 1990
Second Edition 1992
Second Impression 1994
Third Impression 1995
Third Edition 1997
Second Impression 1998
Fourth Edition 2002

Published in 2002 by
Sweet & Maxwell Limited
100 Avenue Road
Swiss Cottage
London NW3 3PF
(http:/ /www.sweetandmaxwell.co.uk)

Typeset by J&L Composition, Filey, North Yorkshire
Printed in Great Britain by MPG Books Ltd, Bodmin, Cornwall

A CIP catalogue record
for this book is available
from the British Library

ISBN 042 1768 800

INTERNATIONAL LAW

AUSTRALIA
Law Book Co.
Sydney

CANADA and USA
Carswell
Toronto

HONG KONG
Sweet & Maxwell Asia

NEW ZEALAND
Brookers
Wellington

SINGAPORE and MALAYSIA
Sweet & Maxwell Asia
Singapore and Kuala Lumpur

To My Mother

FOREWORD

I am very happy, once again to write this Foreword for this, the fourth, edition of Rebecca Wallace's *International Law*, as I admire Rebecca, the name (we are not related) and the book. As she points out in her Preface, the book has more than one use: in her words it is a "narrative companion" to a casebook and a "general introductory test" and I would add that it is a useful first place for a practitioner to come to for a quick orientation. I especially commend Rebecca for keeping the text so very up to date.

Writing as a professor, I give it very high marks as a "narrative companion" to any public international law casebook, even one with ample notes and text. I have used the prior editions in that way. Students want and need such a companion. It is compact and its coverage complete. For professors, it takes off the pressure, so that in class they can work out the problems they wish, emphasize with cases the legal method they want, even the Socratic, and avoid the didactic lecturing on topics such as nature and sources of law which will tend to leave many students cold.

I have also on occasion recommended the earlier editions to students who are not, *horribile dictu*, taking international law at all, but who wish a synoptic view of the field.

For the North American student or other reader, this book appears to have almost as much American material as British, citing U.S. cases, sources such as International Legal Materials and American (and Canadian) subjects. Thus, the discussion of such American doctrines as the Act of State and the functioning of the executive agreements in the American system is admirable.

The continued use of force on the one hand, and some of the hopes and difficulties surrounding the creation of a permanent International Criminal Court on the other hand, underline, if that is necessary, the abiding importance of law in the international system. The general reader may therefore find the book especially valuable and interesting. And in Rebecca's words to an earlier edition of the book, it is written "clearly and simply". The book also continues to serve the practitioner who wants an introduction in a nutshell to precise subjects of interest to him or her.

I welcome the fourth edition with enthusiasm.

September 1, 2002

Don Wallace Jr., Chairman,
International Law Institute;
Professor of Law,
Georgetown University Law Center;
Of counsel, Morgan, Lewis and Bockius,
Washington D.C.

PREFACE

In the five years which have lapsed since the third edition of this text, the most significant event etched on the memory of many are the events of September 11, 2001. In terms of the international legal perspective, what September 11 highlights and reinforces is the need for rules grounded in legal principle, guaranteed by the international rule of law. The international rule of law is that framework within which the substantive rules of international law operate and are applied. The international rule of law can accommodate breaches of international law but not capricious political behaviour. However, the intervening five years have witnessed other significant developments in the international arena, including the establishment of the International Criminal Court, the adoption of the International Law Commission of Draft Articles for State Responsibility for Internationally Wrongful Acts, a greater awareness of human rights by the business community reflecting the Global Compact, the utilisation of the Law of the Sea dispute settlement mechanism and the agreement between the United States and Russia on the reduction of nuclear arms.

This edition, like its predecessors, paints with a broad brush the basic principles of the international legal system, thereby providing the reader with (i) a lucid and comprehensive exposition of the basic precepts necessary for the understanding of the international legal process; and (ii) a general and integrated overview of contemporary international law. The text remains an introduction to international law. It can stand alone or be used as a narrative companion to the many in-depth source texts which are now available, including D.J. Harris's *Cases and Materials on International Law* (1998).

The production of this edition was greatly facilitated by the research assistance of Jo Kenny and Anne Holliday, to whom I extend my thanks and appreciation. Also, much valued have been the encouragement and understanding patience of the editorial staff at Sweet & Maxwell. As before, principal thanks are due to those across the globe who, through the continued use of the text, made this fourth edition necessary.

The law presented is as of July 31, 2002.

Rebecca M.M. Wallace, Professor of Law,
August, 2002

CONTENTS

TABLE OF CASES

TABLE OF PRINCIPAL
INTERNATIONAL CONVENTIONS

Table of Principal International Conventions

Table of Principal International Conventions

TABLE OF STATUTES

ABBREVIATIONS

A.C.	Appeal Cases (U.K.) 1891–
A.D.	Appellate Division, New York Supreme Court
A.D. 2d	Appellate Division Reports, New York Supreme Court, Second Series
A.J.LL.	American Journal of International Law
All E.R.	All England Reports, 1935–
A.S.I.L.	American Society of International Law
A.U.	African Union. (Replacing the *Organisation of African States*, see below)
B.F.S.P.	British and Foreign State Papers, 1812–
Burr.	Burrow's Reports (King's Bench, U.K.), 1757–71
B.Y.I.L.	British Yearbook of International Law
Cd., Cmnd., Cmnd.	U.K. Command Papers 1900–18, 1919–56, 1956– respectively
Ch.	Chancery Reports (U.K.), 1891–
C.M.L.R.	Common Market Law Reports
Cranch.	United States Supreme Court Reports, 1801–15
C.W.I.L.J.	Californian Western International Law Journal
D.P.P.	Director of Public Prosecution
E.C.J.	European Court of Justice
E.C.R.	European Court Reports, 1954–
E.H.R.R.	European Human Rights Reports
E.J.I.L.	European Journal of International Law
E.R.	English Reports
Eur. Court H.R.	European Court of Human Rights

F (2d)	Federal Reporter, Second Series (US), 1924–
F (J)	Fraser, Justiciary Cases (Scotland), 1898–1906
F Supp	Federal Supplement (US), 1932–
G.A.	General Assembly (United Nations)
G.A.O.R.	General Assembly Official Records
Hague Recueil	Recueil des cours de l'Academie de droit international
Hudson	International Legislation
Hudson World Court Reports	(4 Vols, 1934–43)
I.C.C.	International Criminal Court
I.C.J.	International Court of Justice
I.C.J. Rep.	International Court of Justice Reports, 1947–
I.C.L.Q.	International and Comparative Law Quarterly
I.C.T.R.	International Tribunal for the Prosecution of Persons Responsible for Genocide and Other Serious Violations of International Humanitarian Law Committed in the Territory of Rwanda and Rwandan Citizens Responsible for Genocide and Other Such Violations Committed in the Territory of Neighbouring States, between January 1, 1994 and December 31, 1994.
I.C.T.Y.	International Tribunal for the Prosecution of Persons Responsible for Serious Violations of Humanitarian Law Committed in the Territory of the Former Yugoslavia
I.J.R.I.	International Journal of Refugee Law.
I.L.C.	International Law Commission
I.L.M.	International Legal Materials, 1962–
I.L.R.	International Law Reports
I.M.F.	International Monetary Fund
I.T.L.O.S.	International Tribunal for the Law of the Sea

J.L.S.S.	Journal of the Law Society of Scotland
K.B.	King's Bench (U.K.), 1901–52
L.N.O.J.	League of Nations Official Journal
L.N.T.S.	League of Nations Treaty Series, 1920–45
L.Q. Rev.	Law Quarterly Review, 1885–
Moore Int. Arb.	International Arbitration, 5 Vols, 1898
N.A.T.O.	North Atlantic Treaty Organisation
N.E.	North Eastern Reporter, 1885–1936
N.Y.S.	New York Supplement Reporter, 1888
N.Y.S. 2d	New York Supplement, Second Series, 1937–
O.A.S.	Organisation of American States
O.A.U.	Organisation of African States. (Now known as the African Union, see above)
O.J.	Official Journal of the European Communities
Oppenheim	L. Oppenheim, *International Law*, Vols 1 and 2
P.	Court of Probate
P.C.	Privy Council
P.C.A.	Permanent Court of Arbitration
P.C.I.J.	Permanent Court of International Justice
P.C.I.J. Rep., ser. A.	Permanent Court of International Justice, Judgments and Orders, 1922–30
P.C.I.J. Rep., ser. A/B.	Advisory Opinions, Judgements and Orders, 1931–40
P.C.I.J. Rep., ser. B	Advisory Opinions, 1922–30
P.D.	Probate Division Reports (U.K.), 1875–90
Pet.	Peter's, United States Supreme Court Reports, 1828–42
Q.B.	Queen's Bench Reports (U.K.), 1891–1901, 1952–
Q.B.D.	Queen's Bench Division Reports (U.K.), 1875–80
R.I.A.A.	Reports of International Arbitral Awards, 1948–
S.C.	Security Council

S.C.O.R.	Security Council Official Records
S.C.R.	Supreme Court Reports (Canada), 1876–
S.L.T.	Scots Law Times
T.I.A.S.	Treaties and Other International Acts Series (US), 1950–30
T.L.R.	Times Law Reports (U.K.), 1841–1952
U.K.T.S.	United Kingdom Treaty Series
U.N.	United Nations
U.N.C.C.	United Nations Compensation Committee
U.N.H.C.R.	United Nations High Commission for Refugees.
U.N.T.S.	United Nations Treaty Series, 1946–
U.S.	United States Supreme Court Reports, 1875–
U.S.C.	United States Code
U.S. Dept. State Bull.	United States Department of State Bulletin
U.S.T.	United States Treaties
U.S.T.S.	United States Treaty Series
Ves.	Vesey Juniors Chancery Reports (UK), 1789–1816
Whiteman	Digest of International Law, 14 Vols, 1936–73
W.H.O.	World Health Organisation
W.L.R.	*Weekly Law Reports* (UK), 1953–
W.T.O.	World Trade Organisation
Y.B.I.L.C.	Yearbook of the International Law Commission

1. INTRODUCTION

The subject-matter of this text is international law, that is, public international law as distinct from private international law (conflict of laws).[1]

DEFINITION

Today, international law[2] refers to those rules and norms which regulate the conduct of states and other entities which at any time are recognised as being endowed with international personality,[3] for example international organisations and individuals, in their relations with each other. Such a definition takes account of international law's "youthfulness" and recognises that new actors may be required to participate on the international stage. States, although they remain the primary subjects of international law, are no longer its exclusive subjects as they once were. International

---

[1] Private international law (conflict of laws) is a system of law which is part of states' domestic law and which is utilised to determine how conflicts of laws and jurisdiction are to be resolved.

[2] The term "international law" is something of a misnomer, as statehood and nationhood are not necessarily synonymous.

[3] International personality is dealt with in Ch.4.

law was initially concerned exclusively with regulating inter-
state relations and then only in respect of diplomatic relations and
the conduct of war. This is no longer true.

International law has expanded both in terms of its subjects and
its content. Major problems of international concern have been
tackled collectively by states. This has proved, for example, more
resource effective than attempting individual state action. The
consequence has been a proliferation in the number of international organisations in the years since 1945. Modern technology
has brought states and their populations into closer and more
frequent contact with each other, and rules have evolved to
regulate such contact. The subject-matter of international law has
correspondingly expanded, and international law now has within
its ambit issues which were traditionally regarded as being exclusively within a state's domestic jurisdiction, for example treatment
of one's own nationals. This has had repercussions for individuals.
They are now recognised as possessing some, albeit limited, international personality. The traditional definition of international
law, namely a body of rules governing the relations of independent
states in times of peace and war, is too rigid and outmoded. A
definition of international law must accommodate the developments which the international legal system witnessed in the
twentieth century, and must reflect international law as it is today.

NATURE AND CHARACTERISTICS OF INTERNATIONAL LAW

Is international law law?

The question is not one which the author intends to explore. Any
analysis of the question presupposes a definition of law, and is
therefore one more suited for a jurisprudence class than an international law class. It is sufficient to say here that international law
is law. States acknowledge it as such. Some states refer to international law in their constitutions. States like to be seen acting in
accordance with it, and legal advisers are employed to formulate,
present and defend their state's position in international law.

Others, while recognising international law, purport to deny its
effectiveness. What those who are derogatory of international law
fail to appreciate is that their expectations of international law may
be unrealistic. Law cannot coerce states in matters which are primarily political. International law cannot of itself and by itself dic-
tate the policies of states.

If hostilities break out international law is criticised for not maintaining international peace, yet international law cannot prevent
its own violation any more than the municipal criminal law can
prevent crimes being committed or contract law can prevent

contracts being broken. In other words, the fact that law is violated does not in itself negate a legal system's effectiveness. Law is not a solution in itself, but is rather a means of handling a particular situation. International law is concerned with promoting international co-operation, and achieving co-existence amongst states. When international law breaks down, the fault lies not with international law itself, but with those who operate within the international legal system.

International law receives a bad press, especially when it breaks down. The issues involved are internationally politically sensitive, and so are newsworthy. International law, however, functions very effectively on a day-to-day level. Today, we can switch on the television, and see events "live" from anywhere in the world. Mail is sent and delivered throughout the world. International travel is an everyday occurrence. Such happenings are taken for granted, but they are only made possible through the efficient functioning of international law, whose "low-key" operation is generally overlooked, especially as the media do not regard it as newsworthy.

What are the characteristics of international law?

International law is not imposed on states—there is no international legislature. The international legal system is decentralised and founded essentially on consensus. International law is made primarily in one of two ways: through the practice of states (customary international law) and through agreements entered into by states (treaties).[4] Once international rules are established, they have an imperative character and cannot be unilaterally modified at will by states. The absence of a strong enforcement machinery is highlighted by sceptics as a weakness of international law. There is no international police force, nor is there an international court with compulsory jurisdiction to which states are required to submit. However, the creation of the Permanent International Criminal Court, and the entry into force of the Rome Statute, demonstrate the International communities' commitment to the rule of law. That is not to say, however, that international law is not effective. Sanctions are available which may be employed and which may affect a state's conduct. If international law is violated, there are a number of self-help measures which the victim state may adopt, for example, a treaty may be suspended or terminated, or the assets of an offending state may be frozen. The United Nations Security Council may authorise economic sanctions while force may be used in defined circumstances.

---

[4] See Ch.2, "Sources".

Public opinion can also be an effective sanction. States want to be seen to be adhering to international law: why otherwise do they go to considerable efforts to justify their particular position in international law?

There is an international court (the International Court of Justice) to which states can refer their disputes for settlement. States, however, must agree to submit to the court; there is no legal compulsion on them to do so.

The role of reciprocity in international law observance should not be minimised. It is in a state's own interest to respect, for example, the territorial sovereignty of other states as they in turn will respect its territorial sovereignty.

The international legal system is intrinsically different from municipal law. The principal participants of the international legal system, *i.e.* states are all treated as equally sovereign.[5] The international community is composed not of a homogeneous grouping of states, but rather a heterogeneous group of some 190 states, which differ politically, economically, culturally and ideologically.

States need to co-exist. International law was conceived and born out of such a need, and thus is designed to promote international peace and harmonisation. A system which sought to characterise one state as "guilty" and one as "innocent" would not facilitate the realisation of international peace. International law must be conciliatory rather than adversarial.

The international legal system is a young, immature system which is constantly evolving and developing. It is not simply lawyers' law. Politics play an influential role. Consequently, the study of international law facilitates a greater comprehension of, and gives an insight into, the functioning of the international community.

THE DEVELOPMENT OF INTERNATIONAL LAW

Some observations

International law as a system is of recent origin.[6] Modern international law stems from the rise of the secular sovereign state in Western Europe. As in any community, law was required to regulate the relations of states with each other. The rules of war and those on diplomatic immunity were the earliest expression of international law. The Age of Discovery in the sixteenth and

---

[5] This is a legal fiction, as obviously some states carry more weight then others in the international community.
[6] Although the embryo of international concepts was apparent within Greek city states, *e.g.* it was recognised that citizens of states in other territories had rights. There was, however, no concept of an international community as such.

seventeenth centuries necessitated the evolution of rules governing the acquisition of territory. At the same time, the principle of the freedom of the seas was articulated. International law grew out of necessity, namely as already said, in response to the need of states to co-exist.

International law set the parameters of state action; within these parameters establishing national competence, states enjoyed freedom of action. International law continued to expand as international engagement increased and, by the nineteenth century had become, geographically at least, a universal system. It remained, however, rooted in western European traditions and values and in its concept and content it maintained this European bias. The twentieth century witnessed major changes which have had repercussions for the international legal system. The sovereign independent state has been challenged; universal war has brought devastation twice; previous colonial territories have attained independence. The twentieth century has seen a greater emphasis on international co-operation, whereby states work together rather than individually. Matters once considered exclusively within domestic jurisdiction are now susceptible to international regulation. The use of force has been prohibited except in defined circumstances.

International law is no longer the preserve of some 50 states, but rather embraces some 190 states; nor is it an exclusive western club. International law operates against the backcloth of globalisation, in which new actors express views and adopt stances different from those of the old states. The existence of international law *per se* is not challenged but the substantive content of its expression has been challenged and continues to be so, for example the measure of compensation to be awarded in respect of the expropriation of an alien's property and, within the field of human rights, the articulation of "third generation" rights, the rights of women and children and, in respect of the environment, deforesterisation. The European bias of international law has been destroyed. Political ideologies other than those of the capitalist are now heard within international fora, for example the communist and socialist. Modern technology has not only brought states into more frequent contact with each other, but has created new areas for international regulation, for example outer space, the deep seabed, and the internet, which has precipitated the development of international computer crime. In addition, international law has had to meet new challenges—challenges which demand an international response either at governmental level or, for example, by way of an international organisation as individual state action proves to be inadequate and deficient. Contemporary examples which have been the subject of international regulation are the environment, human rights and terrorism. International regulation will only be effective if states respond by pursuing domestic policies which accommodate prevailing international opinion.

The twentieth century for international law has been one of unparalleled expansion. It is on the international legal system as it exists today, at the beginning of the twenty-first century, that this text focuses.

2. SOURCES

Rules and norms of any legal system derive authority from their source.[1] The "sources" articulate what the law is and where it can be found. In a developed municipal legal system, sources may be readily identifiable in the form, for example, of Parliamentary legislation and judicial decisions. However, on the international plane, there is neither an international legislature which passes international legislation, nor is there an international court to which all members of the international community must compulsorily submit. Furthermore, the international legal system does not, unlike the majority of municipal legal systems, possess a written constitution. There is no international constitution identifying the principal organs of government, investing them with authority and defining the scope of their power and the procedures by which such power may be executed.

In the absence of such "law-giving" sources, how is the legal quality of alleged rules of international law assessed?

A pragmatic response to the question has been found in the provisions of Art.38 of the Statute of the International Court of

---

1 "Sources" may be interpreted in a variety of ways, *e.g.* the underlying reason why laws develop, but here its meaning is confined to that given in the text.

Justice. Art.38 does not mention the word "sources", but rather spells out how the court is to decide disputes which may come before it for settlement. The Statute provides that the court is to apply:

> "(a) international conventions, whether general or particular, establishing rules expressly recognised by the contesting states;
> (b) international custom, as evidence of a general practice accepted as law;
> (c) the general principles of law recognised by civilised nations;
> (d) subject to the provisions of Art.59, judicial decisions and the teachings of the most highly qualified publicists of the various nations, as subsidiary means for the determination of rules of law."

Sources may be characterised as formal or material. Briefly, formal sources constitute what the law is, whereas material sources only identify where the law may be found. Hence, Art.38(1)(a)–(c) (treaties, custom and general principles) are formal sources, whereas Art.38(1)(d) (judicial decisions and juristic teachings) are material sources.

Art.38 is therefore primarily a direction to the International Court of Justice on how disputes coming before it should be tackled. Nevertheless, in spite of the absence of the term "sources", Art.38 is regarded as an authoritative statement on the sources of international law. Art.38 does not stipulate that it is establishing a hierarchy, but it is self-evident that Art.38 is nonetheless establishing a hierarchy of procedure for the application of international law in the settlement of international disputes. Initially, existing relevant treaty provisions between the parties to the dispute must be applied. In the event of no prevailing provision, a custom which is accepted as legally binding should be applied. If neither a treaty provision nor a custom can be identified then "general principles as recognised by civilised nations" may be invoked; while finally, at least under Art.38, judicial decisions and judicial writings may be utilised as a means of determining the rules of international law.

Each category of law spelt out in Art.38 will be examined. Custom, although cited second in Art.38, as it historically preceded treaties, will be considered initially.

CUSTOM

In any society, rules of "acceptable" behaviour develop at an early stage and the international community was no exception. States in their relations with each other did, for whatever motives, what they wanted to do rather than what they agreed to do. However, with increasing contact between states, certain norms of behaviour crystallised into rules of customary international law. Custom, through the absence of an international executive and legislature, has exercised an influential role in the formation of international law. In a mature legal system, custom is considered cumbersome and relatively unimportant, whereas in the international field it has, at least until recently, been a dynamic source of law and its contribution is still witnessed in the provisions of many treaties which mirror previously established rules of international customary law

Definition of custom

What is meant by custom? Custom in international law is a practice followed by those concerned because they feel legally obliged to behave in such a way. Custom must be distinguished from mere usage, such as behaviour which may be done out of courtesy, friendship or convenience rather than out of legal obligation or a feeling that non-compliance would produce legal consequences, for example sanctions imposed by other members of the international community.

How is custom differentiated from behaviour that is motivated by reasons other than legal obligation? A rule of customary international law derives its law hallmark through the possession of two elements: (i) a material and (ii) a psychological element. The material element refers to the behaviour and practice of states, whereas the psychological element is the subjective conviction held by states that the behaviour in question is compulsory and not discretionary.

Accordingly, any alleged rule of customary international law must be assessed as to its (i) material and (ii) psychological elements.

Material element

The material element refers to the behaviour of states, but does that behaviour itself have to satisfy certain criteria? Has it to be practised for a certain length of time? Must it be indulged in frequently or is one act sufficient? Must the behaviour be consistently practised or may there be some divergences from the norm? Must the behaviour be universally practised by all states?

Finally, what, for the purposes of customary international law, constitutes state practice?

Duration of practice. There is no set time limit and no demand that the practice should be engaged in since "time immemorial". The fact that a practice has been engaged in only for a brief period of time will not in itself be a bar to the formation of a customary rule, provided that the other requirements of custom are met. The relative unimportance of time if other criteria are satisfied was highlighted by the International Court of Justice in the *North Sea Continental Shelf Cases*,[2] in which it stated that:

> "... Although the passage of only a short period of time is not necessarily, or of itself, a bar to the formation of a new rule of customary international law ... an indispensable requirement would be that within the period in question, short though it might be, State practice ... should have been both extensive and virtually uniform in the sense of the provision invoked;—and should moreover have occurred in such a way as to show a general recognition that a rule of law or legal obligation is involved."[3]

The length of time required to establish a rule of customary international law will depend upon other factors pertinent to the alleged rule. If, for example, the rule is dealing with subject-matter in which there are no previously established rules, then the duration of the practice will require to be less than if there is an existing rule to be overruled. Time has also become less important as international communication has improved. It is now much easier to assess a state's response to an alleged rule than it was in the past. Time thus may be of little importance in assessing a state's behaviour, and its importance in any given case depends on other factors peculiar to the activity concerned and these will now be looked at below.

Extent of state practice. The International Court of Justice in the *Asylum Case*[4] held that before state practice could be acknowledged as law, it had to be in accordance with a "constant and uniform usage" practised by the states in question.[5] Of course, although a particular pattern of behaviour may be engaged in frequently, it does not follow that the conduct is being practised

[2] I.C.J.Rep. 1969 at 3.
[3] *ibid.* at 43.
[4] I.C.J.Rep. 1950 at 266.
[5] *ibid.* at 277.

out of any legal obligation. Similarly, an activity engaged in, albeit infrequently, may be practised because of a legal compulsion to do so. The importance of frequency of practice will depend upon the circumstances surrounding each alleged rule. For instance, a state which is able to cite two examples of state practice to support its contention that the practice is law, will be in a better position than the state which can cite no such examples. However, a more significant factor than frequency is the consistency of practice. In other words, do those states engaging in the practice in question behave in a like manner, thus demonstrating conformity?

The court's judgment in the *Asylum Case* is again instructive. In that case, the court maintained that there was too much fluctuation and discrepancy in both the practice of and the views expressed regarding diplomatic asylum for a rule of custom to have been established. Consequently, the court concluded that it was impossible to find "any constant and uniform usage accepted as law".[6] The existence of diverging practice proved to be the stumbling block in that particular practice's evolution into law.

Inconsistency *per se*, however, is not sufficient to negate the crystallisation of a rule into customary international law. Any inconsistency must be analysed and assessed in the light of factors such as subject-matter, the identity of the states practising the inconsistency, the number of states involved and whether or not there are existing established rules with which the alleged rule conflicts. Inconsistency of practice is explored in greater depth below, when the question of how customary international law may be amended or modified is discussed.

How many states must be involved in a particular activity before the practice is accepted as law? Universal practice is fortunately not necessary. Art.38(1)(b) speaks not of universal practice, but of a general practice. A practice can be general even if it is not universally followed, and there is no precise formula indicating how widespread a practice must be. What in fact is of more importance than the number of states involved is the attitude of those states whose interests are actually affected. It is the stance adopted by such states which is relevant and which has to be considered, a fact which was emphasised in the *North Sea Continental Shelf Cases*:

"..., an indispensable requirement would be that within the period in question, ..., state practice, including that of states

[6] I.C.J.Rep. 1950.

whose interests are specially affected, should have been both
extensive and virtually uniform . . . ."[7]

Thus, it transpires that the number of states is less consequential
than is the identity of the states involved. Each alleged rule must
therefore be examined and assessed in context. In every activity
certain states carry more weight than others—their interest is
greater than that of other states and their attitude to an alleged
rule is of importance. If an alleged rule is to attain legitimacy, a
favourable response from "leading" states is a pre-requisite.
Hence, for example, Britain's contribution in the nineteenth century to sea law and the role of both the United States and the
Soviet Union in developing the law of outer space. In any given
area, the participation of certain states is needed more than others
before an alleged rule may be transformed into customary international law.

Numbers are more important when the custom is a local,
regional one, involving fewer states than general customary law. A
regional custom is of a more contractual nature than a general one
and therefore requires to be positively acknowledged and supported by all the states involved. Hence, the International Court's
emphasis on a "constant and uniform usage" in the *Asylum Case*.

Can a state choose not to be bound by a rule of customary international law? If a state opposes a rule of customary international
law and shows its opposition to that rule from the time of the
rule's inception, then the state will not be bound. Opposition,
however, must be demonstrated from the outset. Only then can
the state concerned not incur liability. In the *Anglo-Norwegian
Fisheries Case*, the court held that if the particular rule in question
was one of international law, it would be "inapplicable as against
Norway insomuch as she has always opposed any attempt to
apply it to the Norwegian coast".[8]

Dissent which is expressed only after the rule has become
established is too late to prevent the state from being bound, and
likewise, early opposition by a state to a rule, if abandoned, loses
its effectiveness. Dissention, of course, only prevents a rule from
becoming binding on the dissenter and does not affect the rule's
application on other states.

Why is dissent important? Expression of dissent is vital
because attaining a state's consent is in reality fictitious. Being
difficult to prove, consent is inferred, and silence, although it may

[7] Above, n. 2 at 43.
[8] I.C.J.Rep. 1951 116 at 131. Arguably the opportunities for states to opt out of
     customary international law are fewer today than previously, given the increase
     in the use of treaties as a medium of international regulation.

stem from indifference, will be regarded as acquiescence and will serve to reinforce the practice in question as law.

A state which enters the international system after a practice has ripened into an established rule is bound by it, regardless of whether it agrees with it or not. Such a state may seek though to amend or modify the rule in question.

How may this occur? Initially, it can be said that it is easier for custom to develop if there are no pre-existing conflicting rules, for example, in the exploitation of outer space, rules of behaviour quickly evolved because not only were there no pre-existing norms regulating behaviour, there were only two states, the United States and the Soviet Union, who were actively employed in that exploitation. The position is different and more complicated if there exist established rules of behaviour. The "new" rule's future will depend on the number indulging in the behaviour contrary to the established rule relative to the number protesting against the creation of the new rule.

It is not to be expected that in the practice of states the application of the rules in question should have been perfect, in the sense that states should have refrained, with complete consistency, from the use of force or from intervention in each other's internal affairs. The court does not consider that for a rule to be considered as customary, the corresponding practice must be in absolutely rigorous conformity with the rule. In order to deduce the existence of customary rules, the court deems it sufficient that the conduct of states should, in general, be consistent with such rules, and that instances of state conduct inconsistent with a given rule should generally have been treated as breaches of that rule, not as indications of the recognition of a new rule.[9]

This naturally raises the question of how customary international law may be amended or modified if conflicting behaviour acts as a hindrance to the crystallisation of an alleged rule into law. Contradictory behaviour has the effect of throwing uncertainty on the apparently established rule, which in turn produces ambiguity regarding the entire law on the subject-matter, a fact which was highlighted in the *Fisheries Jurisdiction Case (United Kingdom v Iceland) Merits*,[10] heard by the International Court of Justice in 1974, when in a Joint Separate Opinion Judges Forster, Bengzon, Arechaga, Singh and Rudha expressed the view that:

"If the law relating to fisheries constituted a subject on which there were clear indications of what precisely is the rule of

[9] *Military and Paramilitary Activities In and Against Nicaragua (Nicaragua v The United States) Case (Merits)* I.C.J.Rep. 1986 14 at 98.
[10] I.C.J.Rep. 1974 at 3.

international law in existence, it may then have been possible
to disregard altogether the legal significance of certain proposals which advocate changes or improvements in a system
of law which is considered to be unjust or inadequate. But
this is not the situation. There is at the moment great
uncertainty as to the existing customary law on account of
the conflicting and discordant practice of states. Once the
uncertainty of such a practice is admitted, the impact of the
aforesaid official pronouncements, declarations and proposals have an unsettling effect on the crystallisation of a still
evolving customary law on the subject."[11]

It is also possible, as is reflected in the above Opinion, that while
states may behave in contradiction to an established rule, the conflicting behaviour may itself be inconsistently expressed. In such
circumstances, change, if it is to come about, will take longer than
if the states are united in what they want the new rule to be. If
support for the rule is wide and consistent, then the acceptance of
it as law will be relatively smooth and rapid. Similarly, if there is
substantial opposition to the "new rule", the established accepted
rule will retain its law character. However, if the members in
favour of the established rule and the new rule are evenly
divided, then a period of ambiguity as characterised by the court
and as illustrated in the law relating to fishing limits will follow.
Indeed, there may be a time when two rules of customary law
may exist side by side. International customary law can accommodate change, but how quickly that change will occur is
dependent upon the response of states to the proposed alteration
of the law. There may well be a period in the change process when
the established rule and the new rule will be seen to exist simultaneously, a situation which can make it difficult to determine
where the old law ends and the new one begins.

This has the advantage, particularly if states are agreed upon
the change they want, of allowing flexibility, but the disadvantage
of creating uncertainty as to what the law is at any given time.

State practice. Finally, what, for the purposes of establishing
customary international law, constitutes evidence of state practice? Treaties, diplomatic correspondence, statements by national
legal advisers in domestic and international fora are amongst the
indicators of state practice. This was endorsed by Ammoun J. in
his Separate Opinion delivered in the *Barcelona Traction, Light and
Power Company Case*,[12] when he stated that:

[11] I.C.J.Rep. 1974 at 48.
[12] (Second Phase) I.C.J.Rep. 1970 at 3.

"to return to State practice as manifested within international organisations and conferences, it cannot be denied, with regard to the resolutions which emerge therefrom, or better, with regard to the votes expressed therein in the name of States, that these amount to precedents contributing to the formation of custom."[13]

Notwithstanding these indicators of state practice, overt state practice continues to be important, as was emphasised by the International Court of Justice in the *Continental Shelf Case (Libya v Malta)*[14] when the Court stated:

"It is of course axiomatic that the material of customary international law is to be looked for primarily in the actual practice and *opinio juris* of states even though multilateral conventions may have an important role to play in defining and recording rules, deriving from custom or indeed in developing them."[15]

A state's response to a particular resolution may be dictated by the occasion and circumstances pertaining at the time and this should also be borne in mind when utilising resolutions and the like as evidence of the development of practice into law.[16]

This was acknowledged in *Military and Paramilitary Activities in and against Nicaragua (Nicaragua v The United States) Case*[17] where documentary evidence before the court included statements by "high-ranking official political figures, sometimes indeed of the highest rank" which could be "of particular probative value when they acknowledge facts or conduct unfavourable to the state represented by the person who made them".[18] Nevertheless, the court stated that it was natural that such statements should be treated with "caution".[19]

Practice in itself does not establish custom. An alleged rule of customary international law has to manifest not only a material element, but a psychological element, otherwise known as *opinio juris*.

---

[13] *ibid.* at 303. As to the role of Resolutions in providing evidence of *opinio juris*, see statements in the *Nicaragua Case* below, n.22.

[14] I.C.J.Rep. 1985 at p.13.

[15] *ibid.* at 29–30. See, also, the view of D'Amato in *The Concept of Custom in International Law* (1971), p.88.

[16] See, *e.g.* J. Brierly, *The Law of Nations* (1963), p.4.

[17] Above n.9, p.4.

[18] *ibid.* at p.41.

[19] Above n.9, p.41.

Opinio juris sive necessitatis

States in their relations with each other engage in behaviour other than that which is required of them legally. If certain rules are to evolve into law, it is necessary to distinguish rules which are regarded as legally obligatory from those which are not. State behaviour on the international plane may be prompted by reasons of mere courtesy, convenience or tradition rather than by legal obligation. Similarly, humanitarian considerations are insufficient in themselves to generate legal rights and obligations and the International Court of Justice as "a court of law" is competent to take account of moral principles only in so far as these are given a sufficient expression in legal form.[20] *Opinio juris* was introduced as a legal formula in an attempt to distinguish legal rules from mere social usage, and it refers to the subjective belief maintained by states that a particular practice is legally required of them. A practice which is generally followed but which states feel they are legally free to disregard at any time cannot be characterised as law. In the words of the International Court of Justice:

> "... not only must the acts concerned `amount to a settled practice', but they must also be accompanied by the *opinio juris sive necessitatis*. Either the States taking such action or other States in a position to react to it must have behaved so that their conduct is evidence of a belief that this practice is rendered obligatory by the existence of a rule of law requiring it. The need for such a belief, *i.e.* the existence of a subjective element, is implicit in the very notion of the *opinio juris sive necessitatis*."[21]

As the court highlighted in the *Nicaragua Case, opinio juris* may, albeit with due caution, be deduced from, *inter alia*, the attitude of the parties and states towards General Assembly resolutions (and in the instant case particularly Resolution 2625 (XXV) entitled "Declaration on Principles of International Law concerning Friendly Relations and Co-operation among States in accordance with the Charter of the United Nations"). It was emphasised that the effect of consent to the text of such Resolutions cannot be understood as merely that of "reiteration or elucidation" of the treaty commitment undertaken in the Charter. On the contrary, it

[20] *South West Africa Cases (Second Phase)* I.C.J.Rep. 1966 6 at 34.
[21] Above n.9 pp.108–109.

may be understood as an acceptance of the validity of the rule or set of rules declared by the Resolutions.[22]

The problem with *opinio juris* is one of proof. It is frequently difficult to determine when the transformation into law has taken place. How can a state's conviction be proved to exist? Essentially, what must be proved is the state's acceptance, recognition or acquiescence in the binding character of the rule in question. The onus of proof is on the state relying upon the custom (it is the party alleging the existence of custom which must demonstrate that the custom is so established that the other party is bound by it) and insufficient evidence of *opinio juris* is fatal to a case, as for example in the *Lotus Case*[23] and the *North Sea Continental Shelf Cases*.

In the *Lotus Case*, although France identified previous instances where in practice the victim's flag state had refrained from criminal prosecution, France, in the court's view, failed to demonstrate that states refrained from prosecuting because they had been conscious of a duty requiring them to do so.

Similarly, in the *North Sea Continental Shelf Cases*, the International Court of Justice maintained that, although the principle of equidistance was employed in the delimitation of the continental shelf between adjacent states, there was no evidence:

> "that they so acted because they felt legally compelled to draw them in this way by reason of a rule of customary law obliging them to do so—especially considering that they might have been motivated by other factors".[24]

Opinio juris and state practice are complementary in the creation of customary international law.

How may customary international law accommodate change if *opinio juris* demands behaviour in accordance with the law? How may new rules evolve if activity contrary to the established rules is prohibited?

If too rigid a view was taken of *opinio juris*, then obviously the law would become stunted and in time deficient. States, however, do act contrary to established rules and do so in the belief that the

---

[22] pp.99–100. The court took US' support of the Sixth International Conference of American states condemning aggression, ratification of the Montevideo Convention on the Rights and Duties of states 1933 and the Declaration on the Principles Governing the Mutual Relations of states participating in the Conference on the Security and Co-operation in Europe as further evidence of an expression of *opinio juris*. The court's stance that *opinio juris* could be deduced from the acceptance by states of GA Resolutions has been criticised, *e.g.* D'Amato, "Trashing Customary International Law" (1987) 81 A.J.I.L. 101.

[23] P.C.I.J.Rep., ser.A, no.10 (1927).

[24] Above n.2, pp.44–45.

new behaviour, if not already law, is about to become law. What will determine the future of such behaviour—whether it in fact does become law or withers—is the response of other states. Their reaction determines whether the new practice gains the necessary *opinio juris*.

Finally, mention must be made of another category of custom known by the somewhat anomalous term of "instant custom". The term is anomalous, being as it is self-contradictory, but what it is used to describe certainly defies classification as traditional custom. It refers not to behaviour, which is constant, uniform and frequently engaged in, but rather to spontaneous activity practised by a *great* number of states acting as they want to act. Instant custom is relatively rare. Two examples of "instant customary law" are the doctrine of the continental shelf, originating from President Truman's Proclamation in 1945, and the unilateral seaward extension throughout the 1970s by coastal states. The doctrine of the continental shelf became established as customary international law on the basis of assertions (that is, claims of exclusive rights and denial of access to others) and general acquiescence, although in fact there was an absence of much actual practice, since for a long time, continental shelf mining was neither technologically nor economically feasible. The exclusive economic zone became established customary international law in the 1970s. Coastal states particularly concerned with controlling the exploitation and conservation of fishery resources, rather than wait for agreement with UNCLOS III,[25] increasingly took unilateral action and extended their sovereign rights beyond their territorial sea to a maximum limit of 200 miles.[26] "Instant custom" may appear an unsatisfactory term, but the activity it describes, while not fitting into the mould of traditional custom, still falls under the general umbrella of custom, rather than under any "new" source of law and, accordingly, the term in the absence of any other will have to suffice. As stressed already, "instant custom" is an exception from the norm.

Concluding on custom, therefore, it is seen that the character of customary international law is such that uncertainty and ambiguity may prevail regarding the law on any given subject at a particular time. Today, the number of states participating on the international plane has increased from 51 in the middle of the last century to almost 200, and the subject-matter of international law

---

[25] Third United Nations Conference on the Law of the Sea.
[26] See 1982 Convention on the Law of the Sea, Arts 55 and 56. The General Assembly Resolution on the Granting of Independence to Colonial Territories and Peoples (GA Res.1514) led to a significant number of African states being accorded political independence—another example of instant custom?

now extends beyond the traditional realm of diplomatic relations and the rules of warfare and has broken through the national hold on such issues as human rights and welfare law.

In the light of this, coupled with the desire of states to know what they have agreed to, treaties are increasingly utilised as the means for regulating international relations.

TREATIES

Art.38(a) does not mention the term "treaties", but refers to "any international conventions, whether general or particular, establishing rules expressly recognised by the contesting States". The effect of this direction to the court is that, if an existing treaty provision pertains between the parties to the dispute before the court, then if relevant, the treaty provision must be applied.

A treaty, although it may be identified as comparable in some degree to a Parliamentary Statute within municipal law, differs from the latter, in that it only applies to those states which have agreed to its terms, and normally a treaty does not have universal application. In other words opting out, which is not available to individuals under national law, is available to the members of the international community.

Treaties are only examined here in so far as they constitute a source of law.[27] Treaties, as Art.38(a) infers, may be between two states (bipartite) or between several states (multipartite).[28]

A distinction is sometimes drawn between law-making treaties ("traite-lois") and "treaty contracts" ("traite-contracts"). The essence of the distinction lies apparently in the fact that "treaty contracts", being agreements between relatively few parties can only create particular law between the signatories, whereas treaties to which there are many signatories create law *per se*. However, all treaties involve a contractual obligation for the parties concerned, and consequently, create law for all parties agreeing to the terms of the treaty. In other words, a bipartite[29] treaty does not create a *lesser* law than does a multipartite treaty. Multipartite treaties may admittedly have a wider effect, and as such, may be regarded as law-making, in that not only do they have a greater number of signatories, but the provisions of such a treaty may become customary international law, as the Netherlands and Denmark attempted to argue, albeit unsuccessfully, in the *North Sea Continental Shelf Cases*. Multipartite treaties may, although

---

[27] The technicalities of treaty law are examined in Ch.10.
[28] Participation in a treaty is not confined exclusively to states, but states are the only entities which have *locus standi* before the ICJ in contentious cases.
[29] Although the terms "bipartite" and "multipartite" are strictly correct, the terms "bilateral" and "multilateral" are more commonly used.

they may never have the truly legislative effect of municipal legislation, have a quasi-legislative effect which is at least *prima facie* denied to bipartite treaties. The International Court acknowledged in the *Territorial Dispute Case* (*Libya v Chad*)[30] that a principle first enunciated in a treaty (Art.31 of the Vienna Convention) had achieved the status of customary international law. Conversely, a multipartite or bipartite treaty may merely spell out what has been accepted as customary international law, and a provision contained repeatedly in bipartite treaties may provide evidence that a particular rule of customary international law exists. Alternatively, it may be argued that the very fact that states insert the rule in a bipartite treaty is evidence that such a rule does not exist under customary international law.

Treaties represent the most tangible and most reliable method of identifying what has been agreed between states. Treaties regulate a diverse and extensive subject-matter including *inter alia* drug control, space exploitation, the establishment of organisations, extradition and safety regulations in the air and at sea, the rights of the child, the elimination of discrimination against women and the establishment of an International Criminal Court.

Customary law and law made by treaty have equal authority to international law, but, if a treaty and a customary rule exist simultaneously on the issue in dispute, then the treaty provisions take precedence, as is illustrated by the *Wimbledon Case*.[31] In that case, the Permanent Court of International Justice, whilst recognising that under customary international law it was prohibited to allow the passage of armaments through the territory of a neutral state to the territory of a belligerent state, upheld Art.380 of the Treaty of Versailles, which provided that the Kiel Canal was to be "free and open to the vessels of commerce and of war of all nations at peace with Germany on terms of entire equality". In stopping a vessel flying the flag of a state with which she was at peace, Germany was, the court maintained, in breach of her treaty obligations under the Treaty of Versailles.

In other words, unless the parties have expressed otherwise, a rule established by agreement supersedes for them a previous conflicting rule of customary international law. Generally, in the event of inconsistency, the latter, be it custom or treaty, prevails as between the same parties. However, parties to a treaty may agree to adhere to the treaty obligations, even in the light of subsequent general custom. Nevertheless, though modification of customary law by treaty is common, there are few instances of rules of customary law developing in conflict with earlier agreements,

---

[30] 6 I.C.J.Rep. 1994.
[31] P.C.I.J.Rep., ser.A, No.1 (1923).

and, in such cases, the principle that the latter in time prevails will be applied on the presumption that the parties to the treaty have impliedly given their consent.[32] However, where there exists customary international law comprising rules identical to those of treaty law "there are no grounds for holding ... that the latter supervenes the former, so that the customary international law has no existence of its own".[33] Hence, the court in the *Nicaragua Case* conceded that, although it was precluded from considering whether the United States had infringed UN Art.2(4)'s prohibition on the use of force,[34] it was still competent to consider whether the existing customary international law on the use of force had been violated.

A presumption exists though against the replacement of customary rules by treaty and vice versa. Treaties are not intended to derogate from customary law, and a treaty which seemingly modifies or alters established custom should be construed so as to best conform to, rather than derogate from, accepted principles of international law, unless, of course, the treaty in question is clearly intended to alter the existing rules of custom. A treaty will not however prevail over prior customary law if the latter is *jus cogens*.[35]

Whatever their legislative effect, treaties generally do not, unlike municipal legislation, have universal application. This statement must be qualified. There are two types of treaties which, because of their purpose, do produce consequences which non-signatories cannot ignore, namely (i) those establishing a special international regime and (ii) those establishing an international organisation.

In 1920, a Committee of Jurists was appointed by the League of Nations to determine whether Finland, as successor state to Russia, was bound by the 1856 Convention under which Russia had agreed with France and Great Britain to the non-fortification of the Aaland Islands.[36] The Committee concluded that the treaty extended beyond the three contracting parties. The islands enjoyed "a special international status", and that until the 1856 Convention was replaced, every state interested had a right to insist upon it being complied with, while "any State in possession of the Islands must conform to the obligations binding upon it". Treaties of this type are, however, very unusual.

---

[32] One such example was the acceptance as law of the 200 mile exclusive economic zone in conflict with the 1958 Geneva Conventions on the Law of the Sea.
[33] Above, n.17 p.95.
[34] By virtue of the US reservation under Art.36(2) of the ICJ Statute.
[35] See below, p.33 and Ch.10.
[36] *League of Nations Official Journal* (1920), Sp.Supp.No.3 , p.3.

Constitutive treaties establishing international institutions, for example the United Nations, have created organisations which have subsequently been held to possess varying degrees of international personality[37]—a personality which has enabled such entities to operate on the international stage and which has, in certain instances, been enforced against non-Member States, for example in the *Reparations Case*.[38]

"GENERAL PRINCIPLES OF LAW AS RECOGNISED BY CIVILISED NATIONS"

International law as a legal system would be undermined if the International Court of Justice, because of an apparent absence of relevant legal rules, was unable to give a decision based on law (such a situation is referred to as *non liquet*). In a municipal system, such a situation would be tackled by the deducing of relevant rules from already existing rules, or from basic legal principles, such as justice and equity. A "*non-liquet*" situation is, or at least was, more likely to arise in international law[39] than in a developed, mature legal system. Accordingly, "general principles of law ..." was inserted to plug the gaps and to avoid an undermining of international law, which an inability to render judgment through an insufficiency of law would undoubtedly incur.

General principles were those as understood by "civilised nations". "Civilised nations" has today, for obvious reasons, been dropped. Its colonial connotations are unacceptable in today's international community.

What then is understood by general principles? It is not clear whether general principles refers to those of the international legal system or those of municipal legal systems. Such ambiguity is advantageous, as it imposes no restraint on the principles which may be applied.

Rather than dwell on the conceptual arguments that have raged over the definition of general principles, it is more advantageous here to identify instances of when general principles have been employed. What has happened is that legal principles have been drawn from the developed municipal legal systems. This does not mean that judges have to have expertise in every legal system of the world, because, of course, legal systems can be

---

[37] International personality is covered in Ch.4.
[38] "*Reparation for Injuries Suffered in the Service of the United Nations, Advisory Opinion*", I.C.J.Rep. 1949 at 185.
[39] It should always be borne in mind that the Statute of the ICJ is the direct successor of the Charter of the Permanent Court of International Justice and that, in the 1920s, international law was certainly less developed than it is today.

divided into families, and consequently, common elements may be identified within legal systems. The general principles are therefore those which are common to the major legal systems of the world, for example the civilian legal system, the common-law system and the hybrid system (Scottish legal system).

Most of the parallels drawn from municipal law have related to procedural, administrative or jurisdictional situations. Principles applied by international tribunals and the International Court and its predecessor, have been those of a state's responsibility for the acts of its agents,[40] the principle of estoppel (personal bar),[41] no one must be a judge of his own case,[42] and the principle of reparation.[43] Analogies with municipal legal systems have been utilised in recent years in the new areas of international law, for example commercial and administrative law. In the *Barcelona Traction Case*,[44] the International Court of Justice emphasised that:

> "If the Court were to decide the case in disregard of the relevant institutions of municipal law it would without, justification, invite serious legal difficulties. It would lose touch with reality, for there are no corresponding institutions of international law to which the Court could resort. . . . It is to rules generally accepted by municipal legal systems . . ., and not to the municipal law of a particular State, that international law refers".[45]

No precise definition either to the extent or scope of general principles has been universally agreed. The importance of general principles, however they may be defined, is that recourse to them has prevented a case from being shelved on the grounds that international law as it exists lacks, or is inadequate for dealing with, the particular issue raised.[46]

Whether a particular general principle is eligible for absorption by international law will depend upon the development of international law at the time in question, for example the prohibition on the use of torture is now unquestionably part of international law based on the fact that the prohibition is at least *prima facie* common to all legal systems.

---

[40] *Fabiani Case* 10 R.I.A.A. 83 (1986).
[41] *Temple Case* I.C.J.Rep. 1962 at 6.
[42] *Mosul Boundary Case*, P.C.I.J.Rep., ser.B, No.12 (1925) at 32.
[43] *Chorzow Factory Case (Indemnity) (Merits)*, P.C.I.J.Rep., ser.A, No.17 (1928) at 29.
[44] Above, n.12.
[45] Above, n.12 at 37.
[46] Possible general fundamental principles of international law are considered under *"jus cogens"* below, p. 33.

EQUITY[47]

"The Court has not been expressly authorised by its Statute to apply equity as distinguished from law. . . . Article 38 of the Statute expressly directs the application of general principles of law recognised by civilised nations', and in more than one nation principles of equity have an established place in the legal system. . . . It must be concluded, therefore, that under Article 38 of the Statute, if not independently of that Article, the Court has some freedom to consider principles of equity as part of the international law which it must apply".[48]

In the *Rann of Kutch Arbitration*,[49] equity was identified as constituting part of international law, while the International Court of Justice in the *North Sea Continental Shelf Cases* directed the parties involved to seek a solution by reference to "equitable principles".[50] Equitable principles are also referred to in multipartite treaties, for example the 1982 Convention on the Law of the Sea[51] and certain General Assembly Resolutions such as the preamble of the 1974 Charter of Economic Rights and Duties of States.[52]

Principles of equity in the sense of fairness, justice and reasonableness are akin to general principles, and it may be wondered why they should not always be considered under the umbrella of general principles. Equity differs from the general principles most frequently applied in that, while the latter has related mainly to procedural techniques, equity as a concept reflects values, which, though they may be hard to define, may profoundly affect the application of the law. Equity in itself cannot be a source of law in that it does not contribute to substantive law, but it can, nevertheless, affect the way substantive law is administered and applied.

Equity plays a subsidiary role in supplementing existing rules. Equity, as understood above, must be distinguished from the International Court's power "to decide a case *ex aequo et bono*, if

---

[47] Equity is sometimes treated separately as a possible independent source of law.
[48] Separate Opinion of Hudson J. in *The Diversion of Water from the Meuse Case* P.C.I.J.Rep., ser.A/B, no.70 (1937) at 76–77.
[49] 50 I.L.R. 2.
[50] Above, n.2, p.47; see also *Fisheries Jurisdiction Cases (Merits)* I.C.J.Rep. 1974 3 at 33; *Continental Shelf (Tunisia v Libya) Case* I.C.J.Rep. 1982 18 at 60, *Gulf of Maine Case* I.C.J.Rep. 1984 at 246, 314–315 and 325–330. A criticism levied against the utilisation of equity in maritime boundary cases is that it has introduced an "unduly subjective and uncertain element into international law". See also *Denmark v Norway: Maritime Boundary in the Area Between Greenland and Jam Mayen Island* (1993) I.C.J. 38, *ad pasim*.
[51] Arts 59, 74 and 83.
[52] GA Resolution 3281 (XXIX) 14 I.L.M. 251 (1975) which highlights the "need to establish a just and equitable economic and social order".

the parties agree thereto",[53] that is the court may apply equity in precedence over all other rules. A judge can only exercise his power under Art.38(2) if he has been expressly authorised so to do.[54]

In the event of the International Court of Justice's being unable to solve a dispute by reference to treaty law, custom or general principles, Art.38 provides that the subsidiary means of "judicial decisions and the teachings of the most highly qualified publicists of the various nations" may be employed. Judicial decisions and writings are subsidiary means of determining what the law is on a given issue. They constitute the material sources of international law, as distinct from the formal sources. They are not the law as such, but are rather where the law may be found. However, the increasing growth of, in particular, treaty law has witnessed a decline in the employment of both judicial decisions and writings, as will be seen as each is considered individually below.

JUDICIAL DECISIONS

Judicial decisions may be applied "subject to the provisions of Article 59". Art.59 states that ". . . the decision of the court has no binding force except between the parties and in respect of that particular case". There is no rule of *stare decisis* in international law whereby the court is obliged to follow its previous decisions. Nevertheless, in spite of the absence of *stare decisis* in international law, the International Court of Justice and international tribunals examine previous decisions, and do take them into account when seeking the solution to a subsequent dispute. There is obviously value in judicial consistency—it will promote some degree of certainty for those participating in the legal system as to what the law is on a particular issue. Although, strictly speaking, the International Court of Justice is only to apply the law and not to make law, it has delivered a number of judgments and advisory opinions which have been influential in their contribution to the development of international law, for example the *Reparations Case*[55] (legal personality of the United Nations), the *Nottebohm Case*[56] (genuine link between individual and claimant state), the *Anglo-Norwegian Fisheries Case*[57] (baselines from which the territorial sea may be drawn) and the *Legality of the Use by a state of*

---

[53] Art.38(2).
[54] Art.38(2) has never been invoked before the ICJ though some international arbitration awards have been decided *ex aequo et bono*.
[55] *Reparation for Injuries Suffered in the Service of the United Nations*, above, n.38.
[56] I.C.J.Rep. 1955 at 4.
[57] *Anglo-Norwegian Fisheries Case*, above, n.8.

Nuclear Weapons in Armed Conflict.[58] Similarly, arbitration deci-sions have contributed to the growth of international law, for example the *Alabama Arbitration Awards*[59] (duties of a neutral state), and the *Island of Palmas Case*[60] (evidence of territorial sover-eignty). Caution should be exercised when assessing the contribu-tion of a particular decision, for example the court may be equally divided and the casting vote of the President may be necessary for a decision as in the *Lotus Case*. Similarly, the importance of an arbitration decision will depend, for example, on the subject-matter involved and the parties concerned.

Before assessing the contribution of any arbitration decision to the development of international law, reference should be made to the contents of the *compromis*; namely the agreement concluded between the parties to the arbitration which may specify, for instance, the tribunal's jurisdiction and the law to be applied. Law, other than international law, or in addition to international law, may be employed by an arbitration tribunal and, if this is the intention of the parties it must be stipulated in the *compromis*.[61] In the *Trail Smelter Arbitration*,[62] for example, the Tribunal was instructed to "apply the law and practice followed in dealing with cognate questions in the United States of America, as well as international law and practice". It is therefore necessary to remember that an arbitration tribunal, in settling a dispute between two states, may not necessarily be applying interna-tional law or, at least, exclusively international law.

A judicial decision by the International Court of Justice may give the stamp of law to an alleged rule of custom. Again, caution must be exercised. For instance, the International Court of Justice in 1974 pronounced that:

> "... Two concepts have crystallised as customary law in recent years arising out of the general consensus revealed at that Conference [1960 Law of the Sea Conference]. The first is the concept of the fishery zone, ... The second is the concept of preferential rights of fishing in adjacent waters in favour of the coastal State in a situation of special dependency on its coastal fisheries ...."[63]

The evidence produced by the court in support of its contention was unconvincing. The court took existing instances of preferential

---

[58] 35 I.L.M. 809 (1996).
[59] Moore, 1 Int.Arb.495 (1872).
[60] 2 R.I.A.A. 829 (1928).
[61] In the absence of any stipulation, international law will be applied.
[62] 3 R.I.A.A. 1905 (1938/41).
[63] *Fisheries Jurisdiction Case (Merits)*, above, n.10 at 23.

rights at face value, and considered neither the reasons why preferential treatment was granted, nor whether the parties concerned felt any legal obligation to provide preferential treatment for coastal states. The evidence produced in court illustrated that relatively few states put preferential rights into practice—21—and that the practice was confined to a single geographical area (the North Atlantic). The court did not attempt to demonstrate that states felt any legal obligation to act in the way they had done. Nor has state practice since the court's judgment supported the view that the court was giving "judgment *sub specie legis ferendae*" and was anticipating "the law before the legislator had laid it down".[64]

The court also came in for criticism with respect to its assertion in the *Nicaragua Case*, that the necessary *opinio juris* could be deduced from the support of states for certain General Assembly Resolutions.[65]

DECISIONS OF MUNICIPAL COURTS

Art.38 does not limit the judicial decisions that may be employed to those of international tribunals. Thus, if a municipal court decision is relevant, it may be applied. The weight attached to a decision of a national court will depend upon the standing of the Court concerned. The United States Supreme Court is held in high regard and, in its decisions dealing with individual state boundaries, it has not only applied but also played a role in developing the relevant principles of international law. Similarly, decisions of the English Prize Courts contributed to the growth of prize law—law relating to vessels captured at sea during war.

A municipal court decision may also serve as evidence of a state's position on a particular issue. Nevertheless, it must always be borne in mind, that although a national court is apparently applying international law, it may in reality be applying a rule of national law, for example as in questions of sovereign and diplomatic immunity.

WRITERS

"Teachings of the most highly qualified publicists of various nations" may be referred to as a subsidiary means in an attempt to settle a dispute.

---

[64] That this is what the court may have been seeking to do is borne out by Ignacio-Pinto J.'s declaration (at 37) that the court gave him the impression that it was "anxious to indicate the principles on the basis of which it would be desirable that a general international regulation of rights of fishing should be adopted".

[65] See D'Amato, above, n. 22.

Writers have played a considerable role in the development of international law. Their influence has been due, in part, to the absence of an executive and a legislative body and, in part, to the "youthfulness" of the international legal system. Especially in its formative period, writers were, because of insufficient state practice, able to help determine, mould and articulate the scope, content and basic principles of international law, for example Grotius—"freedom of the seas"—in the early seventeenth century and, more recently, Lord McNair (1885–1973) on the Law of Treaties. However, as the substantive law of international law increased via, for example state practice and the growth of customary international law, the role of writers declined. Nevertheless, international law is still a relatively young system and its boundaries are constantly being extended; writers may still make a contribution in identifying and highlighting areas where international regulation should be introduced, for example environmental pollution. Writers may also prompt an assessment of the aims and values of international law. Writings, though they have receded in importance, are utilised not as a source of law in themselves, but as a means of ascertaining what the law actually is on a given subject.[66] They are subsidiary means of determining what the law is on a particular issue at a particular point in time, and, in the absence of any rule of *stare decisis* in international law, writings do not necessarily carry less weight than judicial decisions. Obviously, which publicists are "the most highly qualified" cannot be conclusively proved.

The international community of today is very different from the one which existed when Art.38(1) and its predecessor were initiated. It is relevant, therefore, after having examined all of the possible "sources" identified by reference to Art.38(1), to ask whether these are the only sources. Art.38(1) does not profess to be exhaustive, and it is, especially because of the developing character of international law, quite legitimate to look beyond Art.38(1).

OTHER POSSIBLE SOURCES OF INTERNATIONAL LAW

Acts of international organisations

The multiplication of international organisations is a phenomenon of the last 40 years. The best known, enjoying almost universal

---

[66] See, for instance, reference by Lord Stephenson in *Trendtex Trading Corporation v Central Bank of Nigeria* [1977] 1 All E.R. 881 at 902. Note the International Court's statement on the cognisance to be given to documentary evidence produced in the form of extracts from books, namely that "even if they seem to meet high standards of objectivity", *Nicaragua Case (Merits)* 1986, above, n.9 at 40.

membership, is the United Nations. Every Member State of the United Nations (190 members) possesses one vote within the General Assembly. Voting on important questions requires a two-thirds majority, whilst on all other questions a simple majority will suffice. Only those Resolutions adopted by the Assembly on procedure and budgetary questions are legally binding on members. All other Resolutions are recommendations, statements on a given issue. However, certain General Assembly Resolutions, namely those which are "Declarations of Principle", although they carry no legal obligation, do have considerable moral force, for example Resolution 1514 (XV), "Declaration on the Granting of Independence to Colonial Countries and Peoples",[67] and G.A. "Declaration on Principles of International Law Concerning Friendly Relations and Co-Operation Amongst States in Accordance with the Charter of the United Nations" 1970.[68] Although such Resolutions may contribute to the development of international law, the status of customary international law, was denied to G.A. Resolution 3281 (XXIX) "Charter of Economic Rights and Duties of States" 1974[69] by the arbitrator in the *Texaco Case*.[70] However, other Resolutions cannot be dismissed as being of no legal significance. In the words of Lauterpacht J.:

"It would be wholly inconsistent with sound principles of interpretation as well as with highest international interest, which can never be legally irrelevant, to reduce the value of the Resolutions of the General Assembly—one of the principal instrumentalities of the formation of the collective will and judgment of the community of nations represented by the United Nations—and to treat them, . . ., as nominal, insignificant and having no claim to influence the conduct of the Members. International interest demands that no judicial support, however indirect, be given to any such conception of the Resolution of the General Assembly as being of no consequence".[71]

The legal effect of General Assembly Resolutions remains uncertain but, before any law-making effect can be attributed to

---

[67] GA Resolution 1514 (XV) December 14, 1960; see *"Advisory Opinion—Western Sahara"*, I.C.J.Rep. 1975 12 at 31 et seq. for the effect of GA Resolutions in the evolution of the principle of self-determination.
[68] GA Resolution 2625 (XXV) October 24, 1970.
[69] 14 I.L.M. 251 (1975).
[70] 17 I.L.M. 1 (1978).
[71] Separate Opinion in *"Voting Procedure on Questions Relating to Reports and Petitions Concerning the Territory of South West Africa"*, I.C.J.Rep. 1955 67 at 122.

them, a consistent approach requires to be adopted towards them. This is in contrast to the current selective approach, where their impact is dependent upon such factors as the subject-matter of the Resolution, how large a majority the Resolution commands and to what extent it receives the support of the principally affected states in the given field. However, as it is, a vote in the General Assembly is cast by a state's representative and, as such, will reflect a particular state's position on a given issue. How a state votes can be the means of providing evidence of state practice. Thus, voting within an organisation may be a useful link in the international law-making process, that is, it may provide the evidence necessary for "law" to be attributed to usage. The voting on General Assembly Resolutions may provide an indication of what the law is, or possibly what the law should be, on a particular topic at a given time.

General Resolutions are an instance of what is known as "soft law". Soft law is the generic term used to describe non-legally binding international instruments. The term embraces treaties ("legal soft law") containing general obligations and non-binding or voluntary resolutions, statements of intent and codes of conduct produced by international and regional organisations and statements by individuals, for example groups of eminent international lawyers, purporting to articulate international principles ("non-legal soft law").[72] A requisite of soft law is that it be in written form. The number of instruments which fall within the category of soft law has spawned during the last 30 years, and the subject-matter of such instruments is becoming increasingly diverse and includes, *inter alia*, economic measures and environmental instruments. The Charter of Paris for a New Europe adopted by the Conference on Security and Co-Operation in Europe[73] is a prime example of soft law as is the Rio Declaration on the Environment. An advantage of soft law is that it may be employed to "overcome deadlock in relations between states pursuing conflicting ideological and/or economic aims",[74] whereas an alleged disadvantage is that it may discourage states from undertaking "hard law" obligations. Soft law is intended to mould conduct on the international scene and may be transformed into hard law—subsequent state practice may be such to change the status of the soft law or the soft law may ultimately result in a hard

---

[72] C. M. Chinkin, "The Challenge of Soft Law: Development and Change in International Law" (1989) 38 I.C.L.Q. 850.

[73] 30 I.L.M. 190 (1991).

[74] Seidl-Hohenfeldern, 163 *Hague Recueil* 169 (1979–11).

law treaty being concluded.[75] The 1948 Universal Declaration of Human Rights was a statement of intent but led to the promulgation of the 1966 Covenant of Civil and Political Rights,[76] and the 1966 Covenant on Economic, Social and Cultural Rights.[77]

Regional organisations

Regional organisations, such as the Council of Europe, the European Union, the Organisation of American States and the African Union, can, via their internal measures, demonstrate what they, representing a particular regional grouping of states, consider to be the law. Regional organisations enjoy varying degrees of legal personality and if this should extend to a treaty-making competence, the organisation in question may shape substantive international law by participating in treaties.

The International Law Commission

A criticism levelled against custom is that it is diffuse and lacking in precision. In the light of this, attempts have been made at codification—the Hague Conferences 1899 and 1907 produced Conventions on the law of war and neutrality and in 1930 the Hague Convention on Certain Questions Relating to the Conflict of Nationality Law was drawn up. Codification essentially involves a streamlining of all existing law on a particular subject, and it is distinct from consolidation, which is simply a drawing together of all material on a particular subject. In 1946, the International Law Commission was established, and charged with the task of furthering the progressive development and codification of international law. "Progressive development" is defined in Art.15 of the International Law Commission's Statute as "the preparation of draft conventions on subjects which have not yet been regulated by international law or in regard to which the law has not yet been sufficiently developed in the practice of states". Codification, however, is defined as "the more precise formulation and systemisation of rules of international law in fields where there already has been extensive state practice, precedent and doctrine". All codification has, accordingly, since 1946, been effected via the

---

[75] H. Hartmut "A Fresh Look at Soft Law" (1999) no.10, no.3 E.J.I.L. 499, in which the author identifies that "[E]ven if soft law is not a source of law in the sense of Art.38(1) . . ., it is a self-contained regime where the characteristics depend on the parties' intent.—Although soft law is not subject to international treaty law or the principle of *pacta sunt servanda*, it is not indifferent in legal terms and deserves the lawyer's attention. Such rules of behaviour must be ascertained on a case-by-case basis, depending upon the will of the parties".
[76] U.K.T.S. 6 (1977) Cmnd.6702.
[77] *ibid.* 6 I.L.M. 360 (1967).

International Law Commission. The distinction between "progressive development" and "codification" is easier to maintain in
theory than in practice, as was highlighted by Ad Hoc Sorenson
J. (Dissenting Opinion) in the *North Sea Continental Shelf Case*:

> "It has come to be generally recognised, however, that this
> distinction between codification and progressive develop-
> ment may be difficult to apply rigorously to the facts of inter-
> national legal relations. Although theoretically clear and
> distinguishable the two notions tend in practice to overlap or
> to leave between them an intermediate area in which it is not
> possible to indicate precisely where codification ends and
> progressive development begins. The very act of formulating
> or restating an existing customary rule may have the effect of
> defining its contents more precisely and removing such
> doubts as may have existed as to its exact scope or the
> modalities of its application."[78]

The Commission has 34 members,[79] who sit as individuals rather
than as representatives of their governments.[80] The Commission
may be invited by the General Assembly to look at a particular
field of law. However, this is rare, and the Commission as a rule
normally initiates its work programme for itself. Draft articles are
prepared and subsequently submitted to Member States for their
comments. A conference is convened which will, on the basis of
the draft articles, produce a Convention, which will eventually be
opened for signature.[81]

The value of the International Law Commission's work lies not
only in that a multipartite treaty may be produced, but that, in its
preparatory work, state practice can be identified and, as such,
may assist the formation of customary international law. Again,
the interrelation of treaty law and customary international law
and vice versa is illustrated.

Other agencies apart from the International Law Commission
are engaged in attempts to clarify existing law on given subjects,
for example the United Nations Commission on International

---

[78] Above, n.2 at 42–43.
[79] Increased from 15 members to 21 in 1956, to 25 in 1961 and to 34 in 1981.
[80] Elections are by the General Assembly from lists of national groups and are
    elected with regard, *e.g.* to equitable geographical distribution. Ian Brownlie is
    currently the U.K. member of the Commission. He was re-elected for a further
    5-year term, which began on January 1, 2002.
[81] Conferences may span a number of years, *e.g.* UN Conference on the Law of the
    Sea had its opening session in New York in 1973, but it was not until December
    10, 1982 that a Convention was open for signature. Apart from the Law of the
    Sea, the Commission has considered topics as the law of treaties, diplomatic
    and consular relations and state succession.

Trade Law, the International Labour Organisation and independent bodies such as the International Law Association. Mention, albeit brief, must be made of *jus cogens*.[82]

Jus cogens

Jus cogens is the technical term given to those norms of general international law which are of a peremptory force and from which, as a consequence, no derogation may be made except by another norm of equal weight. A treaty, for instance, which conflicts with such a norm is void[83] and, should a new peremptory norm develop any existing conflicting treaty becomes void and terminates.[84]

How does an international rule gain status as a peremptory norm? The Vienna Convention defines[85] a peremptory norm of general international law as one which is "accepted and recognised by the international community of States as a whole. . .". A peremptory norm may, it would appear, be derived from a custom or a treaty, but not, it is submitted, from any other source.

Jus cogens is the label for what are essentially the "public policy" rules of the international legal system. There is, as might be anticipated, considerable uncertainty as to the scope and extent of *jus cogens*. The prohibition on the use of force as expressed in the United Nations Charter was identified by the International Law Commission as a "conspicuous example of a rule in international law having the character of *jus cogens*",[86] and subsequently indorsed as such by the International Court of Justice in the *Nicaragua Case*.[87] Other examples of instances of norms warranting characterisation as *jus cogens* are the prohibition on genocide and torture[88]; and the realisation of the principle of self-determination.

Of course, the almost universal recognition and acceptance of certain basic principles as fundamental would represent an advancement and refinement in the international legal system, and the system for this step forward does not depend upon itself, but rather upon its principal participants—states.

---

[82] *Jus cogens* is looked at more closely within the context of treaty law—Ch.10.

[83] Vienna Convention on the Law of Treaties, 1969, Art.53.

[84] *ibid.*, Art.64.

[85] For the purposes of the Convention.

[86] Commentary of the Commission to Art.50 of "Draft Articles on the Law of Treaties", *I.L.C. Yearbook*, 1966, II, p.247.

[87] Above n.9 at 100.

[88] See, *Siderman de Blake v Republic of Argentina* 965 F.2d 699, 717 (9th Cr.1992), where the Court said that "the right to be free from official torture is fundamental and universal, a right deserving of the highest status under international law, a norm of *jus cogens*".

3. INTERNATIONAL LAW AND MUNICIPAL LAW

International law today is not confined to regulating the relations between states. The scope of international law continues to extend, and is no longer exclusively concerned with the rules of warfare and diplomatic relations. Today, matters of social concern such as health, education and economics fall within the ambit of international regulation. International law is more than ever aimed at individuals.

But, can individuals invoke international law before domestic courts? Can they gain rights under international law which they can enforce within the municipal legal system?

Essentially, the issue which is to be examined in this chapter is the extent to which municipal courts will give effect within the domestic system to rules of international law which are contrary, or not contrary, to domestic law. The approach of a particular state's municipal courts to international law is characterised by that state's attitude to and reception of international law—an attitude which may, and does, differ according to the type of international law in question—treaty law or customary international law. Strictly speaking, the reception of international law by a state is a matter of municipal law. There is no universal, uniform practice stipulating how states should incorporate international law into their domestic legal system and it is a state's perception of international law which determines the way in which international law becomes part of municipal law. In other words, states differ in the way that their municipal courts are either required or allowed to give effect to international obligations.[1]

Before looking at what happens in practice, mention, albeit brief, must be made of the theories which have evolved on the relationship of municipal law to international law. The theorists traditionally have divided themselves into two principal schools—(i) the monistic school and (ii) the dualistic school.

MONISTIC SCHOOL

Monists have a unitary concept of law and see all law, and consequently international law and municipal law, as an integral part of the same system. In the event of a conflict between international law and municipal law, most monists would contend that international law should unquestionably prevail.

DUALISTIC SCHOOL

Dualists see domestic law and international law as independent of each other. The two systems, it is maintained, regulate different subject-matter. International law regulates the relations of sovereign states while municipal law regulates affairs internal to the state, for example the relations of the executive *vis-à-vis* its citizens and the relations of individual citizens *vis-à-vis* each other. Accordingly, dualists hold that the two systems are mutually exclusive and can have no contact with and no effect on each other. If international law is applied within a state, it is only because it has been expressly incorporated into municipal law. The question of primacy is not one to which dualists address themselves. Dualism, as formulated, does not admit that a conflict can arise between the international legal system and a municipal legal system.

Sir Gerald Fitzmaurice stepped into the debate between monists and dualists in the mid-fifties, when he articulated what has become popularly known as the "Fitzmaurice compromise".[2] Fitzmaurice acknowledged that international law and municipal law have, for the most part, separate fields of operation

---

[1] Strictly the way in which a state makes international law part of its domestic legislation is a matter of municipal law rather than international law.

[2] Fitzmaurice, "The General Principles of International Law Considered from the Standpoint of the Rule of Law" 92 *Hague Recueil* 5.

and that each is supreme in its own domain. Nevertheless, on occasion, they have a common field of application and, should a conflict arise, what is involved Fitzmaurice concluded, is not a conflict of legal systems, but rather a conflict of obligations. If a state is by its municipal law, unable to act in the manner required by international law, it is not its internal law which the municipal courts will uphold, which is called into question, but rather the state's liability on the international plane for the non-fulfilment of its international obligations.[3]

In practice, the differences between international law and a particular municipal system are minimised and every effort is made to achieve a harmonisation between the two systems. In the United Kingdom, there exists ". . . a *prima facie* presumption that Parliament does not intend to act in breach of international law, including therein specific treaty obligations; and if one of the meanings which can reasonably be ascribed to the legislation is consonant with the treaty obligations and another or others are not, the meaning which is consonant is to be preferred".[4] In the United States, such a presumption is an established principle of interpretation, so that "[A]n act of congress ought never to be construed to violate the law of nations, if any other possible construction remains. . . ."[5]

What is meant, if it is said, that a country is monistic or dualistic in its approach to international law? Simply, it is monistic if it accepts international law automatically as part of its municipal law and does not demand an express act of the legislature, whereas if a state is dualistic, international law will only become part of its municipal law if it has been expressly adopted as such by way of a legislative act.

MUNICIPAL LAW IN INTERNATIONAL LAW

On the international scene, international law is unequivocally supreme, as it is borne out by both arbitral and judicial decisions and international conventions which reflect accepted international law.

In the *Alabama Claims Arbitration*,[6] the arbitration tribunal concluded that neither municipal legislative provisions nor the absence of them could be pleaded as a defence for non-compliance

---

[3] As illustrated in *Mortensen v Peters* (1906) 8 F. (J.) 93—see below, p.40.

[4] *Salomon v Commissioners of Customs and Excise* [1967] 2 Q.B. 116, CA—Lord Diplock at 143; also *Post Office v Estuary Radio Ltd* [1968] 2 Q.B. 740, CA.

[5] *Murray v Schooner Charming Betsy* 6 US (2 Cranch.) 64 at 118 (1804). Also *Lauritzen v Larsen* 345 US 571 at 578 (1953). For Canadian authority, see, *e.g. Bloxém v Favre* 8 P.C. 101 at 107 (1883, n.5).

[6] Moore, 1 Int.Arb. 495 (1872).

with international obligations, whilst the Permanent Court of International Justice in an advisory opinion held that:

> ". . . a State which has contracted valid international obligations is bound to make in its legislation such modifications as may be necessary to ensure the fulfilment of the obligations undertaken."[7]

Note, however, that Libya sought to justify its refusal to extradite the alleged perpetrators of the Lockerbie bombing on the grounds, *inter alia*, that the Libyan Constitution prohibits the extradition of nationals.

Art.13 of the Draft Declaration on Rights and Duties of States 1949 provides that:

> "Each State has the duty to carry out in good faith its obligations arising from treaties and other sources of international law, and it may not invoke provisions in its constitution or its laws as an excuse for failure to perform this duty."[8]

Art.27 of the Vienna Convention on the Law of Treaties[9] stipulates that "a party may not invoke the provisions of internal law as justification for its failure to perform a treaty", nor may a state, under Art.46 of the Vienna Convention,

> "invoke the fact that its consent to be bound by a treaty has been expressed in violation of a provision of its internal law regarding competence to conclude treaties as invalidating its consent unless that violation was manifest and concerned a rule of its internal law of fundamental importance."[10]

The overriding conclusion to be extracted from the foregoing is that a state should not seek to evade fulfilling an international obligation because of either the presence or absence of an internal legislative provision. Such must be the standpoint on the international level if international law is to succeed and maintain credibility.

---

[7] *Exchange of Greek and Turkish Populations Case* P.C.I.J.Rep., ser.B., No.10 (1925) at 20. see, also, *Free Zones of Upper Savoy and Gex* P.C.I.J.Rep., ser.A/B, No.46 (1932).
[8] This was prepared by the International Law Commission—Y.B.I.L.C., 1949, pp.286, 288.
[9] U.K.T.S. 58 (1980) Cmnd.7964; 8 I.L.M. 679 (1969). See also Ch.10 below.
[10] A violation is manifest if it shall be objectively evident to any state conducting itself on the matter in accordance with normal practice and in good faith (Art.46(2)).

International tribunals may, of course, choose to look at municipal legislation. Domestic legislation may be employed as evidence of a state's compliance or non-compliance with international obligations. Consideration of municipal law may make it possible to ascertain what a state's stance is on a particular issue at a given time[11] and an international tribunal may, in the absence of relevant international law, be required to refer to domestic law. The latter was stressed by the International Court of Justice in the *Barcelona Traction, Light and Power Co. Case*.[12] The court was confronted with issues pertaining to company law and held that "[I]n this field international law is called upon to recognise institutions of municipal law that have an important and extensive role in the international field . . ."[13]

Turning to the municipal scene, what is the position when municipal tribunals are confronted with international law? How do they apply it? What happens in the event of a conflict between international law and municipal legislation?

INTERNATIONAL LAW BEFORE MUNICIPAL COURTS

United Kingdom practice

There is no written constitution defining the internal status within Britain of international law.[14]

Customary international law

Britain essentially adopts a monistic approach to customary international law. This is however, an over-simplification. Although it was maintained by Lord Talbot in *Buvot v Barbuit*,[15] the true British view was best presented by Lord Alverstone in the *West Rand Central Gold Mining Co. Case*:[16]

"It is quite true that whatever has received the common consent of civilised nations must have received the assent of our

---

[11] Highlighted by the Permanent Court of International Justice in *"Polish Upper Silesia,"* P.C.I.J.Rep., ser.A, no.7, (1926) at 22, *Brazilian Loans Case*, P.C.I.J.Rep., ser.A, no.21, (1929), at 124–125.

[12] I.C.J. Rep. 1970 at 3.

[13] *ibid.* at 33. see also above, Chap. 2, n.45.

[14] *cf.* FRG—Art.25 German Constitution. "The general rules of public international law are an integral part of federal law. They shall take precedence over the laws and shall directly create rights and duties for the inhabitants of the federal territory." See also Arts 65 and 66 of the Dutch Constitution 1953 and 1956.

[15] (1737) Cases t. Talbot 281, "That the law of nations, in its full extent was part of the law of England" and reaffirmed by Lord Mansfield in *Triquet v Bath* (1764) 3 Burr. 1478. Court of King's Bench.

[16] [1905] 2 K.B. at 391.

country, and that to which we have assented along with other nations in general may properly be called international law, and as such will be acknowledged and applied by our municipal tribunals when legitimate occasion arises for those tribunals to decide questions to which doctrines of international law may be relevant. But any doctrine so invoked must be one really accepted as binding between nations, and the international law sought to be applied must, like anything else, be proved by satisfactory evidence, which must show either that the particular proposition put forward has been recognised and acted upon by our own country, or that it is of such a nature, and has been so widely and generally accepted, that it can hardly be supposed that any civilised State would repudiate it . . . that the law of nations forms part of the law of England, ought not to be construed so as to include as part of the law of England opinions of text-writers upon a question as to which there is no evidence that Great Britain has ever assented, and *a fortiori* if they are contrary to the principles of her laws as declared by her Courts."[17]

Lord Alverstone's emphasis was on assent and the need to demonstrate the existence and scope of any particular alleged rule of customary international law—an emphasis which has been reflected consistently in subsequent cases. In *The Cristina Case*,[18] Lord Macmillan held that municipal courts, before acknowledging customary international law as part of domestic law, should initially be satisfied that it (that is, custom) had the hallmark of consent.[19] In *Chung Chi Cheung v The King*,[20] Lord Atkin said:

"It must be always remembered that, so far, at any rate, as the Courts of this country are concerned, international law has no validity save in so far as its principles are accepted and adopted by our own domestic law. There is no external power that imposes its rule upon our own code of substantive law or procedure. The Courts acknowledge the existence of a body of rules which nations accept amongst themselves. On any judicial issue they seek to ascertain what the relevant rule is, and, having found it, they will treat it as incorporated into the domestic law, so far as it is not inconsistent with rules enacted by Statutes or finally declared by their tribunals."[21]

---

[17] *ibid*. at 406–408.
[18] [1938] A.C. 485.
[19] *ibid*. at 490. see also Lord Wright at 502.
[20] [1939] A.C. 160.
[21] *ibid*. at 167–168. Lord Atkin's statement is self contradictory.

Lord Denning in *Thakrar v Home Secretary*[22] said that "In my opinion, the rules of international law only become part of our law
in so far as they are accepted and adopted by us."[23] However,
three years later, in *Trendtex Trading Corporation v Central Bank of
Nigeria*,[24] in considering the two schools, incorporation or transformation, Lord Denning concluded that the doctrine of incorporation was correct. Nevertheless, that case dealing with sovereign
immunity predated the 1978 Sovereign Immunity Act and therefore was governed by judicial decisions. The real question was
whether the rules of precedent applying to rules of English law
incorporating customary international law meant that any
change in international law could only be recognised by the
English courts (in the absence of legislation) within the scope of
the doctrine of *stare decisis*. Lord Denning concluded otherwise
and held that:

> "International law knows no rule of *stare decisis*. If this court
> today is satisfied that the rule of international law on a subject
> has changed from what it was 50 or 60 years ago, it can give
> effect to that change—and apply the change in our English
> law—without waiting for the House of Lords to do it."[25]

The decision in *Trendtex* would appear to allow an exception from
an application of the principle of *stare decisis* in cases where international law has changed since the earlier decision was delivered.
In the light of the *Trendtex Case*, it seems that if international law
has changed then the "new" international law may be applied in
spite of the earlier municipal decision. Lord Denning's submissions in favour of the doctrine of "incorporation" received judicial support in the *Tin Council Case*.[26]

Rules of customary international law inconsistent with municipal law

Any rule of customary international law which is inconsistent
with a British statute will not be enforced in the British courts.
The domestic legislation will be upheld while the state will
incur liability on the international scene, as in *Mortensen v
Peters*,[27] when the court quashed an appeal against a conviction
made under a domestic legislative provision which allegedly

[22] [1974] Q.B. 684.
[23] *ibid.* at 701.
[24] [1977] Q.B. 529.
[25] *ibid.* at 554.
[26] *Maclaine Watson v Dept. of Trade and Industry* [1988] 3 W.L.R. 1033; 80 I.L.R. 49; [1989] 3 All E.R. 523; 81 I.L.R. 671.
[27] (1906) 8 F.(J.) 93.

contravened customary international law. The court, in dismissing the appeal, unanimously held, *inter alia*, that the relationship of municipal legislation and international law was one of construction and "of construction only" and that it was not the function of the court:

> "to decide whether an Act of the Legislature is *ultra vires* as in contravention of generally acknowledged principles of international law . . . an Act of Parliament duly passed by Lords and Commons and assented to by the King, is supreme, and we are bound to give effect to its terms."[28]

The court concluded that, whilst there was a presumption against Parliament violating international law:

> ". . . it is only a presumption, and as such it must always give way to the language used if it is clear, and also to all counter presumptions which may legitimately be held in view in determining, on ordinary principles, the true meaning and intent of the legislation. Express words will of course be conclusive, and so also will plain implication."[29]

Customary international law will be treated as part of UK law, provided that there is no contrary judicial decision of a higher court, save possibly the exception admitted by the *Trendtex Case*, or contrary statutory provision.

Treaties

> ". . . as a matter of the constitutional law of the United Kingdom, the royal prerogative, whilst it embraces the making of treaties, does not extend to altering the law or conferring rights on individuals or depriving individuals of rights which they enjoy in domestic law without the intervention of Parliament. Treaties, as it is sometimes expressed are not self-executing. Quite simply a treaty is not part of English law unless and until it has been incorporated into the law by legislation."[30]

A treaty does not become part of British domestic law unless and until it is specifically incorporated as such by a legislative measure—an enabling Act. The United Kingdom adopts, therefore, a dualistic approach to treaty law.

[28] *ibid.* at 100–101.
[29] Above, n.27 at 103.
[30] Lord Oliver in *Maclaine Watson v Department of Trade*, above, n.26.

Why is an Enabling Act required? Treaty-making power is an executive function coming within the royal prerogative. The legislature does not participate and its consent is not required before Britain can undertake international obligations. An Enabling Act is a safeguard against the possible abuse of executive authority, as it prevents the executive from using its treaty-making competence to introduce domestic legislation without going through the necessary parliamentary procedures. Treaties regulating the conduct of war and the cession of territory do not demand an Enabling Act.[31]

In practice, the Enabling Act giving internal effect to a treaty will be passed before the treaty is ratified and the opportunity will then be taken to bring municipal law into accordance with international law. There is also the practice known as the Ponsonby Rule, whereby a treaty is, following signature, laid for 21 days before both Houses of Parliament before ratification and publication in the United Kingdom Treaty Series.[32] Although expedient to provide this opportunity for discussion, it is not legally required.[33] The reason for the requirement of an Enabling Act was spelt out in the *Parlement Belge Case*[34] by Sir Robert Phillimore, when he concluded that to recognise the immunity granted by a Convention[35] to a vessel other than a public warship as being enforceable in the municipal courts would be ". . . a use of the treaty-making prerogative of the Crown which I believe to be without precedent, and in principle contrary to the laws of the constitution."[36]

As from January 1, 1997, every international agreement laid before the UK Parliament under the Ponsonby Rule has been accompanied by an Explanatory Memorandum (EM), identifying the main features of the Treaty. The aim of the EM is to assist Members of Parliament in understanding the substance of the

---

[31] Treaties involving the cession of territory may be an exception to the principle that parliamentary consent is not required for a treaty. See McNair, *Treaties*, p.97: "it is unlikely that the Crown will agree to cede any territory without being sure that Parliament would approve, or, if in doubt, whether inserting a clause making the cession dependent upon Parliamentary approval."

[32] *Hansard*, HC Deb., Vol.171, cols 2003–2004 (April 1, 1924).

[33] *e.g.* the Rule was not applied when the UK accepted the compulsory jurisdiction of the ICJ there being no requirement for ratification—*Hansard*, HC Deb., Vol.578, cols 1145–1146 (November 27, 1957).

[34] (1879) 4 P.D. 129. Probate, Divorce and Admiralty Division.

[35] Postal Convention Regulating Communications by Post (Belgium and Britain) 1876.

[36] Above, n.34 at 154. See also *Walker v Baird* [1892] A.C. 491; *The Republic of Italy v Hambros Bank Ltd* [1950] Ch. 314, *McWhirter v Att.–Gen.* [1972] C.M.L.R. 882, also illustrate the need for an Enabling Act.

Treaty without reference to the actual text. An EM is not required where a treaty enters into force on signature.[37]

In the event of a conflict between a domestic statute and a treaty, the domestic legislative measure will prevail. Such was the case with the European Convention on Human Rights and Fundamental Freedoms, which was not part of British municipal law until 1998, when the Convention was incorporated by the Human Rights Act.[38] The position prior to 1998 continues to illustrate the stance taken *vis-à-vis* an international obligation which is not incorporated into UK domestic law.[39] In the event of an Act of Parliament containing provisions contrary to an international convention, that Act would prevail, although domestic legislation should always be construed as far as is possible to be in conformity with international obligations. There is a presumption in treaty interpretation that Parliament does not intend to violate the United Kingdom's international obligations.[40] The Human Rights Act also provides redress against public authorities which allegedly violate the Convention.[41]

The incorporation of the European Convention coincided with a major constitutional change within the United Kingdom, namely devolution and the establishment of a Scottish Executive, a legislative Parliament and a non-legislative Welsh Assembly. Under the Scotland Act 1998, all acts of the Scottish Executive and Scottish Parliament must be compatible with the European Convention on Human Rights.[42] Acts of the Westminster Parliament cannot be struck out on human-rights grounds but merely declared "incompatible".[43] However, should the Scottish Parliament enact legislation incompatible with the Convention, that

---

[37] See the Guidelines published by the Foreign and Commonwealth Office, London on Explanatory Memoranda for Treaties and Text of a Parliamentary Statement made by Dr Liam Fox on December 16, 1996 in HC.

[38] The Act entered into force on October 2, 2000. However, see the Scotland Act 1998, below.

[39] *R. v Secretary of State for the Home Department and Another, ex p. Bhajan Singh* [1976] Q.B. 198 at 207. See *R. v Chief Immigration Officer, ex p. Bibi* [1976] 1 W.L.R. 979 at 984, CA; Lord Bridge in *Brind v Secretary of State* [1991] 1 All E.R. 722 at 722–723, HL. *Birdi v Secretary of State for Home Affairs*, unreported, 1975, but quoted in *Singh* at 207; *Kaur v Lord Advocate* 1981 S.L.T. 3222 at 329; *Moore v Secretary of State for Scotland* 1985 S.L.T. 38 ABD 41; *obiter dicta* of Lord Hope in T. Petitioner 1966 S.C.L.R. 897 at 910–911

[40] With respect to the European Convention, all new legislation must include a "compatibility" clause.

[41] Human Rights Act, s.6.

[42] The Scottish Executive came into existence in May 1999, and the impact of the Convention was reflected primarily in the administration of justice, giving Scotland hands-on experience of incorporation some 18 months ahead of the rest of the UK.

[43] Human Rights Act, s.4

legislative measure may be deemed *"ultra vires"*. The Scottish Parliament only has competence in certain areas, namely devolved matters such as tax and education. Reserved matters, foreign affairs and defence are retained by Westminster.

Notwithstanding the competence of Scottish courts mentioned above, British courts are concerned with the application of domestic law and, if their provisions cannot be reconciled with international law, that is a matter solely for the consideration of the legislature and not the judiciary.[44]

Executive certificate

The executive certificate is a statement issued by the Foreign Office relating to "certain categories of questions of fact in the field of international affairs".[45] A certificate may stipulate, for instance, whether a particular foreign state or government is recognised by Britain,[46] whether a particular person is entitled to diplomatic immunity or the existence and scope of British jurisdiction in a foreign country. An executive certificate is accepted as conclusive by the courts, as was held in *The Fagernes*,[47] *Duff Development Co. v Government of Kelantan*[48] and *Post Office v Estuary Radio Ltd*[49] and only reviewable in certain defined circumstances, for example if found not to be genuine: see *R. v Secretary of State for Foreign and Commonwealth Affairs, Ex p. Trawnik*.[50]

An executive certificate is not conclusive in the interpretation of statutes or the construction of documents: *Re Al-Fin Corporation's Patent*.[51] The courts still, however, determine what is the effect of such factual situation, although they may not examine the basis on which the Foreign Office made its decision.

United States practice

American law, with its roots in the English legal system, adopts a similar attitude to international law as that adopted by Britain. Accordingly, with respect to customary international law, the United States is monistic in its approach and, in respect of treaties, dualistic.

---

[44] See *e.g.* Lord Templeman in *Lord Advocate v Scotsman Publishers Ltd* 1989 S.L.T. 705 at 710.
[45] L. Oppenheim, "International Law" (1967) Vol. I, para.357(a).
[46] s.21 of the 1978 State Immunity Act provides that the Secretary of State's certificate is conclusive evidence as to (i) whether a country is a state within the meaning of the Act; (ii) who is the head of State; and (iii) who is the government.
[47] [1927] 311 at 324.
[48] [1924] A.C. 797, HL.
[49] [1968] 2 Q.B. 740.
[50] *The Times*, April 18, 1985, p.4.
[51] [1971] Ch. 160.

Customary international law

Judicial decisions confirm that customary international law is part of United States law.

Marshall C.J., in *The Nercide*,[52] declared that, in the absence of an Act of Congress, the court was bound by the law of nations, which was part of the law of the land, while Gray J. in 1900 pronounced:

> "International law is part of our law, and must be ascertained and administered by the courts of justice of appropriate jurisdiction, as often as questions of right depending upon it are duly presented for their determination."[53]

This acceptance of customary international law was, however, qualified:

> "[T]his rule of international law is one which prize courts, administering the law of nations, are bound to take judicial notice of, and to give effect to, in the absence of any treaty or other public act of their own government in relation to the matter"[54]

and so, in the case of *Garcia-Mir v Meese*,[55] the decision of the Attorney-General detaining illegal Cuban immigrants was held to be a "controlling executive act", although the length of the detention was such as to constitute a violation of customary international law.

The position today remains the same as demonstrated in the case of *United States v Fawaz Yunis*,[56] in which it was stated that "our duty is to enforce the Constitution, laws, and treaties of the United States, not to conform the law of the land to norms of customary international law."

The court proceeded to reiterate its previous judicial pronouncement by declaring that:

> "Statutes inconsistent with principles of customary international law may well lead to international law violations. But within the domestic legal realm, that inconsistent statute simply modifies or supersedes customary international law to the extent of the inconsistency."[57]

---

[52] 9 Cr. 388 (US 1815).
[53] *The Paquete Habana* 175 US 677 at 700 (1900).
[54] *ibid.* at 708.
[55] 688 F.2d 1446 (1986).
[56] Heard by the US Court of Appeals (D.C.) 30 I.L.M. 403 (1991).
[57] *ibid.*

Customary international law is accepted without any legislative measure as part of American law, provided there is neither a domestic judicial decision nor a domestic legislative measure to the contrary. In the event of a conflict between alleged international law and municipal legislation, the domestic courts will uphold the municipal provisions:

> "International practice is law only in so far as we adopt it, and like our common law or statute law it bends to the will of Congress . . . There is one ground only upon which a federal court may refuse to enforce an Act of Congress and that is when the Act is held to be unconstitutional. The act may contravene recognised principles of international law, but that affords no more basis for judicial disregard of it than it does for the executive disregard of it."[58]

What is the internal status of customary international law? Customary international law is accepted as federal law and its determination by the federal courts is binding on the state courts.[59]

Treaty law

Under the American Constitution, the President has "Power by and with the Advice and Consent of the Senate, to make Treaties, provided two-thirds of the Senators present concur."[60]

Unlike in Britain, the American legislature participates in the treaty-making process. The President, in the light of the Constitution, has the power to make a treaty, but he may only ratify a treaty after the Senate has given its advice and approval. "All treaties made or which shall be made under the Authority of the US shall be the supreme law of the land."[61]

What is the status of a treaty within the United States? "Supreme" only places treaties on an equal footing with federal statutes.[62] In the event of a conflict between a treaty and a subsequent statute, the latter prevails. This was made quite clear by the Supreme Court in *Edye v Robertson*,[63] when it refuted the

---

[58] *Schroeder v Bissell* 5 F. (2d) 838 (1925) (US Dist. Ct D.Conn.).
[59] Restatement of Foreign Relations Law (Third) of the US (Revised) § III Reporters' No.3. This is the prevailing view. It has not always been so. State and federal courts decided international issues for themselves and consequently issues of international law were determined differently by courts in different states and the federal courts.
[60] Art.II(2).
[61] Art.6 of the US Constitution.
[62] *Edye v Robertson* 112 US 580 at 599 (1884).
[63] *ibid.*

contention that an Act of Congress, which conflicted with an earlier United States treaty, should be declared invalid. The court unanimously held that a treaty was a law of the land, as an Act of Congress was, and that there was nothing which made a treaty "irrepealable or unchangeable" and that the Constitution gave "it no superiority over an Act of Congress in this respect, which may be repealed or modified by an Act of a later date . . ." Congress, of course, does not enjoy the competence to act on the treaty itself and thus Congress cannot repeal a treaty. What Congress may do, however, is to enact legislation which will subsequently be determined as being inconsistent with the law as previously represented.

A treaty provision cannot "be rendered negatory in any part of the United States by municipal ordinances or state laws."[64] However, a later treaty provision will not be treated as having repealed by implication an earlier statute unless "the two are absolutely incompatible and the Statute cannot be enforced without antagonising the treaty."[65] A treaty is not repealed or modified by a subsequent federal statute unless that is the clearly expressed intention of Congress.[66]

The presumption exists, when interpreting domestic legislation, that Congress does not intend to infringe international law and that acts of Congress should be construed as conforming to international law. Courts strive to interpret acts of Congress so that they do not conflict with earlier treaty provisions. Nevertheless, in *Diggs v Schultz*,[67] although recognising that the Byrd Amendment allowing imports contrary to the UN Security Council embargo on Rhodesian products was in blatant disregard of United States treaty obligations, the court concluded that, under the American constitutional scheme, Congress could denounce treaties if it saw fit to do so and that there was nothing other branches of government could do about it.

In the United States, a distinction is made between *self-executing treaties* and *non-self-executing treaties*.

Self-executing treaties are automatically part of American domestic law—that is, no implementing legislation is required—whereas *non-self-executing treaties* are not incorporated into domestic law until the necessary enabling legislation has been passed. Some provisions of an international agreement may be self-executing, while other provisions in the same agreement may

[64] *Asakura v City of Seattle* 265 US 332 at 341 (1924).
[65] *Johnson v Browne* 205 US 309 at 321 (1907).
[66] *Cooke v The United States* 288 US 102 at 119–120 (1933).
[67] 470 F. (2d) 461 (1972).

be non-self-executing. The distinction was initially made in *Foster and Elam v Neilson*,[68] when Marshall C.J. submitted:

> "A treaty is in its nature a contract between two nations, not a legislative act. It does not generally effect of itself, the object to be accomplished, especially so far as its operation is intraterritorial; but is carried into execution by the sovereign power of the respective parties to the instrument. In the United States a different principle is established. Our Constitution declares a treaty to be the law of the land. It is, consequently, to be regarded in courts of justice as equivalent to an act of the legislature, whenever it operates of itself without the aid of any legislative provision. But when the terms of the stipulation import a contract, when either of the parties engages to perform a particular act, the treaty addresses itself to the political, not the judicial department; and the legislature must execute the contract before it can become a rule for the court."[69]

Similarly, in *Sei Fujii v California*,[70] it was said that, in order to determine whether a treaty is self-executing, courts must look to "the intent of the signatory parties as manifested by the language of the instrument, and, if the instrument is uncertain, recourse may be had to the circumstances surrounding its execution" and that "for a treaty provision to be operative without further implementing legislation and have statutory effect and force, it must appear that the framers of the treaty intended to prescribe a rule that, standing alone, would be enforceable in the courts."

The determining factor as to whether a treaty provision will be self-executing within the United States is the intention of the treaty framers. If the agreement is silent and the intention of the United States is unclear, account must be taken of relevant circumstances surrounding its conclusion, such as any statement issued by the President or any views expressed by the Senate. A treaty provision, to be self-executing, must therefore be:

   (a)   unambiguous,

   (b)   certain, and

   (c)   not forward-looking

---

[68] 27 US (2 Pet.) 253 at 314 (1829).
[69] The treaty in *Foster v Neilson*, which Marshall C.J. held not to be self-executing was later held by him to be self-executing, after the Spanish text was placed before the court. *United States v Percheman* 32 US (7. Pet.) 51 (1833).
[70] 242 P. (2d) 617 (1952); 19 I.L.R. 312 (1952) Supreme Ct of California.

(that is, legally complete and not dependent on subsequent legislation for its implementation).[71]

Generally, agreements which can be readily given effect by executive or judicial bodies, federal or state, without further federal legislation are deemed self-executing, unless a contrary intention is manifest. Treaties covering issues on which Congress has regulated extensively are more likely to be interpreted as non-self-executing.

Self-executing treaties are advantageous in that they prevent delay in the execution of obligations and they obviate the need (i) to include the participation of the House of Representatives (excluded from the treaty-making process by the Constitution), and (ii) to further consult the Senate after having received its consent under the two-thirds majority rule.

Although there is no hard and fast rule as to what may and may not be the subject of a self-executing treaty, there nevertheless appears to be a generally assumed principle that "an international agreement cannot take effect as domestic law without implementation by Congress if the agreement would do what lies within the exclusive law-making power of Congress under the Constitution."[72]

Executive agreements[73]

Executive agreements are international agreements entered into by the President without the advice and consent of Senate. Executive agreements are nevertheless regarded as being of the same force as a treaty and thereby, under international law, can effectively bind the United States. The validity of an executive agreement was upheld in *US v Belmont*[74] and in *US v Pink*.[75] In the latter case, it was held that "A treaty is a law of the Land under the supremacy clause (Art.VI, cl. 2) of the Constitution. Such international compacts and agreements as the Litvinoff Agreement have a similar dignity."[76] Executive agreements may be superseded by

---

[71] Hence in *Sei Fujii, ibid.*, the provisions of the Preamble and Arts 1, 55 and 56 of the UN were held not to be self-executing, as they lacked "the mandatory quality and definitions which would indicate an intent to create justiciable rights in private persons immediately upon ratification", but rather were "framed as a promise of future action by member nations."

[72] Restatement of Foreign Relations Law (Third) of the US (Revised) § III, Comment i; *cf. Missouri v Holland* 252 US 416 (1920). See below.

[73] For definition of "executive agreement", see letter of January 26, 1973 from C. Browne, Acting Legal Adviser to Carl Marcy, Chief of Staff of the Committee on Foreign Relations of the US Senate—*Digest of US Practice in International Law* (1973) p.187.

[74] 301 US 324 (1937).

[75] 315 US 203 (1942).

[76] *ibid.* at 230.

subsequent federal legislation, but whether an executive agreement can supersede a prior treaty or Act of Congress is unclear.[77]
The argument against such an effect is based essentially on the
view that it would be inconceivable that the act of a single person,
the President, could repeal an Act of Congress. However, an
executive agreement is federal law and there are not varying
degrees of status for federal law. "All constitutional acts of power,
whether in the executive or the judicial department, have as
much legal validity and obligation as if they proceeded from the
legislature."[78] If an executive agreement was held to supersede a
statute, Congress could re-enact the statute and thereby supersede the intervening executive agreement as domestic law.[79]

Attempts have been made to subject executive agreements to
greater congressional control, for example the abortive Bricker
Amendment 1953–54, Department of State Circular 175, 1955
(as amended 1966)[80] and the Case Act 1972, as amended in 1977
and 1978. In 1972, the Case Act[81] required that "all international
agreements other than treaties, hereafter entered into by the
US, be transmitted to the Congress within 60 days after the
execution thereof." The 1977 amendment requires that the procedure laid down in the Case Act be applied to agreements made
by any department or agency of the United States Government
and, in 1978, this was extended to cover oral as well as written
agreements.

Congressional executive agreements

A congressional executive agreement is an international agreement made by the President with the backing of a simple majority in both Houses of Congress. Such agreements have an
advantage over the treaty as prescribed by the Constitution in
that their use can simplify the legislative process. For example, a
treaty goes to the Senate for consent and then subsequently often
back to the Senate as well as to the House for implementation,
whereas a congressional executive agreement can go to both
Houses in the first instance, and thus "consent" and implementation are achieved simultaneously. The prevailing view is that the
Congressional executive agreement can be used as an alternative
to the treaty method in every instance. Which procedure should

---

[77] See, *e.g. United States v Guy W. Capps Inc.* 204 F. (2d) 655 (1953) (US CA, 4th Circuit).
[78] *The Federalist*, No.64 (Jay) cited in *US v Pink*, above, n.75.
[79] Above, n.82, § 115 Reporters' N. 5. An executive agreement has been held to
    prevail over a subsequent inconsistent state law—*Territory of Hawaii v Ho* 41
    Hawaii 565 (1957); 26 I.L.R. 557.
[80] *Foreign Affairs Manual*, Vol. III.
[81] P.L. 92–403, 86 Stat. 619; 1 US CA 112b.

be used is a political judgment, made in the first instance by the President, subject to the possibility that the Senate might refuse to consider a joint resolution of Congress to approve an agreement, insisting that the President submit the agreement as a treaty.[82]

Problems peculiar to a federal state

In a unitary state, the authority to enter into international agreements and the competence (subject to legislative approval) to give internal effect to such legislation lies with the central government. This is not the case in a federal state, where legislative competence is divided between the federal government and the individual states' governments. *Missouri v Holland*[83] illustrates how legislation may be introduced by the back door. A 1913 Act of Congress designed to protect migratory wild fowl was declared to be outside the legislative competence of the federal government, and within the residual power of the states' legislatures. In 1916, the United States concluded the Migratory Bird Act with Britain (acting on Canada's behalf) and the Act was given internal effect within the United States by the Migratory Bird Treaty Act 1918. Appeal was made to the Supreme Court following a district court's dismissal of a suit brought by the State of Missouri, attempting to prevent Holland, a game warden, from enforcing the Migratory Bird Act. The Supreme Court held that the Act of Congress being challenged was valid, as:

> "[T]he power of the Federal Government to make and enforce treaties is not a limitation on the reserved powers of States, but is the existence of a power not reserved to the States under the 10th Amendment being both expressly granted to the United States and prohibited to the States."[84]

In other words, there was no limitation on what could be the subject-matter of a treaty, and the enforcement of a treaty, regardless of subject-matter, falls within the exclusive competence of the federal government.

Missouri v Holland may be contrasted with *Attorney-General for Canada v Attorney-General for Ontario*.[85] Canada, like the United States, is a federal state and, in 1937, the Judicial Committee of the Privy Council was required to give its opinion on what was the position when the federal government did not have the

---

[82] Above, n.76, § 303 Comment e.
[83] 252 US 416 (1920).
[84] *ibid*. at 431.
[85] [1937] A.C. 326.

competence to give internal effect to international obligations which it had undertaken.[86] The Committee advised:

> "there is no such thing as treaty legislation as such. The distribution is based on classes of subjects; and as a treaty deals with a particular class so will the legislative power of performing it be ascertained . . .; the Dominion cannot, merely by making promises to foreign countries, clothe itself with legislative authority inconsistent with the Constitution."

and:

> ". . . In a unitary State whose legislature possesses unlimited powers the problem is simple. Parliament will either fulfil or not treaty obligations imposed upon the State by its executive. The nature of the obligations does not affect the complete authority of the Legislature to make them law if it so chooses . . ., in a federal State where legislative authority is limited . . ., or is divided up between different Legislatures . . . the problem is complex . . . The question is not how is the obligation formed, that is the function of the executive; but how is the obligation to be performed. . . .[87]

It may also happen in a federal state that the federal government will undertake an international obligation which is inconsistent with the law of a particular constituent part of the federation. As far as possible, the "offending" legislation will be interpreted as being consistent with international law, but the general principle regarding such a conflict is that it is the central government and not the constituent state which will have to answer to the international community.

A similar problem may arise within the United Kingdom in the wake of devolution. The United Kingdom remains responsible at the international level for (non)fulfilment of international obligations. However, the division in competence brought about by devolution might lead to a situation in which the Westminister Parliament does not have the internal competence to give effect to its assumed international obligations.[88]

---

[86] Legislation designed to give effect within Canada to draft conventions adopted by the International Labour Organisation and the League of Nations was claimed to be invalid, as the Dominion Parliament did not possess the competency to legislate on the subject-matter concerned.

[87] Above, n.85 at 351, 352 and 347. The limited internal competence of the federal government was why Canada did not accede to the UN 1966 Covenants on Economic, Social and Cultural Rights and Civil and Political Rights until 1976.

[88] See, however, the Scotland Act, s.58(1); see also the *Tyrer Case* (1978) 58 I.L.R. 339.

Suggestion

The State Department's "suggestion" is the American counterpart of the British executive certificate. However, the suggestion does not confine itself to merely giving the facts, but may include comments on the situation and indicate the executive's attitude. Although not regarded as conclusive, the suggestion will be accepted as persuasive by the courts.

Act of state doctrine[89]

What if a measure of a foreign state is contrary to international law? The act of state doctrine precludes the court from inquiring into the validity of the public acts of a recognised foreign sovereign power within its own territory: "the Judicial Branch will not examine the validity of a taking of property within its own territory by a foreign sovereign government."[90]

    The essence of the act of state doctrine is that the act of one independent government cannot be successfully questioned by the courts of another: "Redress of grievances by reason of such acts must be obtained through the means open to be availed of by sovereign powers as between themselves."[91] In other words, the judiciary abstains from giving a decision in deference to the executive so as not to embarrass the conduct of the executive foreign relations by questioning the acts of foreign states. The act of state doctrine is similar, but yet distinct from sovereign immunity[92] in that both are based on considerations of respect for the sovereign independence and equality of states, and on perceived limitations on the authority of domestic courts of one state to judge the activities of another state. However, whereas sovereign immunity relates to activities carried out in or related to the state of the forum, the act of state doctrine concerns judicial scrutiny of activities of foreign states in their own territories. Strict adherence to the act of state doctrine was maintained by the United States Supreme Court in the *Sabbatino Case*, even when the State Department has described the Cuban legislative measure as:

"manifestly in violation of those principles of international law which has long been accepted by the free countries of

---

[89] Act of State has a different connotation in British constitutional law—an alien, who is injured abroad by an act authorised or subsequently approved by the Crown, has no remedy in English courts.

[90] *Banco Nacional de Cuba v Sabbatino* 376 US 398 at 428 (1964).

[91] *Underhill v Hernandez* 168 US 250 at 252 (1897).

[92] Discussed below in Ch.6, pp. 121–123.

the West. It is in its essence discriminatory, arbitrary and confiscatory."[93]

The outcome of the *Sabbatino Case* was that the court gave effect to the Cuban decree, in spite of its having been contrary to international law.

The act of state doctrine as understood in the *Sabbatino Case* has its basis in the separation of powers and the raison d'être of the *Sabbatino* position was the need to avoid conflict between the judiciary and the executive on decisions regarding the legal nature of foreign actions.

The *Sabbatino* decision prompted a response from Congress in the form of the "Hickenlooper Amendments" to the Foreign Assistance Act, whereby:

> "no court in the United States shall decline on the ground of the . . . Act of State doctrine to make a determination on the merits giving effect to the principles of international law in a case in which a claim of title or other right to property is asserted by any party including a foreign State (or a party claiming through such State) based upon (or traced through) a confiscation or other taking . . . by an act of that State in violation of the principles of international law."[94]

Accordingly, American courts may review the acts of foreign governments which violate international law and which affect property owned by American citizens. The State Department can express in a "suggestion" that the act of state is to apply in a particular case.

Judicial determination of the legality of the foreign act of state will not necessarily interfere with the executive's conduct of foreign affairs.[95]

In *Alfred Dunhill v Republic of Cuba*,[96] the Legal Adviser to the State Department submitted a letter in which he stated that in the State Department's experience there was little support for the presumption "that adjudication of acts of foreign States in accordance with the relevant principles of international law would embarrass the conduct of foreign policy." Accordingly, he concluded that it would not cause embarrassment to the conduct of

---

[93] Above, n.90 at 403.
[94] s.620(e)(2) of the Foreign Assistance Act of 1965, Pub.L.No.89–171; 301(d)(2), 79 Stat. 653, 659, as amended.
[95] See, *Banco Nacional de Cuba v First National City Bank* US Supreme Ct, 406 US 759 (1972); 92 S.L.T. 1808.
[96] 425 US 682 (1976).

United States foreign policy if the court demanded to follow the holding in the *Sabbatino Case*.[97] In *W. S. Kirkpatrick and Co. v Environmental Tectonics Corp. International*,[98] the US Supreme Court declined to apply the act of state doctrine, stating that:

> "The act of state doctrine does not establish an exception for cases and controversies that may embarrass foreign governments but merely requires that, in the process of deciding, the acts of foreign sovereigns taken within their own jurisdiction shall be deemed valid. That doctrine has no application to the present case because the validity of no foreign sovereign act is at issue".[99]

The act of state doctrine would not apply in respect of war crimes or offences over which there is universal jurisdiction. The act of state doctrine should be distinguished from the political question doctrine, namely that there are certain national issues so sensitive that they are non-justiciable.[1] Cases which raise the political question doctrine are dismissed by the courts, unlike those involving the act of state doctrine which are adjudicated.

The act of state doctrine is one of American municipal law. There is no rule of international law which requires the application of the act of state doctrine.

---

[97] *ibid*. letter of Monroe Leigh, Legal Adviser, Department of State—printed as App.706, 709, 710–711.

[98] 29 I.L.M. 182, (1990).

[99] Scalia J. at 189, *ibid*.

[1] *US v Sisson* 294 F. Suppl.515 (D.Mass. 1968), in which the court concluded that a domestic tribunal was incapable of ascertaining facts pertaining during war and that the defendant had submitted an issue of a political character not within the jurisdiction of the court. The defendant had invoked as his defence to a charge of refusing to serve in the US armed forces that the US operations in Vietnam were contrary to international law. On non-justiciability of political questions, see also *Baker v Carr* 369 US 186 (1962) and *Greenham Women against Cruise Missiles v Reagan* 591 F. Supp. 1332 (1984).

4. INTERNATIONAL PERSONALITY

The possession of international personality means that an entity is a subject of international law, and is "capable of possessing international rights and duties, and has the capacity to maintain its rights by bringing international claims."[1]

A subject of international law owes responsibilities to the international community and enjoys rights, the benefits of which may be claimed, and which if denied, may be enforced to the extent recognised by the international legal system, via legal procedures. That is, the entity will have procedural capacity.

Which entities have international legal personality?

The concept of international personality is neither static nor uniform:

> "The subjects of law in any legal system are not necessarily identical in their nature or in the extent of their rights, and their nature depends upon the needs of the community. Throughout its history, the development of international life, . . ., and the progressive increase in the collective activities of

---

[1] "*Reparations for Injuries Suffered in the Service of the United Nations*" I.C.J.Rep. 1949 at p.174.

States has already given rise to instances of action upon the international plane by certain entities which are not States."[2]

As international law has developed and expanded in scope, so "new" entities have been admitted as "actors" on the international scene. The personality enjoyed by such actors varies considerably. States were once considered the exclusive subjects of international law:

"Since the law of nations is based on the common consent of individual States, and not of individual human beings, States solely and exclusively are the subjects of international law."[3]

Today, however, although they remain its primary subjects, they are no longer the exclusive subjects of the international legal system. Throughout the twentieth century, the scope of international legal personality widened considerably as a consequence of the proliferation of international organisations and the greater international awareness of human rights. However, whilst states possess full international legal personality as an inherent attribute of their statehood, all other entities possessing personality do so only to the extent that states allow: that is, their personality is derived via states.

The personality of states may thus be characterised as *original* and that of other entities as *derivative*.

STATES

States are the principal persons of international law. International law is essentially the product of relations between states, be it through practice forming customary international law, or through international agreements (treaties). States alone may be parties to contentious cases before the International Court of Justice.[4] States alone enjoy the discretion as to whether or not to espouse a claim on behalf of a national who has allegedly been aggrieved by another state; and once a state does take up a claim, the dispute is raised to the international level and becomes one between two states.[5] An individual cannot denounce a state's right to espouse a claim on his behalf should it choose to do so[6] and a state does not act as the agent of its nationals when negotiating a treaty.[7]

---

[2] *ibid.* at 178.
[3] L. Oppenheim, *International Law* (2nd ed., 1912).
[4] Art.34(1), Statute of the International Court of Justice.
[5] See, *e.g. Mavrommatis Palestine Concessions Case* P.C.I.J.Rep., ser.A, No.2 (1924).
[6] *North American Dredging Company Case* 4 R.I.A.A. 26 at 29 *et seq.* (1926).
[7] See, *e.g. Rustomjee v The Queen* (1876) 1 Q.B.D. 487 at 492; *Civilian War Claimants' Association Ltd v The King* [1932] A.C. 14, HL at 26.

What is a state?

A "state" under international law is an entity which has a defined
territory, a permanent population, is under the control of a government and engages in, or has the capacity to engage in, formal
relations with other entities.[8]

The definition reflects the indices of statehood enunciated in
the 1933 Montevideo Convention on Rights and Duties of States.[9]
The Convention, regarded as representing in general terms the
requirements of statehood demanded by customary international
law, was adopted by the Seventh International Conference of
American States (15 Latin American and the United States):

> "The state as a person of international law should possess the
> following qualifications: (a) a permanent population, (b) a
> defined territory; (c) government; and (d) capacity to enter
> into relations with other states."[10]

Permanent population

States are aggregates of individuals and accordingly a permanent population is a prerequisite of statehood. However, no minimum population is required. Nauru, with a population of 9,500
is considered a state, as is Liechtenstein with a population of
30,000.

Defined territory

States are territorial units and:

> "territorial sovereignty ... involves the exclusive right to
> display the activities of a State. This right has a corollary, a
> duty: the obligation to protect within the territory the rights
> of other States, in particular their right to integrity and invi-
> olability in peace and in war, together with the rights which
> each State may claim for its nationals in foreign territory.
> Without manifesting its territorial sovereignty in a manner
> corresponding to circumstances, the State cannot fulfil this
> duty. Territorial sovereignty cannot limit itself to its negative
> side, *i.e.* to excluding the activities of other States, for it
> serves to divide between the nations the space upon which
> human activities are employed, in order to assure them at all

---

[8] The American Law Institute, *Restatement of the Law Third, The Foreign Relations
Law of the United States*, Vol. 1, § 201.
[9] 164 L.N.T.S. 19; U.S.T.S. 881; 28 A.J.I.L., Supp., 75 (1934).
[10] Art.1, Montevideo Convention.

points the minimum of protection of which international law is the guardian . . ."[11]

Art.9 of the Montevideo Convention provides that:

"The jurisdiction of States within the limits of national territory applies to all the inhabitants. Nationals and foreigners are under the same protection of the law and the national authorities and the foreigners may not claim rights other or more extensive than those of the nationals."

However, while territory is necessary, there is no prescribed minimal geographical size. The requirement of territory may be satisfied even if the entity's territorial boundaries are not precisely defined or are to some extent in dispute, for example Israel in 1948 and Kuwait in 1963. This rule, that indefinite boundaries need not defeat a claim to statehood, was noted by the court in the *North Sea Continental Shelf Cases*:

"The appurtenance of a given area, considered as an entity, in no way governs the precise determination of its boundaries, any more than uncertainty as to boundaries can affect territorial rights. There is for instance no rule that the land frontiers of a State must be fully delimited and defined, and often in various places and for long periods they are not . . ."[12]

However, one of the reasons advanced by the British for the non-recognition of Bophuthatswana as an independent state is the fragmentation of its territory within South Africa.[13]

A government

Statehood must be evidenced by the establishment of an effective government, that is, one independent of any other authority and one which enjoys legislative and administrative competence.[14] Non-dependence was stressed by the International Committee of Jurists in 1920 in its Report on the status of Finland. The

[11] *Island of Palmas Case* 2 R.I.A.A. 829, Huber J. at 839 (1928).
[12] I.C.J.Rep. 1969 3 at 32.
[13] Other reasons are the pattern of population, the economic dependency on South Africa and primarily the fact that "the existence of Bophuthatswana is a consequence of apartheid . . .". See, *Hansard*, HC, Vol. 126, cols 760–761. (February 3, 1988); U.K.M.I.L. 1986; 57 B.Y.I.L. 507 (1986).
[14] Again note the British position *vis-à-vis* Bophuthatswana and the latter's economic dependence on South Africa. Bophuthatswana was re-incorporated into South Africa on April 27, 1994 and ceased to exist as a separate political entity and the flag is no longer in use.

Committee highlighted the difficulty of ascertaining the actual date when Finland became, in the legal sense, a sovereign state, but concluded that it certainly was not one:

> "until a stable political organisation had been created, and until the public authorities had become strong enough to assert themselves throughout the territories of the State without the assistance of foreign troops. It would appear that it was in May 1918, that the civil war ended and that the foreign troops began to leave the country, so that from that time onwards it was possible to re-establish order and normal political and social life, little by little."[15]

An established state's statehood will not be nullified if it is without an effective government for a period of time, for example during a civil war (*e.g.* Somalia). Nor does military occupation terminate statehood, for example Germany's occupation of the European states during the Second World War.

Capacity to enter into international relations

This is an important indicator of statehood, but its realisation depends on the response of other actors on the international stage. The satisfaction of the first three criteria is essentially factual, but fulfilment of this criterion depends on recognition:

> "The political existence of the State is independent of recognition by the other States. Even before recognition the State has the right to defend its integrity and independence, to provide for its conservation and prosperity, and consequently to organise itself as it sees fit, to legislate upon its interests, administer its services, and to define the jurisdiction and competence of its courts. The exercise of these rights has no other limitation than the exercise of the rights of other States according to international law."[16]

In other words, an entity may have the capacity to enter into foreign relations, but should other states decline to enter into relations with it, the entity in question is denied the opportunity to demonstrate this capacity in practice. For example, Southern Rhodesia, a British self-governing territory until it declared unilateral independence from Britain in November 1965, had a population, territory, a government and the capacity to enter into

---

[15] L.N.O.J., Special Supp. No.3 (1920) 3.
[16] Art.3, Montevideo Convention, above n.9.

relations with other states. However, no other state was willing to enter into relations with Southern Rhodesia. Southern Rhodesia was refused recognition as a state by the rest of the international community.[17] Similarly, governments consistently refused to enter into relations with the Transkei. The Transkei territory was declared by South Africa in 1976 to be a "sovereign and independent state", but the United Nations General Assembly subsequently adopted a resolution rejecting the "independence" as "invalid".[18] Similarly, recognition had been denied by all states other than South Africa to Bophuthatswana, Venda and Ciskei. The independence of Ciskei was refuted by the Security Council, which issued a statement calling upon "all Governments to deny any form of recognition to the so-called 'independent' bantustans."[19] An entity which possesses the ability to conduct foreign relations does not terminate its statehood if it voluntarily hands over all or part of the conduct of its foreign relations to another state, for example San Marino (Italy) and[19a] Monaco (France). Another "mini" European state is Liechtenstein, which operates within the Swiss economic system and has delegated a number of sovereign powers to Switzerland but nevertheless is still recognised as a sovereign state.[20] Similarly, the personality of a protected state which existed before the conclusion of the agreement, establishing its dependent status is not extinguished. See, for example, *Nationality Decrees in Tunis and Morocco Case*[21] and *Rights of Nationals of the United States in Morocco Case.*[22] Such relationships were characteristic of the British and French Empires, and most were terminated during the decolonisation movement, which gathered momentum after the Second World War. Membership of a regional organisation does not negate the statehood of individual members, for example the European Union,

---

[17] See Security Council Resolution of November 12, 1965, Resolution 216 (1965) S.C.O.R., 20th year, Resolutions and Decisions, p.8 and Security Council Resolution of November 20, 1965, Resolution 217 (1965) S.C.O.R., 20th Year, Resolutions and Decisions, p.8 in which the Smith regime was characterised as illegal, the declaration of independence as of "no legal validity" and UN Members were called upon to refrain from assisting the "illegal racist minority regime".

[18] GA Resolution, GAOR, 31st Session, Supp.39, p.10.

[19] S.C.O.R., 36th Year, Resolutions and Decisions, p.1. The legislation relating to the homelands was repealed in 1993, and the four homelands have since been reabsorbed into South Africa.

[19a] *N.B.* San Marino was admitted to the UN in March, 1992.

[20] Although denied admission to the League of Nations on the grounds that she could not discharge all the international obligations which would be imposed upon her by the Covenant, Liechtenstein has been a party to a case before the ICJ (the *Nottebohm Case*, (1955). Liechtenstein became a member of the UN on September 18, 1990.

[21] P.C.I.J.Rep., ser.B, No.4 (1923).

[22] I.C.J.Rep. 1952, 176.

although admittedly, sovereignty in certain areas of competance may be restricted.

Existing states may refuse "statehood" to an entity which has attained a characteristic of statehood in violation of international law, for example the acquisition of territory by the use of force contrary to Art.2(4) of the United Nations Charter, or to the principle of non-intervention.[23] However, in most instances, whether or not there has been an unlawful threat or use of force will be disputed, and generally it is not an issue which will be authoritatively resolved, for example Indian intervention in Bangladesh was by many governments deemed to be illegal, whilst others argued to the contrary, justifying India's action as supporting the principle of self-determination. Territory acquired by the legitimate use of force, for example in self-defence, and then annexed from the aggressor, *may* (emphasis added) be an exception to the non-recognition-of-conquest rule.

Political self-determination, that is, the principle whereby the political future of a colony or similar non-independent territory is determined in accordance with the wishes of its inhabitants, has, particularly since the 1960s, been taken into account in issues of statehood. The principle, which 20 years ago was articulated as "a formative principle of great potency . . .",[24] has now evolved into a rule of international law.[25] The Declaration on the Granting of Independence to Colonial Territories and Peoples[26] characterised the principle and para.2 reads:

> "All peoples have a right to self-determination; by virtue of that right they freely determine their political status and freely pursue their economic, social and cultural development."

---

[23] See GA Res.2625 (XXV) "Declaration on Principles of International Law Concerning Friendly Relations and Co-operation among States in Accordance with the Charter of the United Nations" G.A.O.R., 25th Session, Supp.28 (A/2028) 121 (1970); 65 A.J.I.L. 243 (1970). The ALMA ATA declaration states. "The Community and its Member States will not recognise entities which are the result of aggression". Guidelines on the Recognition of New States in eastern Europe and in the Soviet Union (1992) 31 I.L.M. 1486.

[24] Schwarzenberger, *Manual of International Law* (6th ed., 1976), p.59.

[25] See decision of the Chamber of the International Court of Justice in the *Frontier Dispute (Burkino Faso/Mali)* I.C.J.Rep. 1986 554 at 566–567, in which the Chamber was required to consider the relationship between self-determination and *uti possidetis*. It has also been suggested that it constitutes a rule of *jus cogens*; see Espiell in UN *Law/Fundamental Rights: Two Topics in International Law* (Cassese ed., 1979) p.167.

[26] GA Resolution 1514 (XV), December 14, 1960, G.A.O.R., 15th Session, Supp.16, p.66. Harris, p.117.

The aim of para.2 was identified in the *Western Sahara Case*.[27] It was acknowledged therein "that the application of the right of self-determination requires a free and genuine expression of the will of the peoples concerned."[28] Dillard J., in a separate Opinion (though concurring in the court's Opinion), stated that:

> "It seemed hardly necessary to make more explicit the cardinal restraint which the legal right of self-determination imposes. The restraint may be captured in a single sentence. It is for the people to determine the destiny of the territory and not the territory the destiny of the people . . ."[29]

However, Resolution 1514 does not purport to negate a title to colonial and similar non-independent territory which does not reflect the wishes of its people, but rather emphasises that "immediate steps" should be taken to ensure independence is attained in accordance with self-determination. The emergence of self-determination, as a cardinal principle in shaping the political future of a colonial or similar non-independent territory, means that such territories can no longer be considered as mere adjuncts of the administering power. They have, according to the 1970 Declaration on Principles of International Law:

> "a status separate and distinct from the territory of the State administering it; and such separate and distinct status under the Charter [*i.e.* UN Charter] shall exist until the people of the colony or non-self-governing territory have exercised their right of self-determination in accordance with the Charter, and particularly its purposes and principles."[30]

This separate identity of an administered people is further reflected in several legal statements relating to the status of South West Africa (Namibia).[31]

South West Africa was placed under a "C" Mandate at the conclusion of the First World War. Mandates were introduced as a novel type of administration for those territories taken from defeated powers and "inhabited by peoples not yet able to stand

---

[27] Advisory Opinion I.C.J.Rep. 1975 12—see also Harris (1991), pp. 113–125 for a fuller exposition of self-determination.

[28] *ibid.*, p.32.

[29] Above, n.27, p.122.

[30] Above, n.23.

[31] For the background and details of the mandated and trusteeship systems established by the League of Nations and the UN respectively, see Harris, pp.125–126. South West Africa became the independent state of Namibia in November, 1990.

by themselves under the strenuous conditions of the modern world."[32] After the conclusion of the Second World War, the mandate system was replaced by that of trusteeship.[33] South Africa, however, refused to place South West Africa under that trusteeship system and this precipitated much political and legal argument on the status of South West Africa.[34] In the 1950 Opinion, McNair J. pronounced that the system involved a:

> "new institution—a new relationship between territory and its inhabitants on the one hand and the government which represents them internationally on the other—a new species of international government, which does not fit into the old conception of sovereignty and which is alien to it."[35]

The sovereignty, McNair J. maintained, was held to be in abeyance until the inhabitants of the territory obtained recognition as an independent state. The issues before the court concerned the responsibilities and duties of South Africa but, against the backcloth of the self-determination movement, there was a move away from the traditional view that a mandated/trusteeship territory only achieved international recognition on attaining independence, to one according such an entity at least a degree of international status—a view which was articulated by Ammoun J. when he concluded that:

> "Namibia, even at the periods when it had been reduced to the status of a German colony or was subject to the South African Mandate, possessed a legal personality which was denied to it only by the law now obsolete . . . It nevertheless constituted a subject of law . . ., possessing national sovereignty but lacking the exercise thereof . . . Sovereignty, . . . did not cease to belong to the people subject to mandate. It had simply, for a time, been rendered inarticulate and deprived of freedom of expression."[36]

---

[32] Covenant of the League of Nations, Art.22.
[33] The system applied only to 11 territories—10 former mandates and Somalia taken from Italy. No other territories were brought into the system as was envisaged by Art.77(1) of the UN Charter.
[34] *International Status of South West Africa Case* I.C.J.Rep. 1950, 128; *Legal Consequences for States of the Continued Presence of South Africa in Namibia (South West Africa) Notwithstanding Security Council Resolution 276 (1970). Advisory Opinion* I.C.J.Rep. 1971, 16.
[35] *ibid*. p.150.
[36] Above, n.34 at p.68.

Ammoun's J. view, representing the Third World illustrates the change in international attitude, namely that non-self-governing territories could no longer be dismissed as adjuncts of the administering power. They cannot, by definition, enjoy full sovereignty until independence has been attained, but they do apparently enjoy some status, be it one that falls short of full sovereignty.[37]

States are the primary subjects of international law, but they are not the exclusive subjects. Other entities are afforded a degree of international legal personality. Of these entities, international organisations are undoubtedly the most important. The application of self-determination outside the traditional context of colonialism has led to a distinction between internal self-determination and external self-determination, as was highlighted in the decision of the Canadian Supreme Court *Re Reference by the Govenor in Council concerning certain questions relating to the succession of Quebec from Canada*.[38] This particular case was concerned with whether the province of Quebec enjoyed the right to secede unilaterally from Canada;[39] the court concluded in the negative and held that any right of self-determination could only arise in strictly limited circumstances and that international law does not support the "right" of entities within an existing state to secede unilaterally. The court accordingly upheld the principle of territorial integrity of existing states. It was also noted that no right of external self-determination would be recognised when full participation in civil and political life is available, namely internal self-determination, which may be interpreted as the right of a minority people to pursue political, economic, social, and cultural development, within the framework of an existing state.[40]

The Arbitration Committee of the International Conference on Yugoslavia[41] (the Banditer Committee) stated "That whatever the circumstances, the right to self-determination must not involve changes to existing frontiers at the time of independence

---

[37] Hong Kong, *e.g.* does not satisfy the criteria for statehood because it was subject to the legal authority of the UK. The Hong Kong Special Administrative Region (HKSAR) was established on July 1, 1997, under the legal authority of China (The PRC). The HKSAR has limited treaty-making competence and is able to conclude agreements independently of China in certain fields, *e.g.* shipping, trade, communications, financial and monetary. Foreign and Commonwealth Office, Paper, London, Application after June 30, 1997 of Multilateral and Bilateral International Agreements, Hong Kong Department, April 1996.

[38] (1998) 161 D.L.R. (4th) 385.

[39] The court was asked whether such a right existed under the Canadian Constitution or by way of existing international law.

[40] See Final Report and Recommendations of an International meeting of Experts on the Further Study of the Concept of the Right of People for UNESCO, February 22, 1990, SNS–89/CONF.602/7.

[41] Opinion No.2, 3 E.J.I.L. (1992) 183–184.

(*uti possidetis juris*) except where the State concerned agreed otherwise".[42]

Caution is demanded in respect of self-determination in contemporary international law and the principle of self-determination is only one consideration—cognance must also be given to the human rights of all parties involved. The right of self-determination has to be tempered, otherwise ". . . if every ethnic, religious or linguistic group claimed Statehood, there would be no limit to fragmentation, and peace, security, and economic well-being for all would be much more difficult to achieve."[43]

An additional factor, which has been introduced to state recognition, has been that of compliance with human rights, and the rights of minorities. The Declaration on the Guidelines on the Recognition of new states in Eastern Europe and the Soviet Union[44] (The Alma Ata Declaration) issued by the Foreign Ministers of the European Economic Council in December 1991, demanded, *inter alia*, ". . . respect for the UN Charter, the Helsinki Final Act, and the Charter of Paris, 'especially with regard to the rule of law, democracy and human rights', ". . . guarantees for the rights of ethnic and national groups and minorities."[45]

INTERNATIONAL ORGANISATIONS

International organisations have proliferated during the twentieth century. An international organisation, for the purposes of international law, is an entity established by agreement and which has states as its principal members.[46] Organisations vary considerably in their competencies, importance and membership. The United Nations, for example, is a global organisation enjoying almost universal membership, whilst the European Council is an example of a regional organisation.

Before an international organisation can make any impact on the international scene, it must be afforded some degree of

---

[42] The Banditer Committee was established by EU States and its mandate was to express its views on certain matters in relation to the peace process following the break up of Yugoslavia. In regards to self-determination, the committee's opinion was sought on whether "The Serbian population in Croatia and Bosnia–Herzegovina, as one of the constituent peoples of Yugoslavia, have the right to self-determination."

[43] UN Secretary General Boutros Boutros Ghali, Agenda for Peace, Reproduced in A. Roberts and B. Kingsbury, *United Nations, Divided World* (2nd ed., 1993).

[44] Above, n.23, p.62.

[45] E.J.I.L. 16 December 1991, p.50. Similar conditions were demanded in respect of those entities claiming recognition as states following the break up of the former Yugoslavia.

[46] Inter-governmental organisations are distinct from non-governmental organisations established by individuals.

international personality. The degree of international personality enjoyed by international organisations varies. An international organisation may enjoy certain rights, but not others, and, while all states enjoy the same degree of personality, this is not true with regard to international organisations.

Determination of personality

International organisations frequently resemble states in the personality which they possess. Their legal personality may, to some extent, parallel that of states. Organisations may have the capacity to own, acquire and transfer property, and to enter into contractual agreements and international agreements with states and other international organisations. They may pursue legal remedies and may enjoy rights and duties under international law. International organisations are restricted though by their constituent Charter, that is, the agreement establishing the organisation. Determination of an organisation's personality thus demands that the constituent document be examined.

The constituent document may expressly provide that an organisation is to have international legal personality.[47] Alternatively, and this is more usual, personality may only be implied from the constituent document and consolidated through the practice of the organisation.

The United Nations

The United Nations Charter is silent on the Organisation's international legal personality. Only two articles in the Charter deal explicitly with legal status, and then only with the United Nations' status within the municipal systems of Member States. Art.104 provides that the United Nations is to enjoy within Member States' territory "such legal capacity as may be necessary for the exercise of its functions and fulfilment of its purposes", whilst Art.105 provides that the United Nations "shall enjoy in the territory of each of its Members such privileges and immunities as are necessary for the fulfilment of its purposes."

Arts 104 and 105 do not grant international legal personality to the United Nations. Arts 104 and 105 have been supplemented by the Convention on the Privileges and Immunities of the United Nations drawn up by the General Assembly in 1946.[48] The agreement is in force between the United Nations and every Member of the Organisation and provides for functional privileges and

---

[47] Exceptionally, a Constituent Document may deny an organisation personality, *e.g.* Art.4 of the Statute of the International Hydrographic Bureau.
[48] 1 U.N.T.S. 15; U.K.T.S. 10 (1950) Cmd.7891; 43 A.J.I.L. Supp.I.

immunities for the United Nations. A similar convention, the Convention on the Privileges and Immunities of the Specialised Agencies,[49] provides for the immunities and privileges of the specialised agencies. The United Nations has also entered into agreements with host states in which it operates, for example the UN/USA Headquarters Agreement.[50]

Headquarters agreements are necessary, as an organisation can only establish itself within a state's territory when it has that state's consent. Such agreements determine the status of the organisation's headquarters and its capacities, privileges and immunities.

The capacity of the United Nations to be a party to agreements with states helped the International Court to conclude that the Organisation indeed enjoyed international legal capacity. The court held that the United Nations:

> "was intended to exercise and enjoy, and is in fact exercising and enjoying, functions and rights which can only be explained on the basis of the possession of a large measure of international personality and the capacity to operate on the international plane."[51]

The court had been given the opportunity to comment on the international personality of the United Nations when it was requested by the General Assembly to give an Advisory Opinion on whether the Organisation had the capacity to espouse an international claim in respect of injury sustained by a United Nations official whilst in the service of the United Nations. The court, before delivering its Opinion, took the opportunity to discuss the question of the United Nations' personality. The court looked at the objectives of the Organisation—the promotion of international peace and security—and concluded that the United Nations could not fulfil the objectives for which it was established if it did not possess international personality. As to whether the Organisation could initiate an international claim, the court arrived at an affirmative conclusion.

The court further confirmed that the United Nations could not only espouse a claim for the damage caused to the interests of the Organisation, that is its administrative machinery, its property

---

[49] 33 U.N.T.S. 261; U.K.T.S. 69 (1959) Cmnd.855.

[50] 11 U.N.T.S. 11 (1947) Supplemented; 554 U.N.T.S. 308 (1966); 687 U.N.T.S. 408 (1969).

[51] Above, n.1 at 179. The ICJ reaffirmed the independent legal personality of the UN, see Advisory Opinion on the Applicability of Art.VI of the Convention on the Privileges and Immunities of the UN 1989 I.C.J.Rep. 177, 29 I.L.M. 98 (1990).

and assets, but could initiate a claim for reparation in respect of damage caused to the UN official or agent, or to persons entitled through him. In reaching this conclusion, the court again made reference to the purposes and functions of the United Nations and held that a UN official could only perform his duties satisfactorily if he were afforded adequate protection. Individual states could not be expected to and, indeed, were not able to offer such protection.

The court upheld that the United Nations enjoyed this right of initiative against a non-Member State (in this case, Israel) because the court maintained the United Nations possessed objective personality as opposed to subjective personality. Objective personality can be enforced *vis-à-vis* the whole world by virtue of the purposes of the Organisation and its almost universal membership.

The court's Opinion proved to be not only a landmark for the United Nations, but for international organisations generally. The court emphasised that the rights and duties of an organisation (that is, any organisation) depend upon the purposes and functions of the organisation as specified or implied in its constituent document and developed in practice. Both the General Assembly and the Economic and Social Council enjoy the legal competence to request the International Court of Justice for an advisory opinion.[52] However, in respect of the World Health Organisation (WHO), the International Court of Justice, in the *Nuclear Weapons Case*,[53] highlighted that ". . . international organisations do not, unlike States, possess a general competence, but are governed by the 'principle of speciality', that is to say, they are invested by the States which create them with powers, the limits of which are a function of the common interests whose promotion those States entrust to them. Besides, the World Health Organisation is an international organisation of a particular kind—a 'specialised agency' forming part of a system based in the Charter of the United Nations, which is designed to organise international co-operation in a coherent fashion by bringing the United Nations, invested with powers of general scope, into relationship with various autonomous and complementary organisations, invested with sectorial powers. The Court therefore concluded that the responsibilities of the WHO are necessarily restricted to the sphere of public 'health' and cannot encroach on the responsibilities of

---

[52] The General Assembly, for instance, asked the ICJ for an advisory opinion concerning the legality of the use of nuclear weapons, 35 I.L.M. 809, The Economic and Social Council asked for an opinion concerning the Applicability of Art.VI of the Convention on the Privileges and Immunities of the UN.

[53] Legality of the Use by a State of Nuclear Weapons in Armed Conflict, 35 I.L.M. 809.

other parts of the United Nations system. And that there is no doubt that questions concerning the use of force, the regulation of armaments and disarmament are within the competence of the United Nations and lie outside that of the special agencies." The Court concluded it did not have jurisdiction to hear the case.

The administration of territories by the United Nations under the trusteeship system and the competence of the Organisation to intervene to maintain or restore international peace and security have served further to reinforce the United Nations' international personality.

One word of caution: while a treaty-making power is evidence of international personality, a general treaty-making power should not be deduced from the possession of some degree of personality. In other words, entities having a treaty-making capacity possess some international personality, but not all international entities necessarily possess a general treaty-making capacity.

The overriding conclusion in respect of international organisations is that no generalisation may be made regarding their international personality. Each organisation has to be looked at individually and its international legal status assessed in the light of its constituent document and the organisation's own practice. The plethora of institutions on the international scene has resulted in the growth of law pertaining specifically to them.[54] The law of international institutions is now a specialised subdivision of international law and can be treated as an autonomous subject.[55]

INDIVIDUALS

Individuals have limited international legal personality, although contemporary international law increasingly recognises that an individual may possess both international rights and duties. The greater awareness of human rights over the last 50 years has promoted the guarantee of human rights for individuals through both international and regional regulations.[56]

Simultaneously, it has been increasingly recognised that individuals may be held responsible for certain conduct. It is no longer believed that states are exclusively the perpetrators of conduct which breaches international law. The legal fiction that

---

[54] A good general text on international institutions is D.W. Bowett, *The Law of International Institutions* (4th ed., 1982).

[55] In a number of educational institutions, the law of international institutions is a separate course, independent of international law.

[56] See Ch.9.

individuals do not participate on the international scene, and consequently could not be held responsible for their acts, has been dented. See, for example, the jurisdiction of the International Tribunal for the Prosecution of Persons Responsible for Serious Violations of International Humanitarian law Committed in the Territory of the Former Yugoslavia (the ICTY), the International Tribunal for the Prosecution of Persons Responsible for Genocide and Other Serious Violations of International Humanitarian Law Committed in the Territory of Rwanda and Rwandan Citizens Responsible for Genocide and Other Such Violations Committed in the Territory of Neighbouring States, between January 1, 1994 and December 31, 1994 (ICTR), the Pinochet case,[57] and the efforts to bring the perpetrators of the Lockerbie incident[58] to justice. Notwithstanding this, piracy has long been established under customary international law as an international crime.[59] Individual responsibility derives from international law and is independent of the law of any state. At Nuremberg the International Tribunal held:

"Crimes against international law are committed by men, not by abstract entities, and only by punishing individuals who commit such crimes can the provisions of international law be enforced."

Similarly, Art.4 of the Convention on the Prevention and Punishment of the Crime of Genocide[60] provides that genocide is punishable as a crime, irrespective of whether those committing it "are constitutionally responsible rulers, public officials or private individuals". The corollary of this acknowledgment that individuals may incur international responsibility is that they are under an obligation to refrain from such conduct.[61] Individuals, therefore, have limited rights and duties on the international scene. Other acts which are now recognised as giving rise to individual responsibility at an international level include, *inter alia*, hijacking, sabotage, terrorism, drug trafficking and acts upon diplomats.[61a] A

---

[57] Regina v Bartle & The Commissioner of Police for the Metropolis & Others, Ex Parte Pinochet 24 March, 1999, [1991] 2 All E.R. 97.
[58] Lockerbie case, (1992) I.C.J. 3, 94 I.L.R. 478.
[59] See Ch.6.
[60] Paris, December 9, 1948; T.S. 58 (1970) Cmnd.4421.
[61] The Statute of the ICTY affirms the principle of *ratione personae*, i.e. a person is not relieved of individual criminal responsibility for a crime because it was committed under superior orders (Arts. 6 and 7). This would only be considered as mitigating circumstances when passing sentence. (See Ch.9 on Human Rights generally.)
[61a] See Chs. 6 and 9.

major handicap to individuals' exercising international personality has been their lack of procedural capacity denied to them because of the reluctance of states to grant them such capacity.

Procedural capacity of individuals

The Permanent Court in the *Danzig Railway Officials Case*[62] recognised that, exceptionally, treaties could create rights for individuals, and that in certain circumstances these rights could be enforced in the municipal courts:

> "the very object of an international agreement, according to the intention of the Contracting Parties, may be the adoption by the Parties of some definite rules creating individual rights and obligations and enforceable by the national courts."[63]

The Central American Court of Justice, established in 1908, was novel in that it was envisaged that the court would deal with disputes between states and private individuals. The court was to have jurisdiction to hear disputes between private individuals of any one of the five Contracting Parties and any of the other Contracting Governments. The Court's importance lay in that it envisaged the potential procedural capacity of individuals. The Court itself ceased to function in 1918 after hearing only five cases—of which four were declared inadmissible while the fifth failed on the merits.

The Treaty of Versailles[64] provided for the espousal of claims by individuals against governments and nationals of the defeated states. However, as part and parcel of the peacekeeping treaty, this cannot be regarded as a major enhancement of the individual's position under general international law.

The tribunal, established under the Upper Silesian Convention was notable in that it was competent to hear cases brought by nationals of a state against their own state.[65]

Contemporary international law affords individuals a greater measure of procedural capacity. Under Arts 34 and 35 of the European Convention on Human Rights, individuals can initiate claims alleging breaches of the Convention by their national

---

[62] P.C.I.J.Rep., ser.B, No.15 (1928) 4–47; 4 A.D. 587; Hudson, *World Court Reports*, Vol. II (1927–32) 237.

[63] P.C.I.J.Rep., ser.B, No.15, (1928) 17; Hudson, p.247; *cf.* the concept of direct effect employed by European Community law, *e.g.* Case 26/62 *Van Gend en Loos v Nederlandse Tarief Commissie* [1963] E.C.R. 1; C.M.L.R. 105, with respect to Art.12 of the EC Treaty.

[64] U.K.T.S. 4 (1919) Cmd.153; 13 A.J.I.L.Supp.151; 16 A.J.I.L.Supp.207.

[65] See *Steiner and Gross v Polish State* 4 A.D. 291 (1928).

state.[66] The right of individual petition is similarly provided for in Art.14 of the 1966 International Convention on the Elimination of All Forms of Racial Discrimination, whilst under the (First) Optional Protocol to the International Covenant on Civil and Political Rights (1966) the Human Rights Committee is competent to receive and consider "communications from individuals claiming to be victims of violations of any of the rights set forth in the Covenant." The Optional Protocol to the Convention on the Elimination of Discrimination Against Women, which entered into force on December 22, 2000,[67] also provides recourse for individual petition. The American Convention on Human Rights provides for the initiation of a petition alleging a violation of the Convention by "any person or group of persons or non-governmental entity legally recognised in one or more Member States."[68]

In addition to the foregoing, individuals enjoy limited procedural capacity before the European Court of First Instance, and the Convention on the Settlement of Investment Disputes between States and Nationals of Other States 1965, provides a mechanism for the settlement of disputes between contracting parties and companies of the nationality of a contracting party on the consent of both sides.[69] Individuals do not, however, enjoy *locus standi* before the International Court of Justice.

The procedural capacity of individuals on the international stage has been extended, but only to the extent that states have been willing to accord them such capacity.

OTHER ENTITIES—SELECTED ANOMALIES

National liberation movements

The most notable of the national liberation movements has been the Palestine Liberation Organisation (PLO)[70] The Palestinian Authority, like its predecessor enjoys permanent observer status at the United Nations—such recognition, however, does not impute recognition by the Member States of the Organisation.

---

[66] Provided, that is, such a right has been recognised by the individual's state of nationality. The European Convention, as modified by Protocol No.11, which entered into force on November 1, 1998. *N.B.* the original Convention entered into force on September 3, 1953.

[67] As of the 26 June 2002, there have been 34 ratifications, 74 signatories and 41 parties to the Protocol.

[68] Art.44.

[69] 4 I.L.M. 532 (1965).

[70] The Palestinian Authority replaced the PLO in January 1996 and has been recognised by the Israeli government. Another instance was the African National Congress (ANC), which is now the majority government of South Africa.

Nevertheless, note the advisory opinion of the International Court of Justice in 1988, concluding that the United States, as a party to the Agreement between the United Nations and the United States of America regarding the Headquarters of the United Nations of June 26, 1947, was under "an obligation in accordance with section 21 of that Agreement, to enter into arbitration for the settlement of the dispute between itself and the United Nations."[71] An obligation was held to be incumbent on the United States towards the PLO, in spite of the former's non-recognition of the Organisation.

The Holy See

The Holy See is another notable example of an entity that possesses limited international personality. The Holy See, of which the Pope is the head, has a population that is neither permanent nor indigenous, and its function is exclusively religious. However, it is a party to international treaties on such diverse subject-matters as arbitration, non-proliferation and monetary matters. Under the "New monetary convention between the Holy See and Italy", signed on December 29, 2000, the Vatican City is authorised to use the Euro as its official currency. The Holy See has also replaced the Fundamental Law of the State of the Vatican of June 7, 1929 with one that entered into force on February 22, 2001. The new law draws a greater distinction among the legislative, executive and judicial powers and makes a closer tie between the Governorate and the Secretary of State, which maintains the international relations of the Vatican City State.

In regard to the United Nations, the Holy See has a permanent observer mission and has a presence at other international organisations, such as the Organisation for American States and the specialised agencies of the UN, for example the World Health Organisation and the International Labour Organisation. Some 170 states have diplomatic relations with the Holy See.

The Holy See is an anomaly on the international scene enjoying and exercising international personality, because other international actors are willing to enter into international relations with it. The same is true of the Sovereign Order of Malta, which performs functions of a charitable nature from its headquarters in Rome.[72]

---

[71] See *Applicability of Obligation in Arbitrate Under section 21 of the United Nations Headquarters Agreement of June 26, 1947* I.C.J.Rep. 1988 12.
[72] *Nanni v Pace and the Sovereign Order of Malta* 8 A.D. 2 (1935–37) Italian Ct of Cassation.

CONCLUSION

There is no prototype international personality. States remain the primary subjects of international law. The international status of states is inherent in their statehood and states possess "the totality of international rights and duties recognised by international law . . .".[73] States are no longer the exclusive subjects of international law and other entities, notably international organisations and individuals, have had to be accommodated within what is to be understood as an international person.

RECOGNITION OF STATES AND GOVERNMENTS

The international community is not static. New states may be created while existing states may become extinct, for example the dissolution of the Socialist Federal Republic of Yugoslavia in 1991/92 and the creation of Bosnia–Herzegovina, Slovenia, Croatia and Macedonia as independent states.[74] Governments come to power and are removed from power. Recognition essentially denotes a willingness on the part of the recognising entity to enter into relations with the entity that is being recognised.

Recognition is of importance as it is concerned with status, that is the status of the entity in question (i) on the international scene, and (ii) within the municipal legal system of the recognising state.

Recognition is a complex issue. Factors other than legal considerations influence decisions to recognise any given entity. Recognition is accorded in the majority of cases by the executive. It is a matter of policy in which the recognising state has discretion: an entity, in other words, cannot demand recognition as of right. An apt description of recognition is that it is a political act which produces legal consequences.

Recognition of states and governments distinguished

Recognition of a state is the formal acknowledgment by another state that the recognised state possesses the attributes of statehood and signifies a willingness to treat the entity as a state.

Recognition of a government is the formal acknowledgment by the recognising state that the regime in question is the effective government and signifies a willingness to treat that regime as such.

---

[73] *Reparations Case*, above, n.1 at 180.
[74] See, Marc Weller for an account of the "International Response to the Dissolution of the Socialist Federal Republic of Yugoslavia" (1992) 86 A.J.I.L. 569. Note that the two states of Serbia and Montenegro are now known as the Federal Republic of Yugoslavia, which was recognised by the UK in April, 1996.

Recognition of a state is normally a one-off act—that is, once an entity has been recognised as a state, that recognition will not usually be retracted if the requirements of statehood continue to be fulfilled. If these requirements cease to be fulfilled, the entity will cease to be a state but derecognition will not be necessary, for example two states may be consolidated into one single state, as in 1990, when the Yemen Arab Republic (North Yemen) and the People's Democratic Republic of Yemen (South Yemen) unified to form the Republic of Yemen. However, the governmental regime of a state may not always be accorded recognition. Refusal to accord recognition to a particular governmental regime does not negate its state's statehood. In normal circumstances, governments will be accorded recognition. The question of recognition is only raised when the regime in question has come to power by unconstitutional methods, for example coup d'état. For example, in *Somalia (Republic) v Woodhouse Drake & Carey (Suisse) SA*, the court held that the plaintiff could not recover any money held by the court as the plaintiff had not been recognised by the United Kingdom as the interim government in power at that time.[75] The judge identified several criteria which should be considered by British courts when determining whether a government is the sovereign government of a state, for example:

(a)   whether the entity is the constitutional government of the state;

(b)   the degree, nature and stability of administrative control, if any, which are exercised over the territory of the state;

(c)   whether the British government has any dealings with that government, and, if so, the nature of those dealings; and,

(d)   in marginal cases the extent of international recognition that has been accorded the government of that state.[76]

An entity may therefore be recognised as a state, but it is possible for its governmental regime not to be accorded recognition. It is clear from this case that the UK courts are able to make an objective decision concerning the international legal personality of a government and are not bound by the official position of the UK government.

Before considering what happens in practice, the two principal schools of thought on recognition must be mentioned, albeit briefly.

[75] [1993] 1 All E.R. 371.
[76] *ibid.* at 372.

Theories

There are two principal theories on recognition: (i) the constitutive school of thought; and (ii) the declaratory school of thought.

(i) The constitutive school. Adherents to this school of thought emphasise the act of recognition itself. They maintain that it is the act of recognition which establishes (is constitutive of) the international personality of the entity in question. The act of recognition is regarded as a precondition to the entity's legal status or, to put it another way, it is the act of recognition which (a) creates a state and (b) determines the legal personality of a new governmental regime. The constituent theory raises two immediate problems. What is the position of unrecognised entities; are they free to act as they like on the international scene unfettered by the obligations which international law imposes? What if an entity is recognised by some states and not by others?

(ii) Declaratory (or evidentiary) school of thought. Adherents to the declaratory school of thought minimise the importance of the act of recognition by other entities. It is regarded as only the formal acknowledgment of already existing circumstances. In other words, the act of recognition is not regarded as one which brings into being, for example, a state which did not previously exist. The UK Secretary of State, at the time of the dissolution of the Socialist Federal Republic of Yugoslavia, stated that the act of recognition was declaratory.[77]

> "It has become clear really in the last few weeks that recognition is not a major matter. . . . The practical effects of recognition as opposed to the psychological are secondary."[78]

State practice supports the declaratory theory. Recognition when granted has retroactive effect—that is, recognition is backdated. For example, the British accorded recognition to the *post*-revolution regime in the Soviet Union in 1921, but when recognition was granted it was backdated to 1917.

---

[77] The Badinter Commission was established by the EC to help resolve the crisis in Yugoslavia. It dealt with the applications by Slovenia, Croatia, Macedonia and Bosnia–Herzegovina, requesting recognition. See Weller, p.576 for an account of the procedural rules of the Commission, above, n.74.

[78] See Statements made to the Foreign Affairs Committee (FAC) First Report, Central and Eastern Europe: Problems of the Post-Communist Era, Vol. II, HC 21–II (1991–92 181) (Evidence of January 14, 1992).

Existing states do treat unrecognised entities as having obligations under international law. They are not free to act as they wish on the international scene, for example, in 1949, Britain demanded compensation from the Jewish State in respect of British aircraft shot down by Jewish airmen over Egypt; in 1957, compensation was demanded by the British from the unrecognised Taiwan government for damage done by Taiwan forces to British vessels; and in 1968, the United States asserted that North Korea, which it did not recognise, had violated international law by attacking a United States vessel, *The Pueblo*.

Is there a duty to recognise?

The most notable exponent of the proposition that if an entity satisfies the formal factual requirements of a state or a government, then recognition should be awarded, was the late Sir Hersch Lauterpacht.[79] He did, however, acknowledge that recognition should be withheld if the entity had come to power through a violation of international law, for example the use of force contrary to Art.2(4) of the UN Charter. Although states do look at the factual criteria which are manifested by an entity, the act of recognition is essentially governed by political expediency. A state is not required to enter into relations with another entity if it does not wish to do so. If there was a legal duty to recognise, recognition would not be discretionary but compulsory. The non-recognition by the United States of the Peking regime as the government of China until 1979 illustrates the possible impact of political factors on a decision of whether to recognise an entity or to withhold recognition.

Criteria for recognition of states

The criteria of statehood have already been considered. States will generally accord recognition to an entity if the latter satisfies the requirements spelt out in the Montevideo Convention-defined territory, as well as other factors which may be employed[80]; permanent population; independent government; capacity to engage in relations with other international persons. If the governmental regime appears effective and stable, then recognition will be accorded. "Effective" refers to the physical control of the territory in question. Does the regime enjoy control over most of the state's territory and is that control likely to continue? An affirmative answer will characterise the control as

---

[79] Lauterpacht, *Recognition in International Law* (1947), Chs 3 and 11.
[80] See pp.61–68.

effective. "Stable", on the other hand, refers to the regime's likelihood of continuing in power (see below, especially distinction between recognition *de facto* and recognition *de jure*). The imposition of additional conditions upon Croatia, Slovenia and Bosnia– Herzegovina by the European Community in 1992, was clearly a political act[81] and is indicative of the constitutive theory.[82] Notwithstanding this, the decisions of the EC Arbitration Commission on Yugoslavia appear to favour the application of the declaratory theory to the dissolution of Yugoslavia.[83] If all the criteria are fulfilled, then when recognition is actually accorded is a matter for the recognising state—and usually the timing is with regard to the recognising state's own national interests, for example commercial.

Recognition of governments

The question of whether to recognise a government does not arise when the government comes to power by constitutional procedures. It only arises when the new governmental regime has assumed power by unconstitutional means.

British practice in the past has been not to look so much at how a government came to power, but to consider whether it displayed the criteria for recognition, namely effectiveness and stability. Recognition by the United Kingdom did not imply approval of the new regime.

The British adopted an "acknowledgment of the facts" stance. The United States, on the other hand, regarded recognition as a political weapon—not as something to be granted as a matter of international obligation. Its granting or refusal was discretionary and could be withheld to further national policy. However,

---

[81] States applying for recognition were required to respect the rule of law, democracy and human rights, to reaffirm the inviolability of frontiers, to protect minorities and to adopt constitutional and political guarantees ensuring that the state has no territorial claim towards a neighbouring Community State. See the EC Guidelines on Recognition of New States in Eastern Europe and the Soviet Union and a Declaration on Yugoslavia. 1991 B.Y.I.L. 62, 559 at 560 particularly and A. V. Lowe and Colin Warbrick, "Recognition of States Part 2" 42 I.C.L.Q. 433.

[82] It is important to acknowledge the unique set of circumstances that the European Community confronted when determining the applications for recognition. Recognition of Bosnia–Herzegovina would inevitably lead to inter-ethnic fighting between the Muslims and the Serbs, whereas a refusal to recognise would deny the Muslims the right to self-determination. The widely held view was that it would be easier to intervene to put an end to aggression when international boundaries had been violated as opposed to intervening in a civil war within the territory of one state.

[83] See (1993) 92 I.L.R. 162.

Britain and the United States now adopt a similar stance in respect of the recognition of governments. Both countries have undertaken to de-emphasise recognition and do not formally recognise new regimes:

> "In recent years, U.S. practice has been to de-emphasise and avoid the use of recognition in cases of changes of governments and to concern ourselves with the question of whether we wish to have diplomatic relations with the new governments."[84]

In 1980, the then British Foreign Secretary, Lord Carrington, announced that the Government had concluded that:

> ". . . there are practical advantages in following the policy of many other countries in not according recognition to governments. Like them, we shall continue to decide the nature of the dealings with regimes which came to power unconstitutionally in the light of our assessment of whether they are able of themselves to exercise effective control of the territory of the State concerned, and seem likely to continue to do so."[85]

In practice, little has changed in that the same tests of effectiveness and likelihood of permanence are still applied. What is different is that there is no formal acknowledgment of recognition.[86]

The general rule is that a new governmental regime will be recognised if it has effective control over the territory which it claims to represent, it has the ability to represent the state in question on the international stage, and it is likely to maintain its control.

De facto and de jure recognition

The practice of differentiating the recognition accorded to either a state or a government evolved in the nineteenth century. The practice was initiated by the British, but was also employed by other countries, such as Canada. The United States has generally accorded only *de jure* recognition. The distinction does not appear in the Foreign Secretary's Statement on Recognition.

---

[84] *Digest of U.S. Practice in International Law* (1977) 19–21.

[85] *Hansard*, HL Deb., Vol. 408, cols 1121–1122 (April 28, 1980); Harris, p.156.

[86] The statement only refers to British practice in recognising governments which came to authority by unconstitutional means.

In reality, of course, it was not the recognition which was either *de facto* or *de jure*—rather the entity which was being recognised. If a government was recognised as the *de facto* government, it implied that the government had effective control and that that control appeared to be permanent, that is there was a likelihood that the regime would be the permanent one. A government which was recognised as *de jure* was one which had effective control and was firmly established. An entity recognised as *de facto* was one which manifested most of the attributes of sovereignty, whereas a *de jure* entity displayed all the characteristics of sovereignty. *De facto* recognition was not a substitute for *de jure* recognition, nor was it a lesser alternative. *De facto* recognition in essence meant that the recognising state recognised with reservations the entity in question.

The distinction was one generally applied in respect of governments rather than states. The State of Israel, however, is an example of a state which was initially recognised *de facto* by some other states, for example Canada, whilst with respect to the Baltic states Britain maintained *de facto* recognition in spite of the 1940 annexation of these territories by the USSR.

The benefit of the distinction was that it allowed the recognising entity to hold back, and see how a particular situation was going to develop. In particular, it prevented a state from according premature recognition. To afford, for example recognition to revolutionaries while the existing government is attempting to quell the revolutionaries is an unquestionable breach of international law. The advantage of the distinction was that it enabled cognisance to be taken of factual circumstances while still acknowledging the *de jure* government—even if that government was not in physical control of every part of a state's territory,[87] or was in exile abroad.[88] In the event of competing authority within a territory, the general rule has been to recognise that the *de facto* regime is competent within the area in which it has physical control, whereas the *de jure* authority remains competent for matters arising outwith that territory.

[87] The UK, during the Spanish Civil War (1936–39) recognised *de facto* General Franco's forces as they extended their control throughout the country, but still recognised the Republican government as the *de jure* regime.
[88] *e.g.* the Polish government in exile in London was recognised as the *de jure* government, though it had no control over Polish territory.

THE EFFECT OF RECOGNITION IN MUNICIPAL LAW

United Kingdom practice

A recognised state or government, *de facto* and *de jure*:

(a) enjoys *locus standi* in the UK courts and it can accordingly raise an action in the UK courts[89];

(b) enjoys immunity from suit[90] in the UK courts and cannot be sued without its consent.

In the *Arantzazu Mendi Case*,[91] the House of Lords held that as the British government recognised Franco's Nationalist government, "a Government which at present exercises *de facto* administrative control over the larger portion of Spain",[92] the Nationalist government could not be impleaded without its consent. This case also illustrates the unfortunate consequences that may arise from recognising a *de facto* government and a *de jure* government in respect of the same territory simultaneously. The Republican government's action seeking repossession of the *Arantzazu Mendi*, which had been requisitioned under a decree by the Nationalist government, accordingly failed.[93] The case was initiated in the English courts as the *Arantzazu Mendi* was in London at the time the Republican government issued its writ of possession;

(c) its legislative and administrative acts will be given effect to within the United Kingdom. In *Luther v Sagor*,[94] the Court of First Instance refused to give effect to a Soviet confiscation decree, as the Soviet regime had not been recognised by the British government. However, by the time the case was heard on appeal, the British government had accorded *de facto* recognition to the Soviet regime:

---

[89] *The City of Berne v Bank of England*, 9 Ves. 347 (1804); 32 E.R. 636 (Ch.).

[90] *Luther v Sagor* [1921] 3 K.B. 532, CA—discussed below.

[91] [1939] A.C. 256, HL.

[92] *ibid.* at 258.

[93] Franco's Nationalist forces were in control of the Basque region of the country. The Republican government issued a requisition decree in respect of all vessels registered in the Port of Bilbao. Some nine months later, the Nationalist government also issued a decree taking control of Bilbao vessels. The owners of the *Arantzazu Mendi* accepted the latter decree, but opposed that of the Republican government.

[94] Above, n.91.

"The Government of this country . . . recognised
the Soviet Government as the Government in
possession of the powers of sovereignty in Russia,
the acts of that Government must be treated by the
Courts of this country with all the respect due to
the acts of a duly recognised foreign sovereign
state."[95]

(d) Recognition once granted, is retroactive. It is backdated
to the establishment of the entity in question. It does not
relate to the time recognition is accorded. In *Luther v
Sagor*, Bankes J. concluded that the Soviet government
assumed the position of a sovereign government as
of December, 1917. British recognition of the Soviet
government was therefore backdated to 1917 and all
legislative and administrative acts of the Soviet Government after that date had to be recognised as valid. *Luther
v Sagor* therefore demonstrates that a government, be it
a *de facto* or a *de jure* government, is entitled to immunity
before British courts; that effect will be given to the legislative and administrative acts of a *de facto* and *de jure*
regime; that recognition is retroactive; and that generally the effects of *de facto* and *de jure* recognition are
essentially the same.

There are, however, two major differences between *de facto* and *de
jure* recognition. *De jure* recognition alone implies full diplomatic
relations and immunities and privileges for representatives.[96]
Only a *de jure* government can recover a public debt or state asset.
It was recognised in *Haile Selassie v Cable and Wireless Ltd* (No. 2)[97]
that only the ousted, but still *de jure*-recognised, government of a
state whose new government was only recognised *de facto*, was
entitled to sue for a debt recoverable in England. However, when
the *de facto* regime, in this case the Italian government, was
recognised *de jure*, because recognition is retroactive, it assumed
the right as the *de jure* regime to pursue the claim, whereas the
former *de jure* regime of Haile Selassie was divested of any such
right.

The retroactivity of recognition can create problems. What if
two governments are simultaneously recognised as the *de jure*
regime of the same state? In reality, this does not happen. One

[95] Above, n.91 at 543.
[96] *Fenton Textiles Assoc. v Krassin* [1922] 38 T.L.R. 259; see the Diplomatic Privileges
Act 1964.
[97] [1939] Ch. 182.

de jure government will be superseded by another *de jure* government. The effect, however, of backdating recognition of a new regime can be to place a state in the position of recognising measures of two *de jure* regimes simultaneously. The question of retroactivity and its raison d'être was considered in the *Gdynia Ameryka Linie Zeglugowe Spolka Akcyjna v Boguslawski Case.*[98] A new provisional government established itself as the *de facto* government of Poland on June 28, 1945 and, at midnight on July 5–6, the British government accorded it *de jure* recognition. Prior to this, the British government had recognised the government in exile in London as the *de jure* government of Poland. The issue which confronted the House of Lords was the effect of the *de jure* recognition of the provisional government on the validity of acts done by the government in London on July 3, 1945 with regard to Polish merchant marine personnel. The Lords emphasised that English courts were required to regard as valid not only acts done by the new government after recognition, but also acts done by it before its recognition in so far as those acts related to matters under its control at the time when the acts were performed. This did not, however, involve invalidating all measures of the old government prior to the withdrawal of recognition. It was, the Lords maintained, "not inconsistent to say that the recognition of the new government has certain retroactive effects, but that the recognition of the old government remains effective down to the date when it was in fact withdrawn."[99] What emerges from *Gdynia Ameryka Linie v Boguslawski* is that retroactivity relates specifically to matters within the effective control of the new government, and that the raison d'être of the retroactivity of recognition is to give validity to the acts of a former unrecognised regime, but *not* (emphasis added) to invalidate the acts of the formerly recognised *de jure* authority.[1]

EFFECT OF NON-RECOGNITION

International law

At the international level, as already stated, non-recognition does not give an entity "carte blanche" to act as it wishes. An unrecognised entity has responsibilities which the international community requires it to discharge.

---

[98] [1953] A.C. 11.
[99] *ibid.* at 45.
[1] See also *Civil Air Transport Inc. v Central Air Transport Corp.* [1953] A.C. 70, Judicial Committee of the Privy Council.

Municipal law

United Kingdom practice

As far as the United Kingdom is concerned,[2] the effect of non-recognition is the converse of the consequences of recognition. An unrecognised state or government does not have *locus standi* in the British courts; does not enjoy immunity from the jurisdiction of the British courts; its legislative and administrative measures will be denied effect by British courts, for example *Somalia (Republic) v Woodhouse Drake & Carey (Suisse) SA*.[3]

The non-recognition of legislative and administrative measures, for example those of a private law nature, can produce severe repercussions for "innocent" persons. Britain withheld recognition from the Smith regime of Rhodesia which declared unilateral independence in 1965, and accordingly, refused to recognise judicial decrees made by judges appointed by the Smith regime. The consequences of this were, for example that English law refused to recognise a divorce granted by a Rhodesian court in 1970.[4] The Rhodesian situation was, of course, a unique one for the British courts. They were confronted with a regime which was in rebellion to the British Crown—hence, the strict enforcement of non-recognition.

The consequences of applying non-recognition to its logical conclusion were identified by Lord Reid in the *Carl Zeiss Stiftung v Rayner and Keeler Ltd (No. 2) Case*.[5] Non-recognition of the measures adopted by the German Democratic Republic would mean that:

". . . the incorporation of every company in East Germany under any new law made by the Democratic Republic or by the official act of any official appointed by its Government would have to be regarded as a nullity, so that any such company could neither sue nor be sued in this country. And any civil marriage under any such new law, or owing its validity to the act of any such official, would also have to be treated as a nullity, so that we should have to regard the children as illegitimate. And the same would apply to divorces and all manner of judicial decisions, whether in family or

---

[2] And also, for instance, Canada.
[3] Above, n.75.
[4] *Adams v Adams* [1971] P. 188. This decision prompted the introduction of an Order-in-Council to give effect to Rhodesian decrees which were concerned with personal status. See also the earlier *Madzimbamiuto Case* [1969] 1 A.C. 645, PC.
[5] [1967] A.C. 855.

commercial questions. And that would affect not only status of persons formerly domiciled in East Germany but property in this country the devolution of which depended on East German law."[6]

The House of Lords in the above case employed a legal fiction and successfully side-stepped, for that particular case, the problem of non-recognition. The respondents argued that, as Britain did not recognise the German Democratic Republic, all its enactments should be considered nullities before the British courts. The House of Lords, however, maintained that as Britain recognised the Soviet government as the *de jure* authority in East Germany, the acts of the unrecognised East German regime could be recognised as those of a subordinate body acting under the authority of the Soviet Union. The German Democratic Republic became irrelevant for the House of Lords. For them, the German Democratic Republic was merely a subordinate, dependent administrative body—created by the *de jure* regime. The House of Lords adopted a pragmatic approach. This approach was endorsed by the Court of Appeal in *Gur Corporation v Trust Bank of Africa Ltd*,[7] when it was held that the unrecognised Ciskei government was acting as a subordinate body of the South African government and accordingly enjoyed *locus standi* in the English courts.[8]

Mitigation of the strict non-recognition rule has been favoured where necessary by Lord Denning. He said, *obiter dicta*, in *Hesperides Hotels v Aegean Holidays Ltd*[9] that effect should be given to laws of a body in effective control, even if not recognised by the British government, which "regulate the day to day affairs of the people, such as their marriages, their divorces, their leases, their occupations and so forth."[10]

The 1980 Statement on Recognition has brought the judiciary into the arena of determining the status of the entity in question. Prior to 1980, recognition was exclusively an act of the executive which was binding on the courts. Now, recognition of governments which assume power by unconstitutional means is to be inferred through the dealings which the British government may have with the new regime. If the courts are in doubt as to the status of a particular regime, they will have to assess the evidence

---

[6] [1967] A.C. 855, at 907.
[7] [1987] Q.B. 599.
[8] See also the HL finding in *Arab Monetary Fund v Hashim (No.3)* [1991] 1 All E.R. 871.
[9] [1978] Q.B. 205, CA.
[10] *ibid.* 218.

available to them, and exercise their judgment in deciding whether the regime is unrecognised or recognised. British courts are no longer bound by the official position of the government. Although the Court in the *Somalia (Republic)* case in 1993[11] did not depart from the UK government's official position, the decision is indicative of the change in the British practice of recognition of governments. Support for the test applied in the aforementioned case was reinforced in *Sierra Leone Telecommunications Co. Ltd v Barclays Bank plc*,[12] in which the test was utilised to determine whether the military junta was the recognised government of Sierra Leone. The Court decided in the negative. The courts may still obtain certificates from the Foreign Office and accordingly, a certificate may include, *inter alia*, confirmation of the dealings which the British government has with the new regime, and, of course, an explicit statement of non-recognition.[13] The courts, when interpreting the terms "state" or "government" in a statute or another document, such as a commercial one, look, of course to the intention of the draftsmen or those of the parties.[14]

United States practice

If the Executive unequivocally denies recognition, the courts must accept this as binding.[15] An unrecognised state or government cannot sue in the American courts. An unrecognised government may be entitled to immunity from the jurisdiction of the American courts, if the regime in question can be shown to exist.[16] The Executive may deny recognition, but may nevertheless in its "suggestion", indicate to the courts that cognisance may be taken of the measures promulgated by the unrecognised regime. Thus, in *Salimoff v Standard Oil Co.*,[17] although the US government's non-recognition of the Soviet regime was confirmed in the State Department Certificate, it was nevertheless acknowledged that the Soviet regime was exercising control and power in the territory of the former Russian Empire and that such a fact could not be ignored. In the absence of either explicit or implied direction to the court, the American courts have shown a willingness to

---

[11] Above, n.75.
[12] [1998] 2 All E.R. 821.
[13] See Colin Warbrick, "Britain and the Recognition of Governments" 39 I.C.L.Q. 568 (1981). Recognition of States Part 1 (1992) 41 I.C.L.Q. 473; Recognition of States Part 2 (1993) 42 I.C.L.Q. 433.
[14] *e.g. Re Al-Fin Corporation's Patent* [1970] Ch. 160; *Reel v Holder* [1981] 1 W.L.R. 1226, CA.
[15] *e.g.* as in *The Maret* 145 F.(d) 431 (1944).
[16] *Wulfsohn v R.S.F.S.R.* 138 N.E. 24 (1923); (1923–1924) 2 A.D. Case No.16.
[17] 186 N.E. 679 (1993); (1993–1934) A.D. Case No.8.

modify the legal consequences of non-recognition being carried to their logical conclusion. In other words, common sense and fairness may demand that legal cognisance be accorded.[18]

MODES OF ACCORDING RECOGNITION

Recognition may be expressed or implied. In the absence of an express formal declaration of recognition, the establishment of diplomatic relations between a state and the entity concerned will be taken to imply recognition. Similarly, the conclusion of a bipartite treaty on a general topic implies recognition. A bipartite treaty for a specific purpose does not imply recognition, nor does participation in a multipartite treaty such as the UN Charter. It is possible for parties to be signatories to a multipartite treaty, even though one party does not recognise the other party. Admission to the UN is an acknowledgment of statehood for the purposes of the Organisation. It does not constitute collective recognition by the international community, or recognition of the entity by individual Member States of the United Nations.[19] The most salient factor at all times remains intention—that is, the intention of the recognising state.

---

[18] See *Sokoloff v National City Bank* 145 N.E. 917 (1924); (1923–1924) 2 A.D. Case No.19; *Upright v Mercury Business Machines* 13 A.D. (2d) 36; 213 (N.Y.S.) (2d) 417 (1961).

[19] Admission of Members is effected by a two-thirds vote of the General Assembly. See, *e.g.* SC Res.777 (1992), December 19, 1992.

5. TERRITORY

"State territory is that defined portion of the surface of the globe which is subjected to the sovereignty of the State. A State without a territory is not possible, although the necessary territory may be very small. . . . The importance of State territory lies in the fact that it is the space within which the State exercises its supreme authority."[1]

Territory is thus a tangible attribute of statehood within which a state enjoys and exercises sovereignty. Territorial sovereignty may be defined as the "right to exercise therein, to the exclusion of any other State, the functions of a State".[2] A state's territorial sovereignty extends over the designated landmass, subsoil, the water enclosed therein, the land under that water, the sea coast to a certain limit[3] and the airspace over the landmass and territorial sea. The means whereby title to territory may be established is

---

[1] L. F. L. Oppenheim, *International Law*, *"Peace"* (8th ed., 1955), Vol.1, pp.451–452.
[2] Arbitrator Max Huber in the *Island of Palmas Case*, Permanent Court of Arbitration, 2 R.I.A.A. 829 at 838 (1928). For further discussion, see "State Jurisdiction", Ch.8, below.
[3] Twelve miles is the maximum allowed under the 1982 UN Convention on the Law of the Sea—Art.3.

essentially of academic interest—until, that is, a dispute arises
and competing claims have to be assessed. Then the mode by
which the parties claim to have established sovereignty over the
territory will gain new relevance, for example in the *Case
Concerning Land, Island and Maritime Frontier Dispute El Salvador v
Honduras, Nicaragua intervening)*[4] both parties agreed to refer the
dispute concerning the boundaries between their respective territories to the International Court for resolution by reference to the
principle *uti possidetis*.[5] The Court's decision had the effect of
converting former colonial boundaries into accepted international frontiers.[6] It is also important to note the special status
attributed to treaties establishing international boundaries. The
boundary will continue to subsist even though the treaty falls.[7]

Historically, the need to demonstrate the existence of a valid
title became imperative during the "Age of Discovery" when the
European powers set sail in quest of new lands. Unfortunately,
claims as to territory have been, and remain, a cause of conflict,
for example the Falkland Islands dispute of 1982, the situation in
the Middle East, Kashmir and, as of yet, the unresolved dispute
over Gibraltar. Turning to the means of establishing a valid title,
discovery alone was not sufficient to establish a superior title.
Occupation was also necessary.

OCCUPATION

Occupation gives a state original title to territory. It is the means
of establishing title to territory which is *terra nullius*, that is
owned by no one and therefore susceptible to acquisition.
Regarding settlement by natives this was of no consequence
provided the indigenous peoples were not administratively so
well organised that they could be said to have a recognisable
government. In the *Western Sahara Case* it was said that state practice of the late nineteenth century was such to indicate:

---

[4] I.C.J.Rep. (1992) 351.
[5] For further discussion of this principle see *the Case Concerning the Frontier
     Dispute (Burkina Faso/Republic of Mali)* I.C.J. Rep. (1986) 554 at 565–567.
[6] See the EC Arbitration Committee on Yugoslavia statement 92 I.L.R. (1993) that,
     except where otherwise agreed, the former boundaries become frontiers pro-
     tected by international law. This conclusion follows from the principle of
     respect for the territorial *status quo*, and in particular, from the principle of *uti
     possidetis*. The use of the principle in this context confirms its application to
     newly independent states.
[7] See *Case Concerning the Territorial Dispute between Libya Arab Jamahiriya/Chad*
     where the ICJ held that "a boundary established by treaty thus achieves a per-
     manence which the treaty itself does not necessarily enjoy." (1994) 33 I.L.M. 571
     at 589; I.C.J.Rep. (1994) 6 at 37.

".. . that territories inhabited by tribes or peoples having a social and political organisation were not regarded as *terrae nullius*. It shows that in the case of such territories the acquisition of sovereignty was not generally considered as effected unilaterally through 'occupation' of *terra nullius* by original title but through agreements concluded with local rulers . . ., such agreements with local rulers . . ., whether or not considered as an actual 'cession' of the territory, were regarded as derivative roots of title, and not original titles obtained by occupation of *terrae nullius*."[8]

Occupation is preceded by discovery. Discovery, *per se*, does not establish a good title, giving only an inchoate and not a definite title of sovereignty. An inchoate title must be completed within a reasonable period by the effective occupation of the territory in question.[9] Publication of discovery can, of course, intimate to the international community a discovering state's prior interest and such a discovery is good against any subsequent title founded on alleged discovery. An "inchoate" title does not prevail over the continuous and peaceful display of authority by another state.

Effective occupation

Effective occupation applies to the actual exercise of sovereignty. What will be regarded as sufficient to establish a good title will vary in each particular instance:

"Manifestations of territorial sovereignty assume, . . ., different forms, according to conditions of time and place. Although continuous in principle, sovereignty cannot be exercised in fact at every moment on every point of a territory. The intermittence and discontinuity compatible with the maintenance of the right necessarily differ according as inhabited or uninhabited regions are involved, or regions enclosed within territories in which sovereignty is incontestably displayed or again regions accessible from, for instance, the high seas".[10]

Max Huber was the sole arbitrator in a sovereignty dispute regarding the Island of Palmas between the United States and the Netherlands. The Island of Palmas, the United States believed, was included in the cession of the Philippines to them by the

---

[8] *Western Sahara Case* I.C.J.Rep. (1975) 12 at 39.
[9] *Island of Palmas Case*, above, n.2 at 846.
[10] *ibid.* at 840.

Spanish in 1898, at the conclusion of the Spanish–American War.
The Dutch claimed the island on the basis of the exercise of
sovereignty over a considerable length of time.

The display of sovereignty required to establish title by
occupation, for example over territory inhospitable to habitation,
may therefore be minimal and in certain circumstances may be
little more than symbolic. Assessing the respective claims of
Norway and Denmark to East Greenland, the Permanent Court of
International Justice[11] highlighted the relative test to be utilised in
establishing occupation and observed:

> "It is impossible to read the records of the decisions in cases
> as to territorial sovereignty without observing that in many
> cases the tribunal has been satisfied with very little in the
> way of the actual exercise of sovereign rights, provided that
> the other State could not make out a superior claim. This is
> particularly true in the case of claims to sovereignty over
> areas in thinly populated or unsettled countries."[12]

Minimal overt action may be sufficient to establish effective occupation over small, uninhabited territory.

An important and necessary condition of occupation is "the
actual, and not the nominal, taking of possession".[13] The form of
the actual taking is dependent on factors such as the geographical
and geological terrain of the particular territory. In the *Clipperton
Island Arbitration*,[14] a declaration of sovereignty made on behalf of
France communicated to the French Consulate in Honolulu and
transmitted to the Government of Hawaii along with publication
of the French claim in the Honolulu journal, *The Polynesian* (in
English), was sufficient to establish a good title to the island for
France.

Discovery must be reinforced by an intention (*animus*) or will to
act as sovereign. How that intention will be inferred depends on
the facts in any particular case. Normally, the exercise of exclusive
authority is evidenced when the state establishes an organisation
capable of making its law respected; however, in respect of
Clipperton Island, it was held that France had done sufficient and
had made it apparent in a precise and clear manner that she considered the island French territory. France had never had the

---

[11] *Eastern Greenland Case* (1933) P.C.I.J.Rep., ser.A/B, No.53, pp.22–147; Hudson, *World Court Reports*, Vol. III (1932–35), p.151.

[12] *Eastern Greenland Case* above, n.11 at p. 46; Hudson, above, n.11 at 171.

[13] *Clipperton Island Arbitration* (1932) 26 A.J.I.L. 390 at 393.

[14] The Arbitrator established that the Island at the date relevant to the dispute was "*territorium nullius* and, therefore, susceptible of occupation."

animus of abandoning the island, and the fact that she had not exercised authority in a positive manner did not imply the forfeiture of an acquisition already definitively perfected. The French title was further substantiated by the absence of any French intention to abandon the territory.

Characteristics of effective occupation

Max Huber's articulation of effective occupation is still regarded as the leading statement on the issue.

In the *Island of Palmas Case*, effective occupation must, it was established, be open and public and involve the continuous, peaceful display of state authority extending over a long period of time. An inchoate title based on such a display of state authority would be regarded as superior to any other claim to title, whatever its basis.

Max Huber went to great lengths to attribute the acts of the Dutch East India Company to the Netherlands state thereby emphasising that occupation must be exercised on behalf of a state if it is to be effective. Private individuals cannot legitimately purport to act on behalf of the state of which they are a national without that state's authorisation.[15] In international law:

"... the independent activity of private individuals is of little value unless it can be shown that they have acted in pursuance of a licence or some other authority received from their Governments or that in some other way their Governments have asserted jurisdiction through them.[16]

The exercise of state functions was similarly emphasised in the *Miniquiers and Ecrehos Case.*[17]

The British claim to sovereignty over the Falkland Islands is "derived from early settlement, reinforced by formal claims in the name of the Crown and completed by open, continuous, effective and peaceful possession, occupation and administration of the Island since 1833 . . ."[18]

---

[15] See Harris, p.200 for the example of the cession of Sarawak to Sir J. Brooke, a British national, by the Sultan of Borneo in 1842.
[16] *Anglo-Norwegian Fisheries Case* I.C.J.Rep. (1951), 116—Lord McNair at 184.
[17] I.C.J.Rep. (1953) at 47.
[18] British Government response to Report on the Falklands, Fifth Report of the Foreign Affairs Committee of the House of Commons, Session 1983–84, HC, Papers 268–1, Vol.1, pp.xiv–xvii; Misc.1 Cmnd.9447 (1985). The Report for its part concluded that the historical and legal evidence available demonstrated "such areas of uncertainty . . ." that it was "unable to reach a categorical conclusion on the legal validity of the historical claims of either country." para.22.

Critical date

The critical date in a territorial claim is the date on which the location of territorial sovereignty is decisive, as the state which can demonstrate an effective title in the period immediately preceding the critical date has the superior claim, for example the critical date was, in the *Island of Palmas Case*, 1898, in the *Western Sahara Case*, 1884 and in the *El Salvador v Honduras Case*, 1821 (the date of independence of the former colonies of Latin America).[19] The responsibility of deciding when the critical date is lies with the adjudicating body charged with the task of deciding the territorial dispute. There is no general rule governing the selection of the critical date and selection, if indeed it is made, is made in the context of the relevant circumstances peculiar to each case.

PRESCRIPTION

Claimants to title of territory based initially on discovery and occupation may invoke the principle of prescription to consolidate their claim.

Prescription is the acquisition of title by a public, peaceful and continuous control of territory. Prescription involves a *de facto* exercise of sovereignty. It is distinct from occupation in that the latter can only arise in respect of virgin territory (*terra nullius*), whilst prescription can work to establish a title over any territory. Prescription can validate an initially doubtful title, provided that the display of state authority is public. It must be public, as a title acquired via prescription implies the acquiescence of any other interested claimant. Protest from such a claimant or a dispossessed sovereign[20] can bar the establishment of title by prescription. What form must such protest take? Previously, force could legitimately be used. Today, diplomatic protests would have to be expressed and probably formally registered in the appropriate international fora.

As to the length of time required before prescription will give good title, there is no accepted prescribed period and much will depend on the circumstances of each particular case, such as the geographical nature of the territory and the existence or absence of any competing claims. There has to date, been no decision of an international tribunal conclusively acknowledging title founded on prescription. The difficulty in establishing good title based on prescription is illustrated in the *Kasikili/Sedudu Island* case.[21] In this instance, Namibia was precluded from utilising prescription to establish title.

---

[19] Above, n.4.
[20] *Chamizal Arbitration* (1911) 5 A.J.I.L. 782.
[21] *Kasikili/Sedudu Island (Botswana v Namibia)* (2000) 49 I.C.L.Q. 964.

CONQUEST

Conquest is a mode of acquisition peculiar to the international community. It has no counterpart in municipal law. Conquest is taking possession of enemy territory by military force in time of war. To be effected, there had to be not only the actual taking over (*factum*), but an intention to take over (*animus*), that is, the conqueror only acquired the territory if he intended to do so. Frequently, the vanquished power would cede territory to the conqueror under treaty. In the absence of a treaty the territory could only be annexed if hostilities between the belligerent parties had ceased.

The sharp-eyed reader will have noted the use of the past tense. Why has it been used? Simply because, although in earlier centuries there were no rules restricting a state's use of force, this is no longer true. The twentieth century witnessed the denunciation of war as legitimate, for example Art.10 Covenant of the League of Nations, the 1928 Kellogg Briand Pact and Art.11 of the 1949 Draft Declaration on Rights and Duties of States, which imposes a duty on every state "to refrain from recognising any territorial acquisition by another State in violation of Article 9".[22]

The 1970 Declaration of Principles of International Law concerning Friendly Relations and Co-operation among states in accordance with the Charter of the United Nations, para.X, provides that:

> ". . . The territory of a State shall not be the object of acquisition by another State resulting from the threat or use of force. No territorial acquisition resulting from the threat or use of force shall be recognised as legal."

This has been interpreted as meaning that territory cannot be acquired legitimately through the use of force, even if the use of that force is in accordance with the UN Charter (that is, in self-defence). The Security Council's denunciation of Israel's retention of territory taken during the 1967 War as unlawful is founded on the principle that force cannot give a good title[23]; accordingly, talks have centred on pre-1967 borders ever since. Nevertheless, it must be acknowledged that *de jure* recognition by other states may validate titles based on conquest, for example Indian control

---

[22] *i.e.* prohibition on the use of war as an instrument of national policy and the use of force contrary to Art.2(4) of the UN Charter. Ch.11 deals with the use of force in international law.

[23] *e.g.* Security Council Resolution on the Middle East, November 22, 1967—Security Council Resolution 242 (XXII), S.C.O.R., 22nd Yr., *Resolutions and Decisions* 1967, p.8.

over Goa, Danao and Diu (Portuguese territories on the Indian subcontinent invaded and taken by India in December, 1961). The United States consistently refused to recognise the incorporation of Estonia, Latvia and Lithuania into the Soviet Union. The three states were independent between the two World Wars but were annexed in 1940. Britain accorded only *de facto* recognition.[24]

Conquest is, under contemporary international law, no longer recognised as a valid means of acquiring territory. Hence, the international condemnation precipitated by the Iraqi invasion of Kuwait and subsequent annexation of that territory in August 1990 culminating in UN Security Council Resolution 660,[25] calling for the immediate and unconditional withdrawal of all Iraqi forces from the territory of Kuwait,[26] declaring the Iraqi annexation as "null and void" having no legal validity "under any form and whatever pretext".

What of territories acquired by conquest when the use of force was accepted under international law? In accordance with the doctrine of intertemporal law, the law applicable when title was allegedly established will be applied. The essence of this doctrine is that "a juridical fact should be appreciated in the light of the law contemporary with it, and not of the law in force at the time when the dispute in regard to it arises or falls to be settled."[27] To do otherwise and to require new doctrines to be of retroactive effect would be "highly disruptive", as "every state would constantly be under the necessity of examining its title to each portion of its territory in order to determine whether a change in the law had necessitated, as it were, a reacquisition."[28]

CESSION

This, the transfer of territory by one sovereign to another, is the most usual form of acquiring derivative title to land. Cession is always effected by treaty—most frequently in a peace treaty at the conclusion of a war as in the Treaty of Versailles, 1919, the Treaty of Peace with Japan, 1951[29] and the cession of Hong Kong by

---

[24] See Ch.4, above, recognition, pp.78 *et seq*. The three states in question now once again enjoy independent status and have been admitted to membership of the UN.
[25] Adopted by 14–0, the Yemen abstaining.
[26] For text of Resolution see 29 I.L.M. 1323 (1990) and Resolution 662 of August 9, 1990, adopted by 15–0; for text, see *ibid*. I.L.M. 1327.
[27] Parry and Grant, *Encyclopaedic Directory of International Law* (Oceana).
[28] P. C. Jessup, "The Palmas Island Arbitration" (1928) 22 A.J.I.L. 735 at 740.
[29] 112 B.F.S.P. 1; 136 U.N.T.S. 45.

China to Great Britain after the Opium War.[30] To some extent, the cession may be forced on the defeated power, in which case the latter's consent to the transfer of sovereignty will be recorded in the cession treaty. Cession requires that one party assumes sovereignty and another relinquishes it. One sovereign state is replaced by another. The acquiring sovereign cannot possess greater rights than those possessed by its predecessor. Should a third state have acknowledged rights in the territory, that is a right of passage, then these must be respected. In the past, land has been ceded under an exchange agreement, for example in 1890, Britain and Germany exchanged Zanzibar and Heligoland, or purchased, as in the cases of Louisiana from France, and Alaska from the Soviet Union. The emergence of the principle of self-determination has made the cession of territory between states less likely.

ACCRETION AND AVULSION

Both accretion and avulsion refer to geographical processes. They refer to relatively rare occurrences and are of minor importance.

Accretion involves the gradual increase in territory through the operation of nature, for example the gradual shifting of a river's course leading to additional territory through the formation of alluvial deposits. Avulsion refers to a violent change, such as a sudden alteration in a river's course, or the emergence by volcanic action of an island in territorial waters, namely the Island of Scutsey, which appeared in Icelandic territorial waters in 1963.

If accretion occurs on a boundary river (that is, between two states), then the international boundary changes, whereas with cases of avulsion the international boundary will remain where it was originally established. If the river is navigable, the boundary will follow the *thalweg*, namely the centre of the navigable channel. If the river is not navigable, the middle of the river stream will constitute the boundary.

NEW STATES

The attainment of independence, in accordance with the principle of self-determination (which may also be invoked to substantiate a claim of title to territory, for example with regard to the British

---

[30] Hong Kong and the new Territories were leased to Britain under Treaty in 1898. Hong Kong was restored to China at a handover ceremony at midnight on June 30, 1997. The ceremony marked the return of Hong Kong to Chinese sovereignty and the establishment of a Hong Kong Special Administrative Region (HKSAR) as provided for by the Sino–British Joint Declaration on the Question of Hong Kong 1984. Under the terms of that Declaration, the British agreed to return the entire territory to China.

claim over the Falkland Islands,[31] or the constitutional granting of independence to former colonial possession), involves the replacement of one sovereign by another and thus gives a derivative title to territory. The recognition of title to territory by an entity which comes to "statehood" by unconstitutional means, for example by revolt, will depend on recognition by the other members of the international community, and title may finally only be established when an "acknowledgement of the facts" stance is adopted.[32]

POLAR REGIONS

The Arctic

The Arctic consists largely of ice rather than land. It is incapable of occupation in the accepted sense of the term, and, below the frozen masses, navigation by submarines is possible. Sovereignty over such land, for example Eastern Greenland, can be established by minimum overt acts. Greenland belongs to Denmark, while Norway exercises sovereign rights over Spitzbergen. The Soviet Union and Canada, both anxious to eliminate any potential foreign and possibly hostile settlement, have made claims in the area. Both have utilised a modification of the contiguity principle (principle whereby the occupying state may claim territory which is geographically pertinent to its area of lodgment), namely the sector principle. By this, the sector principle, all land falling within the triangle between the east–west extremities of a state contiguous to the Pole and the Pole itself should be the territory of that state, unless another state has a previously recognised established title. Both the Soviet Union and Canada have asserted sovereignty over extensive areas in the Arctic region and, in September, 1985, Canada declared its intention to establish straight baselines round the Arctic archipelago from latitude 60°E to the Beauford Sea in the west and thereby all waters, including Hudson Bay and several routes of the North West Passage within the baselines, were designated Canadian as of January 1, 1986. Although the Canadian action did not meet with US approval, an agreement on Arctic Co-operation[33] was concluded between the two countries in 1988 and provides that Canadian permission will be sought before American icebreakers and other vessels navigate the North West Passage.[34] The United States and the other Arctic

---

[31] See statement of the Foreign Secretary, "Our case rests on the facts, on prescription and on the principle of self-determination." (1983) 54 B.Y.I.L. 461.
[32] See, further, Ch.4, generally.
[33] 28 I.L.M. 141 (1989); A.J.I.L. (1989) at 63–64.
[34] *ibid.*, Art.4.

states have not utilised the sector principle. The major argument against claims in the Arctic is that what lie beneath the frozen wastes are high seas and not land and is, therefore, not capable of national appropriation.

In 1991, the Arctic States[35] adopted the Arctic Environmental Protection Strategy (AEPS)[36] designed to promote regional environmental protection of the Arctic region. Eight Arctic States endorsed the AEPS and committed themselves to ensuring "the protection of the Arctic environment and its sustainable and equitable development, while protecting the cultures of indigenous peoples".[37] Environmental issues of particular concern to the Arctic and tackled in the AEPS are identified as persistent organic contaminants, oil pollution, heavy metals, noise, radioactivity and acidification. An Arctic Monitoring and Assessment Programme (AMAP) was established in 1991 to promote research and co-operation. Issues which have been addressed include the conservation of Arctic plant and animal life, for example the Conservation of Arctic Flora and Fauna (CAFF) working group has been in operation since 1992; a working group on Protection of the Arctic Marine Environment (PAME) has been in operation since 1994. Following a ministerial review meeting of the AEPS in 1993, the Nuuk Declaration on the Environment and Development in the Arctic was adopted. The Declaration essentially reaffirms the principles established in the AEPS but does highlight the need for additional co-operation to deal with Arctic marine pollution as well as effective domestic measures. The ATLA declaration on the Arctic Environmental Protection Strategy was adopted in 1997 and re-affirms the recognition of the Arctic States of the importance of co-operation. In 1997, the AEPS was subsumed by the Arctic Council, the Council is now charged with developing the work began by the AEPS. It held its first ministerial meeting in Iqaluit, Canada in 1998, where it adopted a further declaration regarding the promotion of co-operation, co-ordination and interaction of the Arctic States, as well as involvement of Arctic indigenous communities on issues common to the area, such as sustainable development and environmental protection.

Antarctica

All of Antarctica has been the subject of territorial claims, though that made by Admiral Byrd on behalf of the United States has

---

[35] Canada, Denmark, Finland, Iceland, Norway, Sweden, the US and the former USSR.
[36] 30 I.L.M. 1624 (1991).
[37] ibid. at 1629.

never been officially adopted. The United States favours an internationalisation of the area and has not recognised any of the
claims made by other states (Argentina, Australia, Chile, France,
New Zealand, Norway and the United Kingdom). The sectors
claimed by Argentina, Chile and the United Kingdom overlap to
some extent.[38] The other states involved appear to have recognised each other's respective claims. However, in an attempt to
avoid a "scramble for Antarctica", the Antarctic Convention was
drawn up in Washington in 1959,[39] and entered into force in 1961.
The Treaty designates Antarctica exclusively for peaceful purposes and prohibits any measures of a "military nature".[40] The
Treaty also provided for the regular meetings of the Consultative
Parties[41] and these parties have been responsible for some 150
initiatives relating to comprehensive protection of the Antarctic
environment, such as Agreed Measures for the Conservation of
the Antarctic Flora and Fauna 1964[42]; 1972 Convention for the
Conservation of Antarctic Seals[43]; and the 1980 Convention for
the Conservation of Antarctic Marine Living Resources.[44] The
raison d'être of the last, for example, is to curtail the use of
resources by certain restrictive measures, such as open and closed
seasons.[45]

The most extensive agreement with respect to the Antarctic
environment is the 1991 Madrid Protocol on Environmental Protection to the Antarctic Treaty and the four annexes, which form
an integral part of the Protocol.[46] The key Article is Art.7 which
prohibits "any activity relating to mineral resources other than
scientific research". This prohibition will remain in force with no
possibility of review until 50 years have lapsed following the
entry into force of the Protocol. The Protocol entered into force 30
days after ratification by all states who were Antarctic Treaty
Consultative States on the date when the Protocol was adopted.[47]

---

[38] The UK in 1955 initiated proceedings seeking a declaration from the ICJ, but the
  latter struck the case from its list in 1956, as it had not received any response
  from either Argentina or Chile.
[39] Antarctic Treaty 1959, U.K.T.S. 97 (1961) Cmnd. 1535; 402 U.N.T.S. 71; (1960)
  A.J.I.L. 477.
[40] Antarctic Treaty, above, Art.1.
[41] Namely ATCPs, of which there are 26.
[42] 17 U.S.T. 996.
[43] U.K.T.S. 45 (1978) Cmnd.7209; 1080 U.N.T.S. 176; 11 I.L.M. 251 (1978).
[44] U.K.T.S. 48 (1982) Cmnd.8714; 19 I.L.M. 841.
[45] For a synopsis of all measures recommended by Antarctic Treaty Consultative
  meeting and approved by Antarctic Treaty Consultative Parties, see 35 I.L.M.
  1165 (1996).
[46] See 30 I.L.M. 1460 (1991). The annexes are: Environmental Impact Assessment;
  Conservation of Antarctic Fauna and Flora; Waste Disposal and Waste Management; Prevention of Marine Pollution.
[47] Art.23.1. The ptotocol entered into force on January 14, 1998.

Reservations are not permitted.[48] Art.19 provides a choice of dispute settlement, either by reference to the International Court of Justice or the Arbitral Tribunal, as established in accordance with the Schedule to the Protocol.

AIRSPACE

Every state enjoys exclusive sovereignty over the airspace above its territory to a height once thought to be indeterminable. In the wake of outer-space exploitation, it is now recognised that there is an upward limit to airspace, but what this limit is has yet to be established. State sovereignty over airspace quickly became customary international law in the early part of this century, and was crystallised in the 1919 Paris Convention on the Regulation of Aerial Navigation,[49] and Art.1 of the 1944 Chicago Convention on International Civil Aviation.[50] International law does not give a right of innocent passage through airspace, and entry into a state's airspace requires the permission of the host state.

The Chicago Convention, which entered into force in 1947, replaced the 1919 Paris Convention rules on navigation. The Chicago Convention recognises the exclusive sovereignty of *all* states over their airspace, that is regardless of whether or not they are Contracting Parties of the Convention. The Convention applies only to civil aircraft and not state aircraft, which, for the purposes of the Convention, are defined as "aircraft used in military, customs and police services".[51] Such aircraft require authorisation by special agreement.[52] The primary stipulation of the Convention is that contained in Art.6, namely that the scheduled international aircraft of a Contracting State must, before flying into or over the territory of a Contracting State, have that state's permission and comply with any conditions of the said authorisation. Thus, the regulation of airspace is effected via interstate agreement.

The failure of the Chicago Conference to reach agreement on the granting of reciprocal rights of overflight or of transportation of passengers and cargo led to the adoption of two supplementary agreements: (i) the International Air Services Transit Agreement (the "Two Freedoms" Agreement),[53] and (ii) the International Air Transport Agreement (the "Five Freedoms" Agreement).[54] The "Two Freedoms" Agreement refers only to

---

[48] Art.24.
[49] 11 L.N.T.S. 173; U.K.T.S. 2 (1922) Cmd.1609.
[50] U.K.T.S. 8 (1953) Cmd. 8742; 15 U.N.T.S. 295.
[51] Chicago Convention, above, Art.3(b).
[52] *ibid.* Art.3(c).
[53] U.K.T.S. 8 (1953) Cmd.8742; 84 U.N.T.S. 389.
[54] 171 U.N.T.S. 387; 149 B.F.S.P. 1.

transit rights, namely each Contracting State must grant to all other Contracting States:

(a)   the privilege of flying across its territory without landing; and

(b)   the privilege of landing for non traffic purposes (for example, refuelling or maintenance).

The "Two Freedoms" Agreement does not provide for commercial rights in the territory of the grantor state.

The "Five Freedoms" Agreement embraces the forementioned freedoms plus three additional freedoms which are traffic rights. These are:

(c)   the privilege of putting down passengers, mail and cargo taken on in the territory of the state whose nationality the aircraft possesses;

(d)   the privilege of taking on passengers, mail and cargo destined for the territory of the state whose nationality the aircraft possesses; and

(e)   the privilege of taking on passengers, mail and cargo destined for the territory of any other Contracting State and the privilege to put down passengers, mail and cargo coming from any such territory.

The practice has been for the third and fourth freedoms to be granted in conjunction, whilst the fifth freedom, being more extensive, has not been so readily granted.

The state granting the freedoms may require (i) transit flights to follow designated routes,[55] (ii) airlines of states granted the freedoms to provide reasonable services at the airports they use,[56] and (iii) payment for the use of airports.[57] A "host" state may revoke permission granted "to an air transport enterprise of another State in any case when it is not satisfied that substantial ownership and effective control is vested in nationals of a Contracting State." Permission may also be revoked when an air enterprise fails to comply with the laws of the territorial state, or when it fails to perform its obligations under the agreement.[58]

---

[55] Two Freedoms Agreement, Art.1(4).
[56] *ibid.*, Art.1(3).
[57] Above, n.55, Art.1(4).
[58] Above, n.55, Art.1(5).

Aircraft in distress

Aircraft possess the nationality of the state in which they are registered[59] and may only be validly registered in one state.[60] For jurisdiction purposes, it is the state of registration which is competent to exercise jurisdiction over offences and acts committed on board.[61] Contracting States, that is, to the Tokyo Convention, other than the state of registration, may exercise criminal jurisdiction in respect of, for instance offences which have effect on their territory or have been committed by or against one of their nationals or permanent residents.[62] The increase in hijacking and terrorist activities relating to aircraft prompted the adoption of the Hague Convention for the Suppression of Unlawful Seizure of Aircraft 1970,[63] and the ICAO Montreal Convention for the Suppression of Unlawful Acts Against the Safety of Civil Aviation,[64] and the Protocol[65] whereby attacks against individuals in airports are brought within the ambit of the Convention. These Conventions (and the Protocol) which are all in force, require Contracting Parties to exercise jurisdiction[66] or to extradite the alleged offender. In respect of the 1988 Lockerbie aerial incident, Libya maintained that all obligations under the Montreal Convention had been fulfilled.[67]

Contracting Parties are required by Art.25 of the Convention to render assistance to civil aircraft (of other Contracting Parties) which find themselves "in distress" in their airspace.

There are no established rules of international law as to what response a "host" state should make on the appearance of an unauthorised civil aircraft in its airspace. Although, arguably, such an aircraft, not being "in distress" does not come within the ambit of Art.25, it would be untenable to allege that the "host" state could take whatever action it wished. If the host state is not a party to the Convention, there is still, on humanitarian grounds, no reason for a distinction to be made between its position and that of a party to the Convention. Injury and death inflicted on

---

[59] Chicago Convention, Art.17.
[60] *ibid.*, Art.18.
[61] Tokyo Convention on Offences and Acts Committed on Board Aircraft 1963, U.K.T.S. 126 (1969) Cmnd.4230.
[62] *ibid.*, Art.4.
[63] U.K.T.S. 39 (1972) Cmnd.4956; 10 I.L.M. 133 (1971).
[64] U.K.T.S. 10 (1974) Cmnd.5524; 10 I.L.M. 1551 (1971).
[65] Protocol for the suppression of unlawful Acts of violence at airports serving international civil aviation (1971).
[66] The Hague Convention requires the imposition of "severe penalties".
[67] See *Case concerning Questions of Interpretation and Application of the 1971 Montreal Convention arising from the Aerial Incident at Lockerbie* (*Libyan Arab Jamahiriya v United States*) 31 I.L.M. 662 (1992).

innocent air passengers will not be accepted by the international community. Unfortunately, though, the violation of air sovereignty has precipitated some states to shoot first and ask questions later, for example the 1953 Aerial Incident in which an Israeli aircraft was shot down in Bulgarian airspace; the 1973 shooting down of a Libyan aircraft by Israel; the shooting down in 1983 of a South Korean aircraft by the Soviet Union; and the destruction by Indian Air Force planes of a Pakistani aircraft.[68] Such a response, in particular from a Contracting Party of the Convention, is especially regrettable when, under Art.4, Contracting states undertake that civil aviation is not to be used for any purpose inconsistent with the aims of the Convention. Owing to the regularity of such incidents and, in particular, the 1983 incident involving the South Korean aircraft, the Assembly of the International Civil Aviation Organisation (ICAO) adopted unanimously Art.3 *bis* of the 1944 Convention.[69] Under this provision, the use of weapons against civil aircraft in flight is prohibited, save for the derogation allowed under Art.51 of the U.N. Charter.[70] Art.3 *bis* recognised what has become an established rule of Customary International Law. This was endorsed by the Security Council Resolution 1067, which "condemns the use of weapons against civil aircraft in flight as being incompatible with elementary considerations of humanity, the rules of customary international law as codified in *Article 3 bis of the Chicago Convention* and the standards and recommended practises set out in the annexes of the convention".[71] This resolution was issued following the shooting down of two US civilian aircraft by Cuban military aircraft on February 24, 1996. Cuba claimed that it was acting in defence of its sovereign right to protect its borders and that the US aircraft were suspected of forming part of a paramilitary terrorist organisation in war against their country. The United States claimed that the fundamental question was whether it was acceptable to shoot down two unarmed civilian aircraft.

The Convention does not identify any sanctions which are to be adopted against "offending" Contracting Parties, and states are left to take whatever measures they see fit in the circumstances. Thus, following the shooting down of the South Korean aircraft, a number of states refused, for a time, the Soviet airline landing rights and cancelled flights by their own aircraft to the Soviet Union.

---

[68] Ariel Incident of August 10, 1999 (*Pakistan v India*). However, please note that the ICJ held it lacked jurisdiction to judge the case, although it did find that India and Pakistan were obliged to resolve the dispute by peaceful means.

[69] 23 I.L.M. 705 (1984).

[70] See Ch.11.

[71] Security Council Resolution 1067 (1996), July 26, 1996, para.6.

The Chicago Convention initiated the establishment of the International Civil Aviation Organisation (ICAO). ICAO is a specialised agency of the United Nations and is based in Montreal. Its function is primarily to supervise the application of air law, report any breaches of the Convention and conduct research into matters of air transport and navigation which are of international importance.

OUTER SPACE

The launching of the first artificial satellite round the Earth by the Soviet Union in 1957 heralded the beginning of outer space exploration, and the evolution of a legal regime regulating activities in outer space. Contrary to the position in respect of airspace, states have accepted that satellites may pass above their territory and no state has contended that such activity constitutes a violation of airspace sovereignty. The exploration of outer space has modified inevitably the view that airspace extends upwards to an indefinite limit. It is now recognised that national sovereignty must cease at some point.

The United Nations Committee on the Peaceful Uses of Outer Space, established in 1958, has been responsible for the measures adopted regulating outer space activity and all such measures recognise that outer space is (i) to be used for peaceful means; and (ii) that it is the common heritage of all mankind.

The Treaty on Principles Governing the Activities of States in the Exploration and Use of Outer Space, including the Moon and Other Celestial Bodies (commonly referred to as the Outer Space Treaty)[72] affirms that:

> ... exploration and use of outer space including the Moon and other celestial bodies, shall be carried out for the benefit and in the interests of all countries, irrespective of their degree of economic or scientific development, and shall be the province of all mankind."[73]

No area of outer space is to be appropriated by any state,[74] and the exploration is to be conducted "in accordance with international law, "including the Charter of the United Nations . . . ."[75] Art.4 is particularly important in that it prohibits the installation of nuclear weapons or any other weapons of mass destruction in

---

[72] U.K.T.S. 10 (1968) Cmnd.3519; 610 U.N.T.S. 205.
[73] Outer Space Treaty, above, Art.1.
[74] *ibid.*, Art.2.
[75] Above, n.73, Art.3.

outer space. The proposed US "Star Wars" development was justified on the grounds that they were designed to take defensive rather than offensive action. Jurisdiction over an object once launched into space remains with the state of registration.[76] Art.9 requires states to conduct exploration, so as to avoid the harmful contamination of outer space and "also adverse changes in the environment of the Earth resulting from the introduction of extra terrestrial matter . . ." Agreement was reached in 1988 between the representatives of the United States, Canada, Japan and nine Member States of the European Space Agency on the establishment of a permanently manned civil space station.[77] The primary purpose of creating such a station is to promote collaborative efforts in the field of, for example biomedical studies. However, financial constraints were responsible for modifications to the original design and delay in the launching of a permanent base until at least 1998. (The first module was launched 5 December 1998).

The 1967 Treaty has been revised and clarified by the 1979 Moon Treaty (Agreement Concerning the Activities of States on the Moon and Other Celestial Bodies).[78] In particular, the Moon Treaty provides that the natural resources of the moon and other celestial bodies should be exploited as the common heritage of mankind in accordance with an international legal regime. This Treaty entered into force on July 11, 1984. The 1967 Treaty has been supplemented by two further agreements:

(a) the Agreement on the Rescue of Astronauts, the Return of Astronauts and the Return of Objects Launched into Outer Space, 1968[79]; and

(b) the Convention on International Liability for Damages Caused by Space Objects 1972.[80]

The Rescue and Return Agreement is essentially concerned with securing co-operation between Contracting Parties for the rescue and return of astronauts, while the 1972 Convention establishes the strict liability of a launching state "for damage caused by its space object on the surface of the earth or to aircraft in flight",[81] and fault liability "in the event of damage being caused elsewhere

[76] Above, n.73, Art.8.
[77] Agreement on co-operation on the detailed design development operation and utilisation of the permanently manned civil space station.
[78] 18 I.L.M. 1434 (1979).
[79] U.K.T.S. 56 (1969) Cmnd.3997; 63 A/J.I.L. 382 (1969).
[80] 10 I.L.M. 965 (1971); U.K.T.S. 16 (1974) Cmnd.5551.
[81] Liability Convention, Art.II. Art.VI establishes joint and several liability in the event of a joint launch.

other than on the surface of the earth to a space object of one launching state or to persons or property on board such a space object . . .".[82]

Every launch and its intended purpose must be registered by the launching state on a public register maintained by the Secretary General of the United Nations. This is required by the 1975 Convention on the Registration of Objects Launched into Outer Space,[83] introduced when the voluntary registration system initially envisaged, proved unsatisfactory.[84]

An important by-product of space exploration has been the development of telecommunications networks. The operation, co-ordination and monitoring of these telecommunications networks and services falls within the remit of the International Telecommunications Union (ITU), a specialised agency of the United Nations, based in Geneva. One of the primary roles of the ITU is to promote the working together of government and private industry.

CONCLUSION

As has been said, states enjoy territorial sovereignty. However, that sovereignty is not unfettered. A state may, for instance, have to recognise that its territory has to be used for the benefit of another state, for example a right of passage, taking of water for irrigation purposes, or alternatively a state may have to refrain from taking certain action on its territory, for example the stationing of forces. Such rights (servitudes) attached to territory have to be recognised by successor states. Benefits may exist not for a single state, but for the international community, for example international waterways such as the Suez Canal.

The increasing awareness and concern for environmental issues has in recent years led to further restrictions being imposed on a state's territorial sovereignty.[85]

---

[82] *ibid*. Art.III. See Also COSMOS 954 claim *(Canada v USSR)* 18 I.L.M. 899 (1979).
[83] 14 I.L.M. 43 (1975).
[84] The Outer Space Act of 1986 introduced the obligations of the Convention into UK domestic law.
[85] Such restrictions are discussed more fully in Ch.8, State Responsibility, below.

6. JURISDICTION

Jurisdiction is an attribute of state sovereignty. A state's jurisdiction refers to the competence of the state to govern persons and property by its municipal law (criminal and civil). This competence embraces jurisdiction to prescribe (and proscribe), to adjudicate and to enforce the law. Jurisdiction is primarily exercised on a territorial basis, but there are exceptions, for example there will be persons within the territory who will be immune from jurisdiction, whilst there will be occasions when a state may exercise jurisdiction outside its territory. The exercise or the non-exercise of jurisdiction is governed by a state's municipal law. In international law, jurisdiction relating to the allocation of competence between states is an ill-defined concept. International law confines itself to criminal rather than civil jurisdiction. The civil law is the concern of private international law or, more correctly, the conflict of laws, though, in the last resort, civil jurisdiction may be backed by the sanctions of the criminal law. International law does not prescribe rules *requiring* (emphasis added) the exercise of jurisdiction. International law concerns itself principally with the propriety of the exercises of state jurisdiction. The exercise of jurisdiction remains, for the most part, a discretionary matter for the state concerned.

Bases on which jurisdiction may be exercised are:

(a) territorial principle;

(b) nationality principle;

(c) protective (or security) principle;

(d) universality principle; and

(e) passive personality principle.

The first four principles, territorial principle, nationality principle, protective (or security) principle and universality principle, were accepted by the Harvard Research Draft Convention of 1935. The Convention was an unofficial work, produced by a number of American international lawyers. Although not binding on any state, it remains of interest because of the extensive study of state practice which was undertaken. The passive personality principle was not adopted by the Convention.

The bases of jurisdiction are not listed in any hierarchy. No state can claim precedence simply on the principle on which it exercises jurisdiction. A state may legitimately possess jurisdiction concurrently with another state and the state which will exercise jurisdiction will be decided by other facts, for example physical presence of the alleged offender.

What international law today demands is the existence of a tangible link between the alleged offender and/or the forum of the incident and the state exercising jurisdiction.[1]

Territorial principle

This is the favoured basis for the exercise of state jurisdiction. Events occurring within a state's territorial boundaries and persons within that territory, albeit their presence is temporary, are as a rule subject to the application of local law.

An offence may not, however, be entirely committed within the territory of one state. A crime may be commenced in one state and consummated in another. If a person stands near to the border between two countries and fires a gun and thereby injures a person on the other side, which state has jurisdiction? The answer is both. The state from which the gun was fired has jurisdiction under the subjective territorial principle, whilst the state where

---

[1] *Lotus Case* P.C.I.J.Rep., ser.A, No.10 (1927) at 25, in which the court emphasised the need for a prohibition to be evident under international law for a state's jurisdiction to be instituted. Otherwise, the state enjoyed a wide measure of discretion in the exercise of its jurisdiction.

the injury was sustained has jurisdiction under the objective territorial principle.

The subjective territorial principle allows the exercise of jurisdiction in the state where a crime is commenced.

The objective territorial principle gives jurisdiction to the state in which the crime has been completed and has effect—the forum of injury.

Both states may claim jurisdiction and both may do so legitimately. The one which will actually exercise jurisdiction will most probably be the one which has custody of the alleged offender. There is no rule of international law which gives a state, where a crime is completed, exclusive jurisdiction. The state in which the crime was initiated is, in other words, not restricted from exercising jurisdiction. Such a state may bring preparatory criminal acts within the ambit of its criminal law. See for example, in the United Kingdom, the Criminal Justice Act 1993, which permits English courts to exercise jurisdiction over specific crimes where a particular aspect of the crime occurs on UK soil although the effects are felt outside UK territory. There is:

> "No rule of comity to prevent Parliament from prohibiting under pain of punishment persons who are present in the United Kingdom, and so owe local obedience to our law, from doing physical acts in England, notwithstanding that the consequences of those acts take effect outside the United Kingdom."[2]

Nor is there anything:

> "in precedent, comity or good sense that should inhibit the common law from regarding as justiciable in England inchoate crimes committed abroad which were intended to result in the commission of criminal offences in England; therefore conspiracies abroad to commit offences in England constituted offences in English law even though no overt acts pursuant thereto took place in England."[3]

---

[2] Lord Diplock in *Treacy v D.P.P.* [1971] A.C. 537, HL at 561. The case related to attempted blackmail by a letter mailed in England to a person in Germany. See also the case of *R. v Markus* [1974] 3 All E.R. 705.

[3] *Somchai Liangsiriprasert v The Government of the United States of America and Another* Privy Council, *Times Law Report*, July 1990—reaffirmed in *R. v Sanson and Others*, CA, *The Times*, September 27, 1990. See, however, the CA's decision in *R. v Governor of Belmarsh Prison, Ex p. Martin* [1995] 2 All E.R., in which the Court declined to apply a UK Act of Parliament extraterritorially in respect of certain acts occurring outside the relevant territory. The Court declined to do so in the absence of express wording in the Act, as this was held to be contrary to usual policy on the exercise of UK jurisdiction abroad.

A problem, which has demanded a modification of the territorial principle, has been the need to fetter the growth of the so called "child sex industry" (both girls and boys). Unfortunately the growth in this trade has been to meet the demand from countries such as Germany, America, Great Britain, Australia and France.[4] Certain countries' nationals, who rank as alleged principle offenders, have initiated legislative measures to extend the territorial application of the legislation. Australia led the way with the Australian Crimes (Child Sex Tourism Amendment) Act.[5] Other countries, which have followed the Australian lead, have been Sweden, Norway, France and Japan. The reluctance to extend UK legislation abroad is reflected in the United Kingdom's response—the Sexual Offences (Conspiracy and Incitement) Act 1996,[6] whereby it is an offence to conspire, within England and Wales, to commit abroad certain sexual acts against children. Incitement of such acts abroad is also an offence under the legislation.

More controversial has been the exercise of jurisdiction based on the effects principles so as to regulate the affairs of foreign nationals abroad, because such activities have an economic impact in the regulating state. The most frequent application of this principle, which is essentially an extension of the objective territorial principle, has been by the United States, for example anti-trust legislation, but certain European states have invoked the principle and the European Communities have affirmed that what is relevant in the application of EEC competition rules is the place where the agreement is implemented.[7] The response of those critical of the principle[8] has resulted in the US courts modifying their approach by introducing "reasonableness" and a balancing of the national interests when considering the potential application of its jurisdiction.[9] In 1996, President Clinton's administration was severely criticised for the D'Amato Bill which attempted to impose worldwide sanctions on foreign companies making new investments of £26 million or more in oil or gas projects in Iran or Libya. The Bill was targeted at these states as the

---

[4] UNICEF, *The Progress of Nations* (1995).
[5] 1994, Part III A.
[6] Need Ref.
[7] See, *e.g. Wood Pulp Case* [1988] 4 C.M.L.R. 901.
[8] See, *e.g.* the United Kingdom's Protection of Trading Interests Act 1980, c.11.
[9] See, however, *Hartford Fire Insurance Co. v California US Supreme Court* 113 S. Ct 2891 (1993) in which the Supreme Court declined to carry out a balancing exercise between US and UK interests and found in favour of the US court, apparently on the basis that there was no conflict with UK legislation. This was despite the fact that the acts of the UK insurance company were deemed to be lawful in the UK.

alleged principal proponents of international terrorism. The international community condemned the legislation as a "clear violation of the principle of extra-territoriality." Similarly, the OAS concluded that the US Helms-Burton Act 1996 did not conform with the "applicable norms of international law in respect of the exercise of jurisdiction of States and its limits on such exercise."[10]

The trial of the two suspects in the Lockerbie bombing was a unique event in that it was the first occasion where a court had sat as a national court outside its own territory. Although the court sat in the Netherlands (Camp Zeist), it was a Scottish Court applying Scot's law in respect of an offence, which took place within Scottish territory. The venue of the Court was moved to the Netherlands to counter the fears that the suspects would not receive a fair trial in Scotland.[11]

Nationality principle

Jurisdiction exercised on this principle relates to the nationality of the offender. A state may exercise jurisdiction over any of its nationals wherever they may be and in respect of offences committed abroad. Although universally acknowledged as a basis of jurisdiction, it is utilised more extensively by civil-law countries than those with a common-law system. The latter restrict jurisdiction exercised on the nationality principle to more serious crimes, such as, in the case of the United Kingdom, offences committed under the Official Secrets Act 1989 and the Sexual Offences (Conspiracy and Incitement) Act 1996, murder, manslaughter and bigamy.

The United States has similarly restricted prosecutions on the grounds of nationality to such crimes as treason, drug trafficking and crimes by or against the armed forces.

The fact that jurisdiction may be claimed on the nationality principle does not preclude the state in which the offence was committed from exercising jurisdiction on the territorial principle.

Protective (security) principle

On the basis of this principle, a state may exercise jurisdiction in respect of offences which, although occurring abroad and committed by non-nationals, are regarded as injurious to the state's

[10] 35 I.L.M. 1322 (1996) Organisation of American States: Inter-American Juridical Committee Opinion Examining the US Helms-Burton Act of August 27, 1996. The EU has also expressed opposition to the Helms-Burton Act, namely its validity under international law, its extraterritorial reach and its impact on trade interests in the EU. See, 35 I.L.M. 397 (1996).
[11] One suspect was acquitted whilst the other is serving a life sentence in a Scottish prison. Lockerbie case, (1992) I.C.J. 3, 94 I.L.R. 478.

security. Although acknowledged as a justification for the exercise of jurisdiction, it remains ill-defined. It is undoubtedly open to abuse if "security" or "vital interests" are given a broad interpretation. However, the justification lies in the need to protect a state from the prejudicial activities of an alien when such activities are not, for instance, unlawful in the country in which they are being carried out.

Examples of when a state might claim jurisdiction on this principle would be in respect of plans to overthrow its government or counterfeit its currency. The principle was invoked by Israel along with the universality principle in the case against Eichmann (see below), while in the English courts it has been said "no principle of comity demands that a state should ignore the crime of treason committed against it outside its territory."[12] "Lord Haw Haw" was found guilty of treason because of his pro-Nazi propaganda radio broadcasts from Germany to Britain during the war. His duty of allegiance was founded on his having acquired a British passport, albeit fraudulently.

Universality principle

One interpretation of this principle is that it gives jurisdiction to a state (any and every) over all crimes perpetrated by foreigners abroad. Such an interpretation is not regarded as being in conformity with international law. Where the principle may be acceptably invoked is in respect of international crimes, that is, offences which are prohibited by international law and the international community as a whole.

The idea of a universal crime over which all states could exercise jurisdiction, regardless of the alleged offender's nationality, evolved with piracy. Under customary international law, the crime of piracy has long been recognised as one over which all states could exercise jurisdiction, provided that the alleged offender was apprehended either on the high seas or within the territory of the state exercising jurisdiction. The arresting state may also legitimately punish pirates. This rule of customary international law is reaffirmed in Art.19 of the 1958 Geneva Convention on the High Seas and Art.105 of the 1982 Convention on the Law of the Sea. Piracy in international law—*piracy jure gentium*—is strictly defined. This is in contrast to piracy in municipal law, where the term is used somewhat loosely. Piracy, for the purposes of international law, is essentially any illegal act of violence or depredation which is committed for private ends on the

---

[12] *Joyce v D.P.P.* [1946] A.C. 347, HL at 372.

high seas or without the territorial control of any state.[13] Only acts which satisfy this definition of piracy are susceptible to the exercise of jurisdiction on the universality principle. Attempts to commit acts of piracy, even though unsuccessful, will also constitute the offence of piracy.

War crimes and genocide are now widely accepted as being susceptible to universal jurisdiction. No state has exercised jurisdiction exclusively on such a basis.[14] In the *Eichmann Case*,[15] Israel successfully (at least in Israeli courts) claimed jurisdiction on two cumulative grounds:

> "a universal source (pertaining to the whole of mankind), which vests the right to prosecute and punish crimes of this order in every state within the family of nations; and a specific or national source, which gives the victim nation the right to try any who assault its existence."[16]

The Charter of the Nuremberg Military Tribunal, in particular Art.6, which referred to crimes against peace, violations of the laws and customs of war, and crimes against humanity and for which there was to be individual responsibility, and the judgment of the Tribunal are now accepted as international law. Genocide has been unanimously condemned by the General Assembly and the 1948 Convention on the Prevention and Punishment of the Crime of Genocide can be characterised as one of the first human rights instruments. Prohibition of genocide is now recognised as a concept of *jus cogens*. That Convention provides for trial by either the territorial state or by an international penal tribunal, but a state which encourages, practices or fails to punish genocide would today be held guilty of having contravened customary international law of a fundamental nature. The International Law Commission's Draft Code of Crimes Against the Peace and Security of Mankind declares certain crimes, including genocide, as a crime against the peace and security of mankind.[17] However, both the ITCY and the ITCR distinguish between genocide, crimes

---

[13] Art.15 of the 1958 Convention on the High Seas; Art.101 of the 1982 Convention on the Law of the Sea; see pp.152–153 below.

[14] Belgium has been the first country to turn the principle of universal jurisdiction into a reality. On June 8, 2001, four defendants were convicted of international crimes arising from the Rwandan genocide. ASIL, Linda Keller, May 2001.

[15] *Attorney-General of the Government of Israel v Eichmann* 36 I.L.R. 5 (1961).

[16] For Genocide Convention, see U.K.T.S. 58 (1970) Cmnd.4421; 78 U.N.T.S. 277; 4 A.J.I.L. Supp.6 (1951).

[17] See, the Report of the International Law Commission on its Forty-sixth Session, UN G.A.O.R., 49th Sess, Supp.No.10 UN Doc.A/49/10 (1994).

against humanity, and war crimes.[18] This distinction is retained in the Statute of the Permanent Court of the International Criminal Court.[19] Significant steps were taken by the international community in the 1990's towards the creation of a permanent international criminal court with enforcement jurisdiction over individuals for a number of crimes against humanity. Simultaneous to these efforts was the establishment, in 1993 and 1994 by the United Nations, of the aforementioned tribunals with jurisdiction to "prosecute persons responsible for serious violations of international humanitarian law".[20] Nevertheless, these tribunals are limited in jurisdiction, both temporally and geographically, and, of course, are non-permanent. However, not withstanding this, the humanitarian crisis in former Yugoslavia was responsible for rekindling efforts to establish an international criminal-law regime. Televised reports of war camps, rape, genocide and the practise of ethnic cleansing shocked the international community, and led to the creation of the tribunal under Ch.VII of the UN Charter to punish the alleged perpetrators of such crimes. UN Security Council Resolution 827 established the ITCY on May 23, 1993 for the sole purpose of:

> "prosecuting persons responsible for serious violations of international humanitarian law committed in the territory of the former Yugoslavia between 1st January, 1991 and a date to be determined by the Security Council upon the restoration of peace."[21]

The Tribunal was designed to establish a judicial process aimed at preventing the continuation of crimes against humanity and to contribute towards the restoration and maintenance of peace and security in the region. This was the first occasion the Security Council had created an international tribunal using Ch.VII powers and can, therefore be said to be a truly international entity.[22]

The Tribunal differs from its predecessor (Nuremberg) in that it may also hear cases of crimes perpetrated in the course of inter-state war and internal strife. Nuremberg could only deal with crimes committed in international armed conflict.

---

[18] Statute of ITCY and ITCR, Arts 6, 7, and 8. ITCR S1994/87 & S1994/906; ITCY S/25704, 3 May 1994.

[19] Rome Statute of the International Criminal Court (as corrected by the process-verbaux of November 10, 1998 and July 12, 1999).

[20] U.N.Doc.S/Res/827/(1993).

[21] S.C.Res 827, U.N. SCOR, 48th Year, 3217th mtg at 1, reprinted in 32 I.L.M. 1203 (1993).

[22] The Nuremberg tribunal was established in very different circumstances, when there was no government in power.

The Statute of the Tribunal embodies rules and procedures reflecting international human rights and standards, particularly those enshrined in the International Covenant of Civil and Political Rights, for example Art.21(a), which deals with the accused's right to be present at his trial, and Art.25, which provides the accused with a right to appeal. The Tribunal issued its first indictment and warrant for arrest in November, 1994 and passed its first sentence in December, 1996, sentencing a Croatian soldier in the Bosnian–Serb army to 10 years for his part in the slaughter of Muslims in the UN "safe-haven" of Srebrenica. The experience of both the ITCY and the ITCR heightened calls for the creation of a permanent Court and gave the impetus necessary for agreement to be reached. The international efforts towards the creation of the International Criminal Court, culminated in the opening for signature of the Rome Statute[23] in July, 1999 and its entry into force on the July 1, 2002.

THE INTERNATIONAL CRIMINAL COURT

The International Criminal Court (ICC) has jurisdiction over ". . . persons for the most serious crimes of international concern . . ."[24] namely genocide—Art.5(1)(a), crimes against humanity; Art.5(1)(b), war crimes; Art.5(1)(c); and the crime of aggression Art.5(1)(d). The crimes themselves are defined in Arts 6, 7 and 8 respectively. However, aggression has not be defined as yet, state parties to the Statute have still to adopt an agreement as to the definition of aggression and the conditions under which the Court would exercise jurisdiction in respect of aggression. The Court has jurisdiction (as do the Tribunals) which is complimentary to National Criminal jurisdiction—Art.1. In other words, the Court will only exercise its jurisdiction when a national court is unable or unwilling to do so. The ICC is not designed to be a substitute to national courts. The court may exercise its jurisdiction only if "one or more of the parties involved is a state party; the accused is a national of a state party; the crime is committed on the territory of a state party; or a state not party to the statute may decide to accept the court's jurisdiction over a specific crime that has been committed within its territory, or by its national."[25] The Court will, of course, only have jurisdiction once the Prosecutor has referred a situation to it or the Security Council refers to the prosecutor; or the prosecutor initiates an investigation on his own authority—Art.13.

[23] Above, n.9.
[24] Above, n.9, Art.1.
[25] Art.12. However, these conditions do not apply when the Security Council, acting under Ch.VII of the Charter, refers a situation to the Prosecutor.

The court will be based in The Hague in the Netherlands and it is anticipated that a new building for the court will be ready by 2007.

In 1971 a UN resolution (GA Resolution 2784 (XXVI)) characterised apartheid as a crime against humanity and, two years later, a Convention[26] was adopted, identifying apartheid as a crime subject to universal jurisdiction.[27]

Other crimes which are of international concern have been tackled by way of Conventions. The Hague Convention on the Suppression of Unlawful Seizure of Aircraft 1970[28] and the Montreal Convention for the Suppression of Unlawful Acts against the Safety of Civil Aviation 1971[29] were the response of the international community to the problem of hijacking which became acute in the 1960s. Both Conventions have been adhered to by a large number of states, and what they impose is an obligation on Contracting States to punish, "by severe penalties" implemented by way of their domestic law, offenders (or alternatively extradite them) even in such circumstances as when the offence was neither committed in their territory nor committed by a national. Similar provisions are contained in the Convention on the Prevention and Punishment of Crimes against Internationally Protected Persons including Diplomatic Agents,[30] the 1979 International Convention against the Taking of Hostages,[31] the 1984 United Nations Convention Against Torture and Other Cruel, Inhuman or Degrading Treatment or Punishment,[32] and the 1988 Convention against Illicit Traffic in Narcotic Drugs.[33] *ALSO* The European Council Articles on Cybercrime.[34] The latter is the international response to the tackling of crimes committed via the internet and other computer networks, particularly copyright, computer related fraud, child pornography and network-security

---

[26] International Convention on the Suppression and Punishment of the Crime of Apartheid, November 30, 1973; 13 I.L.M. 50 (1974).

[27] *ibid.* Art.1; the Convention has only been adopted by one-third of states. The UK and the US are not parties.

[28] 860 U.N.T.S. 105; U.K.T.S. 39 (1972) Cmnd.4956; 10 I.L.M. 133 (1971); Harris, p.280.

[29] U.K.T.S. 10 (1974) Cmnd.5524; 10 I.L.M. 1151 (1971); see Ch.5, above.

[30] 13 I.L.M. 41 (1974); U.K.T.S. 3 (1980) Cmnd.7765.

[31] U.K.T.S. 81 (1983) Cmnd. 9100; 18 I.L.M. 1456 (1979).

[32] 23 I.L.M. 1027 (1984) and 24 I.L.M. 535 (1985). In *Filartiga v Pena-Irala* 630 F. 2d 876 (1980), a US tribunal held that torture was a recognised crime under international law and that every country could exercise jurisdiction over the alleged offenders of such an offence.

[33] 28 I.L.M. 493 (1989).

[34] Convention on Cybercrime, (ETS no.185) November 23, 2001.

violations.[35] Such agreements are effective only between contracting parties. States do not automatically possess competence under customary international law to apprehend and punish alleged offenders. What the Conventions spell out are the particular situations in which states are required to exercise jurisdiction or alternatively initiate extradition proceedings.

International crimes "proper" are susceptible to universal jurisdiction under customary international law regardless of whether a state is party to any international agreement. There is nothing to preclude offences currently regulated by Convention from crystallising into customary international law, as has happened with genocide.

Passive personality principle

The link between the state exercising jurisdiction and the offence is the nationality of the victim. A state may exercise jurisdiction over an alien in respect of an act which has taken place outwith its boundaries, but against one of its nationals. It has not been widely accepted as a basis of jurisdiction—see Moore J.'s objection in the *Lotus Case*.[36] Civilian legal systems recognise it more readily than common-law systems. The vigorous opposition of countries of the Anglo–American tradition was responsible for the principle not being adopted by the Draft Convention. Nevertheless the passive personality principle has been recognised in Art.4(b) of the 1963 Tokyo Convention on Offences aboard Aircraft[37] and Art.5(1)(c) of the 1984 Convention against Torture and Other Cruel, Inhuman or Degrading Treatment or Punishment[38] and, apparently, the current position of the United States is that, although the principle is not generally accepted for ordinary torts or crimes, it is increasingly accepted as applied to terrorist and other organised attacks on a state's nationals by reason of their nationality, or to assassination of a state's diplomatic representatives or other officials.[39]

[35] Although concluded under the auspices of the European Council, Japan, US, Canada and South Africa have ratified the convention and it will enter into force following ratification of five states, including at least three Member States of the Council of Europe. As of July, 2002, there has been one ratification (Albania).
[36] P.C.I.J.Rep., ser.A, No.10, (1927), pp.141–148.
[37] U.K.T.S. 126 (1969) Cmnd.4230; 704 U.N.T.S. 219.
[38] Above, n.32.
[39] Third Restatement of the Law—The Foreign Relations Law of the United States—para.402g. The US passed the Public Law 107–40 authorizing the use of United Armed Forces against those responsible for the attacks launched against the US (SJ 23 (Sept 18, 2001)). This authorized the US to exercise its rights to self-defence and to protect US citizens both at home and abroad. It also has the Diplomatic Security and Anti-Terrorism Act of 1986.

EXTRADITION

If an alleged offender is in a territory other than the state seeking to exercise jurisdiction, the lawful method of securing his return to stand trial is to request his extradition.[40] Extradition is the handing over of an alleged offender (or convicted criminal who has escaped before completing his prison term) by one state to another.

Extradition as a rule is effected by bipartite treaty. There is no duty to extradite in the absence of a treaty.[41] Extradition treaties normally relate only to serious crimes and impose the same obligations on both the parties concerned, for example the offence must be designated a crime under the domestic laws of both countries. A country's own nationals may be protected from extradition as may be persons who have committed offences of a "political" or "religious" character.

ILLEGAL ARREST

A tribunal does not normally concern itself with the means by which the accused is brought before it. If the alleged offender has been procured by illegal means, for example kidnap or in violation of an extradition treaty, this will not preclude the tribunal from exercising jurisdiction. Unlawful arrest does not affect the court's jurisdiction to hear a case. However, this established rule was modified to some extent in the *Toscanino Case*,[42] in which it was stated that a court was divested of jurisdiction when the accused had been brought before it through the illegal conduct of the law enforcement authorities. Forcible abduction, involving brutality and like behaviour by a state's representatives, could impair a state's exercise of jurisdiction. The norm, however, is that a state will, in the absence of protest from other states, try alleged offenders brought before the courts by irregular means as in the case of *Ex p. Elliott*[43] and *R. v Plymouth Magistrates Court, Ex*

---

[40] *e.g.* Germany submitted an extradition request to Italy in August, 1996 for the return of former SS Captain Erich Priebke to stand trial for alleged war crimes committed during the Second World War.
[41] The ILC's Draft Code of Crimes, above, n.17 seeks to impose an obligation on state to extradite an individual alleged to have committed crimes against humanity (Art.6).
[42] *US v Toscanino* 500 F. 2d. 207 (1974) (US Ct of Appeals, 2nd Circuit.). *cf. United States v Alvarez-Machain* 31 I.L.M. 902 (1992) where a Mexican national was forcibly removed from his country and brought before a US court. The Supreme Ct held that the Federal US court could exercise jurisdiction, despite the flagrant breach of international law as this was a matter to be considered only by the Executive.
[43] [1949] 1 All E.R. 373.

p. Driver.[44] In *R. v Horseferry Magistrates' Court, Ex p. Bennett*,[45] the House of Lords held that where a defendant has been forcibly brought before a court by an abuse of process, the UK courts should refuse to exercise jurisdiction. Bennett had been taken from South Africa to the United Kingdom in a manner which appeared to contravene the Extradition Act 1989, and amount to a violation of international law.[46]

The state whose sovereignty has been violated may initiate an international claim against the offending state. Argentina lodged a complaint with the UN Security Council in protest at the abduction of Eichmann to Israel, and called for the immediate return of Eichmann. The claim was dropped and, in August, 1960, Argentina and Israel announced in a joint decision that any violation of international law which had occurred had been "cured". States will only refrain from exercising jurisdiction over persons illegally brought before their courts from another state if the latter protests.

DOUBLE JEOPARDY

What of the person who is susceptible to the jurisdiction of more than one country? Does conviction or acquittal in one country constitute a bar to a subsequent prosecution elsewhere?

International law does not provide an unequivocal answer, though Art.13 of the Harvard Draft Convention does provide that, at least in respect of exercising jurisdiction under the Draft Convention, no state should prosecute or punish an alien who "has been prosecuted in another state for a crime requiring proof of substantially the same acts or omissions and has been acquitted on the merits, or having been convicted, has been pardoned."

Art.13 refers only to aliens. It does not apply to nationals. Regarding the person who finds himself required to do in one state something which is prohibited in another, Art.14 of the Draft Convention provides that ". . . no State shall prosecute or punish an alien for an act which was required of that alien by the law of the place where the alien was at the time of the act or omission." Art.14 applies only to aliens and not to nationals. Art.12 of the International Law Commission's Draft Code of Crimes Against the Peace and Security of Mankind (1996) upholds the principle of *non bis in idem* in relation to two scenarios, the second being subject to exceptions. The first situation is where an individual is tried for crimes by an international criminal court and is convicted

---

[44] [1986] Q.B. 95.
[45] [1993] 3 All E.R. 138.
[46] See in particular, opinions of Lords Griffiths and Bridge.

or acquitted. The principle of *non bis in idem* applies fully. The second situation is where an individual may not be tried for a crime under the code arising from the same act or omission as was the subject of the national trial unless one of these exceptions applies:

(a) if the individual was tried by a national court for an ordinary crime and not a more serious one (e.g. murder, not genocide); and

(b) if the proceedings in the national court were not impartial or independent.

IMMUNITY FROM JURISDICTION

Sovereign immunity and diplomatic immunity are the two principal exceptions to the exercise of territorial jurisdiction. Sovereign immunity refers to immunities enjoyed by foreign heads of state. Diplomatic immunity refers to the immunities enjoyed by their official representatives.

State immunity

"Par in parem non habat imperium"—one cannot exercise authority over an equal. All states are equal. No state may exercise jurisdiction over another state without its consent. Historically, a sovereign and his state were regarded as synonymous. The ruler of a foreign state enjoys complete immunity—the principle that this extends to acts done in a private capacity was confirmed in *Mighell v Sultan of Johore*[47] and still applies today.

Traditionally, foreign states were likewise immune from the jurisdiction of the courts of other states. States in the twentieth century, however, became increasingly involved in commercial activities until eventually state enterprises enjoyed an immunity not enjoyed by non-state counterparts. Sovereign immunity placed state enterprises in a privileged position. Consequently, a number of states adopted a modified, absolute-immunity policy. A distinction was drawn between the public acts of a state (government acts) *jure imperii*, and private acts (trading and commercial acts) *jure gestionis*. Immunity was granted in respect of *jure imperii* acts, but not in respect of *jure gestionis*. Not all states abandoned the doctrine of absolute immunity. As a result, some states were affording complete immunity to the commercial activities of foreign states, whereas the same privileges were not being reciprocated.

---

[47] [1894] 1 Q.B. 149.

The principle of absolute immunity was established in *The Parlement Belge Case*,[48] in which it was held that *The Parlement Belge*, a mail packet vessel belonging to the Belgian King, was entitled to complete immunity. The principle was confirmed in subsequent cases, for example *The Porto Alexandra*,[49] *The Cristina*,[50] *Krajina v Tass Agency*,[51] *Baccus SRL v Servicio Nacional del Trigo*.[52]

Moves towards the modified state immunity approach

Concerned at the privileged position enjoyed by foreign governments, the courts of a number of European states handed down judicial decisions curtailing the scope of immunity, for example *Dralle v Republic of Czechoslovakia*[53] and the *Empire of Iran Case*,[54] to government acts only (*jure imperii*). The so-called "Tate-letter" issued by the United States State Department in 1952 intimated a similar change in American policy, that is ". . . the immunity of the sovereign is recognised with regard to sovereign or public acts (*jus imperii*) of a State, but not with respect to private acts (*jus gestionis*)."[55] A state acting as a private individual was no longer to be placed in the advantageous position of receiving immunity and was to be liable in the same way and to the same extent as a private individual under similar circumstances. The American Foreign Sovereign Immunities Act of 1976[56] confirms restrictive immunity as American policy. The Act spells out the type of acts which are commercial and those which are private. A notable change of policy is provided for in the Act—the decision as to whether or not sovereign immunity is to be accorded is now the responsibility of the courts rather than the State Department.

An increasing number of states followed the United States and adopted a restrictive immunity policy. The number of states acceding to the 1926 Brussels Convention for the Unification of Certain Rules relating to the Immunity of State Owned Vessels,[57] under which government-owned vessels engaged in commercial purposes are subjected to the same legal regime as private vessels, also increased.

The United Kingdom and Commonwealth countries, however, maintained a strict adherence to absolute immunity—at least

[48] (1879) 4 P.D. 129.
[49] [1920] P. 30.
[50] [1938] A.C. 485.
[51] [1949] 2 All E.R. 274.
[52] [1957] 1 Q.B. 438.
[53] (1950) 17 I.L.R. 155, Austrian S.C.
[54] (1963) 45 I.L.R. 57, Federal Constitution Court, German Federal Republic.
[55] 6 Whiteman, 569–571.
[56] 90 Stat. 2891; P.L. 94–583 (1976); 15 I.L.M. 1388 (1976).
[57] U.K.T.S. 15 (1980) Cmnd.7800.

until the 1970s. Britain, in the 1970s, adopted a restricted immunity policy. The common law was effected by decisions of the courts—*The Philippine Admiral*,[58] *Trendtex Trading Corp. v Central Bank of Nigeria*,[59] and *I Congreso del Partido*.[60] The State Immunity Act was introduced in 1978 and came into effect on November 22 of that year. However, sovereign immunity in Britain is now governed primarily by the statutory law which spells out the instances when, and in respect of what activities, a state will not be immune from proceedings in the British courts.[61] Canada adopted the restrictive doctrine in the State Immunity Act 1982. The State Immunity Act enabled the United Kingdom to become a party to both the 1926 Brussels Convention and the 1972 European Convention on State Immunity.[62]

The 1972 Convention was initiated in an attempt to obtain, amongst states, a uniform approach to the issue of sovereign immunity. The Convention, for instance, specifies the circumstances in which sovereign immunity may and may not be claimed before the courts of Contracting States. Immunity may not be pleaded in proceedings in respect of contractual obligations to be carried out in the state exercising jurisdiction. States are also required, with certain exceptions, to give effect to judgments against them.

Today, most countries have adopted a restrictive immunity approach in respect of state trading enterprises.

At the international level, the International Law Commission has been addressing the issue of state immunity and a set of Draft Articles, following the pattern of the European Convention on State Immunity, was adopted in 1986. The Draft Convention, which represents an attempt to codify the international law of

---

[58] [1977] A.C. 373, JC.
[59] [1977] Q.B. 529, CA.
[60] [1981] 3 W.L.R. 329, HL.
[61] See *Commissioners of Customs and Excise v Ministry of Industries and Military Manufacturing, Republic of Iraq* 43 I.C.L.Q. 194 (1994), where it was held that a contract dealing with parts for an Iraqi supergun . . . fell within s.3(3)(a) of the Act which concerns commercial transactions and is therefore not immune from proceedings. *cf. Kuwait Airways Corporation v Iraqi Airways Company and Another* [1995] 1 W.L.R. 1147, where the English CA held that the forcible confiscation and retention of 10 civilian aircraft from Kuwait by Iraqi Airways Co. as directed by the government of Iraq in 1990, was an activity carried out in the exercise of sovereign authority and thus, immune from the jurisdiction of the UK courts. In March, 1997, the HL refused to grant leave to appeal to Sulaiman al-Adsani against a decision of the Kuwaiti government in which it rejected his claim for compensation for torture. The Lords held that the Kuwaiti government could rely on the defence of state immunity to defeat an allegation of torture. See *The Times*, March 25, 1997, p.41.
[62] U.K.T.S. 74 (1979) Cmnd.7742; 66 A.J.I.L. 923; 11 I.L.M. 470 (1972).

state immunity, expounds a general principle of immunity in Art.5 subject, that is, "to the provisions of the present articles [and the relevant rules of general international law]" which is then further qualified in Arts 10–17, which identify the proceedings in which state immunity cannot be invoked.

Diplomatic immunity

> "... the institution of diplomacy, with its concomitant privileges and immunities, has withstood the test of centuries and proved to be an instrument essential for effective cooperation in the international community, and for enabling States, irrespective of their differing constitutional and social systems, to achieve mutual understanding and to resolve their differences by peaceful means; ... [w]hile no State is under any obligation to maintain diplomatic or consular relations with another, yet it cannot fail to recognise the imperative obligations inherent therein now codified in the Vienna Conventions of 1961 and 1963 ... The rules of diplomatic law ... constitute a self-contained regime which, on the one hand, lays down the receiving State's obligations regarding the facilities, privileges and immunities to be accorded to diplomatic missions and, on the other, foresees their possible abuse by members of the mission and specifies the means at the disposal of the receiving State to counter any such abuse."[63]

The second principal exception to territorial jurisdiction is diplomatic immunity—representatives of a foreign state are immune from the application of the host state's municipal law. International diplomatic law was the earliest expression of international relations, for example diplomatic immunity was enjoyed by representatives from Greek city states. Generally, the privileges and immunities accorded by customary international law have not been controversial and have been adopted and respected by states. The customary law was codified in the 1961 Vienna Convention on Diplomatic Relations.[64]

The Convention, which came into force in 1964, deals with the immunities of foreign missions and foreign personnel in receiving

---

[63] *Case Concerning US Diplomatic and Consular Staff in Tehran (Provisional Measures)* I.C.J.Rep. 1979 7 at 19–20 and *(Judgment)* I.C.J.Rep. 1980 3 at 40.

[64] U.K.T.S. 19 (1965) Cmnd.2565; 500 U.N.T.S. 95; 55 A.J.I.L. 1064 (1961). However, certain Articles of the Convention were regarded as representing progressive development.

states and has been adhered to by the majority of independent states. Diplomatic relations exist only by mutual consent of states. Although all independent states enjoy the capacity to establish diplomatic relations, there is no right to diplomatic relations. The establishment of diplomatic relations will imply unequivocally the recognition of an entity as a state by the recognising state. The cessation of diplomatic relations may be used as an expression of disapproval (an instance of a retorsion, for example the severance of relations between the United Kingdom and Argentina following the Falkland Islands dispute in 1982[65] and the expulsion of four Russian and four British diplomats from the respective countries during a spying disagreement in 1996—but will not negate recognition already accorded).

Diplomatic privileges and immunities have, as their raison d'être, a functional objective—the purpose of such privileges and immunities is not to benefit individuals, but to ensure the efficient performance of the functions of diplomatic missions as representing states.[66] The consent, *agrément*, of the host state must be obtained for the proposed head of the mission.[67] Reasons for refusal of *agrément* need not be given. The receiving state may, at any time and without providing reasons, notify the sending state that the head of the mission or any member of the diplomatic staff of the mission is *persona non grata*, or that any other member of the staff of the mission is unacceptable. The sending state is required to either recall the person concerned or terminate his functions at the mission.

Should the sending state refuse or fail to do this within a reasonable period, the receiving state may refuse to recognise the person concerned as a member of the mission.[68]

Art.3 spells out the functions of a diplomatic mission as consisting of, *inter alia*:

"(a)   representing the sending State in the receiving State;
(b)   protecting in the receiving State the interests of the sending State and of its nationals within the limits permitted by international law;
(c)   negotiating with the government of the receiving State;
(d)   ascertaining by all lawful means conditions and developments in the receiving State, and reporting thereon to the government of the sending State;

---

[65] Relations were resumed in the summer of 1990.
[66] Preamble to the Vienna Convention.
[67] Art.4 of the Vienna Convention.
[68] Art.9.

    (e)   promoting friendly relations between the sending State
and the receiving State, and developing their economic,
cultural and scientific relations."

Art.11 provides that, in the absence of specific agreement, the
receiving state may require that the size of the mission be kept
within reasonable limits.

The premises of a diplomatic mission are inviolable,[69] that is,
premises which are currently being used for the purposes of a
mission—see *Westminster C.C. v Government of Iran*.[70] Agents of
the receiving state may not enter there without the consent of the
head of the mission and the receiving state must "take all appropriate steps to protect the premises of the mission against any
intrusion or damage and to prevent any disturbance of the peace
of the mission or impairment of its dignity."[71] Art.22 further provides that the premises of the mission, their furnishings and other
property and the means of transport of the mission are immune
from search, requisition, attachment or execution. The archives
and documents of the mission are inviolable "at any time and
wherever they may be."[72] The private residence of a diplomatic
agent enjoys the same inviolability and protection as the premises
of the mission.[73] Inviolability also embraces an agent's papers,
correspondence[74] and his property.[75] The receiving state is thus
under a duty to afford a high level of protection (higher than that
afforded to "ordinary" aliens) and must accord "full facilities for
the performance of the functions of the mission."[76]

Respect for the inviolability of a foreign mission precluded the
British police from entering the Libyan "People's Bureau" in
April, 1984. On April 17, 1984, a demonstration against the
Gaddafi regime occurred outside the Libyan "People's Bureau" in
St James's Square, London. Shots were fired from inside the
Bureau and a police constable on duty outside the premises, WPC
Yvonne Fletcher, was hit and died from the injuries which she
sustained. The "People's Bureau"'s inviolability was respected by
Britain[77] and continued to be respected for a limited period after

[69] Art.22(1).
[70] [1986] 1 W.L.R. 979, CH.
[71] Art.22(2).
[72] Art.24.
[73] Art.30.
[74] Subject to the instances covered in Art.31(1)(a)–(c).
[75] Art.30(2).
[76] Art.25. Note also the 1973 Convention on the Prevention and Punishment of
Crimes Against Internationally Protected Persons, Including Diplomatic
Agents, 13 I.L.M. 50 (1974).
[77] The exact legal nature status of a People's Bureau nevertheless remains obscure.

the diplomats had left for Libya, even though the mission premises had been used to endanger the host state's nationals.[78] The diplomats left on April 27, but the diplomatic status of the premises did not cease until midnight on April 29, and at 6 am on April 30, the British police legally entered the "People's Bureau". The sanction invoked by Britain to resolve the situation was that of severing diplomatic relations with Libya and expelling the members of the mission. Inviolability is an absolute principle under the Vienna Convention and entry to mission premises is prohibited in all circumstances, save with the consent or invitation of the head of the mission.[79]

The 1979 Iranian hostages incident is an illustration of a receiving state's failing to afford due protection to a foreign embassy. On November 4, 1979, during a demonstration several hundred armed individuals overran the US Embassy Compound in Tehran. Mission archives and documents were seized and 52 American nationals were taken as hostages. Iranian security personnel failed to counter the attack, and, in the subsequent case before the International Court of Justice, the lack of protection afforded to the mission was held to be directly attributable to the Iranian government, even though the initial seizure was "executed by militants not having an official character."[80]

The Iraqi order, demanding the closure of diplomatic missions in Kuwait and the withdrawal of all privileges and immunities, brought a response from the United Nations in the form of Security Council Resolutions 664 and 667. The former[81] called for an immediate rescission of the Iraqi order, while the latter[82] condemned the acts perpetrated by Iraq against diplomatic premises and personnel in Kuwait, and called for the immediate protection and well-being thereof, and for the cessation of any action hindering the diplomatic and consular mission in the performance of their functions.

Inviolability does not mean extra-territorial jurisdiction. The premises are not an extension of the sending state's territory. Acts committed on mission premises are within the territorial jurisdiction of the receiving state. Only in exceptional cases, will a state

---

[78] Art.41(3) provides that "the premises of the mission must not be used in any manner incompatible with the functions of the mission."

[79] This is not to deny that, although legally prohibited there may be occasions where it might be argued that entry might be justified because, for example a threat to the host state, the embassy in question is being used to store armaments, *e.g.* Pakistani raid on the Iraqi Embassy in 1973.

[80] Above, n. 63, p.30. Consider also the seizure of the Japanese Embassy by rebels in the Peruvian capital of Lima in 1996.

[81] Adopted August 18, 1990 by a vote of 15 to 0; 29 I.L.M. 1323 (1990).

[82] Adopted September 16, 1990 by a vote of 16 to 0, *ibid.*

grant asylum to an individual within an embassy. To do otherwise would be regarded as a grave violation of another state's sovereignty.

Diplomatic staff enjoy free movement and travel within the territory of the host state, subject to laws regulating entry into certain areas for reasons of national security. The receiving state must also allow and protect free communication by the mission for all official purposes and the diplomatic bag, which must be clearly marked as such, must be neither opened nor detained.[83] The absence of "visible external marks" from the crate used in the attempted abduction from the United Kingdom of Mr Dikko, an ex-government minister of Nigeria, legitimised the opening by UK customs officials of the container in question and kept their actions within the bounds of the Convention.[84] The right of challenge in respect of the diplomatic bag, which was accepted practice before 1961, is not included in the Convention. Whether a diplomatic bag should be subject to a degree of scrutiny remains controversial, especially as the bag may be used to import illegally, *inter alia*, drugs and weapons.

The International Law Commission adopted Draft Articles on the Status of the Diplomatic Courier and the Diplomatic Bag Not Accompanied by the Diplomatic Courier in 1989. The Draft Articles are designed to establish a comprehensive and essentially uniform regime applicable to all kinds of couriers and bags employed for official communications involved primarily in diplomatic and consular relations. The central Article is Art.28, which enunciates the basic principle of inviolability. However, the competent authorities of the receiving state or the transit state may, if they have serious reason to believe that the *consular* bag contains something other than correspondence, documents or articles intended exclusively for official use, request the opening of the bag in their presence by an authorised representative of the sending state. If this request is refused, the bag is to be returned to its place of origin.[85] The International Law Commission has proposed to the General Assembly that an international conference be convened with a view to the Draft Articles forming the basis of an international convention on the subject.

The person of a diplomatic agent is inviolable, and is not liable to any form of arrest or detention and the receiving state must treat such a person with due respect and must take all appropriate steps

---

[83] Art.27(3).
[84] Mr Dikko, a member of the overthrown Nigerian government, was kidnapped in London and drugged in the attempt to procure his return to Nigeria where he was wanted on criminal charges.
[85] Draft Art.28(2). N.B.: "consular" bag and not "diplomatic" bag.

to prevent any attack on his person, freedom or dignity.[86] A "diplomatic agent" is, for the purposes of the Convention, the head of the mission or a member of the diplomatic staff of the mission.[87]

A diplomatic agent enjoys absolute immunity from the criminal jurisdiction of the receiving state. Nevertheless, in 1987, the United States took the first steps towards an indictment of an ambassador prior to the termination of official accreditation. Following an accident involving two US nationals, one of whom was seriously injured, Ambassador Abisinito, Papua New Guinea's Extraordinary and Plenipotentiary to the United States was charged by the District of Columbia police with "failing to pay full time and attention to driving". Ambassador Abisinito was recalled by his state on February 17, 1987 and his accreditation to the United States ceased as of February 24. However, it was not until January 1988 that the United States Attorney's Office informed Mr Abisinito's criminal lawyers that prosecution was not currently being contemplated.[88]

The diplomatic agent is also immune from the receiving state's civil and administrative jurisdiction, except in the case of:

"(a) a real action relating to private immovable property situated in the territory of the receiving State, unless he holds it on behalf of the sending State for the purposes of the mission;

(b) an action relating to succession in which the diplomatic agent is involved as executor, administrator, heir or legatee as a private person and not on behalf of the sending State;

(c) an action relating to any professional or commercial activity exercised by the diplomatic agent in the receiving State outside his official functions."[89]

In such instances, immunity from jurisdiction is not available. A diplomatic agent is not obliged to give evidence as a witness.[90] The immunity enjoyed by a diplomatic agent is extended to the members of his family (normally spouse and children under the age of 18) if they are not nationals of the host state.[91] The immunity of a national of the receiving state is limited to official acts

---

[86] Art.29.

[87] Art.1(e).

[88] *Washington Post*, February 14–15, 1987; *Columbia Journal of Law*, 1988; *Legal Times*, May 4, 1987; *Diplomatic Note of the Embassy of Papua New Guinea*, February 24, 1987.

[89] Art.31(1).

[90] Art.31(2).

[91] Art.37.

performed in the exercise of his functions.[92] Immunity is from
jurisdiction and not from liability. The sending state may waive
the right to immunity,[93] as did Thailand in the summer of 1991,
when one of its London embassy staff was apprehended by customs officials at Heathrow Airport for allegedly possessing and
attempting illegally to import heroin. In 1997, a diplomat from the
Republic of Georgia was held responsible for the death of a 16-
year-old American girl in a car accident. The President of Georgia
waived the immunity of the diplomat and stated in the American
press that "the moral principle of just punishment outweighs the
antiquated Cold War-era practice of diplomatic immunity".[94]
Waiver must be express.[95] If a diplomatic agent or other person
enjoying immunity initiates proceedings, they are then precluded
from claiming immunity from jurisdiction in respect of any
counter claim which is connected with the principal claim.[96]
Waiver of immunity from jurisdiction in respect of civil or administrative proceedings does not imply waiver of immunity with
regard to the execution of the judgment. A separate waiver is necessary.[97] A host state always reserves the right to declare a member of the diplomatic mission a *persona non grata*.[98]

Not all the staff of a foreign mission enjoy the same immunities.
The Vienna Convention distinguishes between diplomatic agents,
administrative and technical staff (for example archivists, clerical
and secretarial staff) and service staff (for example kitchen staff).
The administrative and technical staff, if non-nationals of the host
state, enjoy complete immunity from criminal jurisdiction, but
their immunity from civil and administrative jurisdiction extends
only to acts performed in the fulfilment of their duties.[99] Non-
national service staff likewise enjoy immunity only in respect of
their official acts.[1] Distinguishing between mission staff and their
respective immunities was an innovation in the Vienna Convention
and represents a modification of the absolute immunity previously
enjoyed under, for example English law—see *Empson v Smith*.[2]

[92] Art.38.
[93] Art.32(1).
[94] see, ASIL Newsletter, January–February 1997, Letters, p.4.
[95] Art.32(2).
[96] Art.32(3).
[97] Art.32(4).
[98] For example, in 1988 the Cuban ambassador and his commercial attache were
expelled from the UK following a shooting incident in London. The UK government 's decision to hold the ambassador personally liable for the actions of
one of his staff was unprecedented and earned the UK a reputation for taking
tough action on abuses of diplomatic immunity.
[99] Art.37(2).
[1] Art.37(3).
[2] [1966] 1 Q.B. 426, CA.

A diplomat who is either recalled or who is declared by the sending state a *"persona non grata"* is allowed a period of grace during which his immunity continues. Thereafter, if he has not left the country he may be sued for private acts committed during his term of office. Immunity continues to subsist in respect of official acts.[3]

In addition to immunity from jurisdiction, diplomatic agents are, with certain exceptions such as purchase tax, exempt from taxes levied in the host state.[4] Mission premises are similarly exempt from local taxes except for those levied in respect of specific services rendered.[5] The right of immunity carries with it an obligation: it is the duty of all persons enjoying such privileges and immunities to respect the laws and the regulations of the receiving state. Such persons are also required not to interfere in the internal affairs of the receiving state,[6] for example in the political affairs of the host state.

The Vienna Convention was made part of UK law by the Diplomatic Privileges Act 1964 and part of US municipal law by the Diplomatic Relations Act 1978. The American legislation applies the Convention's provisions to all states and not just to those who have become parties to the Convention. The Convention does not preclude states either through practice or agreement, extending to each other more favourable treatment than that afforded by the Convention's provisions.

Heads of State

A number of questions were addressed in the case involving General Pinochet.[7] These can be identified as being;

(a)   is the claim for immunity made by a serving or a former head of state?

(b)   is the claim made in respect of the official government act or a private act?

(c)   is the making of the claim consistent with international law?

---

[3]   Art.39(2).
[4]   Art.34.
[5]   Art.23.
[6]   Art.41.
[7]   *R. v Bow Street Metropolitan Stipendiary Magistrate Ex p. Pinochet Ugarte (No.2)* [2001] 1 A.C. 119, *R. v Bow Street Stipendiary Magistrate Ex p. Pinochet Ugarte (No.3)* [2000] 1 A.C. 147; [1999] 2 WLR 272, *R. v Bartle and the Commissioner of Police for the Metropolis Ex p. Pinochet*, 24 March 1999, [1991] 2 All E.R. 97, *R. v Evans and the Commissioner of the Police for the Metropolis Ex p. Pinochet*, 24 March 1999, House of Lords.

The various facets of the *Pinochet* case illustrate an increasing tension between preserving the traditional absolute-immunity approach and an evolving human-rights culture. One of the issues in respect of General Pinochet was the extent to which a former head of state could enjoy immunity. It was held that a former head of state could only be immune for acts which fell within his functions as a head of state, although it remains unresolved as to which acts may be categorised as official and those which may be deemed personal. It was also held that an individual could not claim immunity, nor could a state, in respect of acts which are prohibited by international convention and in which the state concerned is a contracting party to said convention. Accordingly, Chile could not claim immunity of liability after having signed and ratified the 1984 Convention on Torture.[8] The legacy of the *Pinochet* jurisprudence has been to muddy the waters, at least to some extent, on the issue of the immunity of heads of state.

Consular relations

Consuls represent their state in another state, with the consent of the latter. Consuls are concerned not with political affairs, but rather with administrative issues, for example the issue of visas. They also give various forms of assistance to nationals of the sending state when they are in the territory of the receiving state. Consuls have the right to access and communication of nationals who have been detained in another country.[9] Failure to do so has resulted in action being initiated before the International Court of Justice.[10] They are posted in provincial towns as well as in capital cities.

Consular relations, unlike diplomatic relations between states, were largely governed by bipartite agreements. The Vienna Convention on Consular Relations[11] was adopted in 1963 to regulate, on a universal basis, the position and functions of consuls. The Convention entered into force in 1967. If two states have a bipartite agreement and both are parties to the Vienna Convention, the provisions which extend the greater immunities prevail. Consular immunities, unlike diplomatic immunities, may not be assumed, but must be shown to derive from either the Convention on Consular Relations, or from a bipartite agreement. The

---

[8] The Convention Against Torture and Other Cruel, Inhuman or Degrading Treatment or Punishment 1987, Chile ratified the Convention on September 30, 1988.
[9] The Vienna Convention on Consular Relations (1936), Art.36.
[10] Germany and Paraguay both brought cases against the US. See *Paraguay v US* (1998) I.C.J. 248; and *Germany v US (La Grand case)* 40 I.L.M. 1069 (2001), a judgment was passed on June 27, 2001.
[11] 596 U.N.T.S. 261; U.K.T.S. 14 (1973) Cmnd.5219.

immunities and privileges enjoyed by consuls and consular premises resemble those accorded to diplomatic agents and diplomatic missions; however, they are more limited in their scope.

The principal difference is that, in the absence of special agreement, consuls are immune from arrest, detention and the criminal process only in respect of acts and omissions in the performance of their official functions. A consular officer must appear if summoned before the courts, and later plead and prove immunity on the ground that the act or omission in question was in the performance of his official functions. Some states have, by special agreement and on a reciprocal basis, extended full immunity from criminal jurisdiction to consular personnel, for example the American–Soviet Union Convention. A consular officer may only be arrested or detained in respect of a grave crime and pursuant to a decision by a competent judicial authority.[12] Proceedings against a consular officer should be conducted "with the respect due to him by reason of his official position" and save when charged with a grave crime, "in a manner which will hamper the exercise of consular functions as little as possible".[13] Members of a consul's family do not enjoy the same extensive jurisdictional immunities as the members of a diplomat's family, but they are exempt from such restrictions as immigration controls, customs duties and taxes, if they are not nationals of the receiving state.

Special missions

Special *ad hoc* missions sent by a state to fulfil a specific purpose in another state are a recent innovation. There are no rules of customary international law on the subject. A Convention guaranteeing immunities to special missions was drawn up in 1969.[14] The Convention, which entered into force on June 21, 1985, is based essentially on the 1961 Vienna Convention on Diplomatic Relations. Under Art.8 of the 1969 Convention, the sending state must inform the host state of both the size and composition of the mission, whilst Art.17 provides that the location of the mission must be mutually agreed by the states concerned, or must be in the Foreign Ministry of the receiving state.

International organisations

International organisations enjoy those privileges and immunities from the jurisdiction of a Member State as are necessary for

[12] Art.41(1).
[13] Art.41(3).
[14] 9 I.L.M. 127 (1970).

the fulfilment of the organisation's purposes. Such immunities include immunity from legal process, financial controls, taxes and duties. The immunities and privileges to be enjoyed by the organisation and its personnel *vis-à-vis* Member States are provided for in the constituent charter of the organisation and supplementary agreements adhered to by members of the organisation, for example the General Convention on the Privileges and Immunities of the United Nations 1946.[15] The General Convention gives immunity from the legal process to, *inter alia*, the property and the assets of the United Nations, unless such immunity is waived, as well as immunity from criminal jurisdiction for its representatives.

[15] 1 U.N.T.S. 15; U.K.T.S. 10 (1950) Cmd.7891; 43 A.J.I.L. Supp.

7. THE LAW OF THE SEA

The law of the sea[1] is that law by which states, coastal and land-locked, and/or international organisations regulate their relations in respect of those areas subject to coastal state jurisdiction and in relation to those areas of the sea and the seabed beyond national jurisdiction. The rules governing the sea are drawn from both custom and treaty.

In the 1950s, the profusion of claims, the advance of technology and the need for a protection of conventional sea uses were responsible for the Geneva Conventions on the Law of the Sea. The Conventions were the outcome of the initial work undertaken by the International Law Commission. The four Conventions adopted by the 1958 Conference were the Convention on the Territorial Sea and Contiguous Zone,[2] the Convention on the High Seas,[3] the Convention on the Continental Shelf[4] and the Convention on Fishing and Conservation of Living Resources of

---

[1] As distinct from Admiralty law or maritime law which is essentially concerned principally with relations between private persons involved in the transport of passengers or goods.

[2] U.K.T.S. 3 (1965) Cmnd.2511; 516 U.N.T.S. 205; 52 A.J.I.L. 834 (1958).

[3] U.K.T.S. 5 (1963) Cmnd.1029; 45 U.N.T.S. 82; 52 A.J.I.L. 842 (1958).

[4] U.K.T.S. 39 (1964) Cmnd.2422; 499 U.N.T.S. 311; 52 A.J.I.L. 858 (1958).

the High Seas.[5] The Conventions have all entered into force, though by 1982, three-quarters of the nations of the world were not a party to them. The Conventions, which codified certain existing state practices and also articulated rules of progressive development, proved inadequate, particularly with regard to the continental shelf and the ocean bed which, with advanced technology, came within the potential acquisition of certain states.

The need to preserve the seas as the common heritage of all mankind and the danger of a "scramble for the seas" precipitated the calling of the Third United Nations Conference on the Law of the Sea. The 1982 Convention on the Law of the Sea,[6] adopted on April 30, 1982, was the culmination of nine years' protracted negotiations. The Convention was opened for signature in December 1982, and was designed as a "complete package" with limited provision for reservation.[7] The Convention was the subject of considerable opposition, primarily from western nations who were concerned about the provisions regarding the exploitation of the deep seabed as contained in Part XI.[8] Attempts to resolve disagreement over Part XI were unsuccessful until 1994, when the General Assembly adopted a Resolution and Agreement Relating to the Implementation of Part XI of the UN Convention on the Law of the Sea, on July 28, 1994.[9] The adoption of this Agreement was seen as the key to the implementation of the 1982 Convention and this is reflected in the preamble of the Resolution, which notes "the desire to achieve universal participation" in the Convention. Art.1 of the Agreement proscribes the fundamental obligation on states, namely that Part XI of the 1982 Convention is to be implemented in accordance with the Agreement of which the Annex forms an integral part.[10] Arts 1 and 2 constitute the substantive provisions of the Agreement and the remaining eight deal with *"inter alia"* signature and ratification. The Agreement modifies the terms of Part XI in relation to the deep sea.[11] A state cannot become a party to the Agreement independently of the Convention.

---

[5] U.K.T.S. 39 (1966) Cmnd.3208; 599 U.N.T.S. 285; 52 A.J.I.L. 851 (1958).
[6] Misc. II (1983) Cmnd.8941; 21 I.L.M. 1261 (1982).
[7] See Art.309 of the 1982 Convention. For reservations and their effect, see Ch.10.
[8] The US and the UK were particularly opposed to Part XI of the Convention. For the UK's objections as expressed in HC—see *Hansard*, Vol.69, col.642 (December 6, 1984).
[9] GA Res. 48/263, 121–0 in favour, seven abstentions, 35 I.L.M. 1309 (1994). The Agreement entered into force on July 28, 1996.
[10] The Annex sets out the substance of the Agreement.
[11] The Agreement has also phased out the Preparatory Commission whose role *"inter alia"* was to oversee the entry into force of the Convention. The Commission adopted its concluding report in August, 1994 at its final meeting.

The Agreement has sought to address the concerns of western nations regarding Part XI and reflects the significant change in the economic and political climate since 1982. Specifically, it reallocates international and national responsibilities for the management of deep-sea mining.[12] The 1982 Convention came into force on November 16, 1994 and marked an important event in the progressive development and codification of the international law of the sea.[13] The Convention's entry into force confirmed the General Assembly's competence as the global forum for review of all developments relating to the law of the sea.[14]

Some of the provisions of the 1982 Convention simply restate provisions of the Geneva Convention—representing established customary international law. Others, notably those on the exclusive economic zone, reflect what is now customary international law—reflecting state practice before the 1982 Convention was completed. Other provisions represent a departure from established law and indicate the way in which the law is developing. Any review of the laws of the sea must commence with the Geneva Convention of 1958.

TERRITORIAL SEA

A coastal state enjoys sovereignty over "a belt of sea adjacent to its coast, described as the territorial sea"[15] which extends "to the air space over the territorial sea as well as its bed and subsoil".[16] The consequence of being a coastal state is that it possesses a territorial sea:

> "To every State whose land territory is at any place washed by the sea, international law attaches a corresponding portion of maritime territory consisting of what the law calls

[12] Certain provisions which were the source of controversy, such as production limitation and technological transfer, are eliminated.

[13] For a detailed discussion of the 1994 Agreement, see, generally, J. Charney, "Law of the Sea Forum: The 1994 Agreement on Implementation of the Seabed Provisions of the Convention on the Law of the Sea" and D. Anderson, "Legal Implications of the Entry into Force of the UN Convention on the Law of the Sea" I.C.L.Q. Vol.44 at 313.

[14] As of February 6, 2002, there have been 138 ratifications (including the EC) to the Convention. Part XI has 104 ratifications (including the EC). The UK ratified Part XI on July 26, 1997. The US has yet to ratify it. The Agreement for the implementation of the provisions of the convention relating to the conservation and management of straddling fish stocks and highly migratory fish stocks has 31 ratifications. That Agreement came into force on December 11, 2001.

[15] Art.1 of the Geneva Convention on the Territorial Sea and the Contiguous Zone 1958; Art.1 of the 1982 Convention on the Territorial Sea and the Contiguous Zone.

[16] Art.2 of the 1958 Convention; Art.2 of the 1982 Convention.

territorial waters . . . . International law does not say to a
State: 'You are entitled to claim territorial waters if you want
them.' No maritime States can refuse them. International law
imposes upon a maritime State certain obligations and con-
fers upon it certain rights arising out of the sovereignty
which it exercises over its maritime territory. The possession
of this territory is not optional, not dependent upon the will
of the State, but compulsory."[16a]

Art.3 of the 1982 Convention establishes the breadth of the territorial sea at a limit "not exceeding 12 nautical miles".

Previously, agreement on the breadth of the territorial sea had
eluded definition. State practice had been uncertain and varied.
Some countries, for example the United Kingdom and the United
States, rigidly maintained the traditional 3-mile territorial sea,
while certain Latin American countries made extensive claims to
a maximum of 200 miles. The norm, however, was for states to
claim a territorial sea of a width somewhere between 3 and 12
miles. The uncertainty of state practice was reflected in the 1958
and 1960 Geneva Conferences—neither Conference was successful in defining the breadth of the territorial sea. Various permuta-
tions were suggested, such as the United States formula of
six-plus-six, (that is, a six-mile territorial sea with a six-mile fishing zone), an Asian/Latin American sponsored proposal calling
for a 12-mile territorial sea, and a Soviet proposal whereby every
state would enjoy the discretion to declare the width of its territorial sea as a distance between 3 and 12 miles. None of the proposals was successful. The 12-mile maximum which has been
widely reflected in state practice, including that of the United
Kingdom and the United States,[17] is now accepted as customary
international law—see the *Guinea/Guinea-Bissau Maritime Delimitation Case.*[17a] The advent and acceptance of a coastal state's exclusive economic zone (EEZ—see below) has enabled the territorial
sea question to be settled separately.

In the 1950s and 1960s, increased fishing activity and advanc-
ing technology witnessed anxiety amongst coastal states in
respect of fisheries. There was a need to control fishing, but, at
that time fisheries jurisdiction was very much an integral aspect
of territorial jurisdiction. The failure of the 1958 and 1960 Conferences to reach agreement regarding the territorial sea and fishing zones prompted states to take matters into their own hands

[16a] McNair J. (dissenting opinion), *Anglo–Norwegian Fisheries Case* I.C.J.Rep. 1951 116 at 160.
[17] Territorial Sea Act 1987 (Commencement) Order 1987 (SI 1987/1270).
[17a] 77 I.L.R. 636 at 638; 25 I.L.M. 251 (1988) at 272, para.43.

and unilaterally extend their fisheries jurisdiction beyond the territorial sea.

Measurement of the territorial sea

As a general rule, the baseline employed to determine the breadth of the territorial sea is the low-tide water line, as marked on large-scale charts recognised by the coastal state.[18] The outer limit of the territorial sea is the line every point of which is at a distance from the nearest point of the baseline equal to the breadth of the territorial sea.[19] Geography can present problems, and rules to resolve these have been evolved.

In respect of deeply indented coastlines, the 1958 and 1982 Conventions reflect the International Court of Justice's judgment in the *Anglo-Norwegian Fisheries Case*.[20] This case came before the court because Britain challenged the method employed by Norway to measure its territorial sea. Rather than use the low-water mark, Norway used the baseline system. As a result, waters which would otherwise have been high seas were characterised as territorial sea. The court affirmed the legality of the straight baseline method and that, in delimiting Norway's territorial sea, cognisance had to be given to "geographical realities" and that the drawing of the base-lines had to be adapted to the special conditions pertaining in different regions.[21] The special geographical conditions existing on the west coast of Scotland merit such an application of the straight baseline method.

Both the 1958 and 1982 Conventions acknowledge the derogation from the low-water mark allowed by the court. Straight baselines joining appropriate points may be employed where a coastline is deeply indented,[22] provided that the lines do:

> "not depart to any appreciable extent from the general direction of the coast, and the seas lying within the lines must be sufficiently closely linked to the land domain to be subject to the regime of internal waters."[23]

They may not normally be drawn "to and from low-tide elevations" unless "lighthouses or similar installations which are permanently above sea level have been built on them"[24] or "where

[18] Art.3 of the 1958 Convention; Art.5 of the 1982 Convention.
[19] Art.6 of the 1958 Convention; Art.4 of the 1982 Convention.
[20] Above, n.16a.
[21] *ibid.* at 128.
[22] Art.4(1) of the 1958 Convention; Art.7(1) of the 1982 Convention.
[23] Art.4(2) of the 1958 Convention; Art.7(3) of the 1982 Convention.
[24] Art.4(3) of the 1958 Convention.

the drawing of baselines to and from such elevations has received general international recognition".[25]

Both the 1958 and 1982 Conventions allow account to be taken of a further possible consideration which may be employed in the delimitation of the territorial sea.[26] This was acknowledged by the International Court when it stated that:

"... one consideration not to be overlooked, the scope of which extends beyond purely geographical factors: that of certain economic interests peculiar to a region, the reality and importance of which are closely evidenced by a long usage."[27]

The court recognised that the special economic interests of a region could be taken into consideration. However, such a consideration is only supplementary (that is, special economic interests in themselves cannot be grounds justifying the application of straight baselines) and is at all times optional rather than mandatory. Likewise, under the 1958 and 1982 Conventions, special economic interests may be invoked to support an application of the straight baseline system, but only if their reality and importance are clearly evidenced by long usage.[28]

States are prohibited from applying straight baselines in order to cut off, from high seas or an Exclusive Economic Zone, the territorial sea of another state, and a state using the straight baseline system must publicise by way of charts the lines being employed. The 1982 Convention requires the coastal state to deposit copies of charts and lists of geographical co-ordinates with the Secretary-General of the United Nations.[29]

The 1982 Convention alone provides that:

"Where because of the presence of a delta and other natural conditions the coastline is highly unstable, the appropriate points may be selected along the furthest seaward extent of the low-water line and, notwithstanding subsequent regression of the low-water line, the straight baselines shall remain effective until changed by the coastal State in accordance with this Convention."[30]

[25] Added by Art.7(4) of the 1982 Convention.
[26] Art.4(4) and Art.7(5), respectively.
[27] *Anglo–Norwegian Fisheries Case*, above, n.16a at 133.
[28] Both Conventions are silent on what constitutes real and important.
[29] Art.4(5) and (6) of the 1958 Convention; Art.7(6) and Art.16 of the 1982 Convention.
[30] Art.7(2).

Bays

A bay is defined under Art.7(2) of the 1958 Convention as a:

> "well-marked indentation whose penetration is in such pro-
> portion to the width of its mouth as to contain landlocked
> waters and constitute more than a mere curvature of the
> coast. An indentation shall not, however, be regarded as a
> bay unless its area is as large as, or larger than, that of the
> semi-circle whose diameter is a line drawn across the mouth
> of that indentation."

Art.10(2) of the 1982 Convention reiterates this definition.

A special formula has been evolved in respect of bays which
belong to a single state and are more than mere curvatures of the
coast. The salient feature of the formula is that straight baselines
may be employed "If the distance between the low-water marks
of the natural entrance points of a bay does not exceed 24 miles
. . .".[31] In the event of 24 miles being exceeded, a straight baseline
of 24 miles may be drawn within the bay in such a manner as to
enclose the maximum area of water that is possible with a line of
that length.[32]

Neither Convention refers specifically to historic bays, namely
bays, the waters of which have been treated as internal waters by
the coastal state with the acceptance of other states, such as
Hudson Bay and the Gulf of Foncesca,[33] nor to bays bordered by
more than one state. The legal regime which will be applied in
both instances is dependent upon the response of affected states
but the position *vis-à-vis* the latter is one over which "there exists
a good deal of controversy . . .".

Outermost permanent harbour works (which, under the 1982
Convention do not include "offshore installations and artificial
islands") forming an integral part of the harbour system are to be
regarded as part of the coast for the purpose of delimiting the
territorial sea.[34]

---

[31] Art.7(4) of the 1958 Convention; Art.10(4) of the 1982 Convention.
[32] Art.7(5) of the 1958 Convention; Art.10(5) of the 1982 Convention.
[33] Previous to the 1958 Convention, it had been generally accepted under customary international law that straight baselines could be employed in respect of
bays, but there was uncertainty as to beyond what width the closing line could
not be employed. The ICJ in the *Anglo–Norwegian Fisheries Case*, above, n.16a,
rejected, because of inconsistent state practice, the 10-mile rule (which the UK
was claiming as the maximum width) and refuted that such a rule had ever
acquired the character of international law.
[34] Art.8 of the 1958 Convention; Art.11 of the 1982 Convention.

Islands

An island is defined in Art.10 of the 1958 Convention "as a natu-
rally-formed area of land, surrounded by water, which is above
water at high tide". The territorial sea of an island is decided in
the same way as the territorial sea of mainland territories. The
1982 Convention retains the same definition of an island, but
introduces a "regime of islands".[35] This provides that "the territorial sea, the contiguous zone, the exclusive economic zone and the
continental shelf of an island are to be determined in accordance
with the provisions . . . applicable to other land territory". However, rocks which cannot sustain human habitation or economic
life of their own are denied both an exclusive economic zone and
a continental shelf, though they may continue to have a territorial
sea.[36] Low-tide elevations, on the other hand, do not have a territorial sea of their own, though the low-water mark on such an ele-
vation, if it is within the territorial sea of a coastal state, may be
utilised as a baseline,[37] and Art.6 of the 1982 Convention provides
that:

> "in the case of islands situated on atolls or islands having
> fringing reefs, the baseline for measuring the breadth of the
> territorial sea is the seaward low-water line of the reef, as
> shown by the appropriate symbol on charts officially recog-
> nised by the coastal state."

In the Court of Arbitration decision on maritime delimitation (St
Pierre and Miquelon), the Court considered in some detail the
role of islands in delimitation and declined to adjust the extent
of the maritime rights of the islands by reference to either their
political status or special geographical circumstances.[38]

---

[35] Pt VIII, Art.121.
[36] Art.121(3). This provision would deny an EEZ and continental shelf, *e.g.* to the
area referred to as the Island of Rockall. In the *Jan Meyen Case* (*Denmark v
Norway*) I.C.J.Rep. 1993 38, Denmark asserted that the island in dispute could
not sustain economic or human life but appeared to implicitly accept that it
could have a continental shelf or fishery zone. The UK had, under the Fishery
Limits Act 1976, proclaimed a 200-nautical-mile fishing zone around the Island
of Rockall. However, the UK Government withdrew this claim in 1997 on accession to the Law of the Sea Convention.
[37] Art.11 of the 1958 Convention; Art.13 of the 1982 Convention.
[38] See Court of Arbitration for the delimitation of maritime areas between Canada
and France: decision in case concerning delimitation of maritime areas (St
Pierre and Miquelon), in particular the dissenting opinion of Mr Prosper Weil
interpreting the Court's decision 31 I.L.M. 1145 (1992) at 1216–1218. The issue of
islands and delimitation was also considered in the *Jan Meyen Case*, above, n.36.

Delimitation of territorial seas between opposite or adjacent states

The territorial sea between opposite or adjacent states is determined in one of three ways: by agreement between the states, for example, the Anglo–French agreement relating to the Delimitation of the Territorial Sea in the Straits of Dover[39]; by the median line, every point of which is equidistant from the nearest points on the baselines from which the breadth of the territorial seas of each of the two states is measured[40]; or by another line required by historic title or other special circumstances.[41] The 1982 Convention envisages that a coastal state "may determine baselines . . . by any of the methods provided for . . . to suit different conditions".[42]

Archipelagic states

States such as Indonesia and the Philippines which are made up of a number of islands, have, in the absence of international agreement, drawn straight baselines round the outer limits of their islands. The effect has been to turn what were formerly "high seas" into territorial waters.

International law traditionally side-stepped the problems raised by archipelagic states and the Geneva Convention makes no provision for special treatment of mid-ocean archipelagos. The 1982 Convention, however, does deal separately with such states.[43] An archipelagic state is, for the purposes of the Convention, constituted wholly of one or more archipelagos and may include other islands; "archipelago" means a group of islands, including parts of islands, interconnecting waters and other natural features which are so closely interrelated that such islands, water and other natural features form an intrinsic geographical, economic and political entity, or which historically have been regarded as such.[44] The 1982 Convention recognises archipelago baselines joining the outermost points of the outermost islands. Such baselines may "not exceed 100 nautical miles, except that up to three per cent of the total number of baselines enclosing any archipelago may exceed that length, up to a maximum length of 125 nautical miles" and must "not depart to any appreciable extent from the general configuration of the

---

[39] Cmnd.557.
[40] *ibid.* Guinea and Guinea-Bissau submitted their dispute on the delimitation of the maritime boundary to an arbitration tribunal, 25 I.L.M. 251 (1986).
[41] Art.12 of the 1958 Convention; Art.15 of the 1982 Convention.
[42] Art.14 of the 1982 Convention.
[43] Pt IV, Arts 46–54.
[44] Art.46.

archipelago".[45] The territorial sea, the contiguous zone, the exclusive economic zone and the continental shelf are drawn from the archipelagic baselines.[46] Archipelagic waters enclosed by the archipelago baselines fall within the territorial sovereignty of the archipelagic state,[47] subject to the right of all states to enjoy the right of innocent passage[48] similar to that enjoyed in territorial waters (see below). An archipelago state may designate archipelagic sea lanes for passage and prescribe traffic separation schemes[49] comparable to the right of passage through straits.

The 1982 Convention does not provide for the issue of straight baselines by continental states with archipelagos. Nevertheless, Canada established baselines round the entire Arctic archipelago from latitude 60°E to the Beaufort Sea in the west and designated all water enclosed as Canadian.

Innocent passage

The definition of "passage" contained in Art.18 of the 1982 Geneva Convention elaborates upon the accepted customary international law definition and Art.14 of the Geneva Convention. Art.18 provides:[50]

> "1. Passage means navigation through the territorial sea for the purpose of:
>
>   (a) traversing that sea without entering internal waters or calling at such roadstead or port facility outside internal waters; or
>   (b) proceeding to or from internal waters or a call at such roadstead or port facility.
>
> 2. Passage shall be continuous and expeditious. However, passage includes stopping and anchoring, but only in so far as the same are incidental to ordinary navigation or are rendered necessary by *force majeure* or distress or for the purpose of rendering assistance to persons, ships or aircraft in danger or distress."

The Geneva Convention recognises what had become established under customary international law, namely that a coastal state's sovereignty over its territorial sea is subject to the obligation to

---

[45] Art.47.
[46] Art.48.
[47] Art.49.
[48] Art.52.
[49] Art.53.
[50] *Nicaragua Case (Merits)* I.C.J.Rep. 1986 14 at 111.

allow a right of innocent passage to all foreign ships.[51] Innocent passage is defined in a very general way as that which "is not prejudicial to the peace, good order or security of the coastal State".[52] Fishing vessels are required to observe the laws and regulations of the coastal state[53] and submarines are required to navigate on the surface and to show their flag,[54] otherwise their passage will not be regarded as innocent. The 1982 Convention is more specific in its definition of "innocent" and enunciates a list of activities which, if occurring in the coastal state's territorial waters, would not be characterised as "innocent". Such activities include: any threat or use of force against the sovereignty, territorial integrity or political independence of the coastal state; any exercise or practice with weapons of any kind, any act aimed at collecting information to the prejudice of the defence or security of the coastal state; any act of propaganda aimed at affecting the defence or security of the coastal state; any fishing activities and the carrying out of research or survey activities.[55] The coastal state is under a duty not to hamper innocent passage.[56] The 1982 Convention again is more precise and stipulates that the coastal state shall not:

"(a) impose requirements on foreign ships which have the practical effect of denying or impairing the right of innocent passage; or

(b) discriminate in form or in fact against the ships of any State or against ships carrying cargoes to, from or on behalf of any State."[57]

Under both Conventions, coastal states are required to give appropriate publicity of any dangers to navigation of which it has knowledge within its territorial sea.[58]

Art.17 of the 1958 Convention simply provides that foreign ships engaging in innocent passage must comply with the coastal state's laws and regulations. Again, the 1982 Convention articulates to a greater extent the laws and regulations which a coastal

---

[51] Art.5 of the 1958 Convention and Art.8 of the 1982 Convention provide that, where the straight baseline is employed, because of an indented coastline, and this has led to territorial waters or high seas being designated internal waters, a right of innocent passage shall exist in those waters.
[52] Art.14(4).
[53] Art.14(5).
[54] Art.14(6).
[55] Art.19 of the 1982 Convention.
[56] Art.15 of the 1958 Convention.
[57] Art.24.
[58] Art.15(2) of the 1958 Convention; Art.24(2) of the 1982 Convention.

state may adopt. These may, for instance, include measures on the safety of navigation and the regulation of maritime traffic, the protection of navigational aids and facilities and other facilities or installations, the protection of cables and pipelines, the conservation of the living resources of the sea, and the preservation of the environment of the coastal state and the prevention, reduction and control of pollution thereof.[59]

Two new provisions are included in the 1982 Convention: Art.22 provides that a coastal state may require foreign ships to use such sea lanes and traffic separation schemes as it (that is, the coastal state) may designate or prescribe for vessels, in particular tankers, nuclear-powered ships and ships carrying nuclear or other inherently dangerous or noxious substances, or material, engaged in innocent passage. Art.23 provides that foreign nuclear-powered ships and ships carrying nuclear or like material shall be required to carry documents and observe special precautionary measures established for such ships by international agreements.

A coastal state may take the steps necessary to prevent passage which is not innocent,[60] and may, without discrimination amongst foreign ships, suspend innocent passage temporarily in specified areas of its territorial sea if that is required in the interest of its security.[61] If a vessel is proceeding to internal waters, the coastal state may take the steps necessary to prevent any breach of the conditions to which the admission of the ship to internal waters is subject.[62]

Foreign vessels engaged in innocent passage are only subject to the coastal state's criminal and civil jurisdiction in limited defined circumstances. A coastal state may only exercise jurisdiction:

(a)   if the consequences of the crime extend to the coastal state; or

(b)   if the crime is of a kind to disturb the peace of the country or the good order of the territorial sea; or

(c)   if the assistance of the local authorities has been requested by the captain of the ship or by the consul of the country whose flag the ship flies; or

(d)   if it is necessary for the suppression of illicit traffic in narcotic drugs (or psychotropic substances—1982 Convention only).[63]

---

[59] Art.21.
[60] Art.16 of the 1958 Convention; Art.25 of the 1982 Convention.
[61] Art.16(3) of the 1958 Convention; Art.25(3) of the 1982 Convention.
[62] Art.16(2) of the 1958 Convention; Art.25(2) of the 1982 Convention.
[63] Art.19 of the 1958 Convention; Art.27 of the 1982 Convention.

Civil jurisdiction may not be exercised against either the ship or against a person on board, save in respect of obligations and liabilities assumed by the ship itself in the course of, or for the purpose of, its voyage through the waters of the coastal state, or if the vessel is passing through the territorial sea, after having left internal waters.[64] Government vessels operated for commercial purposes come within the ambit of the foregoing provisions. In respect of warships and government vessels operated for noncommercial purposes, the Convention does not affect the immunities from jurisdiction to which they are entitled.

A foreign warship which does not comply with the coastal state's regulations may be required to leave the territorial sea ("immediately" has been added by the 1982 Convention).[65] Although mention is made of warships, neither the 1958 nor the 1982 Convention expressly grants or denies foreign warships a right of innocent passage. The 1982 Convention does provide, however, that the flag state of a vessel shall incur international liability for "any loss or damage to the coastal State resulting from the non-compliance by a warship or other government ship operated for non-commercial purposes with the laws and regulations of the coastal State . . .".[66]

Passage through straits

What is a coastal state's jurisdiction in international straits bordering its coast?

Art.16(4) of the Geneva Convention on the Territorial Sea prohibits a coastal state from suspending innocent passage in territorial sea straits which are used for international navigation between one part of the high seas and another part of the high seas, or the territorial sea of a foreign state.

The right of innocent passage similar to that provided by Art.14 is retained by the 1982 Convention for straits which are formed by an island of a state bordering the strait and its mainland and where there exists seaward of the island a high seas route or an exclusive economic zone (EEZ—see below),[67] and secondly where the strait is between a part of the high seas or an Exclusive Economic Zone and the territorial sea of a foreign state, namely where there is only territorial sea at one end of a strait.[68] The coastal state may not suspend such innocent passage.[69] However,

---

[64] Art.20 of the 1958 Convention; Art.28 of the 1982 Convention.
[65] Art.23 of the 1958 Convention; Art.30 of the 1982 Convention.
[66] Art.31.
[67] Art.38.
[68] Art.45(1)(b).
[69] Art.45(2).

for straits which are used for international navigation between one part of the high seas or an Exclusive Economic Zone and another part of the high seas or an Exclusive Economic Zone,[70] the 1982 Convention dispenses with the right of innocent passage and provides rather for a right of transit. In other words, the right of transit will only apply in straits which have high seas or an Exclusive Economic Zone at both ends.

Art.38(2) defines transit passage as "the freedom of navigation and overflight solely for the purpose of continuous and expeditious transit of the strait". Ships and aircraft are charged with certain duties when travelling through and over the strait, for example proceeding without delay and refraining from any threat or use of force against the sovereignty, territorial integrity or political independence of states bordering the strait.[71] The strait state may, in the interest of safe passage, prescribe sea lanes and traffic separation schemes, but only after its proposals have been referred to and adopted by the "competent international organisation"[72]: the authority of the strait state is thus more restricted than under the 1958 Convention. The strait state may also adopt laws and regulations designed to prevent, reduce or control pollution. The strait state is, however, under a duty not to hamper transit passage and is required "to give appropriate publicity to any danger to navigation or overflight within or over the strait of which they have knowledge".[73] There may be no suspension of transit passage.[74]

Why are international straits subject to a special regime under the 1982 Convention?[75] The effect of extended territorial seas has been to bring straits, through which there were previously high seas, exclusively within territorial waters. Consequently, maritime powers sought definite guarantees for shipping as a condition to their accepting a 12-mile territorial sea; the 1988 Anglo–French Agreement[76] relating to the Straits of Dover guarantees the right of "unimpeded transit passage for merchant vessels, state vessels and, in particular, warships following their normal mode of navigation . . .". The Geneva Convention is also deficient in that it grants no right of passage to aircraft (under the 1982 Convention all aircraft will enjoy the right of transit) and that submarines have to navigate on the surface and show their flag, whereas the 1982 Convention, would appear, with respect to

---

[70] Art.37.
[71] Art.39.
[72] Art.41.
[73] Art.44.
[74] *ibid*.
[75] The regime does not apply to straits regulated by treaty, *e.g.* the 1936 Treaty of Montreux in respect of the Straits of the Bosphorus and Dardanelles.
[76] Cmnd.557.

warships in time of peace, to support the International Court of Justice's pronouncement in the *Corfu Channel Case (Merits)*[77] that it was generally accepted international custom:

> "that States in time of peace have a right to send their warships through straits used for international navigation between two parts of the high seas without the previous authorisation of a coastal State, provided that the passage is *innocent*."[78]

Contiguous zone

A coastal state, under the 1958 Geneva Convention, may claim a zone of the high seas, not exceeding 12 miles from the territorial sea baselines, contiguous to its territorial sea. A contiguous zone need not be claimed, as in the case of the United Kingdom, but if it is, it must be done so specifically. Although the status of the contiguous zone remains that of high seas, the coastal state may exercise control to prevent or punish infringement of its customs, fiscal, immigration or sanitary regulations within *its territory or territorial sea* (emphasis added). The maximum breadth of the contiguous zone is extended under the 1982 Convention to 24 miles from the territorial baselines.[79]

The equality of states, including those without a sea-coast (some 40 states), on the high seas is enshrined in Art.3 of the Geneva Convention which provides that "states having no sea-coast should have access to the sea". The right of access of land-locked states to and from the sea and freedom of transit is exclusively elaborated upon in Arts 124 and 132, inclusively, of the 1982 Convention.[80]

HIGH SEAS

The high seas constitute "all parts of the sea that are not included in the territorial sea or in the internal waters of a State".[81] This definition has had to be modified with the advent of the Exclusive Economic Zone and the recognition of archipelagic waters. Waters not included in the EEZ, the archipelagic waters of an archipelagic state, the territorial waters or internal waters of a state, constitute the high seas.[82]

[77] I.C.J.Rep. 1949 at 4.
[78] *ibid.* at 28.
[79] Art.33.
[80] See also the 1965 Convention on Transit Trade of Land-locked States, 597 U.N.T.S. 3; 4 I.L.M. 957 (1965).
[81] Art.1 of the Geneva Convention on the High Seas.
[82] Art.86 of the 1982 Convention.

According to classical doctrine, the high seas are free and may not be apportioned by any one nation. The freedom of the high seas, with qualified jurisdiction over adjacent waters by the coastal state, was articulated by Hugo Grotius in *Mare Liberum* (1609). The freedom principle was initially articulated with a view to breaking the monopoly of the Spanish and Portuguese over the seas and was accepted by the major maritime states, such as the United Kingdom, the United States, the Netherlands and Japan, which all sought to keep the territorial waters narrow and the high seas as broad as possible.

The freedoms of the high seas, which may be exercised by both coastal and non-coastal states, are the freedom of navigation, of fishing, to lay submarine cables and pipelines and the freedom of overflight.[83] These freedoms are not exhaustive, and others which are recognised by the general principles of international law and which may be "exercised by all States with reasonable regard to the interests of other States in their exercise of their freedom of the high seas"[84] may also exist.[85]

The 1982 Convention reaffirms the four freedoms[86] (though the freedom of fishing is now subject to the rules governing the EEZ) and acknowledges two additional freedoms: the freedom to construct artificial islands and other installations permitted by international law, and the freedom of scientific research. As under the 1958 Convention, consideration must be given to the rights of other states on the high seas and must be "with respect to activities in the area"[87] (that is, the area of the deep seabed and ocean floor and subsoil—see below).

Nuclear testing

The testing of conventional weapons and nuclear weapons may limit other states from exercising the freedom of navigation. The International Court of Justice in the *Nuclear Test Cases*,[88] brought

---

[83] Art.2, above, n.79.

[84] *ibid.*

[85] Spain instituted proceedings against Canada in the ICJ on March 28, 1995 with respect to a dispute which had arisen relating to the Canadian Coastal Fisheries Protection Act 1985 and various other measures which had been taken on the basis of that legislation, in particular, the boarding on the high seas of a Spanish ship by Canadian officials. Spain contended that these measures seriously affected the principle of the freedom of the high seas and infringed the sovereign rights of Spain. The Court, in December, 1998, declared it had no jurisdiction to hear the case by virtue of the reservation contained in para.2(d) of the Canadian Declaration, May 10, 1994.

[86] Art.87.

[87] Art.87(2) of the 1982 Convention.

[88] I.C.J.Rep. 1974 at 253 (*Australia v France*); I.C.J.Rep. 1974 at 457 (*New Zealand v France*).

by Australia and New Zealand against France, did not address itself to the legality under international law of nuclear testing.[89] Petren J.,[90] however, highlighted the fact that, in spite of the 1963 Nuclear Test Ban Treaty[91] the prohibition on nuclear testing had not evolved into a rule of customary international law. He asserted the signatories to the 1973 Treaty, by mutually banning themselves from carrying out further atmospheric nuclear tests, had shown that "they were still of the opinion that customary international law did not prohibit atmospheric nuclear tests". In an advisory opinion in 1996, the ICJ confirmed that the threat or use of nuclear testing is now considered contrary to contemporary international law.[92] France renewed its nuclear testing activities in the South Pacific in 1996, despite the prohibition.[93]

Nationality of ships

Ships must fly the flag of a state; their nationality is that of the state whose flag they fly. A state may establish its own conditions for the granting of nationality to a ship, but there:

> "must exist a genuine link between the State and the ship; in particular, the State must effectively exercise its jurisdiction and control in administrative, technical and social matters over ships flying its flag."[94]

A ship may sail under the flag of one state only and a ship:

> "which sails under the flags of two or more States, using them according to convenience, may not claim any of the nationalities in question with respect to any other State, and may be assimilated to a ship without nationality."[95]

---

[89] The cases were withdrawn following assurances by France in a number of statements that the tests would cease.

[90] I.C.J.Rep. 1985 at 305.

[91] 480 U.N.T.S. 43; U.K.T.S. 3 (1964) Cmnd.2245; 14 U.S.T. 1313.

[92] 35 I.L.M. 809 (1996). See also Ch.11.

[93] In response to the actions of France, New Zealand submitted a request to the ICJ on August 21, 1995, for an examination of the situation arising from the proposed nuclear testing in accordance with para.63 of the ICJ's judgment in the *Nuclear Tests Case* in 1974. New Zealand argued that renewed nuclear testing action would affect the judgment in that Case. The ICJ dismissed the request on the grounds that the basis of its original judgment was not affected by the proposed course of action. (Order of the Court, I.C.J.Rep. 1995 at 288).

[94] Art.5 of the 1958 Convention; Art.91 of the 1982 Convention.

[95] Art.6 of the 1958 Convention; Art.92 of the 1982 Convention.

A ship is not prohibited from sailing without a flag, but if it does, it cannot invoke diplomatic protection for any international wrong it may have allegedly suffered: *Naim Molvan v Attorney-General for Palestine*.[96] A ship may not normally change its flag during a voyage.

The introduction of the genuine link requirement was prompted by the increase in the use of "flags of convenience"— that is, where ship owners register in a particular state because of less onerous municipal taxation and labour laws. The United Nations addressed the issue and this culminated in the 1986 UN Convention on Conditions for Registration of Ships.[97] The raison d'être of the Convention is to introduce improved standards of responsibility and accountability, thereby reinforcing the "genuine" link requirement.[98] Obligations incumbent on the flag state under the 1958 and 1982 Conventions include, *inter alia*:

> the maintenance of a register of all ships flying its flag; the exercise of effective authority and control over the ships in administrative, technical and social matters; to take those measures necessary to ensure safety at sea, to prevent collisions and to prevent, reduce and control pollution of the marine environment and adopt laws and regulations and to take such steps as are required to achieve conformity with generally accepted standards, regulations, procedures and practices, and to serve their implementation and observance.[99]

It is not always for economic benefits that a ship may seek to fly the flag of a state other than that of its state of nationality. During the Iran–Iraq conflict, Kuwaiti vessels seeking the military protection of British and American naval vessels patrolling the Gulf, re-registered under the UK and the US flags.

Jurisdiction on the high seas

Jurisdiction over ships on the high seas lies with the flag state. The flag state is, for instance, responsible for the manning of ships and the labour conditions of the crew.[1] The 1982 Convention's counterpart Article[2] spells out in greater detail the measures

[96] [1948] A.C. 351; see 369–370.
[97] 26 I.L.M. 1236 (1987).
[98] The Convention requires the ratification of 40 countries before it shall enter into force.
[99] Relevant Arts in the 1958 Convention are 5(1), 10, 11, 24 and 25; in the 1982 Convention, 94, 192, 211 and 219.
[1] Art.10 of the 1958 Convention.
[2] Art.94.

which a flag state is required to take to ensure safety at sea. In respect of a collision on the high seas, neither penal nor disciplinary proceedings may be initiated against either the master or a crew member, except before the judicial or administrative authorities of the flag state or the state of which such person is a national. The ship itself may only be arrested or detained, even for investigation purposes, by the authority of the flag state.[3] Warships and government ships used for other than commercial purposes are accorded sovereign immunity and are subject only to the jurisdiction of their flag state.

Exceptions to the freedom of navigation—interference on the high seas

The most important limitation to the freedom of navigation is that:

> "every State may seize a pirate ship or aircraft, or a ship taken by piracy and under the control of pirates, and arrest the persons and seize the property on board."[4]

Piracy is strictly defined in international law as:

> "(1) Any illegal acts of violence, detention or any act of depredation committed for private ends by the crew or the passengers of a private ship or a private aircraft, and directed:
>
> (a) On the high seas, against another ship or aircraft, or against persons or property on board such ship or aircraft;
>
> (b) Against a ship, aircraft, persons, or property in a place outside the jurisdiction of any State;
>
> (2) Any act of voluntary participation in the operation of a ship or of an aircraft with knowledge of facts making it a pirate ship or aircraft;
>
> (3) Any act of inciting or of intentionally facilitating an act described in sub-paragraph 1 or sub-paragraph 2 of this article."[5]

---

[3] Hence, the EU's condemnation of Canada's actions directed at Spanish trawlers as "international piracy" in March 1995. Art.11 of the 1958 Convention; Art.97 of the 1982 Convention; *cf*. decision in the *Lotus Case* P.C.I.J. Rep., ser.A, No.10 (1927).

[4] Art.19 of the 1958 Convention; Art.105 of the 1982 Convention.

[5] Art.15 of the 1958 Convention; Art.101 of the 1982 Convention. The hijacking of the Italian liner *Achille Lauro* by four Palestinians in October, 1985 did not constitute an act of piracy under international law.

The courts of the seizing state are competent to decide the penalties which may be imposed.[6] If the suspicion for the seizure proves groundless, the state making the seizure is liable for any loss or damage it has caused as a consequence.[7] Only warships or military aircraft or other authorised vessels may carry out such a seizure.

Unless provided for by treaty, a foreign merchant ship may only be boarded by a warship if it has reasonable ground for suspecting:

"(a) that the ship is engaged in piracy; or
 (b) that the ship is engaged in the slave trade; or
 (c) that, though flying a foreign flag or refusing to show its flag, the ship is, in reality, of the same nationality as the warship."[8]

Again, if the suspicions prove unfounded, the boarded ship shall be entitled to receive compensation.

The 1982 Convention requires states to co-operate in the suppression of illicit traffic in narcotic drugs and psychotropic substances engaged in by ships on the high seas contrary to international conventions, and provides that a state:

"which has reasonable grounds for believing that a ship flying its flag is engaged in illicit traffic in narcotic drugs or psychotropic substances may request the co-operation of other States to suppress such traffic."[9]

The *Achille Lauro* incident and fears of escalating maritime terrorism prompted the International Maritime Organisation to produce a Convention for the Suppression of Unlawful Acts Against the Safety of Maritime Navigation[10] and a Protocol for the Suppression of Unlawful Acts Against the Safety of Fixed Platforms Located on the Continental Shelf.[11]

---

[6] *ibid*. Canada's Criminal Code, *e.g.* states that it is an offence, punishable by life imprisonment, to do "any act that, by the law of nations, is piracy" (s.75). The Code also makes it an offence to carry out "piratical acts", which include stealing a Canadian ship or its cargo, starting a mutiny or inciting others to do so (s.76).

[7] Art.20 of the 1958 Convention; Art.106 of the 1982 Convention.

[8] Art.22 of the 1958 Convention; Art.110 of the 1982 Convention—the latter also includes the right of visit in respect of ships suspected of engaging in unauthorised broadcasting—see below.

[9] Art.108.

[10] The Convention entered into force on March 1, 1992 and has 67 Contracting Parties accounting for 54.81% of world tonnage.

[11] The Protocol entered into force on March 1, 1992 and has 60 Contracting Parties accounting for 54.46% of world tonnage.

Art.3 articulates what constitutes an offence for the purposes of the Convention and includes, *inter alia*, the seizure or exercising of control over a ship by force or threat thereof or any form of intimidation.[12] Contracting Parties are required to take such measures as may be necessary to establish its jurisdiction over the offences identified by the Convention when the offence is committed:

(a)   against or on board a ship flying its flag at the time when the offence is committed; or

(b)   in its territory, including territorial sea; or

(c)   by one of its nationals.[13]

Jurisdiction *may* (emphasis added) be exercised by a Contracting Party in the event of the offence:

(a)   being committed by a stateless person who is habitually resident in its territory; or

(b)   resulting in one of its nationals being threatened, injured or killed; or

(c)   being committed in an attempt to compel that state to do or abstain from doing any act.[14]

The Convention requires Contracting Parties to make the relevant offences punishable by penalties appropriate to the gravity of the offences[15] and obliges them to either institute proceedings through the domestic courts or extradite the offender or alleged offender.[16]

The 1982 Convention also tackles the problem of high seas broadcasting (pirate radio), particularly in Art.109(3), which provides that a person:

"engaged in unauthorised broadcasting may be prosecuted before the Court of:
(a)   the flag State of the ship;
(b)   the State of registry of the installations;
(c)   the State of which the person is a national;
(d)   any State where the transmissions can be received; or
(e)   any State where authorised radio communication is suffering interference."

---

[12] Art.3.1.(a). Note the Convention does not apply to warships, state vessels being used as a naval auxiliary or for customs or police purposes; Art.2.
[13] Art.6.1.
[14] Art.6.2.
[15] Art.5.
[16] Art.10.

Art.109(4) confirms the right of visit to ships suspected of engaging in unauthorised broadcasting and provides that any person or ship engaged in unauthorised broadcasting may be arrested and the broadcasting apparatus seized by any state which has jurisdiction under Art.109(3).

Fishing activities on the high seas

The 1982 Convention[17] provides for a management and conservation scheme for the living resources of the high seas. These provisions which consolidate and elaborate on those imposed upon states by the 1958 Geneva Convention on the Fishing and Conservation of Living Resources are, of course, independent of those provisions in respect of the coastal states' rights in the EEZ.

Hot pursuit

The warships, law enforcement vessels or aircraft (the 1982 Convention requires that such vessels and aircraft should be clearly marked) of a coastal state may pursue a vessel leaving its territorial waters when it suspects it of having violated its laws and regulations.[18] Pursuit must be continuous and must cease immediately the pursued vessel reaches the territorial waters of another state, be it the vessel's own state or a third state. If pursuit is initiated in contiguous waters, it must only be because of a violation of the rights for which the contiguous zone was established (see above). Pursuit may only be initiated after the offending vessel has received a visual or auditory signal to stop.

Failure to stop may lead to the use of "necessary and reasonable force for the purpose of effecting the object of boarding, searching, seizing and bringing into port the suspected vessel.[19] Hot pursuit has evolved and is now regarded as a rule of customary international law.

Protection of marine environment

The 1958 Geneva Convention on the High Seas requires every state to draw up regulations to prevent pollution of the seas by the discharge of oil from ships or pipelines or resulting from the exploitation and exploration of the seabed and its subsoil, taking account of existing treaty provisions on the subject.[20]

---

[17] Arts 116–120.
[18] Art.23 of the 1958 Convention; Art.111 of the 1982 Convention.
[19] The *I'm Alone Case* 3 R.I.A.A. 1607 at 1615; 29 A.J.I.L. 326 (1935)—where, in fact, the sinking of the vessel concerned was held to be excessive action which "could not be justified by any principle of international law".
[20] Art.24.

In spite of growing concern on the dangers of oil pollution on the marine environment, it was not until 1954 that an international convention was agreed upon, namely the International Convention for the Prevention of the Pollution of the Sea by Oil (OILPOL).[21] Essentially, the Convention prohibited the discharge of oil or any oily mixture by vessels, and made any such violation subject to the jurisdiction of the state of registration. The 1954 Convention as amended in 1962, 1969 and 1971, has been replaced for parties to both Conventions by the 1973 Convention for the Prevention of Pollution from Ships (MARPOL),[22] which covers not only oil discharges from ships, but discharges such as sewage and garbage and other noxious harmful substances.[23] The Marpol Convention is the most important international convention dealing with pollution from ships. An international convention on liability and compensation for damage in connection with the carriage of hazardous and noxious substances by sea was adopted on May 3, 1996 under the auspices of International Maritime Organisation (IMO). The Convention imposes strict liability upon shipowners for *inter alia* loss of life or personal injury, loss of or damage to property outside the ship and loss or damage by contamination of the environment. The Convention also introduces a system of compulsory insurance.[24]

The *Torrey Canyon* incident of 1967, when the United Kingdom bombed a Liberian tanker stranded off the Cornish coast so as to

---

[21] 327 U.N.T.S. 3; U.K.T.S. 56 (1958) Cmnd.595; 12 U.S.T. 2989.

[22] Misc.26 (1974) Cmnd.5748; 12 I.L.M. 1319 (1973). As of February 18, 2002, Annex I/II has 120 Contracting States (95.90% world tonnage); Annex III has 101 Contracting States (81.4% world tonnage); Annex IV has 85 Contracting States (46.34% world tonnage); Annex V has 106 Contracting States (87.88% world tonnage); Annex VI has 4 Contracting States (14.05% world tonnage).

[23] Technical difficulties in respect of the provisions dealing with noxious liquid substances acted as an obstacle to the ratification of the 1973 Convention. A Protocol was adopted in 1978 (Misc.26 (1974) Cmnd.5748) to facilitate the entry into force of the regulations pertaining to oil discharge. A number of amendments to the Marpol Convention were adopted by the IMO Assembly and entered into force on March 3, 1996. The amendments were designed to improve the application of the Convention and apply to four of the Convention's five technical annexes. Ships can now be inspected in the ports of other Contracting Parties so as to ensure that the crews are competent to perform important procedures relating to the prevention of marine pollution.

[24] The Convention will come into force 18 months after the fulfilment of two conditions. First, that there is acceptance by 12 States of the Convention, 4 of which have not less than 2 million units of gross tonnage and secondly, that the persons in those States who are required to contribute to a general fund established under the Convention have received at least 40 million tonnes of contributing cargo in the preceding year. There are complex arrangements for calculating contributions to the Fund. At present, the Liability Convention, has two Contracting Parties, accounting for 1.89% world tonnage, and has not yet entered into force.

avoid further damage through the spillage of oil, precipitated the 1969 International Convention Relating to Intervention on the High Seas in Cases of Oil Pollution Casualties.[25] The Convention allows parties to:

> "take such measures on the high seas as may be necessary to prevent, mitigate or eliminate grave and imminent danger to their coastline or related interests from pollution or threat of pollution of the sea by oil, following upon a maritime casualty or acts related to such a casualty, which may reasonably be expected to result in major harmful consequences."[26]

The measures taken must be "reasonably necessary" and proportionate to the damage, actual or threatened.[27]

A 1973 Protocol to the Convention[28] authorises intervention with respect to threats of pollution from substances other than oil. The Intervention Convention is supplemented by the Convention on Civil Liability for Oil Pollution Damage.[29] The Convention imposes a regime of strict liability (save in certain circumstances) on the owners of vessels and provides for the payment of compensation in respect of damage caused by oil spillage. The Liability Convention is supplemented by the 1971 Convention on the Establishment of an International Fund of Compensation for Oil Pollution Damage,[30] which established a fund for the payment of compensation in circumstances where the Liability Convention proves deficient. Tanker owners have also established their own compensation schemes, namely the Tanker Owners' Voluntary Agreement concerning Liability for Oil Pollution 1969 (TOVALOP)[31]; and the Contract Regarding an Interim Supplement to Tanker Liability for Oil Pollution 1971 (CRISTAL).[32] Protocols to

---

[25] U.K.T.S. 77 (1975) Cmnd.6056; 26 U.S.T. 765; 9 I.L.M. 25 (1969). The International Convention on Civil Liability for Bunker Oil Pollution Damage (2001) was adopted on March 23, 2001. It will enter into force 12 months after 18 states have signed it without reservation as to ratification or have ratified it.

[26] Art.1.

[27] Art.5.

[28] U.K.T.S. 27 (1983) Cmnd.8924; 13 I.L.M. 605 (1974).

[29] U.K.T.S. 106 (1975) Cmnd.6183; 9 I.L.M. 45 (1970). Amending Protocol 1976, U.K.T.S. 26 (1981) Cmnd.8238; 16 I.L.M. 617 (1977). Replaced by the 1992 IMO Convention on Civil Liability for Oil Pollution Damage, and Protocol (see below).

[30] U.K.T.S. 95 (1978) Cmnd.7383; 11 I.L.M. 284 (1972). Amending Protocol Misc.27 (177) Cmnd.7029; 16 I.L.M. 621 (1977). Replaced by the 1992 IMO Convention on the Establishment of an International Fund of Compensation for Oil Pollution Damage and Protocol (see below).

[31] 8 I.L.M. 497 (1969).

[32] 10 I.L.M. 137 (1971).

the 1969 Civil Liability Convention and the 1971 International Fund Convention provide higher limits of compensation and have a wider scope of application than the Conventions originally envisaged.[33] Both Protocols include the EEZ.

Art.25 of the Geneva Convention required states to take measures to prevent pollution by the dumping of radioactive waste as well as co-operating with competent international organisations. Art.5(7) of the Convention on the Continental Shelf requires coastal states "to undertake, in the safety zones all appropriate measures for the protection of the living resources of the sea from harmful agents." These provisions have been reinforced by international conventions on dumping and pollution from land-based sources, such as the Oslo Convention for the Prevention of Marine Pollution by Dumping from Ships and Aircraft 1972,[34] the London Convention on the Prevention of Marine Pollution by Dumping of Wastes and Other Material 1972,[35] the Paris Convention for the Prevention of Marine Pollution from Land-based Sources 1974,[36] and regional arrangements such as the Barcelona Convention for the Protection of the Mediterranean against Pollution 1976.[37] The UN Environment Programme (UNEP) operates a Regional Seas Programme.

A proposed moratorium on the disposal at sea of decommissioned offshore installations was rejected at the 18th Consultative Meeting of Contracting Parties to the London Convention, December 4–8, 1995. Contracting Parties are to continue to apply the Convention and the IMO Guidelines and Standards which provide that, on or after January 1, 1998, structures should not be erected on any continental shelf or in any EEZ unless, due to the design and construction of the installation or structure, it is feasible to remove it upon abandonment or permanent disuse.

The principal international organisation concerned with vessel pollution issues is the IMO. The IMO is responsible for convening conferences, drafting and revising conventions. Although IMO is one of the smaller UN agencies, it has, through its work, achieved

---

[33] The Protocols entered into force on May 30, 1995 and superseded the Protocols adopted in 1984 on the same matter.

[34] U.K.T.S. 119 (1975) Cmnd.6228; 11 I.L.M. 262 (1972).

[35] U.K.T.S. 43 (1976) Cmnd.6486; 26 U.S.T. 2403; 11 I.L.M. 1291 (1972). A Protocol to the London Convention was adopted at an IMO Conference on November 7, 1996. The Protocol introduces a radical new approach to the regulation of the use of the sea as a depositary for waste materials (see Art.3—"the polluter pays" principle). It will enter into force 30 days after ratification by 26 countries, 15 of whom must be Contracting Parties to the 1972 Convention (Art.25) 36 I.L.M. 1 (1997). To date, there have been 16 ratifications.

[36] U.K.T.S. 64 (1978) Cmnd.7251; 13 I.L.M. 352 (1974).

[37] 15 I.L.M. 290 (1976).

considerable success in reducing oil pollution and improving safety at sea. There are 162 Member States and two Associate Members.[38]

The 1982 Convention envisages a comprehensive regime (provided for in 46 Articles)[38a] for the protection and preservation of the marine environment. Art.192 places states under a general obligation to protect and preserve the marine environment, and to this end, parties will be required to adopt national and international measures. The Convention further provides, *inter alia*, for global and regional co-operation, contingency plans against pollution, studies, research programmes and exchange of information and data, and scientific and technical assistance to developing states. States are required to adopt laws and regulations with regard to pollution from land-based sources, seabed activities, dumping, pollution from vessels and pollution from or through the atmosphere. Enforcement is envisaged by flag states, port states and coastal states. Non-fulfilment of international obligations by a party will give rise to international responsibility. The UN Conference on the Environment and Development held in Rio de Janerio in 1992 endorsed the environmental provisions of the Convention. The link between UNCLOS and Ch.17 of Agenda 21 is seen as critical, as it emphasises the need for international co-operation in this area.

EXCLUSIVE ECONOMIC ZONE (EEZ)

The 1982 Convention acknowledges the EEZ as "an area beyond and adjacent to the territorial sea . . ."[39] which "shall not extend beyond 200 nautical miles from the baselines from which the breadth of the territorial sea is measured."[40] UNCLOS III can be said to have recognised the right to claim an EEZ as one existing under customary law. Subsequent judicial indorsement for the exercise of this right is found in the *Continental Shelf (Tunisia v Libya) Case.*[41]

The concept of the EEZ evolved with the realisation that fishery resources are not inexhaustible, and that thus it was imperative to adopt conservation measures.

---

[38] Arts 192–238.

[38a] IMO was established in 1958 and was primarily charged with the task of improving maritime safety. The increase in oil transportation by sea and a number of serious spills in the 1960s led to IMO's involvement in pollution prevention.

[39] Art.55.

[40] Art.57.

[41] I.C.J.Rep. 1982, p.18 at 74; *Gulf of Maine Case* I.C.J.Rep. 1984 246 at 294–295; *Continental Shelf (Libya v Malta) Case* I.C.J.Rep. 1985 13 at 33; *Guinea/Guinea Bissau Delimitation of the Maritime Boundary* 25 I.L.M. 251 (1986) at 272, para.42.

It was only with the failure of both the 1958 and 1960 Conferences to establish the width of the territorial sea and fisheries zone that the two jurisdictional areas became independent of each other. Fisheries jurisdiction, until then, was an integral part of territorial waters jurisdiction. The failure to reach international agreement saw state practice developing the law of fisheries independently. Iceland, for example, did not wait for the 1960 Conference, but, in 1958, extended its exclusive fishery zone to 12 miles by employing the straight baseline method recognised by the International Court of Justice in 1952 (see *Anglo-Norwegian Fisheries Case* above).

Throughout the 1960s, the trend both within and outside Europe was towards recognition of a 12-mile exclusive fishery zone (with, as a general rule, recognition being given to the rights of foreign vessels which had traditionally fished within these waters).[42] By the end of the 1960s, a coastal state's territorial waters and fisheries jurisdiction were no longer synonymous. Judicial recognition was accorded to a 12-mile exclusive fisheries zone by the International Court of Justice in 1974, when it concluded in the *Fisheries Jurisdiction Case (Merits) (United Kingdom v Iceland)*[43] that the 12-mile fishery zone had in the years subsequent to the 1960 Conference "crystallised as customary international law.[44] The court failed to answer explicitly the question addressed to it, that is whether Iceland's claim to a 50-mile exclusive fishing zone was compatible with international law,[45] but rather characterised Iceland's unilateral extension as "an infringement of the principles enshrined in Art.2 of the 1958 Geneva Convention on the High Seas. . . ."[46] The door was left open for continued expansion by coastal states and so it continued throughout the 1970s. The culmination of such claims is reflected in the 1982 Convention and in state practice.

The right to claim an EEZ is discretionary and not mandatory— the United Kingdom, for example, does not claim an EEZ, the reason being that there would be no advantage in doing so as "the United Kingdom already has a fishery zone extending to a maximum of 200 nautical miles and . . . rights over our continental shelf (which extends well beyond 200 miles) are inherent and do

---

[42] See *e.g.* 1964 European Fisheries Convention 581 U.N.T.S. 57; US legislation Public Law 89–658, 5 I.L.M. 1103 (1966).

[43] I.C.J.Rep. 1974 at 3.

[44] *ibid.* at 23.

[45] The Icelandic government implemented its intention to extend Iceland's exclusive fishing zone to 50 miles by the Resolution of the Althing of February 15, 1972 and Regulations of July 14. See Lay, Churchill and Nordquist, *New Directions in the Law of the Sea*, Vol.1, pp.89–90.

[46] Above, n.43 at 29.

not have to be proclaimed."[47] The United States, on the other hand, does claim an EEZ. The Convention provides the regulatory regime for the EEZ.

Rights of coastal states within the Exclusive Economic Zone

The coastal state does not enjoy complete sovereignty over the EEZ, but only sovereign rights "for the purpose of exploring and exploiting, conserving and managing the natural resources, whether living or non-living, of the seabed and subsoil and the superjacent waters . . ." and jurisdiction, *inter alia*, with regard to "(i) the establishments and use of artificial islands, installations and structures; (ii) marine scientific research; (iii) the protection and preservation of the marine environment."[48]

The coastal state is responsible for determining both "the allowable catch of the living resources in its exclusive economic zone"[49] and "its capacity to harvest the living resources of the EEZ."[50] The coastal state's task is to conserve resources within the EEZ and, to this end, is charged with adopting measures which will:

> "maintain or restore populations of harvested species at lev-els which can produce the maximum sustainable yield, as qualified by relevant environmental economic needs of coastal fishing communities and the special requirement of developing States . . ."[51]

Account must be taken of "the best scientific evidence available" with the coastal state co-operating, where appropriate, with the "competent international organisations, whether sub-regional, regional or global."[52]

The coastal state's most important task as far as foreign states are concerned, is to decide, in respect of the EEZ's living resources, the surplus available over its own harvesting capac-ity.[53] That surplus, the Convention provides, is to be made avail-able to other states, either through agreements or other arrangements to certain criteria which the coastal state is, espe-cially with regard to developing states, to take into account. Such criteria include the "significance of the living resources of the

---

[47] *Hansard*, HL Vol.473, Col. 46 (April 7, 1986).
[48] Art.56.
[49] Art.61(1).
[50] Art.62(2).
[51] Art.61(3).
[52] Art.61(2).
[53] Art.61(2).

area to the economy of the coastal state and its other national interests", the interests of land-locked states and those states "with special geographical characteristics" and the interests of those states "whose nationals have habitually fished in the zone."[54] The final say remains, however, with the coastal state.

The coastal state is responsible for regulating fishing by foreign vessels within the EEZ,[55] and is required to give due notice of conservation and management regulations[56] and to exercise control over foreign vessels granted access.[57] The Convention provides for co-operation in the event of stocks occurring within the EEZ of two or more coastal states.[58] The coastal state enjoys rights within the EEZ, but it is also charged with obligations. The coastal state is not the owner, but rather the guardian of the natural resources within its EEZ.

Rights and duties of other states

Other states enjoy the right of free navigation, overflight and the laying of submarine cables and pipelines in the EEZ, provided they respect the rights and duties of the coastal state and comply with the laws and regulations of the latter.[59] The rights of foreign states are reinforced by the obligation on the coastal state to pay "due regard to the rights and duties of other States . . ."[60]

Delimitation of the Exclusive Economic Zone between states with opposite or adjacent coasts

Art.74 of the 1982 Convention provides that the delimitation of the EEZ between states with opposite or adjacent coasts is to be effected "by agreement on the basis of international law as referred to in Art.38 of the Statute of the International Court of Justice, in order to achieve an equitable solution."[61] The *Jan Meyen Case* affirmed the desirability for a common maritime boundary between the EEZ and the continental shelf. However, Oda J., in his dissenting opinion, stated that, because of the separate and independent legal regimes of the EEZ and the

[54] See Art.62(2); Art.69; Art.70; Arts 69 and 70 do not apply to coastal states whose economy is overwhelmingly dependent on the exploitation of the living resources of its exclusive economic zone.
[55] Art.62(4) gives a list of the measures which the coastal state may take, *e.g.* licensing of fishermen.
[56] Art.62(5).
[57] Art.73.
[58] Art.63(1); Art.63(2); Art.64.
[59] Art.58(1) and (3).
[60] Art.56(2).
[61] Above, n.36.

continental shelf, a common maritime boundary cannot be presumed, (I.C.J. Rep.1993. See, also, *Delimitation of Maritime Areas between Canada and France* (St Pierre and Miquelon) 1992 31 I.L.M. 1145).

In the *Delimitation of the Maritime Boundary in the Gulf of Maine Area*,[62] the Chamber, established to decide the delimitation of both the continental shelf and the fishery zone, submitted that the criteria to be employed should be those which, by their neutral character, were best suited for employment in a multi-purpose delimitation. In the case before it, the Chamber utilised criteria especially derived from geography. Likewise, the practical methods to be employed to give effect to the criteria should, the Chamber held, be "basically founded upon geography and be as suitable for the delimitation of the seabed and subsoil as to that of the superjacent waters and their living resources" and, accordingly, the Chamber concluded that "only geometrical methods" would be utilised. The Chamber denied that the parties' respective scale of fishing or petroleum exploitation could serve as an equitable criterion unless:

> ". . . unexpectedly, the overall result should appear radically inequitable as entailing disastrous repercussions on the subsistence and economic development of the population concerned."[63]

CONTINENTAL SHELF

"Continental shelf" is the geographical term used to describe the gently sloping ledge covered by shallow water projecting from the shoreline of many land masses before a steep descent to the ocean waters. Continental shelves vary considerably in width: off the west coast of the United States, the shelf is less then five miles, whereas the entire area under water of the North Sea is continental shelf.

In accordance with the principle of the freedom of the high seas, all states equally enjoy the right to explore the seabed. Continental shelves are rich in oil reserves and, by the 1940s, states possessed the technology to exploit such resources. Furthermore, economically, exploration had become a viable proposition.

President Truman's Proclamation of September 28, 1945, whereby the United States regarded:

---

[62] I.C.J.Rep. 1984 at 246.
[63] *ibid*. at 342.

"... the natural resources of the subsoil and seabed of the continental shelf beneath the high seas but contiguous to the coasts of the United States as appertaining to the United States, subject to its jurisdiction and control,"

but that "the character as high seas of the waters above the continental shelf and the right to their free and unimpeded navigation are in no way affected",[64] precipitated numerous assertions of coastal states' rights over the continental shelf and marked the beginning of the change in the legal status of the continental shelf.

The claims which followed in the wake of the Truman Proclamation differed in nature. Some were restrained, some asserted exclusive sovereignty by the coast state, whilst Argentina and El Salvador claimed not only the continental shelf, but also the superjacent waters and the airspace above, whereas Chile and Peru claimed sovereignty over the seabed, subsoil and water around their coasts to a limit of 200 miles.[65] It was against the background of such claims that the International Law Commission addressed itself to the issue of the continental shelf.

Art.1 of the Geneva Convention defines the continental shelf as referring:

"(a) to the seabed and subsoil of the submarine area adjacent to the coast but outside the area of the territorial sea, to a depth of 200 metres or, beyond that limit, to where the depth of the superjacent waters admits of the exploitation of the natural resources of the said areas;

(b) to the seabed and subsoil of similar submarine areas adjacent to the coasts of islands."

The 1958 definition emphasises exploitability, whereas the 1982 Convention does not. Art.76 of the 1982 Convention defines the continental shelf as:

"the seabed and subsoil of the submarine areas that extend beyond its territorial sea throughout the natural prolongation of its land territory to the outer edge of the continental margin,[66] or to a distance of 200 nautical miles from the baselines from which the breadth of the territorial sea is measured where the outer edge of the continental margin does not extend up to that distance."

---

[64] 4 Whiteman 756.
[65] Chile and Peru possess no geographical continental shelf.
[66] *i.e.* the continental margin consists of the continental shelf, slope and rise that separates the land mass from the deep ocean floor (abyssal plain).

The continental shelf extends to 200 nautical miles for all states, but retains an advantage for the geographically favoured. However, Art.76(6) provides that the continental shelf shall not exceed 350 nautical miles from territorial baselines. Art.76(7) provides the method of delimitation to be employed where the continental shelf exceeds 200 nautical miles.

Regarding a coastal state's rights over the continental shelf, the 1982 Convention essentially reproduces the provisions of the 1958 Convention. A coastal state's rights are not territorial sovereign rights but are, rather, functional rights for the purpose of exploring and exploiting the natural resources of the continental shelf.[67] The coastal state's rights are exclusive, and exploration and exploitation activities may not be undertaken without the consent of the coastal state. Natural resources are defined as the mineral and other non-living resources of the seabed and subsoil, together with living organisms belonging to sedentary species. The 1982 Convention provides that the coastal state has the exclusive right to authorise and regulate drilling on the continental shelf for all purposes.[68]

The coastal state's rights in the continental shelf do not affect the status of the superjacent waters as high seas, or that of the airspace above those waters,[69] and states, in exercising their rights on the continental shelf, must not impede the laying or maintenance of submarine cables or pipelines and must not result in:

> "any unjustifiable interference with navigation, fishing or the conservation of the living resources of the sea, nor result in any interference with fundamental oceanographic or other scientific research carried out with the intention of open publication."[70]

A coastal state may construct artificial installations on the continental shelf and may establish safety zones around such installations to a maximum of 5,000 metres. Art.82 of the 1982 Convention further restricts the maximum limit of the continental shelf (see above) by providing for the payment of contributions in kind by coastal states in respect of the exploitation of the non-living resources when their continental shelf exceeds 200 nautical miles from the territorial baselines. Payments and contributions are to be made five years after production. Developing

---

[67] Art.2 of the 1958 Convention; Art.77 of the 1982 Convention.
[68] Art.81.
[69] Art.3 of the 1958 Convention; Art.78 of the 1982 Convention.
[70] Art.5(1) of the 1958 Convention; Art.246 of the 1982 Convention applies to research on the continental shelf and the EEZ.

states which are net importers of a mineral resource produced from its continental shelf will be exempt from making such payments or contributions. The payments or contributions shall be made through the Authority (see below) which shall distribute to states who are parties to the Convention "on the basis of equitable sharing criteria, taking into account the interests and needs of developing States, particularly the least developed and land-locked among them."[71]

Delimitations of the continental shelf between states with opposite or adjacent coasts

Art.6(1) and (2) of the 1958 Convention on the Continental Shelf provides formulae for delimiting the outer limit of the continental shelf between opposite and adjacent states. In both instances, the boundary should be determined by agreement between the states concerned, in the absence of which the boundary for opposite coasts "is the median line, every point of which is equidistant from the nearest point of the baselines from which the breadth of the territorial sea of each State is measured" and, for adjacent coasts, "the boundary shall be determined by application of the principle of equidistance from the nearest point of the baselines from which the breadth of the territorial sea of each State is measured." Both rules show a recognised exception, namely that neither the median line nor the principle of equidistance will apply if "another boundary is justified by special circumstances."

The Geneva Convention failed to provide any indication of what would constitute "special circumstances". The International Court of Justice in the *North Sea Continental Shelf Cases*[72] provided that delimitation was to be "effected by agreement in accordance with equitable principles, and taking account of all the relevant circumstances."[73] Relevant circumstances identified by the court were, *inter alia*, the general configuration of the coasts of the parties; so far as known or readily ascertainable, the physical and geological structure and the natural resources of the continental shelf areas involved; the element of a reasonable degree of proportionality, which a delimitation carried out in accordance with equitable principles ought to bring about between the extent of the continental shelf areas pertaining to the coastal state and the length of its coast measured in the general direction of the coastline, account being taken for this purpose of the effects, actual or prospective, of any other continental shelf delimitations between

---

[71] Art.82.[EP]
[72] I.C.J.Rep. 1969 at 3.
[73] *ibid.* at 46.

adjacent states in the same region.[74] However, having identified the possible relevant circumstances, the court concluded that there was:

> "no legal limit to the considerations which States may take account of for the purpose of making sure that they apply equitable procedures, and more often than not it is the balancing-up of all such considerations . . . rather than reliance on one to exclusion of all others."[75]

and that, in the absence of any "imperative rules" recognised by international law for the delimitation of the continental shelf, resort could be made to "various principles or methods, as may be appropriate, or a combination of them, provided that, by the application of equitable principles, a reasonable result is arrived at.[76]

In the *Continental Shelf (Libyan Arab Jamahiriya v Malta) Case,*[77] the parties agreed that the delimitation of the continental shelf had to be effected by the application of equitable principles in all the relevant circumstances in order to achieve an equitable result. Certain principles then identified by the court were: that there should be no question of refashioning geography; non-encroachment by one party on areas appertaining to the other; respect for all relevant circumstances; that equity did not necessarily imply equality nor could there be any question of distributive justice.[78] The court in that case refuted that the respective economic positions of the parties concerned should be taken into account but did acknowledge that the existence of an economic resource and security and defence interests might be given cognisance.[79]

Note that in the *Continental Shelf Case (Tunisia v Libya)* economic and political factors were dismissed, unless to do so would be "radically inequitable". See also *Gulf of Maine Case* in which such factors were dismissed as "ineligible for consideration".[80]

In the *North Sea Continental Shelf Cases*, the court maintained that the equidistance principle was not, in light of the special circumstances exception, a principle of international law, but merely an application in appropriate situations of a more general

---

[74] Above, n.72 at 50–52.

[75] Above, n.72 at 50.

[76] Above, n.72 at 49.

[77] I.C.J.Rep. 1985, p.13.

[78] *ibid.*

[79] Above, n.77.

[80] Above, n.62 at 340. The Court acknowledged that they could be relevant to assessment of the equitable character of a delimitation, first established on the basis of criteria borrowed from physical and political geography.

rule. In the *English Channel Arbitration*,[81] the arbitrators held that Art.6 did not formulate the equidistance principle and "special circumstances" as two separate rules, but rather as a combined equidistance—special circumstances rule.

Relevant circumstances were considered in the *Gulf of Maine Case*.[82] The Chamber adopted the stance that the objective of a delimitation of an equitable maritime boundary should (unless the parties agree otherwise) be to attain "an equal division of areas where the maritime projections of the coasts of the States between which delimitation is to be effected converge and overlap."[83] Unless, that is, there were "special circumstances in the case which would make that criterion inequitable."[84] Both parties (the United States and Canada) made submissions as to what "relevant circumstances" should embrace. These included, *inter alia*, environmental (United States) and economic (Canada) circumstances. In rejecting the arguments advanced, the Chamber stated that, under international law, the equitable criteria for a delimitation were to be derived essentially from geographical factors.[85]

The Tribunal in the *Guinea/Guinea Bissau Arbitration* stated that, as it was concerned only with "a contemporary evaluation, it would be neither just nor equitable to base a delimitation on the evaluation of data which changes in relation to factors that are sometimes uncertain"[86] and that its prime objective had been "to avoid that either Party, for one reason or another should see rights exercised opposite its coast or in the immediate vicinity thereof, which could prevent the exercise of its own rights to development or compromise its security".[87] In the *Continental Shelf (Tunisia v Libya) Case*, the Court maintained that "each continental shelf case in dispute should be considered and judged on its own merits, having regard to its peculiar circumstances."[88]

---

[81] 18 I.L.M. 397 (1979).

[82] Above, n.62 at 246, in which the Chamber was called to decide the "maritime boundary" as between the continental shelves and fishing zones of the two parties. The objective for the establishment of such a boundary was held to be that of attaining "an equitable result".

[83] Above, n.62 at 327.

[84] Above, n.62 at 301.

[85] Above, n.62 at 278.

[86] Above, n.41 at 302, para.122 [1986].

[87] Above, n.41 at para.124.

[88] I.C.J.Rep. 1982 18 at 92; see also *Delimitation of the Maritime Boundary in the Gulf of Maine (Canada v United States of America)*, above, n.62 at 292 "... any agreement or other equivalent solution should involve the application of equitable criteria." The Chamber in this case did not apply the equidistance principle.

The International Court has, in other words, minimised the equidistance principle.[89] This is reflected in the 1982 Convention, which has abandoned the Art.6 formulae and provides that delimitation is to be "effected by agreement on the basis of international law, as referred to in Art.38 of the Statute of the International Court of Justice, in order to achieve an equitable solution.[90] The formula envisaged by the 1982 Convention, was characterised in the *Gulf of Maine Case* as being "singularly concise" but one which served "to open the door to continuation of the development effected in this field by international case law."[91] The way in which the Chamber set about arriving at a solution in the *Gulf of Maine* dispute probably best represents how delimitation disputes will be tackled under contemporary international law. The Chamber acknowledged that there was no "body of detailed rules" in customary international law nor indeed under general international law which would "provide a ready made set of rules" for the solution of delimitation rules and that rather what had to be sought was "a better formulation of the fundamental norm . . . whose existence in the legal convictions not only of the Parties to the present dispute, but of all States, is apparent from an examination of the realities of international legal relations."[92] The fundamental norm in question was identified by the Chamber as meaning that:

    (a)   no maritime delimitation between states may be effected unilaterally by one of the affected states;
    (b)   delimitation is to be sought and effected through agreement, following negotiation conducted in good faith with a genuine intention of achieving a positive result;
    (c)   in the absence of agreement recourse should be made to a third party;

and, in all instances, delimitation is to be effected by:

    (a)   the application of equitable criteria;

---

[89] The equidistance principle has been used in treaties between states, however, see also *Guinea/Guinea Bissau Arbitration*, above, n.41, in which the equidistance method was identified as "just one among many and that there is no obligation to use it or give it priority, even though it is recognised as having a certain intrinsic value because of its scientific value and the relative ease with which it can be applied" at para.102.

[90] Art.83(1); Art.74 articulates a similar formula for the delimitation of the EEZ between states with opposite or adjacent coasts.

[91] Above, n.62 at 252.

[92] Above, n.62 at 299.

(b)   the use of practical methods capable of ensuring, with regard to the geographic configuration of the area and other relevant circumstances, an equitable result.

Provision for the establishment of a Commission on the Continental Shelf is made under Art.76(8) in an effort to obtain international objectivity in the national delimitation of the continental shelf, the limits of which are to be established by a coastal state on the basis of Commission recommendations, which are to be final and binding. Art.298 of the 1982 Convention provides that states may opt to exclude delimitation disputes from procedures involving a binding decision and may refer them instead to "compulsory" conciliation.

DEEP SEABED

The deep seabed and its subsoil is rich in mineral resources, particularly in manganese nodules. The extraction of these resources is close to becoming a reality (albeit still an expensive process).

To whom should the resources belong? Should they belong to those relatively few states which, because of a technological and capital advantage, are able to finance deep-sea mining, or should the resources of the ocean bed belong to all states and should the benefits derived be distributed amongst the international community generally? If the answer is the latter, then what conditions should apply?

The United States, for example, regards deep-sea mining as a freedom of the high seas, whereas developing and technologically disadvantaged states in particular have adopted the view that the deep seabed should be designated an "area" which is the "common heritage of mankind" and whose natural resources should not be liable to appropriation by any state. The years preceding the sessions of UNCLOS witnessed the emergence of two groups—one representing developing states, calling for an international body to conduct all exploitation in the deep seabed and the second, that of the developed states, maintaining that deep-sea activity should be undertaken by states and/or national companies subject to a registration and licensing system. Both groups did, however, agree on the need to avoid a "free-for-all". Accordingly, the General Assembly Declaration of Principles Concerning the Sea Bed and the Ocean Floor and the Subsoil Thereof, Beyond the Limits of National Jurisdiction 1970[93] provided that the area and its resources "are the common heritage of mankind" and that no state or person, natural or juridical, could "claim, exercise or

---

[93] GA Resolution 2749 (XXV) December 17, 1970. 10 I.L.M. 230 (1970).

acquire rights with respect to the area or its resources incompatible with the international regime to be established . . .".[94]

The regime articulated in the 1982 Convention represents a compromise between the demands of the developed and the developing states.

Under the 1982 Convention all deep seabed exploration and exploitation is to be carried out and controlled by an International Sea Bed Authority.[95]

International SeaBed Authority[96]

The organs of the International Sea Bed Authority are the Assembly,[96a] the Council and the Enterprise. The Assembly, with a representative from each Member State, is the supreme policy-making organ, adopting decisions by a two-thirds majority. The Council is made up of 36 Member States elected by the Assembly, representing various special interest groups, such as the largest investors in sea mining, land-locked nations and potential producers. The executive organ of the Authority is the Council, which will take decisions, depending on the subject, by two-thirds, three-quarters or consensus. The Enterprise will be responsible for conducting the activities of the Authority.

The General Assembly decided in the 1994 Agreement relating to Part XI of the 1982 Convention to fund, for an initial interim period, the International Sea Bed Authority from the regular budget of the United Nations.[97]

The Convention also provides for the compulsory settlement of deep seabed disputes, either by judicial settlement (by reference to the International Tribunal for the Law of the Sea) or by commercial arbitration.

INTERNATIONAL TRIBUNAL FOR THE LAW OF THE SEA

The International Tribunal[98] for the Law of the Sea was established under the Convention as an independent judicial body to hear disputes relating to the interpretation and application of the

---

[94] *ibid*. Arts 1 and 3.
[95] Art.153.
[96] Arts 156–188.
[96a] The Assembly of the Authority was inaugurated by the UN Secretary General in Kingston, Jamaica on November 16, 1994 and held its first session on February 27 to March 17, 1995.
[97] Details of the funding arrangements are established in s.1 of the Annex to the 1994 Agreement (para.14) as well as in decisions of the 5th Committee of the General Assembly (A/C. 5/48/90). The long-term objective is that the Authority will fund itself once it has sufficient funds from the proceeds of mining.
[98] Art.287 in accordance with Annex VI.

Convention.[99] The Tribunal sits in Hamburg, Germany and has 21 members. Members are independent and are elected from persons who have a high reputation for fairness and integrity and have a recognised competence in the law of the sea. Each State party may nominate up to two candidates. No two members of the Tribunal may be nationals of the same state and an equitable geographical distribution is ensured. Members are elected for nine years and may be re-elected. Elections are staggered with one third of members being elected every three years. The current British nominated member of the Tribunal is David Anderson whose term of office expires on September 30, 2005. The Tribunal was granted observer status by the General Assembly of the United Nations on December 17, 1996.[1] The Tribunal's jurisdiction extends to all disputes submitted in accordance with the Convention and any other agreements which specifically confer jurisdiction on the Tribunal. Unless provided to the contrary the Tribunal's jurisdiction is mandatory in respect of the prompt release of vessels and crews[2] and provisional measures.[3] The Tribunal may in certain circumstances give an advisory opinion. The first case before the Tribunal was the *M/V Saiga case (Saint Vincent and the Grenadines v Guinea)*. A decision was given on December 4, 1997, ordering the prompt release of the tanker ('Saiga') and its crew from detention by Guinea. Judgement on the merits was given on July 1, 1999, when it was held that Guinea had violated the rights of St Vincent and the Grenadines in arresting their tanker and the Tribunal awarded compensation ($2,123,357). Ten cases have been referred to the Tribunal the most recent being that of *Ireland v The United Kingdom*. The dispute arises from the Irish allegation that the mixed oxide fuel (MOX) facility at Sellafield will have detrimental effects on the marine environment of the Irish sea.[4] An order for provisional measures was granted whereby both parties were required to co-operate, consult, exchange information and to monitor the risks involved.

The Tribunal has, under its Statute, formed the following Chambers:

- Chamber of Summary Procedure

- Chamber for Fisheries Disputes

- Chamber for Marine Environmental Disputes

---

[99] Art.288.
[1] Resolution A/RES/51/204 of December 17, 1996.
[2] Art.292.
[3] Art.290, pending the creation of an arbitral tribunal (*id* para.5).
[4] ASIL, 11 February 2002.

- • A special Chamber to deal with a case between Chile and the EC, namely the case concerning the Conservation and Sustainable Exploitation of Swordfish Stocks in the South-Eastern Pacific Ocean

Disputes relating to the activities in the International Seabed Area are brought before the Seabed Disputes Chamber of the Tribunal. Any party to a dispute within the competence of the Seabed Disputes Chamber may ask that an *ad hoc* chamber be constituted from 3 of the 11 judges who make up the Chamber. The Chamber is also competent to give advisory opinions.

The creation of the International Tribunal has attracted stern criticism, as evidenced by the paucity of states accepting the jurisdiction of the Tribunal as provided for in Art.287.[5] The jurisdiction of the Tribunal is only compulsory with regard to disputes arising over deep seabed mining under Part XI of the Convention.[6]

CONCLUSION

The impact of the Convention's entry into force has yet to be felt. The uncertain financial position of the United Nations has affected the extent of the support that it has been able to provide. Nevertheless, the Convention does create an international ocean regime marking recognition that the seas should be the "heritage of all mankind".

---

[5] The Tribunal sits in Hamburg and has 21 members, experienced in the law of the sea.
[6] See Oda J. of the ICJ, "Dispute Settlement Prospects in the Law of the Sea" (1995) 44 I.C.L.Q. 863.

8. STATE RESPONSIBILITY

State responsibility in international law refers to liability—that of one state to another for the non-observance of the obligations imposed by the international legal systems. A state may incur liability for injury to the defendant state itself. This may be, for example, for breach of a treaty obligation, or for injury to the defendant state's nationals or their property.

State responsibility is a complex issue. The International Law Commission initiated a study of state responsibility in 1949. The Commission's early efforts to produce a draft Convention proved inconclusive.[1] It was not until November 2001, at its 53rd session, that the Commission's work culminated in the adoption of the draft Articles on the Responsibility of States for Internationally Wrongful Acts.[2] These Articles "seek to formulate, by way of codification and progressive development, the basic rules of International Law concerning the responsibility of states for

---

[1] I.L.C. Drafts Arts. on State Responsibility, 1979, II Y.B.I.L.C., (Pt. II), p. 90; 1980, II Y.B.I.L.C., (Pt. II), pp. 14, 70; Arts. 1–32, 18 I.L.M. 1568 (1979); Arts. 33–35, 74 A.J.I.L. 962 (1980). Revised draft articles were adopted by the Commission in 1996 and were more detailed than the draft adopted in 1969.
[2] Adopted by the I.L.C at its fifty-third session (2001).

internationally wrongful acts".[3] The emphasis is on the secondary rules of state responsibility, that is to say, the general conditions under international law for the state to be considered responsible for wrongful actions or omissions, and legal consequences which flow there from. The Articles do not attempt to define the content of international law obligations, breach of which gives rise to responsibility. This is the function of primary rules, whose codification would involve restating most of substantive international law, customary and conventional.

The Articles are divided into four parts. Part One, the Internationally Wrongful Act of a State, which sets out the requirements to be met before international responsibility will be incurred; Part Two, Content of the International Responsibility of a State, deals primarily with the legal consequences for the responsible state for any international wrongful act; Part Three, the Implementation of the International Responsibility of a State, and Part Four deals with the general provisions applicable to the Articles as a whole.

The basic rule is spelt out in Art.1, namely "Every internationally wrongful act of a State entails the international responsibility of that State." This article is supplemented by Art.2 which provides:

"There is an internationally wrongful act of a State when conduct consisting of an action or omission:

(a) Is attributable to the State under international law; and

(b) Constitutes a breach of an international obligation of the State."

Art.3 provides that characterisation of an act of states internationally wrongful "is governed by international law". But that "Such characterization is not affected by the characterization of the same act as lawful by internal law".

Breaches of international obligations by states are dealt with in Art.12 ". . . when an act of the State is not in conformity with what is required of it by that obligation, regardless of its origin or character." However, "An act of State does not constitute a breach of an international obligation unless the State is bound by the obligation in question at the time the act occurs."[4]

However, a state will be deemed liable if implicated in the wrongful acts of another state: that is by assisting, controlling or

---

[3] International Law Commission Commentary, Official Records of the G.A., fifty-sixth session, Supplement No 10 (A/56/10 Chp.IV.E.1).
[4] Draft Art.13.

coercing the activities of the "offending" state.[5] A state cannot relieve itself of responsibility by invoking either provisions or omissions of its domestic legislation.[6] In a federal state, such as Canada or the United States, the Federal Government is responsible on the international plane and will incur international liability for any actions or omissions of its Member States which result in international injury. A federal government may not exonerate itself from responsibility by submitting that individual Member States are independent or autonomous.

Recognised defence pleas which may be utilised by a state to deny responsibility are consent, reprisal, force majeure, distress, necessity and self-defence.[7]

NATURE OF LIABILITY

A notable absence from the 2001 Draft Articles is the distinction between international delict and international crimes, which were previously identified in Draft Art.19.[8] The more generally framed Draft Art.12 is designed to define what constitutes a breach of an international obligation.

The origin of an internationally unlawful act is, as noted above, irrelevant. The origin neither affects the characterisation of the act as unlawful nor does it affect the international responsibility of the state concerned.[9] The basic principle contained in Art.1 spells out a rule of Customary International Law; this rule was acknowledged in the *Chorzow Factory Case (Indemnity) (Merits)*,[10] when the Court maintained that ". . . any breach of an engagement involves an obligation to make reparation."[11] See also Draft Art.31 and below.

Is state responsibility absolute or must there be fault? In other words, is liability strict or must there be a degree of blameworthiness which can be attributed to the state? Must there be intention or negligence?

The customary international law rule on these questions is not clear. While evidence in the form of arbitral and judicial decisions can be found in support of both standpoints, conclusive evidence in support of either theory is absent. Fault liability appears to

---

[5] Draft Arts 16 and 17.

[6] *Free Zones of Upper Savoy and the District of Gex* P.C.I.J.Rep., ser.A/B. No.46 at 167 (1932) Art.3.

[7] See Arts 20–25; please also note A26, regarding the requirement to comply with peremptory norms.

[8] I.L.C. Draft Arts on State Responsibility, 1979, II Y.B.I.L.C. (Pt II).

[9] See draft Art.12, above.

[10] P.C.I.J.Rep., ser.A, No.17 (1928).

[11] *ibid*. at 29.

have received support in the *Home Missionary Society Claim*[12] and the *Corfu Channel Case (Merits)*,[13] while the Claims Commission in the *Caire Claim*[14] supported absolute liability. State practice throws little light on the issue which is, anyway, essentially theoretical and one of largely academic interest. The proliferation of state organs and agencies has seen an increased application of strict liability. Fault liability has, because of the extension of state activities, become too complicated to apply in practice. However, note that Draft Art.39 states that, "In the determination of reparation, account shall be taken of the contribution to the injury by wilful or negligent action or omission of the injured State or any person or entity in relation to whom reparation is sought." In the LaGrand case, the ICJ recognised that the conduct of the claimant state could be pertinent in determining the extent of reparation due.[15]

Imputability

"Imputability" in the context of state responsibility means "attributable" and is dealt with in Ch.II of the Draft Articles, where:

> "Article 4 states the basic rule attributing to the State the conduct of its origins. Article 5 deals with conduct of entities empowered to exercise the governmental authority of a State, and article 6 deals with the special case where an organ of one State is placed at the disposal of another State and empowered to exercise the governmental authority of that State. Article 7 makes it clear that the conduct of organs or entities empowered to exercise governmental authority is attributable to the State even if it was carried out outside the authority of the organ or person concerned or contrary to instructions. Articles 8–11 then deal with certain additional cases where conduct, not that of a State organ or entity, is nonetheless attributed to the State in international law. Article 8 deals with conduct carried out on the instructions of a State organ or under its direction or control. Article 9 deals with certain conduct involving elements of governmental authority, carried out in the absence of the official authorities. Article 10 concerns the special case of responsibility in defined circumstances for the conduct of insurrectional movements. Article 11 deals with conduct not attributable to

---

[12] 6 R.I.A.A. 42 (1920).
[13] I.C.J.Rep. 1949 at 4.
[14] 5 R.I.A.A. 516 (1929).
[15] LaGrand Case (*Germany v United States*) 40 I.L.M. 1069 (2001).

the State under one of the earlier articles which is nonetheless adopted by the State, expressly or by conduct, as its
own."[16]

A state is only responsible for acts or omissions which can be attributed to it as its own. What, for the purposes of state responsibility,
constitutes the state?

In international law, a state is thus responsible for the actions of:

(a) the government;

(b) any political sub-division of the state;

(c) any organ, agency official employee or other agent of its
     government or of any sub-division acting within the
     scope of their employment.

Imputability is a legal fiction assimilating the acts of those identified above to the state as if they were its own.

A state is not responsible for acts committed by one of its
nationals (provided, that is, he is a private individual and is not,
for example, a policeman) against a foreigner. The individual
may, of course, be liable to prosecution in the domestic courts and
indeed the government concerned may be held internationally
liable if it fails to discharge its duty "of diligently prosecuting and
properly punishing".[17] Acts of private persons performed on their
own initiative in an emergency, for example a natural disaster, are
attributable to the state.[18] An individual can, however, now be
held responsible for certain crimes under international law. Both
ICTY and ICTR, for example, have jurisdiction to prosecute
individuals responsible for grave breaches of the Genocide
Convention, laws of war and crimes against humanity.[19]

A state cannot deny responsibility for an international wrong
on the grounds that the act is, under its domestic law, *ultra vires*.
A state can be held liable for the conduct of an official, even when
official competence has been exceeded, provided that is, the officials acted with apparent authority as competent officials or
organs and the powers or methods used were appropriate to this
official authority.[20] For example, in *Southern Pacific Properties*

[16] *International Law Commission Commentary*, p.83. See also the judgment in the
    Nicaragua case (*Nicaragua v The United States*) *Case* (*Merits*) I.C.J. Rep. 1986.
[17] *Noyes Claim* 6 R.I.A.A. 308 at 311 (1933); see also the *Zafiro Case* 6 R.I.A.A. 160
    (1925).
[18] Draft Art.8(b).
[19] Art.20 of the Tribunals' Statute. (See further Chs 4 and 9).
[20] Draft Art.7; *Caire Claim*, above n.17.

(Middle East) Ltd v Arab Republic of Egypt (1993), the International Centre for Settlement of Investment Disputes rejected the argument submitted by Egypt that it could not be held responsible for the acts of certain high-ranking officials as they had not followed the correct procedures required under Egyptian law.[21] The Tribunal stated that:

> "the principle of international law which the Tribunal is bound to apply is that which establishes the international responsibility of States when unauthorized or *ultra vires* acts of officials have been performed by State agents under cover of their official character. If such unauthorized or *ultra vires* acts could not be ascribed to the State, all State responsibility would be rendered illusory."[22]

In the *Youmans Claim*,[23] Mexico was held liable for the conduct of certain members of its militia who acted in defiance of orders and, instead of affording protection to a group of Americans, opened fire on the house where the latter were seeking refuge. The United States–Mexican General Claims Commission maintained that the Mexican Government was liable for the soldiers' unlawful acts, even though the soldiers had exceeded their powers.

A state is responsible for the acts of all its officials irrespective of their rank[24] and, as is illustrated by the *Rainbow Warrior Case*,[25] a state is responsible for the acts of its security services. A state is not held liable for the activities of insurrectionaries,[26] but, should the insurrectionaries be successful in their objective and become the subsequent government, they (as the legitimate government) will be held liable for any wrongful act committed during their struggle for power.[27] A state will only be held responsible for actions, which it is bound by, as previously stated in Draft Art.13, thus dealing with the question of intertemporal law regarding state responsibility. Ch.IV defines exceptional cases in Art.17, ". . . where one State is responsible for the internationally wrongful act of another State . . .".[28] The legal consequences of an internationally wrongful

---

[21] 32 I.L.M. 933.
[22] See Art.20 of the International Criminal Tribunal for the former Yugoslavia and the International Criminal Tribunal for Rwanda. (See, further Chs 4 and 9), and Art.30 of the Statute of the International Criminal Court.
[23] Draft Art.7; *Caire Claim*, above, n.12.
[24] *Massey Case (U.S. v Mexico)*, 4 R.I.A.A. 155 at 157 (1927).
[25] 26 I.L.M. 1346 (1987).
[26] *Sambaggio Case (Italy v Venezuela)*, 10 R.I.A.A. 499 at 513 (1903).
[27] Draft Art.10. See *Short v Iran* (1987) 16 Iran-USCTR 76; *cf. Yeager v. Iran* 17 Iran-USCTR 92.
[28] *International Law Commission Commentary*, p.152.

act are primarily twofold, namely the responsible state should cease from the wrongful conduct and secondly to make full reparation for the injury as stated in Draft Arts 30 and 31. One should also note that Draft Art.41 provides that states are charged with co-operating to ". . . bring to an end through lawful means any serious breach within the meaning of Article 40."[29] Furthermore, "No state shall recognize as lawful a situation created by a serious breach within the meaning of Article 40, nor render aid or assistance in maintaining that situation."[30]

Erga omnes

Whilst the foregoing is concerned with the obligation owed by one state to another, contemporary international law also recognises the concept of *erga omnes*—that is, obligations owed by every state to the international community as a whole. These obligations were identified by the International Court of Justice in the *Barcelona Traction Case*[31] as deriving from "the outlawing of acts of aggression, and of genocide . . ." and from "rules concerning the basic rights of the human person, including protection from slavery and racial discrimination."[32] Thus, by their nature, such obligations are the concern of all states and, because of the importance of the rights involved, all states have a legal interest in their protection. This decision prompted the International Law Commission to include Draft Art.19, which distinguished between civil and criminal liability, but as noted previously this distinction has been omitted in the 2001 Draft Articles. What the Draft Articles do recognise, discussed in the Commentary, is that there are:

". . . certain consequences flowing from the basic concepts of peremptory norms of general international law and obligations to the international community as a whole within the field of State responsibility. Whether or not peremptory norms of general international law and obligations to the international community as a whole are aspects of a single basic idea, there is at the very least substantial overlap between them . . . . While peremptory norms of general international law focus on the scope and priority to be given to a certain number of fundamental obligations, the focus of obligations to the international community as a whole is

---

[29] Draft Art.41(1).
[30] Draft Art.41(2).
[31] I.C.J.Rep.1970 at 3.
[32] *ibid.* at 32.

essentially on the legal interest of all States in compliance—
i.e., in terms of the present Articles, in being entitled to
invoke the responsibility of any State in breach. Consistently
with the difference in their focus, it is appropriate to reflect
the consequences of the two concepts in two distinct ways.
First, serious breaches of obligations arising under peremptory norms of general international law can attract additional
consequences, not only for the responsible State but for all
other States. Secondly, all States are entitled to invoke
responsibility for breaches of obligations to the international
community as a whole."[33]

The second of these topics are dealt with in Draft Article 48.

Reparation

Diplomatic negotiation may produce an apology or an assurance
that the offending breach of international law will not recur. If,
however, material loss has been sustained by a state or one of
its nationals, the question of reparation frequently has to be
determined.

The object of reparation should be to wipe out, as far as possible, "all the consequences of the illegal act and re-establish the situation which would in all probability have existed if the act had
not been committed."[34] Reparation is designed to restore previous conditions and, if this is not possible, to compensate for the
injury itself.

Reparation may be awarded through restitution in kind and, if
restitution is not possible, through:

> "payment of a sum corresponding to the value which a resti-
> tution in kind would bear; the award, if need be, of damages
> for loss sustained which would not be covered by restitution
> in kind or payment in place of it—such are the principles
> which should serve to determine the amount of compensation
> due for an act contrary to international law."[35]

Restitution in kind is infrequent.[36] More frequently, monetary
compensation is awarded to cover the cost of the injury suffered.

---

[33] *International Law Commission Commentary*, pp.281–282.
[34] *Chorzow Factory Case (Indemnity) (Merits)* P.C.I.J.Rep., ser.A, No.17 (1928) at 47.
[35] *ibid.*
[36] Restitution in kind was ordered in the *Martini Case (Italy v Venezuela)* 2 R.I.A.A.
975, 1002 (1930) and in the *Temple Case*, I.C.J.Rep.1962 at 6—restitution is dealt
with in Draft Art.35.

In the *Chorzow Factory Case* (*Indemnity*),[37] the Permanent Court of International Justice held that the rules of law governing reparation should be:

> "the rules of international law in force between the two States concerned, and not the law governing relations between the State which has committed a wrongful act and the individual who has suffered damage. Rights or interests of an individual the violation of which rights causes damage are always in a different plane to rights belonging to a State, which rights may also be infringed by the same act. The damage suffered by an individual is never therefore identical in kind with that which will be suffered by a State; it can only afford a convenient scale for the calculation of the reparation due to the State."[38]

Compensation is normally a matter of negotiation. There are no established principles for calculating the sum to be paid. In respect of material loss, the sum awarded is generally commensurate with the loss sustained and will take account of "loss of profits . . . as compared with other owners of similar property.[39]

Damages have been awarded for non-material loss, but international tribunals have been reluctant to grant exemplary or punitive damages:

> ". . . Counsel has failed to point us to any money award by an international arbitral tribunal where exemplary, punitive, or vindictive damages have been assessed against one sovereign nation in favour of another presenting a claim on behalf of its nationals."[40]

In the *Lusitania Case*, the United States–Germany Mixed Claims Commission refused to award punitive damages. The Commission did not impose a penalty and only awarded reparation in respect of the injury suffered. However, in the *I'm Alone Case*,[41] $25,000 was awarded against the United States as a "material amend in respect of the wrong suffered by Canada".

A state will be liable to another state if it, *inter alia*, breaches a treaty obligation, violates its territorial integrity, injures its

[37] Above, n.32. See also Draft Art.31 above, and for various forms of reparation. See Draft Art.34 and Draft Art.37 for reparation in the form of an apology.

[38] *ibid.* at 28.

[39] *Norwegian Shipowners Claim* (*Norway v U.S.*) 1 R.I.A.A. 307 at 338 (1922).

[40] *Lusitania Case* (*United States v Germany*) 7 R.I.A.A. 32 at 38–44 (1956), Parker J.

[41] (*Canada v United States*) 3 R.I.A.A. 1609 (1933/35); 29 A.J.I.L. 326 (1935).

diplomatic representatives or mistreats one of its nationals or causes injury to the property of one of its nationals.

It is in the context of the treatment of aliens and aliens' property that the issue of state responsibility will be examined.

TREATMENT OF ALIENS—THE TREATMENT OF NATIONALS OF OTHER STATES

If an individual allegedly sustains injury while in another state, redress may only be sought through the individual's state of nationality. (See nationality of claims rule below.) An individual cannot force a state to espouse a claim on his behalf. It is a matter of state discretion whether a claim is taken up and if a state does pursue a claim on behalf of an individual, it is not required to hand over any damages which may be received.[42] Nor can an individual prevent a state from exercising its rights of diplomatic protection if it (the state) feels its right to have its nationals treated properly has been violated:

> ". . . an alien . . . cannot deprive the government of his nation of its undoubted right of applying international remedies to violations of international law committed to his damage. Such government frequently has a larger interest in maintaining the principles of international law than in recovering damage for one of its citizens in a particular case, and manifestly such citizen cannot by contract in this respect, tie the hands of his Government."[43]

In other words, in espousing a claim on behalf of an individual, a state is protecting one of its own rights, which must be respected, namely that its nationals be treated in a particular manner. Once a state has taken up a claim on behalf of an individual, it enjoys exclusive control over the handling and presentation of a claim[44] and the claim becomes one between two states:

> "it is true that the dispute was at first between a private person and a State . . . Subsequently, the Greek Government took up the case. The dispute then entered upon a new plane; it entered the domain of International Law, and became a dispute between two States . . . Once a State has taken up a case on behalf of one of its subjects before an international tribunal in the eyes of the latter the State is the sole claimant."[45]

---

[42] *Civilian War Claimants Association v The King* [1932] A.C. 14.
[43] *North American Dredging Co. Case (U.S./Mexican)* 4 R.I.A.A. 26 at 29 (1926).
[44] See *e.g. Administrative Decision No. V (U.S. v Germany)* 7 R.I.A.A. 119 (1924).
[45] *Mavrommatis Palestine Concessions Case*, P.C.I.J.Rep., ser.A, No.2 (1924) at 12.

Standard of treatment

A state is not required to admit foreign nationals. Immigration control is a matter of national law. Once aliens are admitted, however, if a state should then fail to treat foreign nationals in a required way, it may be held guilty of having breached an international obligation. This was indorsed by the General Assembly in 1985, in the Declaration on the Human Rights of Individuals who are not Nationals of the Country in which they Live,[46] which articulates the fundamental human rights to be observed by the host state. Aliens are assured of certain rights, such as the right of equality within the judicial process and protection from torture, cruel or inhuman treatment. Aliens are, of course, required to observe the laws of the host state and to do so with respect for the customs and traditions of that country.

By what standard is the treatment to be gauged? There are two views, one representing that of developing "new" states and the other representing that of developed states.

The national treatment standard

Originally supported by the Latin American countries during the nineteenth and early-twentieth centuries, this view is favoured today by eastern European socialist states and some developing states. According to the national treatment standard, aliens are to be treated in the same way as nationals of the state concerned. Obviously, if applied consistently, this would be to the advantage of aliens. However, international law does not regulate a state's treatment of aliens in all activities, for example aliens in the United Kingdom may not vote nor may they be admitted to public office.

The disadvantage of the national treatment standard is obvious. A state could subject an alien to inhuman treatment and justify such treatment on the grounds that nationals could be similarly treated. Thus, international arbitration tribunals and developed western states have denied that a state can exonerate itself by pleading that nationals are treated likewise, if the treatment of aliens falls short of the international minimum standard.[47]

International minimum standard

The international minimum standard is difficult to define. International law has not provided a definition, although an attempt to do so was made in 1957 when the International Law Commission debated the Second Report on State Responsibility

---

[46] GA Res. 144 (XL), G.A.O.R., 49th Sess., Supp.53, p.253.
[47] *Roberts Claim* 4 R.I.A.A. 77 (1926).

of its Special Rapporteur.[48] In the Report, an Article which embraced both the national minimum standard and the international minimum standard was proposed. States were to afford to aliens the same treatment as that enjoyed by nationals, but in no circumstances was such treatment "to be less than the 'fundamental human rights' recognised and defined in the contemporary international instruments". However, the proposal was too far-reaching and, since then, the International Law Commission has concentrated its attention on the codification of general principles of responsibility.

To violate the international minimum standard, a state's treatment of foreign nationals must fall so short of established civilised behaviour "that every reasonable and impartial man would readily recognise its insufficiency".[49]

A state may incur responsibility if an alien is physically ill-treated,[50] or if an alien's property is damaged.[51] A state may also incur responsibility if an alien suffers a maladministration of justice, for example is denied assistance of counsel,[52] or denied adequate protection. Liability will only be incurred if the lack of protection has been either wilful or due to neglect.[53]

States are required to afford a higher degree of protection to internationally protected persons[54] than to "ordinary" aliens.

Although international law is against the arbitrary and unjustified expulsion of aliens,[55] states do enjoy a discretion to deport aliens if the presence of such aliens is a threat to the public interest. Art.12 of the EC Treaty[56] prohibits discrimination between the nationals of Member States on the grounds of nationality and Arts 48–51 of the Treaty provide for the free movement of workers. Member States can deny the exercise of that right on the grounds of public health, public security and public order. However, when deported, the individuals concerned should be

---

[48] Y.B.I.L.C., 1957, II, p.104.

[49] *Neer Claim* 4 R.I.A.A. 60 at 62 (1926).

[50] *Roberts Claim*, above, n.45; *Quintanilla Claim (Mexico v U.S.)* 4 R.I.A.A. 101 (1926).

[51] *Zafiro Case*, above, n.18 Art.9, Harvard Draft Convention on the International Responsibility of States for Injuries to Aliens 1961, 55 A.J.I.L. 548 (1961).

[52] *Pope Case*, 8 Whiteman 709.

[53] *Noyes Claim (U.S. v Panama)*, above, n.18; *Janes Claim (U.S. v Mexico)* 4 R.I.A.A. 82 (1926).

[54] See the Convention on the Prevention and Punishment of Crimes Against Internationally Protected Persons including Diplomatic Agents 1973, 13 I.L.M. 42 (1974); Misc.19 (1975) Cmnd.6176.

[55] See Art.3. 1955 European Convention on Establishment, 529 U.N.T.S. 141; U.K.T.S. 1 (1971) Cmnd.4573; Fourth Protocol of the European Convention of Human Rights 1963, Misc.6 (1964) Cmnd.2309; 58 A.J.I.L. 334 (1964).

[56] As amended by the Treaty of Nice.

advised of the reasons for their deportation, save where to do so would be contrary to national security.[57]

Nationals

If nationals of a state are expelled from another state, the state of nationality is obliged to receive them, unless they are willing to go to another state and that state is willing to admit them. It was in acknowledgment of this obligation imposed by international law that the United Kingdom, in 1972, admitted all East African Asians who were not Ugandan nationals.

Refugees

International law does not require states to admit asylum seekers,[58] but, under the 1951 Convention Relating to the Status of Refugees[59] and the 1967 Protocol Relating to the Status of Refugees,[60] Contracting Parties undertake to accord refugees treatment no less favourable than that accorded to aliens generally and no individual may be expelled to territory "where his life or freedom would be questioned".[61] To fall within the ambit of the refugee Convention, the individual must show a well founded fear of persecution because of race, religion, nationality, member of a particular social group or political opinion and is outside the country of nationality and is unable or unwilling to invoke the protection of that country.[62] The office of the United Nations High Commissioner for Refugees (UNHCR) was created in December 1950 and has responsibility for providing international protection to refugees and also to finding longer-term solutions to the displacement of refugees.[63] Of particular contemporary concern to UNHCR is the displacement of civilians in their own country of

---

[57] Regulation No.72/194 EEC Council Directive of May 18, 1972, [1972] O.J. L121/32 (May 26, 1972).

[58] It was significant that Article 14 of the United Nations Declaration of Human Rights was omitted from further international instruments.

[59] 189 U.N.T.S. 150; 39 (1954) Cmd.9171.

[60] 606 U.N.T.S. 267; U.K.T.S. 15 (1969) Cmnd. 3906; 6 I.L.M. 78 (1967); 63 A.J.I.L. 385 (1969). Currently two-thirds of the international community have ratified either or both the Convention and the Protocol.

[61] See Statute of the Office of the United Nations High Commissioner for Refugees, GA Res 5/428, annex, G.A.O.R. 5th Sess., Supp.20 p.46, UN Doc A/1775 (1950) adopted December 1950. The office came into existence on January 1, 1951.

[62] Art.1A(2) of the Convention Relating to the Status of Refugees 1951.

[63] See 87 A.J.I.L. 157 (1993). The Cairo Declaration was adopted by consensus at the I.L.A. Conference in Cairo, April 20–26, 1992. There have been eight High Commissioners and the position is currently held by Prof. Dr Ruud Lubbers, a Dutch national who assumed office in 2001.

origin. It is estimated there are some 26 million internally displaced persons in the world today. However, there are no specific international instruments to cover them, but the United Nations has produced a booklet called *Guiding principles on internally displacement*. This contains 30 pointers for governments. Although it is not legally binding, the UNHCR notes that it is increasingly accepted by states.

The 1993 Vienna Declaration reaffirmed the right of an individual to seek asylum from persecution in other countries and the right to be able to return home.[64] The granting of refugee status is a matter of individual states subject to Art.33(1). The 1951 Convention was introduced to deal with a specific problem arising in Europe in the wake of the Second World War; regional organisations have promulgated the refinements of the 1951 definition, for example as by the Organisation of American States,[64a] the Organisation of African Unity[64b] and the European Union adopted a Joint Position on March 4, 1996, relating to the implementation of the Convention criteria for refugee status, subsequent developments include a common asylum procedure and a uniform status, valid throughout the union for persons granted asylum.[64c] International Refugee Law is not static and continues to evolve and address issues such as gender-related persecution, unaccompanied minors, the scope and meaning of "particular social group".[64d]

Expropriation of the property of aliens

Expropriation is the compulsory taking of private property by the state. Initially the definition of property was said to include "all moveable and immovable property, whether tangible or intangible, including industrial, literary and artistic property, as well as rights and interests in any property"[65] but not, however, rights derived from contracts. Nevertheless, the jurisprudence of the United States–Iran Claims Tribunal has apparently extended the definition to include contractual rights.[66]

---

[64] Above, n.60, Art.32(1). Art.32(1) will not apply if the "individual is reasonably suspected of being a security risk or having been finally convicted of a particular serious crime, constitutes a danger to the Community"—Art.33(2).

[64a] Definition of Refugee Status (Cartagena Declaration) OAS/SER.I/ V/II.66, doc.10, rev.1, pp.190–193, adopted by 10 Latin American states in 1986.

[64b] (OAU) Convention Governing the Specific Aspects of Refugee Problems in Africa, UNTS.14, 691 entered into force June 20, 1974.

[64c] Communication for the Commission to the Council and the European Parliament COM (2002) 755 Final.

[64d] Further examination of these topics is out with the scope of this text.

[65] Art.10(7), 1961 Harvard Draft Convention, above, n.49.

[66] See *e.g. Starrett Housing Corp. v Iran (Interlocutory Award)* 4 Iran-USCTR 122; 23 I.L.M. 1090 (1984); *Amoco International Finance Corp. v Iran* 15 Iran-USCTR 189; 82 A.J.I.L. 358 (1986).

Expropriation extends beyond the actual physical taking of property to include any action which unreasonably interferes with "the use, enjoyment or disposal of property . . .".[67] The application of taxation and regulatory measures designed specifically to deny the effective use of private property may be referred to as "creeping", "constructive" or indirect expropriation.[68]

Expropriation, particularly in the *post*-colonial period, became an important issue in international law. Possibly more than any other issue, expropriation has highlighted the opposing views of the capitalist developed countries, the socialist states and the "new" developing states. Capitalist developed countries seek a guarantee of protection and security before investing abroad, whilst the latter (that is, socialist and developing states) are reluctant to allow too much foreign investment and wish to retain control over their own resources. Both developed and developing states recognise that every state has a legitimate right to expropriate property, but, while the developed states of the western tradition maintain that expropriation is only legitimate if it complies with an international minimum standard and if, in particular, it is accompanied by effective compensation, the developing "new" states deny this.

The position of the capitalist developed states is represented in General Assembly Resolution 1803 on Permanent Sovereignty over Natural Resources.[69] The Resolution recognises the right of peoples and nations "to permanent sovereignty over their natural wealth and resources . . ."[70]

Art.4 of the Resolution, which is regarded as reinforcing customary international law, provides that:

> "[N]ationalisation, expropriation or requisitioning shall be based on grounds or reasons of public utility, security or the national interest which are recognised as overriding purely individual or private interests, both domestic and foreign. In such cases the owner shall be paid appropriate compensation in accordance with the rules in force in the State taking such measures and in accordance with international law."

In other words, expropriation, in order to be valid, should be for public purposes, should not be discriminatory (not specified but implied in Art.4) and should be accompanied by compensation

[67] Art.10(3)(a), 1961 Harvard Draft Convention, above, n.49.
[68] See the *Starrett Case*, above, n.63.
[69] (1962) G.A.O.R., 17th Session, Supp.17, p.15.
[70] Art.1.

assessed in accordance with the rules in force in the appropriate state *and* international law.

Public purpose

The requirement that nationalisation should be for a public purpose for it to be valid under international law was identified in the *Certain German Interests in Polish Upper Silesia Case*[71] and more recently in *Amoco International Financial Corp. v Iran*.[72] The concept of a "public purpose" whereby expropriation is lawful remains undefined and consequently states enjoy considerable discretion in its application. In the *BP Case* of 1974,[73] the British challenged Libyan nationalisation measures on the grounds, *inter alia*, that they were not motivated by considerations of a political nature related to the international well-being of the taking state. In that case, the arbitrator confirmed that the measures in question violated international law as they were made for purely extraneous political reasons.[74] However, three years later in the *Liamco Case*,[75] the arbitrator dismissed the independent public purpose requirement, on the grounds that "it is the general opinion in international law that the public utility principle is not a necessary requisite for the legality of a nationalisation."[76] In practice, public purpose has not been predominant in international claims and where it has featured, it has been of secondary importance. Public purpose is a broad concept which is not readily susceptible to objective examination by states.

Discrimination

Nationalisation[77] which discriminates against foreigners, or foreigners of a particular nationality, or particular foreigners, has been regarded by developed states as being contrary to international law.[78] Discrimination is difficult to prove. There may, for example, be no comparable enterprises owned either by local nationals of other countries. Like public purpose, arguments inferring discrimination have not predominated when expropriation has been challenged and, in the *Amoco Case*,[79] although

[71] P.C.I.J.Rep., ser.A, No.7, (1929), p.22.
[72] above, n.63.
[73] 53 I.L.R. 297 (1974).
[74] *ibid.* at 329.
[75] 20 I.L.M. 1 (1981).
[76] *ibid.* 58–59.
[77] Nationalisation is used synonymously with expropriation and requisitioning.
[78] See UK's objections in the *Anglo–Iranian Oil Co. Case* I.J.C.Rep. (Pleadings) 1951 at 81; also in the *BP Case*, above, n.70; US's argument in the *Liamco Case*, above, n.72, also arbitrator's findings in that case.
[79] Above, n.63.

acknowledged as being prohibited, an element of discrimination may be tolerated in certain circumstances, for example, being reasonably related to the public purpose.[80]

Compensation

What has been decisive has been whether or not compensation has been paid and whether, if paid, it complies with the standard prescribed by international law. To comply with international law as represented by western developed states, compensation must be "prompt, adequate and effective".[81] These terms have been used in many bilateral commercial treaties. The expression "appropriate compensation" was adopted in Resolution 1803 and has been subsequently endorsed as reflecting the standard demanded under customary international law in the *Texaco Case*[82] and the *Aminoil Case*.[83] "Appropriate compensation" is, according to the Tribunal in the latter case, to be assessed in the light of the circumstances peculiar to the particular case. Compensation has traditionally been considered as involving payment equivalent to the full value of the property taken, possibly with a margin allowed for future loss of profits. Payment should be made in a readily convertible currency (that is, the recipient should be in a position to use and benefit from the compensation) either before or at the time of the takeover. Deferred payment will only be allowed if the amount to be paid is fixed promptly and provision is made for the payment of interest.

This traditional approach has been challenged and, to some extent, rejected by developing countries. The position of these states is reflected particularly in Art.2(c) of the 1974 Charter of Economic Rights and Duties of States,[84] which provides that "appropriate compensation should be paid by the state adopting such measures, taking into account its relevant laws and all circumstances, that the state considers pertinent." Art.2(c) further provides that in the event of a dispute arising over compensation it should be decided, unless otherwise mutually agreed, by the

[80] *ibid.* at para. 145.
[81] See *e.g.* Statement of US Secretary of State, Hull, in letter to Mexican Government, Harris, p.568 and *Anglo–Iranian Oil Co. Case*, above, n.75 at 105.
[82] 53 I.L.R. 389 (1977); 17 I.L.M. 1 (1978).
[83] *Kuwait v American Independent Oil Co.* 21 I.L.M. 976 (1982). More recently, in *Southern Pacific Properties (Middle East) Ltd v Arab Republic of Egypt* 32 I.L.M. 933 (1993), the International Centre for Settlement of Disputes held that "fair" compensation was the standard that should be applied when assessing compensation in a lawful expropriation.
[84] GA Res. 3281 (XXIV) 14 I.L.M. 251 (1975); see also GA Res. 3171 (XXVIII) 1973, 68 A.J.I.L. 381 (1974); GA Res. 3201 (S-VI) Declaration on the Establishment of a New International Economic Order 1974, 13 I.L.M. 765 (1974).

domestic law of the nationalising state. However, note that the 1974 Charter has, as yet, been denied the status of current international law[85] and recent trends demonstrate a tendency to adopt a middle of the road stance.

In the *Amco Indonesia Case*,[86] it was stated that compensation should be awarded for the loss suffered (*damnum emergens*) and expected profits (*lucrum cessans*). It is important to distinguish between expropriation which is lawful and unlawful. The distinction was highlighted in the *Amoco Case* as being necessary "since the rules applicable to the compensation to be paid by the expropriating state differ according to the legal characterisation of the taking".[87] In accordance with the established rules of state responsibility, unlawful expropriation should merit full restitution in kind or, alternatively, the equivalent pecuniary value and, in some instances, a payment for loss or an expected loss of profits. On the other hand, lawful expropriation would only warrant compensation reflecting the value of the property taken at the time of takeover. However, a by-product of the collapse of the former communist powers has been to remove considerable ideological opposition to the payment of compensation.[87a]

"Creeping expropriation"

The increasing uncertainty regarding the customary international laws of expropriation has prompted bilateral treaties between developed and developing states guaranteeing, for example, provision of compensation in the event of expropriation. The United States and other developed western capital-exporting countries also operate insurance schemes for nationals engaged in foreign investment.

Settlement of disputes

Frequently, disputes will be resolved by a compromise settlement, whether settlement is by straightforward negotiation between the parties or by a lump-sum settlement. Lump-sum settlements have found increasing favour during the last 40 years, for example United Kingdom–U.S.S.R. Agreement on the Settlement of Mutual Financial and Property Claims. Under lump-sum settlements, the expropriating state agrees to pay the investor state a lump sum in respect of all subsisting claims by nationals of the investor state. The investor state is

---

[85] See Arbitrator's finding in the *Texaco Case*, above, n.79.

[86] *Amco Asia Corporation v The Republic of Indonesia* 24 I.L.M. 1022 (1985).

[87] *Amoco International Finance Corp. v Iran*, above, n.63 at 246.

[87a] See O'Brien, p.385.

then responsible, normally via a national claims commission (for example, in the United Kingdom the Foreign Compensation Commission and in the United States the Foreign Claims Settlement Commission of the United States), for adjudicating upon and settling, in accordance with international law, individual claims.

In 1981, an international tribunal was established at The Hague to settle the claims of US nationals against Iran and the claims of Iranian nationals against the United States.[88]

In August 1991, the United Nations established a compensation fund to settle war claims against Iraq arising from the hostilities in the Gulf. The UN Claims Commission gave its first decision in 1996.[89]

In 1965, the Convention on the Settlement of Investment Disputes between States and Nationals of Other States[90] established the International Centre for the Settlement of Investment Disputes in Washington, DC. The Convention, through the Centre, provides, for parties who agree, procedures for the settlement of disputes between contracting parties and companies of the nationality of a contracting party. The procedures established by way of the International Centre for the Settlement of Investments Disputes (ICSID) have been endorsed by states as an appropriate mechanism for the settlement of investment disputes. This is reflected in the provisions of an increasing number of Bilateral Investment Agreements (BIAs).

Breach of contract

Contracts between a state and an alien as a rule are governed by the national law of the former and consequently seldom involve international law. A state will only, therefore, incur liability if it denies the foreigner concerned access to an effective domestic forum for adjudication of the alleged dispute.

A contract between a state and an alien, however, can be "internationalised". A contract may be "internationalised" if a state legislates to abolish or repudiate its contractual obligations. The state can by its unilateral action, place itself on a different level than the

---

[88] The Tribunal was set up under the Claims Settlement Declaration made on January 19, 1981 by the Governments of Iran and the US—see 20 I.L.M. 230 (1981).

[89] 30 I.L.M. 846 (1996), see also p.292. As regards the UN compensation fund regarding Iraq: on December 10, 1999, the Council of the Compensation Fund approved compensation claims totalling just under $2 billion. It observed that total compensation awarded so far had been $414.6 billion, out of which $4.5 had been paid.

[90] U.K.T.S. 25 (1967) Cmnd.3255; 575 U.N.T.S. 159; 4 I.L.M. 532 (1965).

other party to the contract. In the *Norwegian Loans Case*,[91] such was the alleged effect of Norwegian legislation on the contract between Norway and French bondholders.[92] Others maintain that the insertion of a clause that a concession agreement is to be governed not by the law of the state party to the agreement, but, for example by "general principles of the law of nations" or "principles of the law of the concessionary state not inconsistent with international law", removes the contract from the municipal plane and "internationalises" it. One view, for example, is that such a clause transforms the agreement into an international agreement and breaches of contract into breaches of international law.[93] Developing states in particular refute such arguments and do not accept such clauses as valid, as they deny a state its sovereign right to control its natural resources. Accordingly, the norm is that a contract between a state and a foreigner will be governed by the domestic law of the state concerned.

The "Calvo" Clause

The "Calvo" Clause, which was named after its originator, an Argentinian jurist and statesman, was frequently included in agreements between Latin American states and foreigners. Under the Calvo Clause, foreigners accepted in advance that, in the event of a dispute, they would not attempt to invoke the assistance of their national state. The Calvo Clause purported to deny a state its right to exercise diplomatic protection on behalf of one of its nationals. The validity of the Calvo Clause has been refuted by international tribunals, which have maintained that an individual is not competent to fetter his/her state in such a way and that the right of diplomatic protection and of its exercise belong exclusively to the state of nationality.[94] The requirements to exhaust local remedies still exist.[94a]

Nationality of claims rule

Nationality is important in the context of state responsibility. A state may only espouse a claim against another state on behalf of one of its nationals. International law lays down no definition of nationality, as the granting of nationality is exclusively a matter

---

[91] I.C.J.Rep. 1957 9.
[92] The Court did not decide on the merits of the case, but individual judges considered the internationalisation of the contract; Read J. at 87–88; Lauterpacht J. at 38.
[93] See *e.g.* Arbitrator in *Texaco Case*, above, n.79.
[94] *North American Dredging Co. Claim* (1926), above, n.41 at 29.
[94a]See below, p.198.

of domestic law.[95] A state is free to determine for itself who are to be deemed its nationals.[96] In spite of this *prima facie* unfettered discretion, a state may have its grant of nationality challenged when it attempts to raise a claim against another state. A state's right to afford diplomatic protection may be challenged on the grounds that the link between it and its alleged national is only tenuous and not genuine. In the absence of such a link, a claimant state will be prohibited from proceeding with an international claim. The need for there to be an obvious genuine link between the claimant state and the individual concerned was emphasised in the *Nottebohm Case*. In that case, Liechtenstein attempted to exercise diplomatic protection, on behalf of Nottebohm, against Guatemala. Nottebohm had become a naturalised Liechtenstein citizen after only a few weeks' residence in that state and Guatemala challenged Liechtenstein's right to espouse a claim on his behalf. The International Court maintained:

"... a State cannot claim that the rules it has thus laid down are entitled to recognition by another State unless it has acted in conformity with this general aim of making the legal bond of nationality accord with the individual's genuine connection with the State ..."[97]

The Court characterised nationality as:

"a legal bond having as its basis a social fact of attachment, a genuine connection of existence, interests and sentiments, together with the existence of reciprocal rights and duties. It may be said to constitute the juridical expression of the fact that the individual upon whom it is conferred, either directly by the law or as the result of an act of the authorities, is in fact more closely connected with the population of the State conferring nationality than with that of any other State."[98]

From the *Nottebohm Case*, it emerges that, not only must an individual possess the claimant state's nationality, but that the nationality must be effective. The *Nottebohm* judgment extended the concept of "genuine connection", which previously had been

---

[95] Nationality may be acquired in a variety of ways but the two most common ways of attaining nationality are (i) by descent from parents (*jus sanguinis*), or (ii) by birth in the territory of the state (*jus soli*).
[96] Art.1 of the 1930 Hague Convention on Certain Questions Relating to the Conflict of Nationality Laws, 179 L.N.T.S. 89; U.K.T.S. 33 (1937) Cmd.5553.
[97] *Nottebohm Case (Second Phase)*, I.C.J.Rep.1955 4 at 23.
[98] *ibid.*

utilised to resolve problems of dual nationality,[99] to the issue of diplomatic protection generally.

The general rule is that a state will only espouse a claim on behalf of an individual if the latter is a national at the time when the injury occurs and at the time when the claim is presented.[1]

In respect of an individual possessing dual nationality, the traditional view has been that a claim by one national state against another national state would not be entertained. The United Kingdom has conceded, however, that it may take up a claim against the state of nationality if the latter has treated the claimant as a UK national.[2]

In respect of claims against a third state on behalf of an individual with dual nationality, it is not altogether clear which of the national states has the right to espouse the claim. In the *Merge Claim*,[3] it was suggested that only the state with which the individual had the closest connection could espouse a claim on his behalf, whereas in the *Salem Case*[4] it was suggested that both states could do so. More recently, the Iran–United States Claims Tribunal spoke in terms of "dominant and effective nationality" as a basis for exercising jurisdiction. The British attitude is that, although the government of the day may take up a claim on behalf of an individual possessing dual nationality, it prefers to do so jointly with the other national state.[5]

The absence of nationality, that is statelessness, means that a state which inflicts injury against a stateless person cannot be held internationally responsible nor is any state competent to intervene on such a person's behalf.

"Genuine link" is not limited to individuals. Accordingly "ships have the nationality of the State whose flag they are entitled to fly. There must exist a genuine link between the State and the ship."[6]

Companies and shareholders

Which state may espouse a claim on behalf of a corporation? A company has traditionally been regarded as having the nationality of "the State under the laws of which it is incorporated and in

---

[99] See *Canevaro Case* (*Italy v Peru*) 11 R.I.A.A. 397; 6 A.J.I.L. 746 (1912) Translation.
[1] See *e.g.* Rule I of the Rules Regarding International Claims issued by the British Foreign and Commonwealth Office 1985.
[2] Rule III, *ibid.*
[3] 22 I.L.R. 443.
[4] (*Egypt v U.S.*) 2 R.I.A.A. 1161 (1932).
[5] Rule III, above, n.1.
[6] Art.5 of the Geneva Convention on the High Seas 1958—see above, See also Chicago Convention 1944, Arts 12 and 18.

whose territory it has its registered office".[7] However, these are not the only two criteria whereby a link between a company and a state may be evidenced. For example:

"it has been the practice of some States to give a company incorporated under their law diplomatic protection solely when it has its seat (*siege social*) or management or centre of control in their territory, or when a majority or a substantial proportion of the shares has been owned by nationals of the State concerned."[8]

The Court concluded in the *Barcelona Traction Case* that, with respect to "the diplomatic protection of corporate entities, no absolute test of the 'genuine connection' has found general acceptance".[9] In the *Barcelona Traction Case*, the International Court was confronted with the question of whether Belgium could intervene on behalf of Belgian nationals and shareholders in a company, Barcelona Traction, which was incorporated in Canada and where it maintained its registered office. The losses sustained had been as a result of measures taken by Spain, the country in which the company operated. Canada initially intervened, but subsequently withdrew and did not proceed with a claim. The Court upheld Spain's objection to Belgian intervention on the grounds that Canada's failure to act did not increase Belgium's right. According to the Court's judgment, the state whose nationality a company possesses, even if it operates in a foreign country and is controlled by foreign shareholders, has the right to make the claim on its behalf. It was the company which had suffered the injury, but the company was not defunct and, therefore, whether or not to espouse a claim on behalf of the company remained within Canada's discretion. Regarding shareholders, the general rule is that a state may not pursue a claim on behalf of nationals who suffer injury as a consequence of a measure taken against foreign companies in which they own shares. The International Court in the *Barcelona Traction Case* concluded that to recognise diplomatic protection on behalf of shareholders would result in confusion, as the shares of international companies are "widely scattered and frequently change hands".[10] The Court did admit one exception to the general rule, namely if the company ceased to exist. In such circumstances, the Court recognised that the national state of the shareholders could initiate a

---

[7] *Barcelona Traction, Light and Power Co. Case*, I.C.J.Rep.1970 3 at 42.
[8] *ibid.*
[9] Above, n.7.
[10] Above, n.7. at 49.

claim on behalf of the shareholders in respect of losses sustained by them as a result of the injury to the company.[11] The Court's judgment failed to acknowledge that a state in which a company is incorporated may have little interest in pursuing a claim on its behalf. A company may be incorporated in a particular state as a matter of convenience. In that event, the state whose nationals are shareholders may indeed have considerable interest in espousing a claim.

The United Kingdom Rules Regarding International Claims[12] provide that where a UK national has an interest as a shareholder or otherwise in a company incorporated in another state and the company is injured by a third state, a claim will normally only be espoused by Britain in conjunction with the state in which the company is incorporated. Independent intervention will only take place exceptionally when the company concerned has ceased to exist.[13] If a state in which a company is incorporated injures the company and a UK national is a shareholder, the British Government may intervene to protect the interests of the UK national.[14] There are, therefore, two exceptions in UK practice to the Court's denial of any right to intervene on behalf of share-holders. In instances where capital in a foreign company is owned in various proportions by shareholders of several nationalities including British nationals, Britain will seldom intervene, unless those states whose nationals hold most of the capital support its representations. Art.44(a) of the Draft Articles provides "The responsibility of a State may not be invoked if: (a) The claim is not brought in accordance with any applicable rule relating to the nationality of claims." It also reflects an established rule of Customary International Law, namely that of exhaustion of local remedies.[15]

Exhaustion of local remedies

It is an established rule of customary international law that before diplomatic protection is afforded, or before recourse may be made to international arbitral or judicial processes, local remedies must be exhausted. The raison d'être of the rule is:

(a)   to allow the state concerned the opportunity to afford redress within its own legal system for the alleged wrong;

[11] Above, n.7. at 41.
[12] Above, n.1.
[13] Above, n.1. Art.V.
[14] Above, n.1. Art.VI.
[15] Draft Art.44(b).

(b) to reduce the number of possible international claims;

(c) respect for the sovereignty of states.

Local remedies means:

> "not only reference to the courts and tribunals, but also the use of the procedural facilities which municipal law makes available to litigants before such courts and tribunals. It is the whole system of legal protection, as provided by municipal law . . .".[16]

An individual must, therefore, employ "all administrative, arbitral or judicial remedies".[17] Only effective remedies which could affect the final outcome of the case need be exhausted.[18] The exhaustion of local remedies has been strictly applied, but local remedies need not be exhausted if it is evident that there is no justice to exhaust, or where it is apparent that any attempt to seek redress would be thwarted.[19] If it is apparent that a UK national, in exhausting municipal remedies, has encountered prejudice or obstruction and, accordingly, a denial of justice, the British Government may intervene in order to seek redress on his behalf.[20] The exhaustion of local remedies is not required when the alleged wrong is a direct injury by one state against another state. The requirement to exhaust local remedies may be dispensed with by treaty, but this must be explicitly stated and not merely implied.

STATE RESPONSIBILITY FOR THE ENVIRONMENT

Since the early 1970s, there has been increasing concern for the environment and a realisation that protection, to be effective, must be based on international co-operation. The international community has more recently focused on preventative measures. This is in contrast to the traditional approach whereby responsibility was attributed to the state deemed to have caused the harm. The regulation of the international environment has increased dramatically in the last 30 years and the new preventative

---

[16] *Ambatielos Arbitration (Greece v U.K.)* 12 R.I.A.A. 83 (1956); 23 I.L.R. 306 (1956).
[17] See Draft Art.19, 1961 Harvard Draft Convention on International Responsibility of States for Injuries to Aliens.
[18] *Finnish Ships Arbitration* 3 R.I.A.A. 1479 (1934); *cf. El Oro Mining and Railway Co. Case (Great Britain v Mexico)* 5 R.I.A.A. 191 (1931); *Interhandel Case (Preliminary Objections)* I.C.J.Rep.1959 6 at 26–29.
[19] *Robert E. Brown Case* 6 R.I.A.A. 120, 129 (1923). See Rule VII, above, n.1.
[20] Rule VIII, above, n.1.

approach is reflected in the plethora of arrangements both at an international and regional level (see below). The United Nations in 1972 established UNEP (United Nations Environment Programme) to implement the Action Programme adopted at the Conference that year on the Human Environment. This international "legislative" activity has been accompanied by regional developments. The expansion of international/regional environmental norms is reflected in the focus it now receives within the increasing number of academic programmes. Initially, the international community tackled responsibility for the environment by way of customary international law and imposed certain restrictions on the enjoyment of a state's recognised right "in accordance with the Charter of the United Nations and the principles of international law, . . . to exploit their own natural resources pursuant to their own environmental policies".[21] The responsibility incumbent on states, under customary international law is expressed in Principle 21 as being "to ensure that activities within their jurisdiction or control do not cause damage to the environment of other States or of areas beyond the limits of national jurisdiction"[22] It is currently reiterated in Principle 2 of the Rio Declaration.[23] Art.30 of the Charter of Economic Rights and Duties of States also provides:

> "The protection, preservation and enhancement of the environment for the present and future generations is the responsibility of all States. All States shall endeavour to establish their own environmental and developmental policies in conformity with such responsibility . . . All States have the responsibility to ensure that activities within their jurisdiction or control do not cause damage to the environment of other States or of areas beyond the limits of national jurisdiction. All States should cooperate in evolving international norms and regulations in the field of the environment."[24]

Art.24 of the African Charter on Human and Peoples' Rights (the Banjul Charter) 1981 heralds as a right of all people "a general satisfactory environment favourable to their development".

---

[21] Declaration on the Human Environment (Stockholm, 1972) 11 I.L.M. 1416 (1972), Principle 21.

[22] *ibid.*

[23] The Rio Declaration on the Environment was adopted on June 14, 1992, at the UN Conference on Environment and Development, Rio de Janeiro, June 3–14, 1992. It was attended by 176 states; see 31 I.L.M. 814 (1992).

[24] It may be recalled that the status of the Charter under international law is not fully established.

The extent and scope of a state's responsibility under customary international law was illustrated in two cases involving the United States and Canada, the *Trail Smelter Arbitration*[25] and *Gut Dam Arbitration*.[26]

The *Trail Smelter Arbitration* related to damage caused in the State of Washington by sulphur dioxide emitted since 1925 from a smelter plant at Trail on the Columbian River, 10 miles from the United States/Canadian border on the Canadian side.

In the Tribunal's final decision in 1941, a general principle of international law was recognised, namely that "a State owes at all times a duty to protect other States against injurious acts by individuals from within its jurisdiction".[27] The Tribunal concluded from decisions of the US Supreme Court in controversies between Member States of the Union, that there existed as a principle of US law and of international law that:

> "[N]o State has the right to use or permit the use of its territory in such a manner as to cause injury by fumes in or to the territory of another or the properties or persons therein, when the cause is of serious consequences and the injury is established by clear and convincing evidence."

The Gut Dam, on the international boundary between the United States and Canada, raised the water levels of Lake Ontario between 1947 and 1952 and resulted in considerable damage being sustained to properties on the lake shore. Following the re-establishment of an international arbitral tribunal, Canada agreed to pay compensation in respect of the damage caused to the property of US citizens.

Similarly in the *Corfu Channel Case*,[28] it was maintained that incumbent on every state is the duty "not to allow knowingly its territory to be used for acts contrary to the rights of other states".[29]

Principle 22 of the Stockholm Declaration required states to co-operate in the further development of international law on liability and compensation for the victims of pollution and extra-territorial damage, while Principle 24 called upon states to

[25] 3 R.I.A.A. 1905.
[26] 8 I.L.M. 118 (1969).
[27] above, n.29 at 1963.
[28] I.C.J.Rep.1949 at 4.
[29] *ibid.* at 22. See also the ICJ acknowledgment that a state's territorial sovereignty is restricted by obligations towards the environment. This is now part of the corpus of international law relating to the environment, as was stated in the *Nuclear Weapons* case, *per* Weeramantry J. See also the separate opinion of Weeramantry J. in the *Nagymaros* case.

act in a co-operative spirit for the protection and improvement of the international environment. The requirement to co-operate is a recurring theme in contemporary international agreements.[30]

In 1992, the United Nations convened a Conference on Environment and Development (UNCED) in Rio de Janeiro in response to the growing recognition that environmental problems should be addressed at an international level. The Conference endorsed the concept of sustainable development[31] and introduced a number of general principles in its Declaration on Environment and Development (the Rio Declaration) in particular the obligation on states to take precautionary measures (Principle 15), the polluter pays principle (Principle 16) and environmental impact assessment (Principle 17). The Declaration also imposes obligations upon states to notify emergencies and engage in consultation where there is a risk of transboundary pollution. The Conference also adopted a Programme of Action (Agenda 21), a Convention on Biological Diversity, a Convention on Climate Change and a Statement of Principles on Forests. Agenda 21, although not a legally binding instrument, is regarded as a comprehensive plan of action for the international community and combines environmental and development concerns in 40 chapters. A Commission on Sustainable Development was created in 1992 to monitor progress concerning the implementation of Agenda 21.[32] A review of the progress made in the implementation of what was agreed at Rio in 1992 was the focus of the World Summit on Sustainable Development, which was held in Johannesburg, South Africa, between August 26 and the September 4, 2002. The preparatory process for the Johannesburg summit was encouraged by the General Assembly to "ensure a balance between economic development, social development and environmental protection as these are interdependent and mutually reinforcing components of sustainable development."[32a] It will be some time before the principles enunciated in the Rio

---

[30] *e.g.* Art.5 of the 1979 Long-Range Transboundary Air Pollution Convention; and Vienna Convention on Early Notification of a Nuclear Accident 1986—see below.

[31] Sustainable development can be described simply as meeting the needs of present generations without compromising the ability of future generations to do the same. See, the Bruntland Report of the World Commission on Environment and Development (WCED) 1987, titled *Our Common Future*. With the population of the earth set to double in the next 50 years, sustainable development is regarded as vital to the survival of the planet. See Ch.39 of Agenda 21 generally.

[32] UN GA *res* 47/191, Dec. 22, 1992. Based on Ch.38 of Agenda 21 on International Institutional Arrangements.

[32a] General Assembly Ten-year review of progress achieved in the implementation of the outcome of the UN Conference on Environment and Development, A/RES/55/199, December 20, 2000, point 4.

Declaration and Agenda 21 are fully implemented. International environmental law is, however, no longer confined to the adoption of measures to regulate states' behaviour. Instead, it is increasingly concerned with implementation, environmental impact assessment and the development of effective dispute resolution techniques. The recognition by the international community of the link between the environment and development has already produced a substantial body of law and is one of the fastest-growing areas of international law in contemporary society.

In addition to the issues identified at the Rio Conference, as priorities for the international community, other problem areas of concern include, *inter alia*, desertification, transboundary air pollution, global warming/depletion of the ozone layer, the transfer and disposal of hazardous waste and control of nuclear activities. Special conditions and environmental problems which some Third World countries face have been recognised by the United Nations in a Convention to Combat Desertification in those Countries Experiencing Serious Drought and/or Desertification, particularly in Africa.[33] The purpose of the Convention is to identify the factors contributing to desertification and the practical measures necessary to it and the mitigation of the effects of drought through international co-operation and partnership agreements. The problem of drought is viewed by the international community as having far-reaching repercussions for economic growth, social development and poverty eradication.[34]

The 1979 Convention on Long-Range Transboundary Air Pollution and its 1985, 1988 and 1994 Protocols[35] tackled the problem of transboundary air pollution and contracting parties agreed to "endeavour to limit and, as far as possible, gradually reduce and prevent air pollution including long-range transboundary air pollution". The Convention defines transboundary air pollution as that which originates:

> "within the area under the national jurisdiction of one State and which has adverse effects in the area under the jurisdiction of another State at such a distance that it is not generally possible to distinguish the contribution of individual emission sources or groups of sources."

---

[33] 33 I.L.M. 1328 (1994).
[34] See, Ch.12 of Agenda 21 generally.
[35] 18 I.L.M. 1442 (1979); 27 I.L.M. 707 (1988). Adopted in Oslo, June 14, 1994, 33 I.L.M. 1540 (1994).

The Convention does not address the issue of liability for pollution across state frontiers, but rather emphasises research and the exchange of information.[36]

The 1985 Protocol required contracting parties to reduce, by 1993 at the latest, sulphur emissions by at least 30 per cent, while the 1988 Protocol required a reduction, by the end of 1994, in the annual emission of nitrate oxides or their transboundary fluxes to a minimum of the 1987 level. The 1994 Protocol establishes an implementation committee to "review the implementation of the present protocol and compliance by the parties with their obligations".[37]

In a further effort to minimise transboundary pollution, the United Nations adopted a Convention on Environmental Impact Assessment in 1991.[38] The obligation incumbent on contracting parties is to "either individually or jointly, take all appropriate and effective measures to prevent, reduce and control significant adverse transboundary environmental impact from proposed activities".[39]

Throughout the 1980s, the issue of global warming and the depletion of the ozone layer was widely recognised by governments and individuals alike as requiring urgent attention. The need to protect the ozone layer brought an international response and culminated in the 1985 Vienna Convention for the Protection of the Ozone Layer,[40] the 1987 Montreal Protocol on Substances that Deplete the Ozone Layer,[41] and the 1989 Helsinki Declaration on the Protection of the Ozone Layer.[42] The Vienna Convention entered into force in 1988 and essentially provides for co-operation, scientific research and the exchange of information, whilst the 1987 Protocol, as amended in 1990, entered into force in 1990 and stipulates maximum consumption levels of chlorofluorocarbons and imposed a freeze on the use of halons. However, the Helsinki Declaration requires a phasing out of CFCs by the year 2000 and, as soon as practical, other ozone harming materials. The most notable international measures regarding global warming are the Hague Declaration on the Environment 1989,[43] calling for the

---

[36] 18 I.L.M. 1442 (1979).

[37] Art.7.

[38] 30 I.L.M. 800 (1991).

[39] *ibid.*, Art.2.1.

[40] 26 I.L.M. 1516 (1987).

[41] *ibid.* at 1541. The 1987 Montreal Protocol was amended at the Fourth Meeting of the Parties to the Protocol at Copenhagen in 1992. Besides shortening the deadlines for already scheduled substances, the adjustments also provided for new rules on other substances. See UN: Montreal Protocol on Substances that Deplete the Ozone Layer—Adjustments and Amendments, Copenhagen, November 23–25, 1992 32 I.L.M. 874 (1993).

[42] 28 I.L.M. 1335 (1989).

[43] 28 I.L.M. 1308 (1989).

establishment of an international body exclusively dedicated to the consideration of such issues, and the Framework Convention on Climate Change, agreed on May 9, 1992.[44] The primary objective of the Convention was to stabilise greenhouse gas concentrations in the atmosphere while recognising that some climate change was inevitable. While the Convention did not impose binding provisions on the reduction of emissions, states are required to adopt national measures to limit the emission of greenhouse gases. These measures are then to be reviewed at an international Conference by all parties.[45] The Kyoto Protocol to the Convention was adopted on the December 10, 1977.

The UN Convention on Biological Diversity was negotiated under the auspices of UNCED[46] and was designed to protect the planet's biodiversity by promoting its sustainable use (Art.2). The Convention establishes a number of obligations upon states, including national monitoring of biological diversity, national *in situ* and *ex situ* conservation measures, environmental impact assessments and national reports, from countries concerned, on the steps they have taken to implement the Convention.

A number of international measures regulate the transfer and dumping of hazardous waste.[47] The 1989 Basle Convention on the Control of Transboundary Movements of Hazardous Wastes and Their Disposal,[48] for instance, controls and, in certain circumstances prohibits the transfer of such material between contracting parties. A Convention establishing a liability regime for Hazardous Waste Accidents was opened for signatures on March 25, 2000.

In 1992, the United Nations adopted a Convention on the Transboundary Effects of Industrial Accidents.[49] The Convention applies to the prevention of and response to industrial accidents capable of causing transboundary effects, including the effects of such accidents caused by natural disasters. An industrial accident is defined as an event resulting from an uncontrolled development in the course of any activity involving hazardous substances (Art.1(a)) either in an installation (Art.1(a)(i)) or during

[44] The Convention was signed by 155 states and entered into force on March 24, 1994. It was the first international environmental agreement to be negotiated by almost all of the international community. 31 I.L.M. 849 (1992).

[45] Art.7 of the Convention establishes the Conference of the Parties as the body responsible for monitoring the implementation of the Convention and to taking any necessary decisions to ensure implementation is effected. National measures are to be reviewed at the end of 1998.

[46] 31 I.L.M. 818 (1992) entered into force on December 29, 1993.

[47] For those relating to the protection of the marine environment, see Ch.7 above.

[48] 28 I.L.M. 649 (1989).

[49] Adopted March 17, 1992, in Helsinki, 31 I.L.M. 1330 (1992).

transportation (Art.1(a)(ii)). The Convention also sought to promote international co-operation concerning mutual assistance, research and development, exchange of information and exchange of technology in the area of industrial accidents. It does not apply to, *inter alia*, nuclear accidents or oil spillages.[50]

An item on the agenda of the International Law Commission has been the law regarding the use of International Watercourses,[51] these seek to regulate the use of said watercourses and to protect ecosystems and the marine environment.[52] The Draft Articles were produced in 1994 and the Convention on the Law of Non-navigational Uses of International Watercourses was adopted by the General Assembly in 1997.[52a] A Convention on the Protection and Use of Transboundary Watercourses and Lakes was adopted in 1992 under the auspices of the U.N. Economic Commission for Europe.[53] The Convention codifies regional rules concerning the protection and use of watercourses and contributes to the progressive development of the law relating to the conservation and restoration of ecosystems and pollution control, for example the polluter-pays principle.

Nuclear weapons and the environment

Fears of radioactive fall-out prompted the 1963 Treaty Banning Nuclear Weapons Tests in Outer Space and Under Water.[54] Art.1(1)(b) of the Treaty forbids testing "in any . . . environment if such explosion causes radioactive debris to be present outside the territorial limits of the State under whose jurisdiction or control such explosion is conducted".[55]

Australia in the *Nuclear Tests Cases*[56] advanced the argument that there existed a rule of customary international law prohibiting atmospheric nuclear testing and that the prohibition was expressed in absolute terms, thus constituting an obligation *erga omnes*—an obligation owed to the international community as a whole and not just to one state.[57] The International Court of Justice declared, in 1996, that the threat or use of nuclear weapons

---

[50] See, Art.2 generally.
[51] For a commentary of these Draft Articles, see Reports of the Commission in II Yearbook of the I.L.C. (1993) and (1994).
[52] See, Pts II and IV of the Draft Articles.
[52a] GA Res. 51/229, May 21, (1997).
[53] 31 I.L.M. (1992) 1312.
[54] 480 U.N.T.S. 43; U.K.T.S. 3 (1964) Cmnd.2245.
[55] Discussed further in Ch.7. See also Ch.11—The Use of Force.
[56] I.C.J.Rep.1973, Pleadings, at 333–336.
[57] The ICJ, on the basis of France's undertakings to refrain from any further testing, declined to give a ruling on the claims presented to it—see I.C.J.Rep.1974 253.

is "contrary to the rules of international law applicable in armed conflict"[58] and that there is now a customary obligation upon states to negotiate in good faith for nuclear disarmament.[59]

The 1986 Chernobyl incident highlighted the inadequacies of the international nuclear safety regime and brought an almost immediate international response in the form of the Vienna Convention on Early Notification of a Nuclear Accident[60] and the Convention on Assistance in the Case of a Nuclear Accident or Radiological Emergency.[61] As may be apparent, the ensuing obligations relate to the provisions of information and assistance.

The Convention on Nuclear Safety was opened for signature by the General Conference of the International Atomic Energy Agency (IAEA) in Vienna, 1994.[62] The Convention does not establish an internationally binding regime and was originally intended as a framework convention. The Convention instead introduces a system of accountability and states are required to take appropriate measures in order to implement their obligations under the Convention. Responsibility for nuclear safety rests with the State having jurisdiction over a nuclear installation, for example a nuclear power plant.[63]

The conduct of hostilities does not relieve states of their responsibilities to the environment. The 1977 Convention on the Prohibition of Military or Any Other Hostile Use of Environmental Modification Techniques[64] and Protocol 1 of the 1980 Conventional Weapons Treaty[65] prohibit modes of warfare having a severe and long-term effect on the environment and requires respect to be shown for the natural environment and its protection from severe widespread and lasting damage. For example, in 1993, the United Nations adopted a Convention on the Applicability of the Development, Production, Stockpiling and Use of Chemical Weapons and on their Destruction, the

[58] 35 I.L.M. 809 (1996). This was in response to a request from the GA. The Court in 1993 was asked by WHO to give an advisory opinion concerning the legality of the use of nuclear weapons in armed conflict on the grounds that the request as submitted by WHO "did not relate to a question within the scope of [the] activities of that Organisation."

[59] *ibid.* See Declaration of President Bedjaoui. See also Ch.11 for further discussions on nuclear weapons.

[60] 25 I.L.M. 1370 (1986).

[61] *ibid.* at 1377.

[62] 33 I.L.M. 1514 (1994).

[63] Experts have warned, however, that, despite international co-operation on the issue of nuclear safety, the threat of a serious nuclear accident remains, due to the exceptionally poor condition of dozens of nuclear sites across Russia. *The Times*, April 11, 1996.

[64] 16 I.L.M. 88 (1977).

[65] 19 I.L.M. 1529 (1980).

purpose of which was to prohibit and eliminate all chemical weapons.[66] Para.39.6(a) of Agenda 21 also highlights this issue by calling on states to adopt measures which address the problem of large-scale destruction of the environment during international armed conflict.[67]

International liability for the injurious consequences of acts not prohibited by international law

Akin to responsibility, but not identical to it, is the possible liability of states for the injurious consequences of acts which are not prohibited by international law. The essence of the distinction between responsibility and liability is that the prerequisite to the former is an act breaching international law, while the latter is concerned with harmful effects of an activity which is not *per se* a violation of international law. The International Law Commission has had this matter on its Agenda since 1978 and much of its work has been focused on such liability for harm to the environment. At the 53rd Session, 2001, the International Law Commission adopted Draft Articles on the Prevention of Transboundary Harm from Hazardous Activities. The activities to which the convention applies are those "not prohibited by international law which involve a risk of causing significant transboundary harm through their physical consequences."[68] This convention only applies to instances where there is risk of significant harm arising in the territory of a state other that the state in which the activity is undertaken. The commentaries to the Draft Articles provide valuable insight into the interpretation of the terms used within the convention, for example, the Commentary highlights ". . . that the element of 'risk' is concerned with future possibilities and thereby implies some element of assessment or appreciation of risk. The notion of risk is thus to be taken objectively as denoting an appreciation of possible harm resulting from an activity which a properly informed observer had or ought to have had."[69] States remain reluctant to pursue claims against other states for environmental damage despite there being a solid legal basis for such an action, for example the *Chernobyl* incident in 1986. International conventions that have sought to address this issue have tended to focus on liability for oil pollution.

---

[66] Adopted in Paris, January 13, 1993, 32 I.L.M. 800 (1993).
[67] above, n.32.
[68] Art.1.
[69] Commentaries to the Draft Articles on Prevention of Transboundary Harm from Hazardous Activities, p.385, Report of the International Law Commission on the work of its fifty-third session, *Official Records of the General Assembly, Fifty-sixth session, Supplement No. 10* (A/56/10), Ch.V.E.2

International environmental law continues to be a changing paradigm. While the Stockholm Conference drew the world's attention to the environment, the Rio Summit recognised that contemporary environmental problems stem from underdevelopment, hence the attention now given to the concept of "sustainable development". This shift in approach is evident from recent international conventions and other legal instruments. The international community has also recognised the particular problems that developing countries face when adopting international standards for regulation of the environment and some Third World countries have received preferential treatment in international conventions.

9. HUMAN RIGHTS

WHAT ARE HUMAN RIGHTS?

"All human rights are universal, indivisible and interdependent and interrelated."[1]

Human rights are difficult to define. Generally speaking, they are regarded as those fundamental and inalienable rights which are essential for life as a human being. There is, however, no consensus as to what these rights should be. What human rights may be interpreted as being differs according to the particular economic, social and cultural society in which they are being defined. Human rights have, therefore, escaped a universally acceptable definition, presenting a problem to international regulation. However, under contemporary international law, human rights are increasingly sub-divided into three classifications: "first, second and third generation" rights. Civil and political rights constitute the "first generation" rights; economic, social and cultural rights, the "second generation"; whilst group rights are

---

[1] Pt I, para.5 of the Vienna Declaration and Programme of Action, adopted, following the UN World Conference on Human Rights, Vienna, June, 1993.

characterised as "third generation" rights. The distinguishing feature of the latter is that the focus is on collective as opposed to individual rights. The right to development and the right to self-determination are two of the principal examples of "third generation" rights. The Vienna Conference in June 1993 affirmed the right to development as a fundamental human right. This was endorsed by the UN Secretary General, Boutros Boutros Ghali, who pledged his personal commitment to development in his "Agenda for Development".[2] The concept of "third generation" rights originated in the 1970s and remains controversial with the primary protagonists being the developing states. The problem with third generation rights is: how can such a right be enforced and indeed defined? However human rights are defined, they have now permeated the vocabulary of international business and globalisation, and have been responsible for the increase in the number of businesses demonstrating corporate social accountability. This is not to say that businesses have become altruistic and are now involved with philanthropy. The truth lies in greater availability and transparency of corporation documents, a greater accessibility of shareholders who can, and frequently are the target of pressure groups and intense media exposure. Expansion in the marketplace demands global competitiveness of which social accountability is a critical dimension.[2a]

In addition to definition, a major contributing difficulty has been that many states regard human rights as falling within domestic jurisdiction, and not a matter to be tackled by international law. In other words, treatment of one's own nationals should not, according to those states, be the focus of external review. The international law position is that *severe* violations of human rights can no longer fall within the exclusive jurisdiction of states.[3]

Human rights is a subject of contemporary international law and the efforts to regulate human rights at an international level only gained momentum after World War II. It should be noted that human rights are not a static concept, as was highlighted by the European Court of Human Rights in the decision of *'Selmouni'*, regarding the characterisation of treatment as torture, which previously would have escaped such a label.[3a] The

---

[2] Report of the Secretary General A/48/935, May 6, 1995. In response to the Secretary General's Agenda, the General Assembly adopted a resolution which created an ad hoc open ended working group with the specific purpose of "elaborating further an action-oriented comprehensive agenda for development." A/Res/49/126, January 20, 1995.

[2a] See guidelines for Cooperation between the United Nations and the Business Community, issued by the Secretary-General of the UN, July 17, 2000.

[3] See pp.262 *et seq.*

[3a] *Selmouni v France*, European Court of Human Rights, 25803/94, July 28, 1999.

importance of human rights on the political agenda is reflected, for example, in the United Kingdom by the publication, since 1998, of an annual report on Human Rights. This report is undertaken by the Government and published by the Foreign and Commonwealth Office.

Rights of the individual recognised by international law

Pre-1945

Minority groups, that is those people of a different race, religion or language from the majority group within a state, came to be guaranteed certain rights, such as equality of treatment, by way of Minority treaties such as those concluded in Albania, Finland and Poland. Minority treaties were not renewed after the Second World War. Freedom from slavery has been recognised under customary international law since 1815 and was reaffirmed in international Conventions, such as the 1926 Slavery Convention[4] and the 1956 Supplementary Convention on the Abolition of Slavery, the Slave Trade and Institutions and Practices Similar to Slavery.[5] Trafficking women and children was similarly prohibited by Convention,[6] but, with the exception of such isolated ad hoc intervention, there was no attempt to regulate human rights at an international level until after 1945. Prior to the Second World War, minority groups and foreign nationals were in a privileged position *vis-à-vis* majority groups and nationals of the host state. They were recognised as deserving at least a minimum standard of treatment.

Post-1945

The signing of the United Nations Charter marked the formal realisation that human rights is a matter for international concern. One of the purposes for which the United Nations was founded was "to achieve international co-operation . . . in promoting and encouraging respect for human rights and for fundamental freedoms for all without distinction as to race, sex, language or religion,"[7] whilst Arts 55 and 56 charge the United Nations and Member States with achieving, *inter alia*, "universal respect for, and observance of, human rights and fundamental freedoms for all without distinction as to race, sex, language and religion." The

---

[4]   60 L.N.T.S. 253; U.K.T.S. 16 (1927) Cmd.2910.
[5]   266 U.N.T.S. 3; U.K.T.S. 59 (1957) Cmnd.257.
[6]   *e.g.* International Convention for the Suppression of Traffic in Women and Children, 60 U.N.T.S. 416; U.K.T.S. 26 (1923) Cmd.1986; the 1947 Protocol 53 U.N.T.S. 13.
[7]   Art.1(3) of the UN Charter.

language of the Charter is vague, and, although Members pledged themselves to the realisation of human rights, they were not required to do so within a particular time period. The UN Charter acknowledges certain benefits which individuals should enjoy. It does not confer rights upon them.[8]

The protection of human rights in contemporary international law including the conferring of rights and the provision of the machinery whereby rights, if infringed, may be enforced, has been tackled at both an international and regional level. (This chapter deals only with international efforts.)

UNITED NATIONS

One of the initial resolutions adopted by the UN General Assembly was the Universal Declaration of Human Rights,[9] adopted on December 10, 1948. The Declaration spells out a series of political, civil, economic, social and cultural rights. As a resolution, it is not, of course, legally binding. It was never intended to be, but rather, in the words of the United States representative to the General Assembly and Chairman of the United Nations Committee on Human Rights during the drafting of the Declaration, Mrs Eleanor Roosevelt, was to act as a "common standard of achievement for all peoples of all nations." The Declaration has been tacitly accepted by all Member States and has served as the blueprint for the constitutions of many newly independent states. It is arguable today that some, if not all, the rights and freedoms enunciated in the Charter have become accepted as customary international law. The rights spelt out in the Universal Declaration are diverse and include, *inter alia*, the right to life, liberty and security of the person; freedom from slavery or servitude; freedom from torture or cruel, inhuman or degrading treatment or punishment; recognition as a person before the law; the right to nationality; the right to own property; freedom of thought, conscience and religion; the right to participate in government; the right to social security; the right to work and the right to education. The rights and freedoms are to be enjoyed without "distinction of any kind, such as race, colour, sex, language, religion, political or other opinion, national or social origin, property, birth or other status"[10] and are only to be curtailed by:

---

[8] See *Sei Fujii v California* (1952) 19 I.L.R. 312; see also *Filartiga v Pena-Irala* 630 F. 2d. 876 (1980); 19 I.L.M. 966 (1980).

[9] GA Res.217 (III), G.A.O.R., 3rd Session, Pt I, Resolutions, p.71. December 10 is celebrated annually as Human Rights Day.

[10] Art.2.

"such limitations as are determined by law solely for the purposes of securing due recognition and respect for the rights and freedoms of others and of meeting the just requirements of morality, public order and the general welfare in a democratic society."[11]

In June 1993, a conference was convened in Vienna to further the protection and promotion of human rights in the international community.[12] The World Conference on Human Rights (the Vienna Conference) provided an opportunity for an extensive analysis of the international human rights system and the machinery used to afford such protection. The Vienna Conference culminated in a Declaration on Human Rights and the adoption of an Action Programme[13] which identified particularly vulnerable groups of individuals as being women, minorities, children, refugees, indigenous people, prisoners and persons with disabilities. The Action Programme emphasises the need for frequent review and appraisal of the measures taken by the international community to ensure that the rights of these groups are adequately protected.[14] The Vienna Conference considered "human rights education, training and public information essential for the promotion and achievement of stable and harmonious relations among communities" and in December 1994, the General Assembly pronounced 1994–2004 as the United Nations Decade for Human Rights Education.[15]

The Vienna Declaration and the Programme of Action were reviewed in 1998.[15a] The conclusion was that implementation of human rights throughout the world remains inconsistent. The end of apartheid in South Africa and the emergence of governments in Central and eastern Europe symbolise advances made towards "making human rights a reality".[15b] On the other hand, national laws are still in force and legislation still adopted which "discriminate against women, fails to recognise economic, social and cultural rights and does not adequately protect individuals in proceedings".[16]

The rights and freedoms set out in the Universal Declaration have been articulated more precisely in two separate international

---

[11] Art.29(2).
[12] The conference marked the 45th anniversary of the Declaration of Human Rights. See 32 I.L.M. 1661 (1993).
[13] Adopted by the Conference on June 25, 1993 by 171 representatives.
[14] For the relevant international instruments protecting the rights set out in the Vienna Declaration, see below, p.222.
[15] GA Res.48/127, December 20, 1993.
[15a] Part II(F), para.100.
[15b] Note by the UN Secretary-General, September 11, 1998 on presenting the Report of the UN High Commissioner for Human Rights, to the General Assembly.
[16] RMM Wallace, *International Human Rights, Text and Materials*, p.589.

Covenants: the Covenant on Civil and Political Rights 1966,[17] which entered into force in March 1976; and the Covenant on Economic, Social and Cultural Rights 1966,[18] which entered into force in January 1976.[19] A General Assembly Resolution was adopted in 1985 regarding the human rights of individuals who are not nationals of the country in which they live.[20]

Under the Covenant on Civil and Political Rights, Contracting Parties undertake "to respect and to ensure to all individuals within its territory and subject to its jurisdiction the rights recognised in the present Covenant",[21] whereas the Covenant on Economic, Social and Cultural Rights requires a Contracting Party "to take steps . . . to the maximum of its available resources, with a view to achieving progressively the full realisation of the rights recognised in the present Covenant."[22]

An initial difference between the two Covenants is that the obligations assumed by a state under the Covenant on Civil and Political Rights are required to be implemented immediately upon ratification of the Covenant by a state, while the Covenant on Economic, Social and Cultural Rights provides that the realisation of the rights it recognises may be achieved progressively. The fulfilment of economic, social and cultural rights depends upon a state's economic development. The right to recognition as a person before the law can be put into effect upon implementation of the appropriate legal measures.

Rights protected

The Civil and Political Covenant prescribes certain rights and freedoms which, if the characterisation described above is employed, would be "first generation rights". The rights include the right to life, to liberty and security, to equality before the courts, to peaceful assembly, to marry and found a family and to vote; whereas the freedoms articulated include those of association and, of thought, conscience and religion. The Covenant explicitly prohibits torture, cruel, inhuman or degrading treatment or punishment,[23] slavery, servitude and forced or compulsory labour.

---

[17] U.K.T.S. 6 (1977) Cmnd.6702; 6 I.L.M. 368 (1967).
[18] U.K.T.S. 6 (1977) Cmnd.6702; 6 I.L.M. 360 (1967).
[19] The UK is a party to both.
[20] GA Res.144 (XL), G.A.O.R., 49th Session, Supp.53, p.253; see also p.184 above.
[21] Art.2(1).
[22] Art.2(1).
[23] This guarantee is supplemented by the UN Convention Against Torture and Other Cruel, Inhuman or Degrading Treatment or Punishment (New York, February 4, 1985) Misc.12 (1985) Cmnd.9593; 23 I.L.M. 1027 (1984); for amended text 24 I.L.M. 535 (1985).

The exercise of right may be subject to restriction, but these limitations must be provided by law and must be necessary to protect national security, public order, public health or morals, or the rights and freedoms of others, for example Art.12(3) which concerns limitations on freedom of movement and residence within a country, and the right to leave a country. Derogation is allowed in times of public emergency, for example in 1989, the United Kingdom intimated a derogation with respect to Northern Ireland.

In 1989, the second Optional Protocol to the Covenant Aiming at the Abolition of the Death Penalty[24] was adopted. This Protocol entered into force in July 1991 on receipt of the 10th ratification.[25]

The Covenant on Economic, Social and Cultural Rights guarantees those "second generation rights" originally spelt out in Arts 22–27 of the Universal Declaration, for example the right to work, to just and favourable conditions of work and rights to medical and social services and social security. Art.4 of the Covenant provides that these rights are subject "only to such limitations as are determined by law only in so far as this may be compatible with the nature of these rights and solely for the purpose of promoting the general welfare in a democratic society."

Both Covenants recognise the right of all peoples to self-determination and the right to "freely dispose of their natural wealth and resources." These provisions do not appear in the Universal Declaration.

Implementation machinery

- *Reporting system*—common to both Covenants.

- *Inter-state complaint*—Art.41 of the Covenant on Civil and Political Rights.

- *Individual communication to the Committee of Human Rights*—(First) Optional Protocol to the Covenant on Civil and Political Rights

Reporting system. A reporting system as a medium for enforcing the rights guaranteed is common to both Covenants and states are required to submit periodic reports. In the case of the Covenant on Civil and Political Rights states are required "to submit periodic reports on the measures they have adopted which give effect to the rights recognised herein and on the

---

[24] For the First Optional Protocol, see below.
[25] The UK became a party to the 2nd optional protocol on December 10, 1999.

progress made in the enjoyment of those rights: (a) within one year of the entry into force of the present Covenant for the state parties concerned."[26] Art.40 is the only compulsory supervisory system to which states submit on ratifying the Covenant.

The Human Rights Committee is a body of 18 individuals elected by the Contracting Parties, but who sit as individuals not as government representatives. The Committee's task is to study the reports received and transmit a report and "such general comments as it may consider appropriate to the States Parties." Additional information may be requested from the state by the Committee and will be provided either by a state representative who will be present at the Committee's discussions, or at a later date by the government concerned. The reporting system is essentially a means of providing information which may provide the basis for the Committee to issue such "general comments as it may deem appropriate."[27] These comments have concerned, *inter alia*, freedom of speech and freedom from torture as guaranteed by the Covenant[28] and the interpretation of discrimination for the purposes of the Covenant. Although, for the most part, non-controversial the Committee, in the Second General Comment on the right to life as guaranteed by Art.6, stated that nuclear weapons, their production, testing, possession and deployment, should not only be prohibited but should be "recognised as crimes against humanity." States submit subsequent reports whenever required to do so by the Commission—currently every five years.

State parties to the Covenant on Economic, Social and Cultural Rights are also required to submit reports:

> "in stages, in accordance with a programme to be established by the Economic and Social Council within one year of the entry into force of the present Covenant after consultation with the States Parties and the specialised agencies concerned."[29]

Reports are submitted not to the independent Human Rights Committee, but rather to the Economic and Social Council Committee established in 1985 by ECOSOC to assist it in fulfilling its

---

[26] Art.40.
[27] Art.40(4).
[28] Arts 19 and 7, respectively. For details on all general comments, see Compilation of General Comments and General Recommendations Adopted by the Human Rights Treaty Bodies, Economic and Social Council, HRI/1/Rev.5, April 26, 2001.
[29] Art.17.

duties under the Covenant. The Committee is composed of 18 independent experts in the field of human rights. The main task of the Committee is to examine reports submitted by states in accordance with Art.16 of the Covenant. Reports are examined with a view to ensuring that states are adopting suitable measures to implement the rights set out in the Covenant and the Committee will negotiate with the state concerned to discuss how implementation may be improved. The Committee submits an annual report to the Council.

The Committee on Economic, Social and Cultural Rights concluded consideration of a Draft Optional Protocol to the Covenant on Economic, Social and Cultural Rights in 1996. The Protocol when adopted will grant the right of individuals or groups to submit communications (complaints) concerning noncompliance with the Covenant.

Inter-state complaint—Art.41, covenant on civil and political rights. Art.41 is not compulsory for states. Acceptance of Art.41 by a state is independent to its ratification of the Covenant. Art.41 provides for optional inter-state petitions. A state may accept the right of other states to bring before the Human Rights Committee a claim alleging its violation of the Convention. The initiation of the Art.41 procedure is dependent upon:

(a)　the condition of reciprocity—both states, the one alleging the violation and the alleged offender, must have accepted Art.41; and

(b)　the exhaustion of local remedies.

The Committee makes its good offices available to the states and within 12 months, submits a report indicating the facts and solution reached. If no solution is achieved, the report will be confined to the facts, along with the submission of the two parties. In the absence of a solution, the Committee may, with the prior consent of the states concerned, appoint an ad hoc Conciliation Commission.[30] If the Commission is used, but a solution is not achieved, the Commission produces a report which is not binding, but in which the Commission may indicate "its views of the possibilities of an amicable settlement."[31] When compared to its European Convention counterpart,[32] Art.41 lacks teeth. There is no provision for reference to a judicial body or for the taking of a

[30] Art. 42.
[31] Art. 42(7)(c).
[32] Art. 24.

decision in accordance with judicial procedures. Conciliation
remains the primary aim.

Art.41 entered into force on March 28, 1979 and to date it has
been accepted by the United Kingdom. Art.41 has yet to be
utilised.

**Individual communications to the Committee of Human
Rights**—(First) Optional Protocol to the Covenant on Civil and
Political Rights.[33] Under the First Optional Protocol to the
Covenant on Civil and Political Rights,[34] the Committee is com-
petent to receive and consider communications from individuals
who claim to be victims of a violation by a state party to the
Covenant, provided that the latter is a party to the Optional
Protocol.[35] A communication must:

- not be anonymous;

- concern an alleged violation of one of the rights provided for in the Covenant;

- not relate to a matter which is under consideration in
  any other international forum (this provision is designed
  to prevent the simultaneous consideration of petitions
  by the Human Rights Committee and, for instance, the
  European Commission of the Council of Europe); and

- all domestic remedies must have been exhausted, unless
  the application of such remedies is unreasonably pro-
  longed.[36]

The Optional Protocol makes no provision for reference to a
Court, nor does the Committee perform a conciliatory role. The
Committee's function is simply to receive applications, examine
them and subsequently "forward its views to the State Party concerned and the individual" on whether the Covenant has been
breached. The Committee considers applications in private. There
are no oral hearings. The Committee's views, which are not
binding, are published as annexes to its annual report. A majority
of the applications considered by the Committee were against
Uruguay (for example, the *Weinberger Case*)[37] but the Committee has also confirmed alleged breaches, *inter alia*, by Canada,

[33] U.K.T.S. 6 (1977) Cmnd.6702; 6 I.L.M. 383 (1967); 61 A.J.I.L. 870 (1967).
[34] Art. 1 of the 1966 Covenant; the Committee is also competent under Art. 5 of the
Second Optional Protocol (1990).
[35] 991 Communications from individuals, as of July, 2001.
[36] Arts 3 and 5.
[37] Report of the Human Rights Committee, G.A.O.R., 36th Session, Supp.40, p.114.

220   *Human Rights*

Mauritius and Finland. In the *Lovelace Case*,[38] a provision of
Canada's Indian Act, denying an Indian woman from returning
to her native Indian reserve on the break up of her marriage to a
non-Indian, was held to be in violation of Art.27 of the Covenant.
In the *Mauritian Women Case*,[39] Mauritian legislation placing
Mauritian women married to foreign husbands, but not Mauritian men married to foreign women, at risk of deportation was
found to be contrary to Arts 2(1), 3 and 26 in relation to Arts 17(1)
and 23(1) of the Covenant. As for compliance, Uruguay made
little consistent effort, whereas Canada and Mauritius amended
their "offending" legislation. Several states have now made
changes to their own laws as a result of decisions by the Human
Rights Committee on complaints from individuals under the
Optional Protocol.

The Optional Protocol entered into force in March 1976 and
has been adopted by more than 100 parties. Neither the United
Kingdom nor the United States has accepted the Optional Protocol. The General Assembly adopted a resolution in 1993 creating
the post of the High Commissioner for Human Rights to promote
and protect civil, cultural, economic, political and social rights.[40]
The first UN High Commissioner for Human Rights was Mr Jose
Ayala–Lasso, the Ecuadorian Ambassador to the United Nations
at the time. Mary Robinson, former president of Ireland, was his
successor. She took up office in 1997.

Human Rights Commission. An important body engaged in
the examination of alleged violations of human rights is the
Human Rights Commission, a subsidiary body of ECOSOC. The
Commission comprises representatives of 53 Member States, cho-
sen to reflect an equitable geographical distribution. A notable
function of the Commission is its competence under ECOSOC
Resolution 1235 (XLII) adopted in 1967 to "examine information
relevant to gross violations of human rights" and to study
"situations which reveal a consistent pattern of violations of
human rights". This power has been utilised by the Commission
to undertake public investigations against particular states for
alleged violations of human rights. Normally, the Commission
operates on an ad hoc basis, for example Iran, 1990, but, if a particular situation warrants it a standing working group may be
established—for example, suppression of political opposition in
Chile. The Human Rights Commission held its 58th session in
April, 2002. At that session, it was decided to appoint a Special

[38] 1981 Report of the Human Rights Committee, p.166.
[39] *ibid.* p.134.
[40] A/Res.48/141 adopted December 20, 1993.

Rapporteur on the right to health; establish two new working groups dedicated to racism, as agreed at the World Conference against Racism held in South Africa (the Durban Declaration and Programme of Action); also establish a voluntary fund to provide, amongst other things, additional resources for the effective implementation of the Durban Declaration and Programme for Action. Colombia was also discussed and the mandates of the Special Representatives on Human Rights in Equatorial Guinea and Iran were terminated. There have also been five special sessions (as authorised by ECOSOC in resolution 1990/48, May 25, 1990) held since 1992. In October, 2000, a session was called to discuss Grave and Massive violations of the Human Rights of the Palestinian people by Israel and terrorism in the wake of September 11, 2001. In addition to Resolution 1235, there exist the investigatory procedures introduced by Resolution 1503 (XXVIII). Under Resolution 1503, the Economic and Social Council authorised the Human Rights Commission's Sub-Commission on the Prevention of Discrimination and Protection of Minorities to appoint a working group to examine private individual petitions received and to report to the Sub-Commission on those which appear to reveal a "consistent pattern of gross and reliably attested violations of human rights." Resolution 1503 has proved essentially ineffective as, although several situations have been referred to the Commission, they have only been considered in private by the Commission with no further action having been taken.

Do the Optional Protocol and Resolution 1503 overlap? Although, *prima facie*, there may appear to be a potential overlap, there does remain a fundamental difference between the two procedures. The Optional Protocol is concerned primarily with individual, identifiable violations of human rights, whilst Resolution 1503 is concerned with an examination of situations. Also, the latter is applicable to all states and concerns violations of all human rights embodied in the Universal Declaration of Human Rights, whereas the former applies only to States Parties to the Optional Protocol and only to those civil and political rights mentioned in the Covenant on Civil and Political Rights.

The Commission has also established working groups which have the raison d'être of investigating particular subject areas of concern, such as religious intolerance, torture, minority rights conscientious objection to military service, integration of human rights of women and the gender perspective, and indigenous issues.

Notwithstanding the foregoing competencies, the Commission's powers remain limited. The Commission has no competence to enforce its findings, its recommendations are simply that, namely recommendations and Commission delegations have no mandatory authority to enter a territory or examine witnesses.

OTHER UNITED NATIONS CONVENTIONS GUARANTEEING PARTICULAR HUMAN RIGHTS

A number of international conventions guaranteeing specific human rights have been concluded under the auspices of the United Nations. Such conventions include the 1948 Genocide Convention,[41] 1966 Convention on the Elimination of All Forms of Racial Discrimination,[42] 1973 Convention on the Suppression and Punishment of the Crime of Apartheid,[43] 1979 Convention on the Elimination of All Forms of Discrimination Against Women,[44] 1984 Convention Against Torture and Other Cruel, Inhuman or Degrading Treatment or Punishment,[45] 1989 Convention on the Rights of the Child, supplemented by two additional protocols, namely the Optional Protocol to the Convention of the Rights of the Child on the involvement of Children in Armed Conflict (GA Res. A/RES/54/263, 25 May 2000 and came into force on 12 February 2002) and the Optional Protocol to the Convention on the Rights of the Child Concerning the Sale of Children, Child Prostitution and Child Pornography (GA Res. A/RES/54/263, 25 May 2000 and came into force on 18 January 2002). and the 1990 Convention on Migrant Workers.[46] All the foregoing Conventions are in force. Enforcement is primarily by the submission of reports by Contracting Parties to a relevant Committee, however, under the Convention Against Torture and Other Cruel, Inhuman or Degrading Treatment or Punishment, there is provision for inter-state and individual petition, subject to the state concerned accepting the competence of the Committee in this respect. There is now an Optional Protocol to the Convention on the Elimination of All Forms of Discrimination against Women, which provides for individual petition against a consenting Contracting Party.[47]

Of particular note is the enforcement procedure of the Convention on the Elimination of All Forms of Racial Discrimination, which provides for an optional system of individual petition whereby an individual, or group of individuals, can lodge a complaint within the Convention (Art.14). Thirty-eight states have made a declaration recognising the competence of the Committee to receive such complaints. This can only occur if the alleged offending state has accepted the optional individual complaint

---

[41] U.K.T.S. 58 (1970) Cmnd.4421; 79 U.N.T.S. 277; see also Chs 4 and 6, above.
[42] U.K.T.S. 77 (1969) Cmnd.4108; 60 U.N.T.S. 195.
[43] 13 I.L.M. 50 (1974).
[44] Misc.1 (1982) Cmnd.8444; 19 I.L.M. 33 (1980).
[45] Misc.12 (1985) Cmnd.9593; 23 I.L.M. 1027 (1984); 24 I.L.M. 535 (1985).
[46] 28 I.L.M. 1448 (1989).
[47] Art.2. The Protocol was opened for signature on October 6, 1999, and entered into force December 22, 2000. GA RES. A/54/4.

procedure. The right of individual petition was employed successfully in *Yilmaz-Dogan v Netherlands*.[48] There is a compulsory inter-state complaint procedure, but this has never been utilised. The Committee on the Elimination of All Forms of Racial Discrimination, a body of 18 independent experts, is central to the enforcement of the Convention. It receives reports from Contracting Parties and forwards to the General Assembly suggestions and general recommendations as it sees fit. Art.22 of the Convention provides for compulsory reference to the International Court of Justice in the event of any "dispute between two or more States Parties with respect to the interpretation or application of this Convention ... unless the disputants agree to another mode of settlement." This represents an interesting attempt at strengthening international enforcement. However, the lodging by states of reservations to this provision undermines its potential.

A state which is a party to two or more instruments on human rights may be required to submit a number of reports and this has prompted the suggestion that there should be a standardisation of reports, to the effect that such states could refer to documents already supplied, thereby preventing a duplication of information in the preparation of reports. The Vienna Conference identified a number of fundamental human rights which the Conference felt required international attention, some of which are briefly considered here. For instance, the elimination of racism and discrimination was highlighted as a priority for the international community.[49] The Vienna Conference indorsed the appointment by the Commission on Human Rights of a Special Rapporteur to consider contemporary forms of racism, racial discrimination, xenophobia and related intolerance.[50]

Women were identified at the Vienna Conference as a group particularly vulnerable in the international community. The Conference confirmed that the full and equal participation of women in political, civil, economic, social and cultural life at national, regional and international levels and eradication of all forms of discrimination on grounds of sex was an important objective.[51] The Declaration adopted at the Vienna Conference coincided with a Declaration on the Elimination of Violence Against Women which recognised that violence against women because of their

---

[48] C.E.R.D. Report, G.A.O.R., 43rd Session, Supp.18, p.59 (1988).
[49] The most recent World Conference on Racism, being held in South Africa in September 2001, culminating in the Durban Declaration and Programme of Action.
[50] The UN Commission on Human Rights adopted Res.1993/20, February 26, 1993 at its 49th, session when Mr Dossou was appointed Special Rapporteur.
[51] Pt I, para.18 of the Declaration.

gender was a specific problem.[52] This Declaration urges states to ratify the 1979 Convention on Elimination of Discrimination[53] and leaves implementation of the objectives to states. The Fourth UN Conference on Women, held in Beijing in September, 1995, looked specifically at areas of particular concern to the advancement of women and adopted a Platform of Action to tackle these issues.[54] The Platform of Action "is an agenda for women's empowerment"[55] and includes actions to eradicate poverty, eliminate violence and inequality in education, promote women's human rights and ensure access to relevant health care.[56] In June, 2000, Beijing Plus Five was discussed in a special session of the General Assembly. At the end of the session, a political declaration was adopted, by consensus, confirming the political will to implement the Beijing Declaration and Platform for Action.

The United Nations adopted a Draft Declaration on the Rights of Indigenous Peoples in 1994,[57] which was submitted to the Commission on Human Rights in 1995 for further consideration.[58] The Declaration is unprecedented in its recognition of group rights of indigenous peoples. The United Nations declared 1994–2004 as the International Decade of the World's Indigenous People.

The international protection of human rights does not lie exclusively with the United Nations. Regional bodies have promulgated regional instruments, the most notable of which is the European Convention on Human Rights,[59] which has a sophisticated enforcement mechanism and has developed an extensive jurisprudence. Human Rights also features on the agenda of other bodies, for example the Red Cross and certain of the specialised agencies of the United Nations, such as the International Labour Organisation.

---

[52] Adopted by GA Res.48/104, February 23, 1994.

[53] See below, at n.57.

[54] A/CONF.177/20, October 17, 1995; 35 I.L.M. 401 (1996).

[55] Ch.1, Mission Statement.

[56] See Ch.IV, paras 45–285 which contain the Strategic Objectives and Actions.

[57] Res.1994/45, adopted August 26, 1994 by the UN Sub-Commission on Prevention of Discrimination and Protection of Minorities, 46th Session, 1994. See 34 I.L.M. 541 (1995).

[58] The Human Rights Commission had on its agenda at the 53rd session in Geneva from March 10 to April 18, 1997, a report of the Secretary General on the possible establishment of a permanent forum for indigenous people within the UN. This was established and held its first meeting on May 13, 2002.

[59] 213 U.N.T.S. 221; U.K.T.S. (1953) Cmd.8969.

HUMAN RIGHTS AND INTERNATIONAL CRIMINAL LAW

The League of Nations in 1937, for instance, initiated a Convention for the Prevention and Punishment of Terrorism[60] and a Convention for the Creation of an International Criminal Court,[61] but the former received only one ratification, while the latter received none. Televised reports of war camps, rape, genocide and the practice of ethnic cleansing shocked the international community, and led to the creation of an ad hoc International Tribunal under Chapter VII of the UN Charter to punish the alleged perpetrators of such crimes. The International Tribunal for the Prosecution of Persons Responsible for Serious Violations of International Humanitarian Law Committed in the Territory of the Former Yugoslavia (the ICTY) was established by UN Security Council Resolution 827 on May 23, 1993 for the sole purpose of:

> "prosecuting persons responsible for serious violations of international humanitarian law committed in the territory of the former Yugoslavia between 1st January, 1991 and a date to be determined by the Security Council upon the restoration of peace."[62]

The Tribunal was designed to establish a judicial process aimed at preventing the continuation of crimes against humanity and to contribute towards the restoration and maintenance of peace and security in the region.

The Tribunal has jurisdiction under the Convention on the Prevention and Punishment of the Crime of Genocide[63] to prosecute individuals responsible for grave breaches of the Convention, laws of war, and crimes against humanity.[64] The Tribunal differs from its predecessor (Nuremberg) in that it may also hear cases of crimes perpetrated in the course of inter-state war and internal strife. Nuremberg could only deal with crimes committed in international armed conflict. It is the first time the Security Council has created an international tribunal using Chapter VII powers and can therefore be said to be a truly international entity.[65]

---

[60] 7 Hudson 862.

[61] 7 Hudson 878. For a synopsis of events precipitating the crisis see, Marc Weller, "The International Response to the Dissolution of the Socialist Federal Republic of Yugoslavia" 86 A.J.I.L. 568.

[62] S.C.Res 827, UN SCOR, 48th Year, 3217th mtg at 1, reprinted in 32 I.L.M. 1203 (1993).

[63] Adopted December 9, 1948.

[64] Arts 2, 3, 4 and 5 of the Genocide Convention and Art.20 of the Tribunal's Statute (see below).

[65] The Nuremberg tribunal was established in very different circumstances when there was no government in power.

Human Rights

The Statue of the Tribunal[66] embodies the most detailed rules and procedures ever drafted for an international criminal tribunal.[67] The rules reflect international human rights standards, particularly those enshrined in the International Covenant on Civil and Political Rights, for example Art.21(a), which deals with the accused's right to be present at his trial and Art.25, which provides the accused with a right of appeal.

The Tribunal issued its first indictment and warrant for arrest against a former commander of the Susica camp in the Republic of Bosnia–Herzegovina, Dragan Nikolic, in November, 1994. It also requested the deferral by the Federal Courts of Germany of criminal proceedings against Dusko Tadic, emphasising the international community's desire to create a truly international entity. Art.9(2) of the Statue provides that the ICTY shall have primacy over national courts. This applies to situations where the tribunal requests the national courts to transfer the accused and the investigation to its jurisdiction. Jurisdiction is otherwise concurrent with national courts.

Eleven judges were elected by the General Assembly in September 1993 and took office on November 17, 1993.[68] Art.16 makes provision for a prosecutor who is charged with:

> "the investigation and prosecution of persons responsible for serious violations of international humanitarian law committed in the territory of the former Yugoslavia since January 1, 1991. Arts 23 and 24 confer sentencing powers on the Judges who must make their decision public along with a reasoned opinion. Convicted persons may be imprisoned but there is no death sentence."[69]

The work of the Tribunal has been greatly impeded by a number of shortcomings, in particular unsatisfactory funding arrangements.[70] Problems have also arisen concerning the apprehension of alleged war criminals and the enforcement of international

---

[66] Adopted by Security Council Res.827, May 25, 1993, reproduced in 32 I.L.M. 1192 (1993).

[67] Rules and Procedure and Evidence, adopted pursuant to Art.15 of the Statute of the Tribunal, which came into force, March 14, 1994; 33 I.L.M. 484 (1994). They have been amended on several occasions since, *e.g.* see 35 I.L.M. 1342 (1996).

[68] Art.12. Judges are assigned to chambers for a period of one year, after which they will rotate.

[69] Art.24.

[70] This is no longer the case in respect to Yugoslavia, as the following figures reinforce—1993, $276,000; *cf.* 2002–03, $223,169,800.

arrest warrants.[71] The ICTY passed its first sentence in December 1996 sentencing a Croatian soldier in the Bosnian Serb army to 10 years in prison for his part in the slaughter of Muslims in the UN "safe-haven" of Srebrenica, and Tadic was sentenced on July 14, 1997 to 20 years' imprisonment. However, one of the most wanted, Slobodan Milosevic, the former president of Serbia, was apprehended and handed over to the Tribunal in June, 2001.

The events precipitating the creation of the International Tribunal for the Prosecution of Persons Responsible for Genocide and Other Serious Violations of International Humanitarian Law Committed in the Territory of Rwanda and Rwandan Citizens Responsible for Genocide and Other Such Violations Committed in the Territory of Neighbouring States, between January 1, 1994 and December 31, 1994, (ICTR) were, according to one Report, "a pre-planned execution of severe human right violations, including systematic, widespread and flagrant breaches of international humanitarian law, large-scale crimes against humanity and genocide."[72] The estimated death toll in the 1994 massacre was approximately one million people.

ICTR was established on November 8, 1994 by UNSC Resolution 955.[73] Despite efforts to extend the Statute of the ICTY to cover crimes perpetrated in the territory of Rwanda and maintain a single Tribunal to cover both Yugoslavia and Rwanda, the Rwandan government objected due to pressure from the Rwandan people to be seen to punish the perpetrators of genocide in the territory of Rwanda itself.[74] ICTR does, however, share the same chief prosecutor and appeals chamber as the ICTY. The first prosecutor was Louise Arbour of Canada, who has been succeeded by Carla del Ponte of Switzerland.

Notwithstanding the criticisms, the establishment of these Tribunals was undoubtedly a significant step towards the establishment of a permanent international criminal tribunal and endorsed a willingness amongst UNSC members to co-operate in apprehending and prosecuting alleged perpetrators of international crime.

---

[71] Those convicted of genocide and crimes against humanity include the Rwandan former Prime Minister and Head of Interim Government in 1994, Me. Jean Kamboda.

[72] Preliminary Report of the Independent Commission of Experts established in accordance with Security Council Resolution 935 (2994) UN Doc.S/1994/1125 of October 4, 1994, para.42.

[73] S.C.Res. 955, UN SCOR, 49th year, 3453d mtg at 1. UN Doc.S/RES/955 (1994).

[74] It was eventually decided to establish the Tribunal in Arusha in the United Republic of Tanzania.

A permanent international criminal court

The experience of both the ICTY and the ICTR heightened calls for the creation of a permanent Court.[75] The General Assembly, for example, adopted a resolution on January 16, 1997, which confirmed its commitment to establish an international criminal court. The General Assembly renewed the mandate of the Preparatory Committee[76] and decided to convene a diplomatic conference of plenipotentiaries to be held in Italy in 1998 with a view to finalising and adopting a convention on the establishment of a permanent international criminal court.[77]

The Permanent International Criminal Court.

The Convention was finalised and opened for signature at the conclusion of the Conference. The Convention has now received the requisite number of ratifications to enter into force and will do so on July 1, 2002.[78] The establishment of the Court is regarded as making good a deficiency in the international legal system. It will also remove the need for ad hoc tribunals such as ICTY and ICTR and guard against what has been referred to as "tribunal fatigue". Delays are characteristic of any ad hoc system, but expeditious procedures are essential in criminal law. Otherwise memories fade and, as a consequence, evidence is difficult to obtain. The Court will be established in the Hague, the Netherlands by 2003. The Court will be constituted by 18 judges elected for a 9 year term. The jurisdiction of the Court is set out in Art.5.1 and is "genocide", crimes against humanity, war crimes and crimes of aggression. The various terms are defined in Articles 6 (genocide), 7 (crimes against humanity), and 8 (war crimes) and crimes of aggression.[79] The

---

[75] See the Draft Statute for an International Criminal Court, in the Report of the International Law Commission on Its Forty-sixth Session, UN G.A.O.R., 49th Sess., Supp.No.10 at 43, UN Doc.A/49/10 (1994). See 33 I.L.M. 253 (1994). The ILC has also been asked in the context of its work on the Draft Code of Crimes Against the Peace and Security of Mankind to address the question of a permanent international criminal court. GA Res.48/31 UN G.A.O.R., 48th Sess., Supp.No.49, at 328, UN Doc.A/48/49 (1993).

[76] The Preparatory Committee was established by GA Res.50/46, December 11, 1995 with the specific task of preparing the text of an international convention for a permanent international criminal court.

[77] 51st session, UN GA Res.A/Res/51/207, January 16, 1997.

[78] The UK is a Contracting Party. The US, in April, 2002, withdrew notwithstanding the Clinton administration's acceptance as reflected in its signing the Convention in October, 2000.

[79] The Court shall exercise jurisdiction over the crime of aggression once a provision is adopted in accordance with Arts 121 and 123, defining the crime and setting out the conditions under which the Court shall exercise jurisdiction with respect to this crime. Such a provision shall be consistent with the relevant provisions of the Charter of the UN.

Court will have jurisdiction in respect of crimes which occur after July 1, 2002.[80]

The establishment of the court is evidence that the international community recognises that there is a role for a permanent international regime. To be effective, this demands the recognition that certain crimes are of international concern and arguably are more effectively dealt within an international forum. However, as highlighted, "No provision . . . relating to individual criminal responsibility shall affect the responsibility of states under international law."[81]

CONCLUSION

Human rights in the twenty first century have been seen in the international global context. The facts are not palatable and certainly do not suggest a world which respects human rights. The task confronting the international community is to work together to achieve a world in which there is mutual respect for all individuals as individuals and an absence of arbitrary discrimination. International human rights instruments in themselves will not prove the ultimate panacea but they do highlight awareness, which hopefully, with the passage of time, will cascade to all levels of society and will provide, at the very least, a minimum standard which will become the norm for all rather than the exception.

---

[80] For the jurisdiction of the Court, see Ch.6.
[81] Art.25.4 of the Statute.

10. THE LAW OF TREATIES

The importance of treaties has already been acknowledged. Treaties are increasingly utilised to regulate relations between international persons and the expansion in the subject-matter of international law is reflected in the diversity of subject-matter regulated by treaty.

Treaty law is, for the most part, non-controversial. As the international law of contract, it is essentially lawyer's law. What is a treaty? How is a treaty concluded? How is a treaty to be interpreted?

The law relating to these questions is best considered against the backcloth of the 1969 Vienna Convention on the Law of Treaties.[1] The Convention, which entered into force in January, 1980, was the product of 20 years' work by the International Law Commission. The Convention is regarded as essentially codifying customary international law, though some of the provisions are seen as representing progressive development, for example Art.53.

The Convention, as a convention, does not have retroactive effect, but because it spells out established rules, the Convention may be applied to agreements pre-dating the Convention, for

---

[1] U.K.T.S. 58 (1980) Cmnd.7964; 8 I.L.M. 679 (1969); A.J.I.L. 875 (1969).

example in the League of Nations Mandate in the *Namibia (South West Africa) Case*,[2] and similarly in the *Beagle Channel Arbitration*,[3] the Convention's rules were applied to the 1881 Argentina/Chile Treaty.

A Convention on the Law of Treaties Between States and International Organisations or Between International Organisations was adopted on March 21, 1986,[4] but has not yet entered into force.[5] The Convention's provisions closely parallel those of the 1969 Convention.

DEFINITION OF A TREATY

"Treaty" is the generic term used to embrace convention, agreement, arrangement, protocol, and exchange of notes. International law does not distinguish between agreements identified as treaties and other agreements. The name accorded to an agreement is not in itself important and is of no legal effect.[6]

For the purposes of the Convention " 'treaty' means an international agreement concluded between States in written form and governed by international law . . .".[7]

The Convention concerns itself only with written agreements. But can states enter into oral agreements?

Treaties invariably are in written form. It cannot be stated unequivocally, however, that an oral agreement has no legal significance. Oral statements have been held to be binding.

In 1919, the Danish Government informed the Norwegian Government, through their representative in Norway, that they would not raise any objection at the Paris Peace Conference to the Norwegian claim over Spitzbergen, if Norway would not challenge Danish claims of sovereignty over all Greenland. The then Norwegian Foreign Minister, M. Ihlen, subsequently reported to his Danish counterpart that "the Norwegian Government would not make any difficulty." Denmark argued before the Permanent Court of International Justice in the *Legal Status of Eastern*

---

[2] I.C.J.Rep. 1971 16 at 47.

[3] 17 I.L.M. 632 at 645 (1978).

[4] Misc. 11 (1987) Cm.244; 25 I.L.M. 543 (1986).

[5] The Convention shall enter into force on the 30th day following the date of deposit of the 35th instrument of ratification or accession by States or by Namibia, represented by the UN Council for Namibia, in accordance with Art.85(1). Instruments of formal confirmation deposited by international organisations are not counted towards the entry into force of the Convention. The UK has been a party since June 20, 1991.

[6] Within a municipal system "treaty" may have a specialised meaning as, *e.g.* in the US.

[7] Art.2(1)(a). Note the comments of the ICJ in the *Maritime Delimitations and Territorial Questions Case (Qatar v Bahrain)* 1994 J.C.J.Rep.112 with respect to what may constitute an international agreement at pp.121–122.

Greenland[8] that Norway had, by the "Ihlen Declaration", recognised Danish sovereignty. The court denied that the "Ihlen Declaration" constituted a recognition of Danish sovereignty, but did, however, maintain that Norway had incurred a legally binding obligation to refrain from contesting Danish sovereignty over Greenland. The Permanent Court did not, however, characterise the "Ihlen Declaration" as an oral agreement, nor did it define the circumstances, if any, in which a unilateral statement could be binding. The Court rather emphasised the contemporaneous acceptance by Denmark of the Norwegian claims over Spitzbergen.

The International Court of Justice was confronted with the legal nature of unilateral declarations in the *Nuclear Tests Cases*,[9] in which Australia and New Zealand sought a decision from the court against France, that the latter's testing of nuclear weapons in the atmosphere was contrary to international law. The Court found that the series of public statements made by France announcing that she would refrain from further testing, was sufficient to commit her and negate Australian and New Zealand objections.

Not all written agreements necessarily establish binding relations. The Charter of Paris for a New Europe, adopted at the Conference on Security and Co-operation in Europe,[10] is an instance of soft law.[11]

Art.102 of the UN Charter provides for the registration[11a] with the Secretariat of the United Nations of every treaty and international agreement entered into by any Member State and, unless a treaty or international agreement is registered, it cannot be invoked before any organ of the United Nations. Registration provides tangible evidence that the agreement is to be regarded as a treaty and that that is the intention of the parties concerned; for example, the Charter of Paris for a New Europe[12] provides that the Charter is "not eligible for registration under Art.102 of the Charter of the United Nations . . .". Non-registration or late registration does not affect the binding nature of the agreement between the parties concerned.[13]

---

[8] P.C.I.J.Rep. ser.A/B, No.53 (1933).

[9] I.C.J.Rep. 1974 253, 457. see, also comments of the ICJ in the *Frontier Dispute Case* (*Burkina Faso v Mali*) I.C.J.Rep. (1986), 554 in which the court stated that unilateral statements could only bind a state where it was apparent that the state intended to be bound, *i.e.* only in exceptional circumstances.

[10] 30 I.L.M. 190 (1991).

[11] See Ch.2, above, p.31.

[11a] Approximately 40,000 treaties have been registered.

[12] Above, n.10.

[13] *Maritime Delimitation and Territorial Questions Case* at 122, above, n.7.

For the Vienna Convention to apply to an international agreement, the latter must be in written form, must reflect the intention of the parties to be bound and must be governed by international law.[14]

TREATY-MAKING COMPETENCE

Municipal law

Arrangements for the exercise of a state's treaty-making powers are left to each state and the constitutional requirements with respect to the ratification of treaties vary widely. A state may not plead a breach of its constitutional provisions relating to treaty-making so as to invalidate an agreement, unless such a breach was manifest and "objectively evident to any state conducting itself in the matter in accordance with normal practice and in good faith."[15]

International law

A state representative may conclude a treaty on behalf of a state if (a) he possesses full powers, or (b) if, from the practice of the states concerned or from other circumstances, it can be deduced that he enjoys full powers.

"Full powers" refers to the document:

> "emanating from the competent authority of a State designating a person or persons, to represent the State for negotiating, adopting or authenticating the text of a treaty, for expressing the consent of the State to be bound by a treaty, or for accomplishing any other act with respect to a treaty."[16]

Heads of State, governments and foreign affairs ministers are regarded as possessing by virtue of their office "full powers".[17]

An act relating to the conclusion of a treaty performed by a person who cannot be considered as enjoying "full powers" and thereby authorised to represent a state for that purpose is without legal effect, unless afterwards confirmed by that state.[18]

---

[14] Treaties may be employed as a vehicle for the expression of soft law.
[15] Art.46.
[16] Art.2(1)(c).
[17] In *Qatar v Bahrain*, above, n.7 at 121–122, the court denied the claim of Bahrain's Foreign Minister that he had no authority under Bahrain's constitution to conclude a treaty as the existence of a valid treaty had to be determined objectively.
[18] Art.8.

Adoption and confirmation of the text of a treaty

The text of a treaty may be adopted by the consent of all states participating in the drafting or, alternatively, by the majority vote of two-thirds of states present and voting, or by a different procedure if the two-thirds majority so agree.[19]

Expression of consent

A state may indicate its consent to be bound by a treaty in a variety of ways, for example signature, signature *ad referendum*, ratification and accession.

Simple signature may be sufficient to bind parties, but, frequently, signature *ad referendum* is employed, that is signature subject to later ratification. Although lacking legal effect, *ad referendum* implies political approval and a moral obligation to seek ratification. Ratification in international law refers to the subsequent formal confirmation (subsequent to signature) by a state that it is bound by a treaty. Ratification is employed most frequently by those states (for example, the United States) which are required to initiate some parliamentary process to gain approval to their being bound by the international agreement in question. Between signature and ratification, a state is under an obligation to refrain from acts which would defeat the object and purpose of the treaty.[20]

Accession

A state may, in acceding to a treaty, express its consent to be bound by the terms of the treaty, that is a non-signatory state may subsequently become a party under a procedure provided for in the treaty concerned. The term "adhesion" may also be encountered. Adhesion is distinct from accession in that it refers to a state's acceptance of either only certain aspects of the treaty or certain principles contained in it.

Reservations

Treaties may be likened to legislation, but, unlike municipal law, where legislative measures apply uniformly to all, international law allows a state to become a party to a treaty while, nevertheless, opting out from the application of certain provisions.

Art.2(1)(d) of the Vienna Convention defines a reservation as a "unilateral statement, however phrased or named, made by a State, when signing, ratifying, accepting, approving or acceding

---

[19] Art.9.
[20] Art.18(a).

to a treaty, whereby it purports to exclude or to modify the legal effect of certain provisions of the treaty in their application to that State."

A reservation is distinct from an "interpretative declaration" in that the latter is simply a statement by a party to the treaty as to the position it adopts concerning some aspect of the treaty. It is not an attempt by the state in question to achieve derogation from the application of the treaty.[21]

Reservations only apply in respect of multipartite treaties. They cannot apply with regard to bipartite treaties, where the rejection of a proposed provision constitutes the refusal of an offer made and therefore demands a renegotiation of the proposed term.

Traditionally, it was maintained that a reservation could only be inserted if all Contracting Parties to the treaty consented. In the absence of unanimous agreement, the reservation was null and void. However, with the increase in the number of states and the simultaneous growth in the complexity of treaty subject-matter, achieving the concurrence of all the states involved became a problem. What was required, if states were not to reject completely treaties which contained a particular provision to which they took exception, was a more flexible approach to reservations. The Advisory Opinion requested in respect of *Reservations to the Convention on Genocide Case*[22] heralded the necessary change in approach.

The court was of the view that a state, making a reservation to which one or more but not all parties to the Convention, had raised an objection, could be regarded as a party to the Convention *provided* (emphasis added) the reservation was compatible with the object and purpose of the Convention. As to the effect of a reservation between the reserving state and (i) those objecting and (ii) those accepting the reservation, the court's response was:

"(a) that if a party to the Convention objects to a reservation which it considers to be incompatible with the object and purpose of the Convention, it can in fact consider that the reserving State is not a party to the Convention;

(b) that if, on the other hand, a party accepts the reservation as being compatible with the object and purpose of the Convention, it can in fact consider that the reserving State is a party to the Convention."[23]

[21] For further discussion, see D. McRae 49 B.Y.I.L. 155 (1978) and the case of *Belilos v Switzerland* E.C.H.R., Series A, No.132, Judgment of April 20, 1988—see below. See also the general comments of the UN Human Rights Committee on the effect of reservations made to the International Covenant on Civil and Political Rights and the Optional Protocols, 34 I.L.M. 840 (1995).

[22] I.C.J.Rep. 1951 15.

[23] *ibid.* at 29–30.

The court's opinion introduced the test of compatibility. This test, which is applied by states themselves, in the light of the court's opinion, is a matter of subjective interpretation. The court's opinion marked a sharp contrast to the previous approach, namely one of unity and a minimising of deviance from treaty provisions. The court's opinion opened up the possibility of different legal relationships existing between different parties to the same agreement.

The Vienna Convention allows reservations unless:

"(a)   the reservation is prohibited by treaty;" for example Art.64 of the European Convention on Human Rights prohibits "reservations of a general character"[24];

"(b)   the treaty provides that only specified reservations, which do not include the reservation in question, may be made; or

(c)   in cases not falling under sub-paragraphs (a) and (b), the reservation is incompatible with the object and purpose of the treaty."[25]

Incompatibility with the object and purpose of the treaty can relate either to substantive provisions of the treaty, or to the nature and spirit of the treaty. For a case dealing with the "object and purpose" issue, see the *Restrictions to the Death Penalty Case*.[26] A convention may provide a mechanism for deciding whether a provision is compatible or not, for example the Convention on Racial Discrimination deems a reservation to be incompatible if at least two-thirds of Contracting Parties object to it.[27]

Acceptance of and objection to reservations

A reservation which is expressly authorised by a treaty does not demand the subsequent approval of other contracting parties unless required by the treaty.

---

[24] See *Belilos v Switzerland*, above, n.21 in which the Swiss reservation was declared invalid, *inter alia*, because it was "couched in terms that are too vague or broad for it to be possible to determine their exact scope or meaning", thus it was a "reservation of a general character".

[25] Art.19. In the *Effect of Reservations Case*, it was stated that Art.75 of the American Convention on Human Rights 1969 had impliedly incorporated Art.19(c) and thus allowed reservations which were not "incompatible with the object and purpose of the treaty." Art.75 provides that the American Convention on Human Rights "shall be subject to reservations only in conformity with" the Vienna Convention on the Law of Treaties.

[26] 23 I.L.M. 320 (1983).

[27] Art 20 of the International Convention on the Elimination of All Forms of Racial Discrimination 1966, U.K.T.S. 77 (1969) Cmnd.4108.

If, however, it is apparent from the limited number of states concerned and from the object and purpose of the treaty "that the application of the treaty in its entirety between all the parties is an essential condition of the consent of each one to be bound by the treaty", then any reservation must be accepted by *all* the parties.

In respect of a treaty which is the constituent instrument of an international organisation, a reservation, unless it is otherwise provided, must be accepted by the competent organ of the relevant organisation.

The general rules to be followed in other cases are that:

"(a)   acceptance by another Contracting State of a reservation constitutes the reserving State a party to the treaty in relation to that other State if or when the treaty is in force for those States;

(b)   an objection by another Contracting State to a reservation does not preclude the entry into force of the treaty as between the objecting and reserving States unless a contrary intention is definitely expressed by the objecting State;

(c)   an act expressing a State's consent to be bound by the treaty and containing a reservation is effective as soon as at least one other Contracting State has accepted the reservation."[28]

If a state does not object to a reservation (a) within 12 months of having been informed of the reservation, or (b) within 12 months of having expressed consent to be bound by the treaty—depending on which is later—that state will be deemed to have expressed its consent to be bound by the treaty.[29]

Legal effects of reservations and of objections to reservations

The effect of a reservation established with regard to another party is that it:

"(a)   modifies for the reserving State in its relations with that other party the provisions of the treaty to which the reservation relates to the extent of the reservation; and

(b)   modifies those provisions to the same extent for that other party in its relations with the reserving State."[30]

---

[28] Art.20(4).

[29] Art.20(5).

[30] *e.g.*, Libya's reservation to the Vienna Convention on Diplomatic Relations, whereby the diplomatic bag could be intercepted in suspicious circumstances,

If a state objects to a reservation, but does not oppose the entry into force of the treaty between itself and the reserving state, the provisions to which the reservation relates do not apply as between the two states to the extent of the reservation. The provisions of the treaty for the other Contracting Parties are not modified by the reservation.[31] The effect of Art.21(3) is illustrated by the Arbitration Tribunal's decision in the *Anglo–French Continental Shelf Case*[32]:

> "the combined effect of the French reservations and their rejection by the United Kingdom is neither to render Art.6 [that is, Art.6 of the 1958 Geneva Convention on the Continental Shelf] inapplicable *in toto*, as the French Republic contends, nor to render it applicable *in toto*, as the United Kingdom primarily contends. It is to render the Article inapplicable as between the two countries to the extent of the reservations."[33]

The effect in practice of a reservation is that a multipartite agreement becomes fragmented. States will be parties to the same agreement, but in effect, one agreement will exist between some Contracting Parties while another agreement will exist between other parties. In other words, under the umbrella of one multipartite convention, several separate agreements may evolve. The overall purpose of the reservation system is to induce as many states as possible to adhere to a multipartite agreement.

A reservation, and an objection to a reservation, must be expressed in writing, but may be withdrawn at any time, unless otherwise provided for in the treaty. The withdrawal of a reservation becomes operative only when the state(s) concerned receive notice of the withdrawal. Similarly, the withdrawal of an objection to a reservation only has effect when received by the reserving state. An express acceptance of a reservation must also be formulated in writing.

Entry into force

A treaty enters into force in such a manner and upon such a date as it (the treaty) may provide, or as the negotiating states may agree.[34]

---

would by the operation of the principle of reciprocity have entitled the UK to exercise the same right; see *Libyan People's Bureau Incident*.
[31] Art.21(3).
[32] 18 I.L.M. 397 (1979).
[33] *ibid*. at 341.
[34] Art.16.

A multipartite treaty normally comes into force following receipt of a stipulated number of ratifications or accessions, for example the Vienna Convention provided for its own entry into force "on the thirtieth day following the date of deposit of the thirty-fifth instrument of ratification or accession."[35] Once the required number of ratifications has been received, a treaty will normally provide how soon after receipt of consent an agreement enters into force at the international level for the states concerned, for example, the 1982 Law of the Sea Convention entered into force one year after the 60th ratification, namely on November 16, 1994; The Rome Statute, establishing a Permanent International Criminal Court, will enter into force on July 1, 2002, 60 days after the 60th state has become party to the Statute through ratification or accession.

OBSERVANCE AND APPLICATION OF TREATIES[36]

States are charged with performing and fulfilling their treaty obligations, which are binding in good faith—*pacta sunt servanda* is the maxim which expresses this basic canon of treaty observance. As a rule, treaties do not have retroactive effect. If they are to have such effect, this will be expressly stated. Unless otherwise provided, a treaty applies to all the territory of a Contracting Party. The Vienna Convention did not address itself to the question of dependencies. An agreement may spell out the dependencies to which it is to apply, for example the EEC Treaty. If silent, then, for example under US law, an agreement will be deemed to apply to all dependencies of the United States. Parties to a multipartite treaty may agree to conclude a new treaty and accordingly negate any preceding agreement.

All is well if all states consent. However, there may be parties to the old treaties which do not accede to the new agreement. The relationship between two such states will be governed by the treaty to which both states are parties (that is, the former).[37]

TREATY INTERPRETATION

How is a treaty to be interpreted? There are three main approaches in international law to treaty interpretation:

    (a)   the "objective" approach—interpretation in accordance with the ordinary use of the words of the treaty;

---

[35] Art.84(1).
[36] Art.26.
[37] Art.30(4)(b).

    (b)   the "subjective" approach—interpretation in accordance with the intention of the parties to the treaty;

    (c)   the "teleological" approach—interpretation in accordance with the treaty's aims and objectives.

Although characterised as distinct, the three approaches are, in practice, not mutually exclusive. In practice, credence may be given to the principles of the three approaches, as is reflected in the international jurisprudence which has emerged.

The Vienna Convention adopts an integrated approach to interpretation, but nevertheless gives emphasis to the ordinary-meaning approach. Art.31 of the Convention articulates the general rule of interpretation as being that:

> "A treaty shall be interpreted in good faith in accordance with the ordinary meaning to be given to the terms of the treaty in their context and in the light of its object and purpose."

Art.31 allows the use of the teleological approach, but only to shed light on the ordinary meaning of the words of the treaty provisions.[38] It is invoked as an ancillary aid in interpretation and not as an independent approach of interpretation. A special meaning may be given to a term if it is evident that that is what the relevant parties intended. "Context" includes the text of the treaty, the preamble, any annexes and also:

    "(a)   any agreement relating to the treaty which was made between all the parties in connexion with the conclusion of the treaty;

    (b)   any instrument which was made by one or more parties in connexion with the conclusion of the treaty and accepted by the other parties as an instrument related to the treaty."[39]

In addition, account may be taken of:

    "(a)   any subsequent agreement between the parties regarding the interpretation of the treaty or the application of its provisions;

---

[38] The ICJ recognised the provisions of Art.31 as customary international law in the *Territorial Dispute Case* (*Libya v Chad*) I.C.J.Rep. 1994 6; see also the *Kisikili/Sedudu Island* (*Botswana v Namibia*) case, I.C.J., October 13, 1999.

[39] Art.31(2).

    (b)   any subsequent practice in the application of the treaty which establishes the agreement of the parties regarding its interpretation;

    (c)   any relevant rules of international law applicable in the relations between the parties."[40]

If giving the ordinary meaning in the terms of the treaty would lead to an ambiguous or obscure meaning, or would produce a manifestly absurd and unreasonable approach, supplementary means of interpretation may be invoked.[41] Supplementary includes "the preparatory work of the treaty and the circumstances of its conclusion."[42]

Preparatory work—*travaux préparatoires*—is not defined in the Vienna Convention, but the term, it is accepted, refers to records documenting the treaty's drafting and includes the records of negotiations between the participating drafting states.

In certain cases, the opinion of expert bodies may also be utilised. "Circumstances" of its "conclusion" refer not only to contemporary circumstances but also to the historical context against which the treaty was concluded, for example as in the *Anglo-Iranian Oil Co. Case*.[43]

Interpretation of treaties authenticated in two or more languages

A text is equally authoritative in each language, unless the agreement provides and the parties agree that, in the case of divergence, a particular text shall prevail. One text may be designated as authoritative whilst other versions may only be recognised as having the status of "official texts" (that is, a text signed by the negotiating states, but not adopted as authoritative). If there is doubt as to the meaning between texts, the more limited interpretation and the one which will least restrict a state's sovereignty is preferred.

THIRD STATES

Pacta tertiis nec nocent nec prosunt—a treaty does not create either obligations or rights for a third state without its consent. This rule of customary international law is spelt out in Art.34 of the Vienna Convention. This does not preclude a provision contained in a

---

[40] Art.31(3).
[41] The ICJ has rejected supplementary evidence when the text of the treaty is clear, see the *Maritime Delimitation and Territorial Questions Case*.
[42] Art.32.
[43] I.C.J.Rep. 1952 3 at 105.

treaty from becoming law for a non-party when the provision has crystallised into international law. The non-party is bound, not by the treaty, but rather by customary international law.[44] Art.34 contains the general rule—there are exceptions—that special territorial arrangements may produce obligations which third parties are obliged to respect (for example, the Aaland Islands). Art.2(6) of the UN Charter provides that:

> "the organisation shall ensure that States which are not members of the United Nations act in accordance with these principles so far as may be necessary for the maintenance of international peace and security."

Art.2(6) today is regarded as a part of customary international law and any state acting contrary to Art.2(6) would be violating customary international law.

A treaty can produce obligations for a third state "if the parties to the treaty intend the provisions to be the means of establishing the obligation and the third State expressly accepts that obligation in writing."[45] A third state may derive rights from a treaty, for example those guaranteeing freedom of passage through the Suez and Kiel Canals, if that is the intention of the parties to the treaty and the assent of the third state has been secured. In contrast, however, to the assent of states on which an obligation is incumbent, the assent of a benefiting state "shall be presumed so long as the contrary is not indicated, unless the treaty otherwise provides."[46]

AMENDMENT AND MODIFICATION

Both amendment and modification relate to a revision of treaty terms by parties. Amendment is the more formal process involving at least, *prima facie*, all parties to the treaty, while modification is a "private arrangement" between particular parties and in respect of particular provisions.

Amendment

In a bipartite treaty, amendments are straightforward, but, in a multipartite treaty, the agreement of all states to a proposed amendment may be difficult to secure. Art.40 lays down the procedure which, if not provided by the treaty, is to be followed.

---

[44] Art.38.
[45] Art.35.
[46] Art.36(1).

Art.40 allows for amendment by less than all Contracting Parties to the original treaty by permitting amendment between those parties in agreement *after* (emphasis added) all states have been given the opportunity to participate in considering amendment proposals. An amending agreement does not, of course, bind a state which, although a party to the original treaty, fails to become a party to the amending agreement.

Modification

Art.41 allows two or more parties to a multipartite treaty to conclude a modifying agreement between themselves, provided that the possibility of modification is recognised by the treaty, is not prohibited by the treaty and does not affect the rights of other parties, or does not relate to "a provision, derogation from which is incompatible with the effective execution of the object and purpose of the treaty as a whole."[47]

VALIDITY OF TREATIES

The Vienna Convention stipulates five grounds on which the validity of an agreement may be challenged. The Convention is exhaustive—states may not invoke other grounds of invalidity. The five grounds are:

(a) non-compliance with municipal law requirements;

(b) error;

(c) fraud and corruption;

(d) coercion;

(e) *jus cogens.*

Non-compliance with municipal law requirements

See above at p.233.

Error

Error is of limited significance. It plays a much less important role in international law than error in the municipal law of contract. Error may only be invoked by a state if "the error relates to a fact or situation which was assumed by that State to exist at the time when the treaty was concluded and formed an essential basis of its consent to be bound by the treaty."[48]

---

[47] Art.41(1)(b)(ii).
[48] Art.48(1).

Error has been invoked almost exclusively in respect of bound-ary questions. A state which contributed by its behaviour to the error, or should have known of a possible error, cannot relieve itself subsequently of its treaty obligations.[49] Errors in the work-ing of the treaty are not a ground for invalidating the treaty. These must be corrected in accordance with Art.79 of the Convention and by a procedure which may be quite informal.

Fraud and corruption

Like error, fraud and corruption are of little significance. Art.49 provides that a treaty may be invalidated "if a State has been induced to conclude a treaty by the fraudulent conduct of another negotiating State . . .". Art.50 provides that a treaty may be inval-idated if a state's consent to a treaty "has been procured through the corruption of its representative directly or indirectly by another negotiating State." Neither "corrupts", "fraudulent conduct" nor "corruption" are defined in the Convention or by international jurisprudence.

Coercion

A treaty will be of *no legal effect* (emphasis added) if a state's con-sent "has been procured by the coercion of its representative through acts or threats directed against him . . .".[50] The use of coercion against a state's representative is rare, especially as Art.51 is concerned with coercion of the representative's person, rather than with coercion by way of a threat of action against his state.

Acceptance of a treaty through coercion, and the threat of coer-cion against a state "in violation of the principles of international law embodied in the Charter of the United Nations", renders a treaty void.[51] Art.52 reflects modern international law's prohibi-tion on the use of force. The Vienna Convention refers explicitly to the use of force as contained in Art.2(4) of the Charter of the United Nations. Political and economic coercion were not included, in spite of the efforts of the less developed countries. To have extended Art.52 would have been to open the "flood gates" and would have undermined the basic tenet, *pacta sunt servanda*.

Jus cogens

Jus cogens refers to peremptory norms of international law. A peremptory norm is defined, for the purposes of the Convention,

---

[49] Art.49(2); see also the *Temple Case*, I.C.J.Rep. 1962 6 at 26.
[50] Art.51.
[51] Art.52.

as one which is "accepted and recognised by the international community of States as a whole" and from which "no derogation is permitted and which can be modified only by a subsequent norm of general international law having the same character."[52] Any treaty which conflicts at the time of its conclusion with such a norm will be deemed void. Should a new peremptory norm of general international law develop, any existing treaty which is contrary to that norm becomes void and terminates.[53]

The Vienna Convention establishes that there are certain rules of international law which are of a superior status and which, as such, cannot be affected by treaty. What these peremptory norms are remains unidentified and uncertain. What is certain is that the norm must not only be accepted by the international community, but it must also be accepted as being of peremptory force. Rules which might be categorised as *jus cogens* are those prohibiting genocide, slavery and the use of force.[54]

TERMINATION OF A TREATY

A treaty may be terminated as provided for by the treaty or by the consent of the parties. Material breach of one of the parties may also terminate or suspend a treaty as may a supervening impossibility or a substantial change in circumstances.

Termination by treaty provision or consent

A treaty may provide for termination. A treaty which is silent regarding termination may not be denounced unless it is apparent that the parties intended to admit the possibility of denunciation or withdrawal, or where such a right may be implied by the nature of the treaty. Two or three parties to a multipartite treaty may at any time conclude an agreement suspending the operation of certain provisions temporarily between them, provided that the treaty allows it, it does not restrict the rights of other parties and it is not incompatible with the object and purpose of the treaty.[55] It is common today for a treaty either to be for a fixed term, for example, the treaty establishing the European Coal and Steel Community has a term of 50 years and expires in July, 2002, or to provide that a party may withdraw after giving a certain period of notice. If all parties to a treaty conclude a later treaty relating to the same subject-matter, the original treaty will be considered terminated—similarly, where it appears that the matter

---

[52] Art.53.
[53] Art.64.
[54] For further discussion thereof, see Ch.2, above, at p.33.
[55] Art.58(1).

should be governed by the later treaty, or where the provisions of the later treaty "are so far incompatible with those of the earlier one that the two treaties are not capable of being applied at the same time."[56]

Material breach

A mere breach of a treaty provision is not sufficient to terminate a treaty. Art.60(3) of the Vienna Convention defines a material breach as one constituting either:

> "(a) a repudiation of the treaty not sanctioned by the present Convention; or
> (b)   the violation of a provision essential to the accomplishment of the object or purpose of the treaty."

In a bipartite treaty, material breach may be invoked by the innocent party to terminate the treaty or suspend its operation in whole or in part. Material breach of a multipartite treaty allows the "innocent" parties to suspend, by unanimous agreement, the operation of the treaty, in whole or in part, or to terminate it either "(i) in the relations between themselves and the defaulting State, or (ii) as between all the parties."

The party particularly affected by the breach may invoke the breach as reason for suspending the operation of the treaty in whole or in part in the relations between itself and the defaulting state, while any party other than the defaulting state, may invoke the breach so as to suspend the operation of the treaty in whole or in part with respect to itself, if the treaty is of such a character that a material breach of its provisions by one party radically changes the position of every party with respect to the further performance of its obligations under the treaty. Neither the definition of material breach nor the consequences of such a breach apply to:

> "provisions relating to the protection of the human person contained in treaties of a humanitarian character, in particular to provisions prohibiting any form of reprisals against persons protected by such treaties."[57]

The 1949 Geneva Red Cross Conventions are instances of such treaties. Art.46 of Convention I states that "Reprisals against the wounded, sick, personnel, buildings, or equipment protected by the Convention are prohibited."[58]

---

[56] Art.59(1).
[57] Art.60(5).
[58] See below, Ch.11.

The breach by one party of its obligation under a humanitarian or human rights convention does not entitle other parties to either terminate or suspend their own obligations arising from the convention. As to whether there has been a breach: each party may decide for itself, except where the treaty provides a procedure for doing so.

Supervening impossibility of performance

Art.61 of the Vienna Convention, which provides for termination of a treaty on the grounds of a supervening impossibility of performance, was designed to cover such relatively rare happenings as the "submergence of an island, the drying up of a river or the destruction of a dam or hydro-electric installation indispensable for the execution of a treaty."[59] Performance may become impossible because a party ceases to exist as a state (for the position when this occurs see "State Succession", below). If the impossibility is temporary, it may be invoked only as a ground for suspending the operation of the treaty. Impossibility of performance may not be invoked by a party if that party has been responsible for making performance impossible.

Fundamental change of circumstances

The doctrine of *rebus sic stantibus* may be invoked to terminate a treaty. The operation of this doctrine, which literally means "things remaining as they are", rests on the assumption that a treaty may be denounced if circumstances change profoundly from the ones prevailing at the time of the treaty's conclusion. In the *Fisheries Jurisdiction Case*,[60] Iceland challenged the court's jurisdiction to hear the dispute between herself and Britain and Germany on the grounds that there had been a fundamental change of circumstances since the conclusion of the 1961 Exchange of Notes, which contained, *inter alia*, a compromissory clause providing for reference to the International Court of Justice. Iceland alleged that there had been a fundamental change of circumstances as a consequence of changes in fishing techniques. The court identified the changes of circumstances which would be recognised as fundamental or vital as those "which imperil the existence or vital development of one of the parties."[61]
The court held, however, that:

---

[59] Y.B.I.L.C. 1966, II, p.256.
[60] *Fisheries Jurisdiction Case (Jurisdiction)*, I.C.J.Rep. 1973 at 3.
[61] *ibid.* at 19.

"apprehended dangers for the vital interests of Iceland, resulting from changes in fishing techniques, cannot constitute a fundamental change with respect to the lapse or subsistence of the compromissory clause establishing the Court's jurisdiction,"[62]

and that, for a change of circumstances to justify termination of a treaty, there would have to be:

"a radical transformation of the extent of the obligations still to be performed. The change must have increased the burden of the obligations to be executed to the extent of rendering the performance something essentially different from that originally undertaken."[63]

The changed circumstances doctrine will only be successfully invoked when it applies to circumstances which were not contemplated by the parties when the treaty was concluded. In the *Fisheries Jurisdiction Case*, the court maintained that not only had the jurisdictional obligation not been radically transformed, it had remained precisely as it was in 1961. The compromissory clause indeed anticipated a dispute such as the one that had arisen. Similarly in the *Danube Dam Case*,[64] the Court held that prevalent political conditions were not sufficiently related to the object and purpose of the Treaty so as to constitute an essential basis of the consent of the parties, and, thus, although changed, it did not radically alter the extent of the objectives to be performed; the same was also held to be true of the economic system in force at the time the said treaty was concluded in 1977. The Court also denied that advances in the law of environment were completely unforseen. *Rebus sic stantibus* may not be invoked in respect of a boundary settlement or by a state which has caused the fundamental change.

Severance of diplomatic or consular relations

The severance of diplomatic or consular relations between parties to a treaty does not affect legal relations between the parties, except in so far as the existence of diplomatic or consular relations is vital for the treaty's application.[65]

Termination of an agreement normally applies to the whole treaty, unless the treaty provides otherwise. This is the norm

---

[62] Above, n.60 at 20.
[63] Above, n.60 at 21.
[64] *Gabcikovo-Nagymaros Project (Hungary v Slovakia)* (1997) I.C.J. 7; 38 I.L.M. 162.
[65] Art.63.

reflected in Art.44. Exception is admitted if the ground for termination relates to particular clauses which can be separated from the rest of the treaty. These clauses may be terminated if their acceptance was not an essential basis of the consent of the other parties to be bound, and if continued performance of the remainder of the treaty would not be unjust. A party, a victim of fraud or corruption, has the option of invalidating the agreement as a whole or in part. Such an option is not available in respect of the use or threat of force or violation of *jus cogens*.

A state loses its right to initiate a claim for invalidating, terminating, withdrawing from or suspending the operation of a treaty if, subsequent to becoming aware of the fact, it has expressly agreed that the treaty is valid, or, by its conduct, it can be said to have acquiesced in the validity of the treaty.[66]

CONSEQUENCES OF INVALIDITY, TERMINATION OR SUSPENSION

A treaty which is established as invalid is void. The provisions of a void treaty have no legal force. If, however, acts have been performed in reliance upon such a treaty:

"(a)   each party may require any other party to establish as far as possible in their mutual relations the position that would have existed if the acts had not been performed;

(b)   acts performed in good faith before the invalidity was invoked are not rendered unlawful by reason only of the invalidity of the treaty."[67]

The above does not apply "with respect to the party to which the fraud, the act of corruption or the coercion is imputable."[68]

Termination of a treaty, unless otherwise provided, releases the parties concerned from any future obligations, but does not affect any right, obligation or legal situation of the parties created through the execution of the treaty prior to its termination. If a treaty is declared void under Art.53 (conflict with a peremptory norm) the parties are charged with eliminating as far as possible the consequences of any act performed in reliance on the offending provision, and with bringing their mutual relations into conformity with the peremptory norm of general international law. If Art.64 is invoked to terminate a treaty, the parties are released from any further obligation to perform the treaty, but the rights, obligations and legal situation of the parties created prior

---

[66] Art.45.
[67] Art.69(2).
[68] Art.69(3).

to the treaty's termination are not affected, provided that "those rights, obligations or situations may thereafter be maintained only to the extent that their maintenance is not itself in conflict with the new peremptory norm of general international law."[69]

Suspension has, for the period of suspension, a similar effect to termination. During the period of suspension, parties are to refrain from acts which would be likely to obstruct the resumption of the treaty's operation.

Parties to the Vienna Convention are called to seek a peaceful solution to disputes relating to the validity of treaties. This general rule is reinforced by Art.66, which provides that, if a solution is not achieved on the lapse of 12 months, the parties shall submit to the International Court of Justice, to arbitration or to the consultation procedure provided for in the Convention's Annex.

STATE SUCCESSION

What happens to a state's treaty obligations when it is replaced by another state on the international plane? In 1978, the International Law Commission produced the Vienna Convention on the Succession of States in Respect of Treaties.[70] The Convention reflects predominantly the views of the "newer" states and, as such, represents progressive development rather than a codification of existing law. Essentially, the "clean-slate" view is favoured with respect to successor states—that is, a state is not to be tied by its predecessor. The obligations maintained by a state's predecessor by way of multipartite or bipartite agreements are not automatically incumbent on a state. A state has the option of assuming the multipartite treaties of its predecessor. It is not required to do so. The continuance of a bipartite treaty depends upon agreement, either express or implied, between the parties, that is the succeeding state and the other Contracting State.

There is, however, an exception to this general rule. It does not apply in respect of treaties establishing boundaries, territorial regimes and to those imposing restrictions on a territory for the benefit of another state. To apply the clean-slate principle in such instances would prove too disruptive. Accordingly, a successor state is bound by such treaties to which its predecessor has been a party. In the event of states uniting or separating, the Convention stipulates that treaties continue in force for the territory concerned unless the parties have agreed otherwise, or the result would be inconsistent with the object and purpose of the treaty and would

---

[69] Art.71(2).
[70] Misc.1 (1980) Cmnd.7760; 72 A.J.I.L. 971 (1978); The Convention entered into force on November 6, 1996. The UK is not a party.

radically change the conditions for its operation.[71] State property, archives and debts are dealt with in the 1983 Vienna Convention.[72]

Under Art.11 of the German Unification Treaty,[73] West and East Germany took the position that international treaties of the Federal German Republic would remain in effect, and that rights and obligations arising therefrom would also apply in the former German Democratic Republic. Under Art.12, international treaties of the German Democratic Republic were to be reviewed with the Contracting States as to their applicability, modification or termination, with due regard to the aspects of *pacta sunt servanda*, the interests of the Contracting States, and the contractual obligations of West Germany and the European Communities.

The transfer of Hong Kong to China in 1997 presented a unique situation in international treaty law, namely the continued application of Hong Kong's treaty obligations. Arrangements for the application of multilateral and bilateral international agreements after the transfer of the government of Hong Kong to China on June 30, 1997 were established in the 1984 Sino–British Joint Declaration on the Question of Hong Kong. The Declaration provides the Hong Kong Special Administrative Region (HKSAR) with a high degree of autonomy, able to conclude international agreements with states, regions and relevant international organisations in a number of areas, using the name "Hong Kong China".[74]

Hong Kong therefore continues to have some treaty-making competence in the international legal system, independently of the Chinese relationship. Notwithstanding the position of newer states, it appears to be generally accepted that treaties relating to human rights apply to the successor state. This is reinforced by the UN Human Rights Committee General Comment (No.26), namely "once the people are accorded the protection of the rights under the Covenant, such protection devolves with territory and continues to belong to them, notwithstanding change in government of the State Party, including dismemberment in more than one state or state succession or any subsequent action of the State Party designed to divest them of their rights guaranteed by the Covenant."[75]

---

[71] State succession raises issues other than those raised by succession to treaties, but these are outside the subject-matter of this text.

[72] UN DOC. A/Conf. 117/?; 22 I.L.M. 306.

[73] FRG:GDR: Treaty on the Establishment of German Unity, at Berlin, August 31, 1990, entered into force on September 29, 1991; 30 I.L.M. 457 (1991).

[74] Foreign and Commonwealth Office, London. Paper on the Application after June 30, 1997 of Multilateral and Bilateral International Agreements, Hong Kong Department, April 1996, para.26 of the Joint Declaration.

[75] Human Rights Committee General Comment 26 (61), UN Doc. A/53/40, Annex VII, December 8, 1997, para.4.

11. THE USE OF FORCE

The use of force (that is, *jus ad bellum*—the right to wage war)[1] is prohibited by international law. The UN Charter requires Member States to settle disputes amongst themselves by peaceful means, and to refrain in their international relations with each other from either the threat of or the use of force.[2] The serious breach of an international obligation of essential importance for the maintenance of international peace and security has been characterised by the International Law Commission in its Draft Articles on Responsibility of states[3] for internationally wrongful acts.[4] Contemporary international law may prohibit the use of force, but international law cannot prevent the use of force any more than municipal criminal law can prevent murder. International law consequently aims to control the use of force, and so there is accordingly a widely accepted distinction between the legitimate and illegitimate use of force. Nevertheless, prohibition on the use of force remains the general rule with the exceptions

[1] *Jus ad bellum* is to be distinguished from *jus in bellum* relating to the conduct of hostilities—discussed below, p. 278.
[2] United Nations Charter, Arts 2(3) and 2(4).
[3] See Ch.8 above.
[4] Draft Arts 40 and 41.

admitted by international law clearly defined. This, however, has not always been the case.

THE LAW BEFORE 1945

In earliest history, a just war was regarded as a legitimate use of force. St Augustine (A.D. 354–430) articulated the just war as one designed to avenge injuries which had been sustained and which: "the nation or city against which warlike action is to be directed has neglected either to punish wrongs committed by its own citizens or to restore what has been unjustly taken by it." The just war was founded in theological doctrine. However, the breakdown of the Church's authority was followed by the emergence of the sovereign nation state. The right to use force was recognised as an inherent right of every independent sovereign state. International law placed no restraints on the use of force; factors other than legal considerations obviously would affect a state's resort to force and the use of force was a legitimate action for any state to adopt.

The unprecedented devastation of the First World War prompted states to establish an international forum in which states could discuss their problems. It was hoped thereby to reduce the possibility of a resort to force. Consequently, the League of Nations was founded. The Covenant of the League of Nations, signed in 1919, did not abolish war, but rather placed limitations upon the use of force. In the event of a dispute which was potentially disruptive, Member States agreed under the Covenant to submit the dispute to arbitration or judicial settlement or to inquiry by the Council of the League. War was not to
· be resorted to until three months after the award by the arbitrator, the judicial decision, or the Council's report had been made. In this way the Covenant provided a cooling-off period for protagonists. Members also agreed not to go to war with fellow Members of the League who complied with either an arbitral award, judicial decision or with a unanimous report of the Council. The Covenant required Member States "to respect and preserve as against external aggression the territorial integrity and political independence of all Members of the League."[5] In 1928, the international community was successful in agreeing to a comprehensive ban on war as an instrument of national policy. Sixty-three states signed the General Treaty for the Renunciation of War (also known as the Kellogg–Briand Pact or the Pact of Paris),[6] in which parties agreed to seek a peaceful solution to all disputes

---

5 Art.10 of the Covenant, U.K.T.S. 4 (1919) Cmd.153.
6 U.K.T.S. 29 (1929) Cmd.3410; 94 L.N.T.S. 57; 22 A.J.I.L. Supp.171.

arising between them. Nevertheless, the right of self-defence still existed. The Treaty, although it has never been terminated, has been superseded by Art.2(4) of the UN Charter. Treaties, however, cannot prevent wars and the Second World War broke out in 1939 only 11 years after the signing of the Renunciation Treaty.

THE LAW AS OF 1945

Art.2(3) of the UN Charter requires all Member States "to settle their international disputes by peaceful means in such a manner that international peace and security, and justice are not endangered", while Art.2(4) demands that all Member States:

> "refrain in their international relations from the threat or use of force against the territorial integrity and political independence of any State, or in any manner inconsistent with the purposes of the United Nations."

Art.2(4), as a provision of the UN Charter, is addressed to all Members of the United Nations; however, the prohibition on the use of force is now regarded as a principle of customary international law, which has attained the character of *jus cogens*, and, as such, is addressed to all members of the international community.[7]

Extent of the prohibition contained in Art.2(4)

Art.2(4) prohibits the use of force. It is not concerned only with the outlawing of war: Art.2(4) does not distinguish between war and the use of force falling short of war, for example reprisals.[8] Art.2(4) thus embraces all threats of and acts of violence without distinction.

The Article specifically refers to the threat or use of force "against the territorial integrity or political independence of any State . . .." Can force be used to enforce a right when force is not employed against territorial integrity or political independence? Can force be used to protect human rights? Art.2(4) should be read as a whole within the context of the UN Charter. Force contrary to "the purposes of the United Nations" is also prohibited.

---

[7] Endorsed by the International Court of Justice in the *Case Concerning Military and Paramilitary Activities in and against Nicaragua (Merits)* I.C.J.Rep. 1986 14 at 100.

[8] A declaration of war is seldom made by states parties to hostilities. War is a technical term. Acknowledgment of war produces consequences under international law, *e.g.* role of neutral states, and municipal law, *e.g.* the status of aliens.

The purposes of the United Nations are spelt out in Art.1 of the Charter. The purposes include respect for the principle of equal rights and self-determination and respect for human rights, but nevertheless the overriding purpose of the United Nations remains:

> "[T]o maintain international peace and security, and to that end: to take effective collective measures for the prevention and removal of threats to the peace, and for the suppression of acts of aggression or other breaches of the peace, and to bring about by peaceful means, and in conformity with the principles of justice and international law, adjustment or settlement of international disputes or situations which might lead to a breach of the peace."[9]

The emphasis is on the maintenance of peace and security and on solving both potential and actual conflict by peaceful means.

Art.2(4) has been supplemented by the 1970 General Assembly Declaration on Principles of International Law Concerning Friendly Relations and Co-operation Among States in Accordance with the Charter of the United Nations.[10] The Resolution is only a resolution and therefore is not legally binding on Members. Nevertheless it is regarded as representing the consensus of the international community on the legal interpretation to be given to the principles enunciated in the UN Charter. This Declaration adds flesh to the prohibition on the use of force. It provides, *inter alia*, that:

> A war of aggression constitutes a crime against the peace for which there is responsibility under international law. Every state has the duty to refrain from the threat or use of force to violate the existing international boundaries of another state or as a means of solving international disputes, including territorial disputes and problems concerning frontiers of states. States have a duty to refrain from acts of reprisal involving the use of force. Every state has the duty to refrain from any forcible action which deprives peoples of realising equal rights and self-determination.
>
> Every state has the duty to refrain from organising or encouraging the organisation of irregular forces or armed bands, including mercenaries, for incursion into the territory of another state.

---

[9] UN Charter, Art.1(1).
[10] GA Res.2625 (XXV), October 24, 1970—see also Resolution on the Definition of Aggression 1974, GA Res. 3314 (XXIX); 69 A.J.I.L. 480 (1975).

Every state has the duty to refrain from organising, instigating, assisting or participating in acts of civil strife or terrorist acts in another state or acquiescing in organised activities within its territory, directed towards the commission of such acts, when the acts involve a threat or use of force.

The territory of a state shall not be the object of military occupation resulting from the use of force. The territory of a state shall not be the object of acquisition by another state resulting from the threat or use of force. No territorial acquisition resulting from the threat or use of force shall be recognised as legal.

The International Law Community's response to the September 11 terrorist attacks is reflected in Security Council Resolution 1373,[10a] which calls upon all states, *inter alia*, "to prevent and suppress the financing of terrorist attacks; refrain from providing any form of support, active or passive, to entities or persons involved in terrorist acts, including suppressing recruitment of members of terrorist groups and eliminating supplies of weapons to terrorist."[10b] States were also called upon to engage in greater co-operation through the Convention For Suppression of the Financing of Terrorism, 1999.[10c]

To put it simply, any threat or use of force by a state, other than in accordance with the exceptions provided for under the UN Charter, is contrary to, and prohibited by contemporary international law.

Does Art.2(4) only prohibit use of armed force?

Force does not necessarily have to refer to armed force. Force can be economic and/or political. Does Art.2(4) confine itself to prohibiting only the use of armed force or are other categories of force similarly prohibited?

The preamble of the UN Charter and Art.51 (on a state's inherent right of self-defence, considered below) specifically mentions "armed force". The 1970 Declaration, on the other hand, is inconclusive. It recalls the duty of states to refrain in their international relations from military, political, economic or any other form of coercion, but in the section on the use of force, force is not qualified. The imprecision of definition reflects the dichotomy which

---

[10a]28 September 2001. See also GS Res.A/Res./56/88 (on the report of the Sixth Committee (A/56/593)) and Security Council Resolution 5IRES/1368 (2001).
[10b]1A and 2A.
[10c]December 9, 1999.

existed essentially between developed and developing states. The latter would have interpreted force to encompass economic and political force,[11] whilst the former maintained that it was only armed force which was outlawed. However, the former group of states did concede that economic and political pressure could constitute illegal intervention, but although economic coercion is prohibited in the 1970 Declaration's section on non-intervention, it remains undefined and, in the *Nicaragua Case*, the International Court of Justice denied that American economic sanctions against Nicaragua constituted "a breach of the customary-law principle of non-intervention."[12]

As far as Art.2(4) and the legal regime envisaged by the United Nations Charter is concerned, the prohibition is one aimed at outlawing armed force and "gunboat diplomacy" in relations between states.

Exceptions to the prohibition on the threat or use of force

The use of force only remains legitimate under international law in particularly well defined circumstances:

- in self-defence either individual or collective—in accordance with Art.51 of the UN Charter;

- collective measures taken under the auspices of the United Nations; and

- if authorised by a competent organ of the United Nations.

Self-defence

Customary international law recognised a state's right of self-defence, but the extent of that right was ill-defined. It was only as restrictions were imposed on the employment of force by states that the need to articulate the concept of self-defence in international law became more acute.

Under customary international law, the use of force had to be justified if states were at peace. The use of force by one state against another with which it was not at war was, *prima facie*, unlawful. The circumstances which allowed the exercise of self-defence were articulated in the now famous communication of the US Secretary of State Webster to the British Government following the *Caroline* incident.[13]

---

[11] See also para.4(e) of the 1974 Declaration on the Establishment of a New International Economic Order, 13 I.L.M. 715 (1974).

[12] Above, n.7, at 126.

[13] 29 B.F.S.P. 1137–1138; 30 B.F.S.P. 195–196.

The *Caroline* was a vessel which operated from US territory supplying rebel insurrectionaries in Canada. A British force destroyed the *Caroline* and two US citizens were killed. A British subject, Mcleod, was charged with murder and arson.

In his letter, Secretary Webster emphasised that the success of the British government's defence was dependent on their action being justified on grounds of "the necessity of self-defence and preservation." It had to be demonstrated that the need for self-defence was "instant, overwhelming, leaving no choice of means, and no moment for deliberation." It was also necessary for Britain to show that the Canadian authorities had done nothing "unreasonable or excessive; since the act, justified by the necessity of self-defence, must be limited by that necessity, and kept clearly within it."

To summarise, the exercise of force in self-defence was justified under customary international law provided that the need for it was:

(a)   instant;

(b)   overwhelming;

(c)   immediate; and

(d)   there was no viable alternative action which could be taken.

The extent of force used in self-defence had to be commensurate with the violation it was being utilised to repel. The above criteria still apply today as the *Nicaragua Case* affirms.

Article 51, United Nations Charter. Art.51 of the UN Charter acknowledges the right of self-defence as an inherent right of every state:

> "Nothing in the present Charter shall impair the inherent right of individual or collective self-defence if an armed attack occurs against a Member of the United Nations, until the Security Council has taken measures necessary to maintain international peace and security. Measures taken by Members in the exercise of this right of self-defence shall be immediately reported to the Security Council and shall not in any way affect the authority and responsibility of the Security Council under the present Charter to take at any time such action as it deems necessary in order to maintain or restore international peace and security."

Self-defence is permissible if an armed attack has taken place and
Art.51 confines itself to self-defence only in this situation. When
does such an attack occur? What constitutes an armed attack?

"There now appears to be general agreement on the nature of
the acts which can be treated as constituting armed attacks.
In particular, it may be considered to be agreed that an armed
attack must be understood as including not merely action by
regular armed forces across an international border, but also
'the sending by or on behalf of a State of armed bands,
groups, irregulars or mercenaries, which carry out armed
force against another State of such gravity as to amount to'
(*inter alia*) an actual armed attack conducted by regular
forces, 'or its substantial involvement therein . . . .' The Court
sees no reason to deny, that in customary law, the prohibition
of armed attacks may apply to the sending by a State of
armed bands to the territory of another State, if such an operation, because of its scale and effects, would have been clas-
sified as an armed attack rather than as a mere frontier
incident had it been carried out by regular armed forces. But
the Court does not believe that the concept of 'armed attack'
includes not only acts by armed bands where such acts occur
on a significant scale but also assistance to rebels in the form
of the provision of weapons or logistical or other support.
Such assistance may be regarded as a threat or use of force,
or amount to intervention in the internal or external affairs of
other States."[14]

Can a state resort to force in anticipation of an armed attack?
Anticipatory self-defence is excluded from Art.51. Does that
mean it is prohibited? The right of self-defence, which Art.51
acknowledges as "inherent", exists under customary international
law—that is, independently of Art.51. Does, therefore, the right
of anticipatory self-defence exist under customary international
law?

States do employ force in anticipation of an alleged armed
attack, for example Israel's strike on the United Arab Republic in
June 1967. The justification for anticipatory self-defence can be
reconciled with the obligation on UN Member States to refrain
from either "the threat or use of force". States which are threatened with the use of force may take appropriate anticipatory
measures to repel such a threat, but such measures can only be
justified if:

[14] Above, n.7 at 103–104.

(a)   a state is the target of hostile activities of another state;

(b)   the threatened state has exhausted all alternative means of protection;

(c)   the danger is imminent;

(d)   the defensive measures are proportionate to the pending danger.

States enjoy the right of self-defence in the event of an armed attack under Art.51 of the UN Charter. Under customary international law they also enjoy the right to use force in circumstances falling short of an armed attack—the International Court of Justice did not feel it necessary to address the issue of anticipatory self-defence in the *Nicaragua Case*.

However, whatever rights states enjoy with respect to the use of force, they are at all times required by the UN Charter and customary international law to settle their disputes by peaceful means.

Use of force to protect nationals abroad. What if a state's nationals or property are harmed abroad? Does that state have a right to intervene to defend its nationals when its territory has not been the object of an armed attack?

The Anglo–French invasion of Suez, the Israeli raid on Entebbe Airport (1976), the abortive US rescue mission of the hostages in Iran and the US intervention in both Grenada (1983) and Panama (1989) are instances of force being used by the intervening state to protect its nationals. The legitimacy of intervention to afford such protection is not firmly established in international law. Such intervention can be reconciled with the doctrine of self-defence, if the basic concept underlying diplomatic protection is stretched, so that an imminent threat of danger to nationals abroad may be regarded as an imminent threat to the national state itself. In other words, by invoking a legal fiction, intervention on behalf of one's nationals can be reconciled with self-defence.

Non-fulfilment by the host state of its international duty to safeguard, to at least a minimum international standard, the interests of aliens, may lend support to intervention by the national state. Thus, in the Security Council debate, held in July 1976, on the Entebbe incident an Israeli representative maintained that Uganda had "violated a basic tenet of international law in failing to protect foreign nationals on its territory."[15]

---

[15] See 15 I.L.M. 1228 (1976).

Intervention to protect nationals is open to obvious abuse, particularly as it involves a subjective interpretation by a state of when its nationals are in danger. Even if protective intervention is accepted, it must be recognised as the exception rather than the norm, not least because it involves violations of another state's territorial integrity and sovereignty. Protective intervention is more likely to be accepted by the international community if the danger to the rescuing state's nationals can be shown to be overwhelming. A successful mission, although it may not be legally condoned, is more likely to be accepted as expedient than one which fails—for example, compare the Entebbe raid with the US abortive mission to rescue the American hostages in Iran. As with self-defence, the force used in such circumstances must be proportionate to the danger.

Intervention in civil wars. Civil wars are not prohibited by international law. Art.2(4) prohibits the use of force in respect of international relations only. International law does, however, have something to say on participation by other states. The general rule is one of non-intervention. The General Assembly's Declaration on the Inadmissibility of Intervention in the Domestic Affairs of States and the Protection of their Independence and Sovereignty prohibits any state from intervening:

> "directly or indirectly, for any reason whatever, in the internal or external affairs of any other State ... no State shall organise, assist, foment, finance, incite or tolerate subversive, terrorist or armed activities directed towards the violent overthrow of the regime of another State, or interfere in civil strife in another State."

The prohibitions enunciated in the 1965 Declaration were reaffirmed in the 1970 Declaration on Principles of International Law.

States may, for a variety of political reasons, intervene to support the rebels, or alternatively, to support the established authorities. Policy, rather than law, will determine a state's decision to intervene. Non-intervention is undoubtedly the best policy. The danger of intervention by a state in support of one party is that it will attract counter-intervention by another state in support of the other party and, consequently, an internal matter can escalate into an international war.[15a]

[15a] The threat to peace and security in a particular region may be such that the most appropriate response is through the UN, *e.g.* Sierra Leone.

Classical humanitarian intervention. Humanitarian intervention is distinct from protective intervention in that it involves intervention to protect another state's nationals (or a group of nationals) and possibly those of the territorial state. The intervening state is, in other words, not protecting its own right. Although it may be contended that, at least superficially, the intervening state is playing a more objective role than when intervening to protect its own nationals, humanitarian intervention is equally open to abuse. The intervening state may ostensibly intervene to promote an altruistic interest, but, in reality, intervention may be prompted by political motives and an anxiety to secure for itself some long-term benefit.

Protagonists of humanitarian intervention support its use for the prevention of serious violations of basic human rights, normally the right to life, or instances of torture.

Contemporary humanitarian intervention[16]

The demise of the Cold War transferred the spotlight to the increasing number of internal conflicts, which unfortunately remain a feature of the contemporary global community. Media images of human suffering in Somalia, Rwanda, Haiti, the former Yugoslavia and Sierra Leone have heightened public awareness of the humanitarian dimension of civil war. The doctrine of humanitarian intervention and its interpretation has, as a consequence, been substantially revised, with a prominent role being given to the United Nations.[17]

"Operation provide comfort"—Northern Iraq

The first crisis in which intervention was based on humanitarian concerns was the UN relief operation in Northern Iraq following the Gulf War in 1990–91. Reports of the deaths of over 1,000 Kurdish refugees a day fleeing Iraqi troops[18] and a growing concern in international, political circles that this was largely a man-made disaster prompted the UN Security Council to pass Resolution 688.[19] The resolution condemned the repression of the Iraqi civilian population and insisted that Iraq allow immediate access by international humanitarian organisations to those in need of help. Resolution 688 triggered a multinational operation,

---

[16] The importance of this doctrine in contemporary international law, merits greater consideration than is possible here.
[17] Scholarly debate supports the view that humanitarian intervention by the UN is the preferable course of action. See Ian Brownlie, *International Law and the Non-Use of Force* (1963).
[18] *The New York Times*, April 10, 1991, A1, col.4.
[19] UN SC Res. 688, 30 I.L.M. 858 (1991).

co-ordinated by the United Nations, to set up "safe-havens" in
Northern Iraq to protect the Kirdish people. Despite consterna-
tion among academic scholars and UN circles that this operation
did not establish a legal precedent for future humanitarian interventions, largely due to the unique events that preceded it, it was
the first time the UN Security Council had authorised military
support to ensure humanitarian relief to civilians. By linking
human suffering with threats to international peace and security,
Resolution 688 created a new rationale for forcible humanitarian intervention.[20] Subsequent events demonstrated that the
humanitarian crisis in Northern Iraq was not an isolated incident.

The former Yugoslavia

Humanitarian considerations initially played little part in the
conflict which broke out in Yugoslavia.[21] UN Member States initially saw the crisis as an internal matter which fell within Art.2(7)
of the Charter[22] and were reluctant to authorise the use of military
force to provide humanitarian aid. As the crisis escalated, however, with reports of war camps, rape and ethnic cleansing across
Bosnia–Herzegovina, humanitarian issues dominated Security
Council resolutions and various other international statements.[23]
The international response, however, fell short of a full-scale military invasion under Chapter VII, leading many to conclude that,
far from establishing a legal basis for humanitarian interventions,
the crisis affirmed the inviolability of the principles of sovereignty
and non-interference as far as human suffering was concerned.
The UN Interim Administrative Mission in Kosovo (UNMIK)[23a]
was established with the aim of providing interim administrative
help. UNMIK has 4,517 international police and 4,619 Kosovo
police-service officers deployed throughout the province and
border crossings. The mission is made up of 49 countries.[23b]

---

[20] Res. 688 stated that the flow of refugees, "threatens international peace and
security, reflecting the language of Chapter VII".
[21] For a comprehensive analysis of events leading to the dissolution of Yugoslavia,
see Marc Weller, "The International Response to the Dissolution of the Social
Federal Republic of Yugoslavia" A.J.I.L. 1992 at 569. Documents regarding the
conflict can be found in 31 I.L.M. 1421 (1992).
[22] This argument is not tenable. Recognition of Croatia as an independent state
with international borders transformed the crisis from an internal war to one of
international concern. Croatia, Bosnia–Herzegovina and Slovenia have since
been admitted to the UN.
[23] UNPROFOR's mission from the outset, *e.g.* was "to ensure the security and
functioning of Sarajevo airport and the delivery of humanitarian assistance."
UNSC Res.764, July 13, 1992. UNPROFOR ceased to exist in March, 1995.
[23a] SC Res.1244 1999, June 10, 1999.
[23b] As of July 2, 2002.

"Operation restore hope in Somalia"

In 1992, a two-year drought and the overthrow of the government contributed to Somalia's descent into anarchy. The international response to what was described as the greatest human emergency in the world placed particular emphasis on humanitarian considerations and was perceived by many as a successful, humanitarian intervention. Humanitarian aid was distributed quickly by US soldiers under the authority of UN resolutions, to starving civilians caught up in a bitter civil war. It soon became apparent that military action was required to ensure safe delivery of humanitarian supplies, many of which had been confiscated by the warring factions. UN Security Council Resolution 794 authorised Member States to use "all necessary means to establish as soon as possible a secure environment for humanitarian relief operations in Somalia" and became the first UN resolution to explicitly authorise a massive military intervention into a sovereign state[24] without a request from the host government. Public opinion at home prompted the United States to withdraw its troops rather than become involved in protracted fighting with Somali rebels. The Somalian crisis may be perceived as a successful humanitarian intervention due to the swift response of the international community in mobilising a force. Yet it also highlighted the dangers of sending an international force without a clear mandate[25] into a civil war.

Conclusion

The international community has demonstrated its willingness to use humanitarian concerns as a basis for intervention into what are essentially civil-war conflicts. The alleviation of human suffering would appear to be taking precedence over the principle of state sovereignty. Nevertheless, the international response to humanitarian crises in the 1990s has been inconsistent and considerable criticism has been directed at operations by the UN. Intervention in any future crisis will require Security Council authorisation. For example, the UN intermediate Administrative Mission in Sierra Leone (UNMASIL),[25a] which has, as its main remit, co-operation with

---

[24] It is arguable whether Somalia was a sovereign state in the absence of a viable government.

[25] The UN was condemned in the former Yugoslavia by the Serbian government for appearing to side with the Muslims and, yet, was heavily criticised by the international community for its failure to allow the Muslims to arm themselves against the might of the Serbian army.

[25a] SC Res.1270 (1999), October 22, 1999.

the government to restore law and order and stabilise the internal political situation.[25b]

Collective self-defence. The right of collective self-defence is recognised by Art.51. Collective self-defence is something of a misnomer, as it refers to the right of each state to use force in defence of another state. The force is therefore employed on behalf of another state.

Collective self-defence refers, strictly speaking, to collective defence rather than self-defence. Art.51 is the legal basis of collective agreements such as the NATO Alliance, in which an attack on one member is treated as an attack on all. Under Art.5 of the North Atlantic Treaty,[26] the Contracting Parties:

"agree that an armed attack against one or more of them in Europe or North America shall be considered an attack against them all; and consequently they agree that, if such an armed attack occurs, each of them, in exercise of the right of individual or collective self-defence recognized by Art.51 of the Charter of the United Nations, will assist the Party or Parties so attacked, by taking forthwith, individually, and in concert with the other Parties, such action as it deems necessary, including the use of armed force, to restore and maintain the security of the North Atlantic area."

The bombing of Yugoslavian territory under the auspices of NATO resulted in the legality of the use of such force being raised, by Yugoslavia, in the International Court of Justice. The states in question were Belgium, Canada, France, Italy, the United Kingdom, the Netherlands, Portugal, Spain and the United States.

All measures adopted by Member States in self-defence must be reported to the Security Council and the use of force in individual or collective self-defence may only be employed until the Security Council has taken appropriate measures to maintain international peace and security. The right of collective self-defence was recognised by the International Court of Justice in the *Nicaragua Case* as existing under customary international law, but its legitimate exercise depended on (a) the declaration

---

[25b]See also UN Mission in Ethiopia and Eritrea, (UNMEE), established by UN Res. S/Res./1312 (2000), July 31, 2000.

[26] U.K.T.S. 56 (1949) Cmd.7789; U.N.T.S. 243. The eastern European countries, Poland, the Czech Republic and Hungary were admitted into NATO in July, 1997. Further enlargement of NATO is envisaged and, currently, nine European countries have expressed an interest in joining. Enlargement of NATO is on the agenda of the NATO Summit of 2002.

by the alleged victim that it had been attacked; and (b) the request by that state for assistance.[27] In the same case, the court held that intervention by a third state could only be regarded as lawful ". . . when the wrongful act provoking the response was an armed attack."[28] The armed response (Operation Desert Storm) to liberate Kuwait was the exercise by the latter of its legal right to collective self-defence.[29]

Regional arrangements. The right of states to make regional arrangements to deal with matters of international peace and security is protected by the UN Charter and, in particular, by Art.52.

Art.52(1) provides:

> "Nothing in the present Charter precludes the existence of regional arrangements or agencies for dealing with such matters relating to the maintenance of international peace and security as are appropriate for regional action, provided that such arrangements or agencies and their activities are consistent with the Purposes and Principles of the United Nations."

Art.52(2), however, charges members of regional organisations with making "every effort to achieve pacific settlement of local disputes through such regional arrangements or by such regional agencies before referring them to the Security Council." Action taken via regional organisations will only be legitimate if it is consistent with the purposes and principles of the UN Charter, and does not amount to "enforcement action", unless this has been authorised by the Security Council. The Security Council must, under Art.54, be kept fully informed at all times "of activities undertaken or in contemplation under regional arrangements or by regional agencies for the maintenance of international peace and security."

---

[27] *Nicaragua Case*, above, n.7 at 110.

[28] *ibid.*

[29] Commentators have maintained that the Gulf War was a collective self-defence operation legitimised by the Security Council and that it would be wrong to call it a UN collective security operation. See Dr Max Hilaire, "Use of Force Against Iraq: Collective Security or Collective Self-Defence Under the United Nations Charter and Customary International Law? I.L.R., April/June 1993, No.2 and Eugene Rostow, "Until What/Enforcement Action or Collective Self-Defence?" 85 A.J.I.L. 510 (1991). See also UN SC Res.661 (1990) in which the Security Council recognised for the first time that collective self-defence applied, even when the assisting state had not been attacked and there is no special treaty arrangement to provide help. UN Doc.S/Res/661, August 6, 1990.

The Organisation of Eastern Caribbean States' peace-keeping mission which, with the support of Barbados, Jamaica and the United States, landed in Grenada on October 25, 1983, is an instance of action being taken under the auspices of a regional organisation. Arguments supporting the legality of the invasion are founded, *inter alia*, on its legitimacy as a regional peace-keeping mission under Art.52 of the UN Charter, especially as it was prompted by the breakdown of government authority and its response to a request by the Governor General, Sir Paul Scoon.[30]

The legitimacy of the 1962 US quarantine imposed in respect of vessels destined for Cuba, is purported to be based on Art.52, namely through the authorisation of the Organisation of American States.

Regional organisations can play a vital role in the maintenance of international peace and security. For example, in the crisis in the former Yugoslavia, there was evidence of a growing utilisation of regional agencies. UN SC Resolution 787 authorised states "acting nationally or through regional agencies" to use appropriate measures to enforce the UN economic sanctions against Serbia and Montenegro. NATO also played a significant part in this crisis and was specifically charged with the task of enforcing the no-fly zone over Bosnia in support of UN SC Resolution 816. Although the delegation of powers from the UN force in Bosnia at the time (UNPROFOR) to NATO troops (IFOR) was not strictly an authorisation to a regional organisation under Art.53, it was, nevertheless, evidence of the Council's willingness to delegate the maintenance of international peace and security to a regional organisation.[31]

The crisis in Liberia was a further example of the increased systematic co-operation between the United Nations and a regional organisation. The UN Security Council gave its support to the regional organisation, the Economic Community of West African States, known as ECOWAS, in March, 1993, by imposing a "general and complete embargo on all deliveries of weapons and military equipment to Liberia until the Security Council decides otherwise."[32] Nigeria and its African neighbours have spent an estimated

[30] For some of the arguments for and against the lawfulness of the Grenada invasion, see 78 A.J.I.L. 131–175 (1984); see also W. C. Gilmore, *The Grenada Intervention* (Mansell, 1984).

[31] NATO is specifically mentioned in the Annexes to the Resolution. It has been suggested that NATO was utilised in Bosnia only because the SC was prevented from taking unanimous action due to the reluctance of Russia to authorise force against one of its traditional allies.

[32] See the Report of the Secretary General on the Question of Liberia, UN Doc. S/25402 (1993) generally for the background to this war. See also UN SC Res.788 (November 19, 1992 and UN SC Res.866 (1993) September 22, 1993 which established the UN Observer Mission in Liberia (UNOMIL).

half a billion dollars on the peacekeeping operation in Liberia. This is one of the largest peacekeeping efforts in the world and is notable, as it does not operate under the auspices of the United Nations.[32a]

Reprisals. Reprisals (now more commonly referred to as counter-measures) are acts which, in themselves are illegal under international law and adopted by a state in response to its having been the victim of an unlawful act by another state. They were defined in the *Naulilaa Case*[33] as:

> "acts of self-help by the injured State, acts in retaliation for acts contrary to international law on the part of the offending State, which have remained unredressed after a demand for amends. In consequence of such measures, the observance of this or that rule of international law is temporarily suspended in the relations between the two States. They are limited by considerations of humanity and the rules of good faith, applicable in the relations between States. They are illegal unless they are based upon a previous act contrary to international law. They seek to impose on the offending State reparation for the offence, the return to legality and the avoidance of new offences."[34]

Reprisals involving armed force have now to comply with the contemporary international law on the use of force if they are not to be contrary to international law—the Declaration on Principles of International Law Concerning Friendly Relations and Co-operation Among States in Accordance with the Charter of the United Nations expressly prohibits reprisals and provides that states "have a duty to refrain from acts of reprisal involving the use of force."[35]

Retorsions. Retorsions are distinct from reprisals in that they are acts which, in themselves, although unfriendly, are not unlawful. They are a lawful means of expressing displeasure at the conduct of another state, for example the severance of diplomatic relations or foreign aid.[36]

[32a] ECOWAS has been instrumental in addressing issues, which will assist Liberia in overcoming the effects of eight years of civil war.

[33] 2 R.I.A.A. 1012 (1928).

[34] *ibid.* at 1026. See also *Air Services Agreement Case* 18 R.I.A.A. 416.

[35] GA Res.2635 (XXV), October 24, 1970.

[36] See also the ILC's Draft Articles which permit states to take counter-measures against another state which has committed an internationally wrongful act. See also the ILC's Draft Articles on Responsibility of States for Internationally Wrongful Acts, 2001, Arts 49 and 50.

Collective measures through the United Nations

Under the UN Charter, the primary responsibility for peacekeeping lies with the Security Council.[37] Member States agree, under Art.25, to accept and carry out the decisions of the Security Council. The Security Council can act either under Chapter VI or Chapter VII of the Charter.

Under Chapter VI, the Security Council can make recommendations with the objective of achieving a peaceful settlement to disputes.

Chapter VII deals with the enforcement measures which the Security Council can adopt. Under Art.39, the Security Council is empowered to determine "the existence of any threat to the peace, breach of the peace, or act of aggression . . .."

What constitutes aggression? A General Assembly Resolution adopted in 1974[38] defined aggression as "the use of force by a State against the sovereignty, territorial integrity, or political independence of another State, or in any other manner inconsistent with the Charter of the United Nations . . .". Examples of acts that would be identified as aggression include the invasion or armed attack by one state against the territory of another state, the blockade of the ports or coasts of a state by the armed forces of another state, the sending by or on behalf of a state of armed bands, groups, irregulars or mercenaries, to employ armed force against another state.[39]

Following an affirmative decision under Art.39, the Security Council can make recommendations or decide what measures are to be taken in accordance with the Charter to maintain peace and security. In practice, the Security Council seldom discusses the issue of whether it enjoys jurisdiction under Art.39, and, consequently, which aspect (that is, "threat to the peace" or "breach of the peace") it is basing its action on is not identified. "Threat to the peace", which should be read as international peace, has become of minimal significance in the light of the Security Council's characterisation of the situation in Southern Rhodesia and South Africa (essentially an internal matter) as threatening international peace and security. A "breach of the peace" has only been specifically identified in four cases: Korea (1950), the Falklands (1982), Iran–Iraq (1987) and, most recently, in the Gulf crisis

---

[37] Art.24.
[38] GA Res.3314 (XXIX) above, n.10. See also Draft Code of Crimes Against the Peace and Security of Mankind, Art.15, which deals with the international crime of aggression. 83 A.J.I.L. 153 (1989).
[39] *ibid.* Art.3.

(1990–91), when the invasion of Kuwait by Iraq was characterised as an act breaching "international peace and security".[40] Art.40 provides that the Security Council may call upon the parties concerned to comply with such provisional measures as it deems necessary or desirable, for example the Security Council could call for a cease fire. The enforcement action which the Security Council may consider necessary may be either:

    (i)   measures not involving the use of force (Art.41); or

    (ii) armed force (Art.42).

(i) Acting under Art.41, the Security Council may call upon Members of the United Nations to employ economic sanctions or diplomatic sanctions against a "defaulting" state. The economic sanctions imposed against Iraq represent the most comprehensive action of the United Nations under Art.41.[41]

Resolution 661,[42] prompted by Iraq's failure to withdraw from Kuwait, called upon Member States to abstain from the importation of all commodities and products originating in Iraq or Kuwait and the exportation to those states of all products, save those "supplies intended strictly for medical purposes, and, in humanitarian circumstances, foodstuffs". Supervision of Resolution 661 was entrusted to a Committee established by the Security Council and, under Resolution 666,[43] that Committee was charged with overviewing the supply of foodstuffs designated as falling within the humanitarian exception. Such supervision was undertaken in co-operation with humanitarian agencies such as the International Committee of the Red Cross. Resolution 665[44] called upon those Member States with maritime forces in the region "to use such measures commensurate with the specific circumstances to halt all

---

[40] SC Res.660, (1990) adopted August 2, 1990 by 14–0 (Yemen abstained), 29 I.L.M. 1325 (1990).

[41] Sanctions against South Africa and Southern Rhodesia (British colony which became independent Zimbabwe in 1979) were also based on Art.41. Recent examples of sanctions are the arms embargo imposed against Rwanda in 1994. UK Order SI 1994 1637 and the international economic sanctions against Serbia, UN SC Res.757 September 30, 1992. The sanctions against Serbia were tightened further in UN SC Res. 1993 820. A significant aspect of these measures was the prohibition on the provision of services, both financial and non-financial to any person or body for the purposes of business in Serbia and Montenegro, the only exceptions being telecommunications, postal services, certain legal services and services whose supply may be necessary for humanitarian purposes on a case by case basis by the UN Sanctions Committee.

[42] (1990) adopted by 13–0 (Cuba and Yemen abstained) August 6, 1990; 29 I.L.M. 1325 (1990).

[43] (1990) adopted September 13, 1990, *ibid.* at 1330.

[44] (1990) adopted August 25, 1990, above, n.42 at 1329.

inward and outward maritime shipping in order to . . . inspect and verify their cargoes and destinations." This was for the purpose of enforcing the sanctions. Subsequently, Iraq's continued presence in Kuwait led to stricter measures, namely the requirement that all states deny clearance (that is, permission to take off from, or fly over) to cargo-carrying aircraft bound for either Iraq or Kuwait.[45] Resolution 748, adopted on March 31, 1992, requiring Libya to comply with Resolution 731 (namely to co-operate in determining responsibility for the terrorist activities which culminated at Lockerbie), was also adopted under Chapter VII, as was the mandatory arms embargo established against Yugoslavia by Security Council Resolution 713 in September, 1991, and SC Resolution 2001 1373 in relation to September 11.

(ii) If the Security Council considers that Art.41 measures would be, or have proved, inadequate, it may take such action by air, sea or land forces as may be necessary to maintain or restore international peace and security. Such action may include demonstrations, blockades and other operations by air, sea, or land forces of Members of the United Nations.

Art.42 is supplemented by Art.43, according to which states undertake to provide, under special agreements with the Security Council, armed forces assistance, and facilities, including rights of passage, to the extent necessary for maintaining peace and security.

The force which operated in Korea in 1950 was designated a UN force, but whether it was one in the true sense remains doubtful. The Security Council Resolutions calling upon Members to assist the United Nations in securing the withdrawal of the North Korean forces, to furnish "such assistance to the Republic of Korea as may be necessary to repel the armed attack and to restore international peace and security in the area", and authorising the use of the UN flag, were adopted through the fortuitous absence of the Soviet Union representative in the Security Council.[46] Control over the forces, provided by 16 states, was maintained throughout by the United States and, indeed, the troops were provided pursuant to agreements made by the United States and the countries involved. Operation Desert Storm, on the other hand, never professed to be a UN force.

Under the Charter, the General Assembly may discuss any questions relating to the maintenance of international peace and security, provided the matter is not before the Security Council.[47]

---

[45] Res. 1990 670 adopted September 25, 1990, above, n.42 at 1334.
[46] The Soviet Union representative was absent in protest at the seating of the Nationalist Chinese delegation.
[47] Arts 11 and 12.

Whilst the Security Council can make decisions, the General Assembly can only make recommendations. Under the Charter, the role envisaged for the General Assembly was a less active one than that envisaged for the Security Council, but, in practice, the Security Council has been rendered impotent by the use of veto and this, to some extent, has resulted in a more active role than that originally anticipated being assumed by the General Assembly.

It is generally accepted that the current membership of the Security Council does not accurately reflect the balance of economic power within the international community. Germany and Japan have been lobbying for a permanent seat since the Gulf crisis, when both countries contributed financially to the UN operation without having any decision-making responsibility. Nations like India, Brazil and Nigeria are also potential Security Council members, whose admission would improve the image of the United Nations in the Third World.

The United Nations Secretary General

The UN Secretary General has an increasingly important role to play in the maintenance of international peace and security. On January 31, 1992, at a Security Council meeting, the former Secretary General, Dr Boutros Boutros Ghali, was invited to "prepare" "his analysis and recommendations on ways of strengthening and making more efficient within the framework and provisions of the Charter, the capacity of the United Nations, for preventative diplomacy, for peacemaking[48] and for peacekeeping". The request from the Security Council reflected the growing need for the United Nations to adopt a more systematic and intrusive approach towards internal strife and aggression. The Secretary General responded on June 17, 1992, by identifying important interconnected UN security functions in a Report entitled "An Agenda for Peace"[49] which included, *inter alia*:

- preventative diplomacy;
- peacemaking;
- peace building in its differing contexts;
- rebuilding institutions and infrastructures of nations divided by civil war and strife; and

---

[48] UN Doc.S/23500.
[49] An Agenda for Peace: "Preventative Diplomacy, Peacemaking and Peacekeeping." June 17, 1992 31 I.L.M. 953 (1992) U.N.Doc.A/47/277,S/24111 (1992).

- addressing the causes of conflict, for example economic deprivation, social injustice and political oppression.

The Secretary General also called for the creation of permanent peace-enforcement units under Art.43 of the UN Charter with the ability to respond to aggression immediately. These would be constituted by troops from all Member States and would be placed under the auspices of the Secretary General. Deployment of these units would be on the basis of provisional measures in Art.40 of the Charter. The UN Security Council endorsed the Report in principle, but have yet to adopt the recommendations.[50]

Dr. Ghali's successor is Kofi-Annan, who is the first UN Secretary-General to be appointed from an African state.[51] As the former Under-Secretary-General for peacekeeping, he is also the first to have worked his way up through the ranks in the United Nations. His mandate for his second term of office is the unrolling of what will be the United Nations' agenda for the next 10–15 years, mainly tackling AIDS, education, environmental issues, governance and human rights.[52]

The veto. Every member of the Security Council has one vote.[53] Procedural issues in order to be adopted must receive the affirmative vote of nine members, while non-procedural matters require nine votes, including the concurring vote of the Five Permanent Members (that is China, France, the United Kingdom, the United States and, as of December 1991, the Russian Federation (RSFSR)). Absence and abstention are taken as concurrence. The decision as to whether a matter is or is not procedural is itself a non-procedural issue, that is, the concurring vote of the Five Permanent Members is required.

The possibility of exercising a double veto is therefore open to a Permanent Member. If, because of the veto, the Security Council is unable to make any decisions, then the General Assembly, with residual authority for the maintenance of peace, can assume

[50] To this date, no UN Member State has signed an Art.43 special agreement with the UN despite the fact that the text of Art.43 asks Member States to sign such agreements "as soon as possible".
[51] Kofi-Annan comes from Ghana.
[52] The Secretary General's strategy is designed to implement and achieve the UN Millennium Declaration—"Road Map towards the implementation of the Millennium Declaration". Report of the Secretary-General September 6, 2001. (The General Assembly Resolution 53/202, December 17, 1998, designated 55th Session of the General Assembly "The Millennium Assembly of the United Nations".) An integral part of the millennium assembly was the Millennium Summit, September 6–8, 2000, and addressed the theme "The Role of the United Nations in the Twenty First Century".
[53] Art.27.

the responsibility which the Security Council is unable to discharge. The inability of the Security Council to take further action for the management of the Korean campaign (because of the return to his seat of the Soviet Union representative and his consequent use of the veto) led to the Uniting for Peace Resolution in November 1950.[54]

The Uniting for Peace Resolution provided that, in the event of the Security Council being unable, because of a lack of unanimity of the Permanent Members, to discharge its primary responsibility for the maintenance of international peace and security, the General Assembly could, where there appears to be a threat to the peace, breach of the peace or act of aggression:

> "consider the matter immediately with a view to making appropriate recommendations to Members for collective measures, including in the case of a breach of the peace or act of aggression the use of armed force when necessary, to maintain or restore international peace and security."

If the General Assembly is not in session at the time, an emergency session may be called. An emergency session may be requested by the Security Council on the vote of any nine members, or by a majority of the Members of the United Nations. The General Assembly has invoked the Uniting for Peace Resolution on a number of occasions, for example the Suez Question (1956), the Congo Question (1960), the Pakistan Civil War (Bangladesh) (1972), Afghanistan (1980), Namibia (1981) and alleged violations of the fourth Geneva Convention relating to the protection of civilian persons in times of war—Israel (1999). The Uniting for Peace Resolution was more effective in allowing issues to be discussed in the General Assembly, rather than as a means of preventing crises and preserving international peace and security.

Traditional peacekeeping forces. The UN Charter does not provide those peacekeeping forces—that is, forces which are designed to maintain peace rather than take enforcement action— which have made an important contribution in major crises. Peacekeeping forces, which consist of troops given voluntarily by UN Member States, must remain at all times impartial. They have been responsible for supervising a cease fire, as was the UN Emergency Force (UNEF) in the Middle East in 1956, and the UN Iran–Iraq Military Observer Group (UNIMOG), established in 1988, assisting a return to peace, as did the UN Force

---

[54] Res. 377 (V), November 3, 1950; G.A.O.R., 5th Session, Supp.20, p.10.

in the Congo (ONUC) in 1960, and the UN Protection Force in Yugoslavia (UNPROFOR) 1992, in patrolling a buffer zone, as did the UN Iraq–Kuwait Observation Mission (UNIKOM) in 1991, supervising a withdrawal of occupying forces as did the UN Angola Verification Mission (UNAVEN) in 1989 and in the supervision of the attainment of independence, UN Transition Assistance Group (UNTAG established 1978, operational 1989) with respect to Namibia, the performance of basic civilian administrative functions (UNMIIC) in 1999 and a return to political stability (UNAMSIL) in 1999. In practice UN peacekeeping forces traditionally only operate in a territory as long as the host state consents.

The constitutionality of peacekeeping forces was affirmed in the *Certain Expenses of the United Nations Case*.[55] The International Court of Justice was requested by the General Assembly to give an advisory opinion on the legality of expenses levied on members for the purpose of financing the UN forces in the Middle East (UNEF) and the Congo (ONUC), following the refusal of a number of states, including the Soviet Union and France, to make their contributions. The International Court held that the expenses were legitimate as they were made for the fulfilment of a purpose of the United Nations.[56]

Regarding the respective roles of the Security Council and General Assembly in the maintenance of international peace and security, the court emphasised that, while the Security Council enjoyed a primary responsibility, its responsibility was not exclusive. The court did, however, acknowledge that only the Security Council could "require enforcement by coercive action against an aggressor."[57] In other words, the authorisation of enforcement measures involving the use of force is the prerogative of the Security Council. The General Assembly's competence is, in the light of the court's opinion, limited to action which falls short of enforcement action *per se*. The General Assembly may not be competent to authorise enforcement measures which involve the use of force, but it can nevertheless recommend action when that does not involve "enforcement action" but rather the establishment of a peacekeeping force designed to maintain the peace.

Under the UN regime, although the Security Council is the organ exclusively competent to authorise the use of force, the General Assembly enjoys residual competence to recommend action falling short of coercive or enforcement action.

---

[55] I.C.J.Rep. 1962 151.
[56] *ibid.* at 172.
[57] Above, n.55 at 163.

Peace-enforcement[58]

The number of UN soldiers participating in peacekeeping operations increased four-fold in the first half of 1992. The peacekeeping force (UNPROFOR) deployed in Bosnia–Herzegovina was the
largest UN operation to date[59] and had far-reaching implications
for the way in which UN peacekeeping operations would be conducted in the future. UNPROFOR was asked to engage in activities, ancillary to the basic nature of peacekeeping. In Somalia, the
US-led military operation eschewed *established* UN peacekeeping
practices, by which force could only be used in self-defence. Both
operations demanded that peacekeepers protect the delivery of
humanitarian supplies to civilians caught up in internal strife.[60]

These conflicts demonstrated that *traditional* peacekeeping
forces cannot deal with the provision of humanitarian aid in a
civil war. New tasks demanded of UN peacekeepers conflict with
their traditionally perceived image of mediators. The international community is now demanding that peacekeepers demar-
cate   boundaries,   disarm   warring   factions   and   deliver
humanitarian aid with or without the consent of the parties to the
conflict. As these are tasks which demand more powerful peacekeepers to enforce the peace, there is a growing body of opinion
that the United Nations should concentrate efforts on creating a
credible international enforcement mechanism under Art.43, a
provision of the Charter which, until recently, was stultified by
the Cold War powers.[61]

In Agenda for Peace, Secretary General Boutros Boutros Ghali
recommended the deployment of "peace-enforcement units from
Member States, which would be available on call and would

---

[58] This subject warrants greater attention than is permissible here. For further
detail, see generally Andrew Miller, "Universal Soldiers: A UN Army"
Georgetown Law Journal, March, 1993 at 773–828 and W. M. Reisman "Peacemaking" *Yale Journal of International Law* Vol. 18:415 1993.

[59] The establishment of a UN Protection Force was approved by the Security
Council in Res.743 February 21, 1992 and full deployment was authorised by
Res.749 (April 7, 1992). By April 1992, 8300 members of UNPROFOR were
deployed and, by July 23 of that year, almost all of the 14,000 members were in
place. See above, n.23.

[60] The humanitarian crisis in Rwanda necessitated similar assistance from the
international community in late 1996. It was only when Rwandan refugees
began returning home at their own volition that the UN decided not to deploy
a peacekeeping force.

[61] On April 30, 1947, the Military Staff Committee submitted a report to the SC, in
which it set out principles for implementing a UN force under Art.43. Although
SC members provisionally adopted many of the Articles, the five permanent
members failed to agree on many aspects of the composition and organisation of
armed forces that would be committed under the agreement. See the Report from
the MSC to the President of the Security Council, Yearbook of the UN, 1945 at 403.

consist of troops that have volunteered for such service",[62] the idea being that UN military forces would provide an effective means of deterring aggression and containing humanitarian crises.[63] There is no evidence to suggest that the political will exists to implement any such proposal.

Domestic jurisdiction limitation. Art.2(7) of the UN Charter prohibits the United Nations from intervening in matters which are essentially within the jurisdiction of any state. This limitation does not apply in respect of Chapter VII enforcement action. Domestic jurisdiction has been interpreted restrictively, and Art.2(7) has not impeded the work of the United Nations.[64]

For instance, severe violations of human rights are no longer considered to be solely within a state's domestic jurisdiction and are therefore excluded from Art.2(7).[65] During Security Council debate concerning UN Resolution 688 in the Gulf crisis, it was declared that Art.2(7) does not apply to matters which are not fundamentally domestic, such as human rights protection.[66] Intervention by the international community to prevent human suffering is however, beset with conceptual difficulties. What constitutes human suffering? How widespread would it require to be before intervention would be triggered?

Certainly, the principles of state sovereignty and non-interference in internal affairs are no longer sacrosanct in a world where increased international telecommunications prevent governments hiding behind the shield of the sovereign state.

Force authorised by a competent organ of the United Nations

A state may be authorised by the Security Council to use force, even in circumstances when the use of force would otherwise be illegal. This is the conclusion to be drawn from the Security Council Resolution 221 (1966) which called upon the United Kingdom:

---

[62] Agenda for Peace doc, supra n. 49.

[63] Note, jurisdictional immunity from the International Criminal Court (ICC), for personnel participating in situations authorised by the UN now exists. Exemption applies to personnel from countries who do not accept the jurisdiction of the ICC, *e.g.* the US. See SC Res. 1422, July 12, 2002.

[64] For example, UN SC Res. 687, which was passed in the aftermath of the Gulf crisis, was considered particularly intrusive and authorised the destruction of Iraq's nuclear, chemical and biological weapons. See Lawrence D. Roberts, "United Nations Security Council Resolution 687 and Its Aftermath: The Implications for Domestic Authority and the Need for Legitimacy" [1993] 25, *International Law and Politics* 593.

[65] On human rights as an international concern beyond the domestic jurisdiction of states, see M. N. Shaw *International Law*, (4th ed., 2001), p.202.

[66] See UN Doc.S/PV 2982 at 58 (1991) (providing text of the Resolution debates).

"to prevent by the use of force if necessary ... vessels reasonably believed to be carrying oil destined for Rhodesia, and ... to arrest and detain the tanker known as the Joanna V upon her departure from Beira in the event her oil cargo is discharged there."[67]

Apparently, as Art.42 authorises the Security Council to use force in circumstances where force would normally be illegal, the Security Council can authorise states to do likewise.

JUS IN BELLUM

In the event of states' turning from the procedures prescribed by international law for the settlement of their disputes, hostilities may occur. However, there still exist rules which states are required to respect—*jus in bellum*. These fall into two categories— those relating to the actual conduct of hostilities, and those which afford a minimum protection to the individual (humanitarian law). The former are to be found principally in the Hague Conventions 1899 and 1907 while the 1949 Four Geneva Conventions ("Red Cross") and two additional protocols (adopted in 1977) comprise the latter.

Conduct of armed conflict

Declarations of war have ceased to be the norm. The UN Charter does not distinguish between war and other modes of armed force, nor do the Geneva Conventions, and the 1977 Protocols, and the expression "armed conflict" is today frequently employed. However, a characterisation of the nature of the conflict may be important for neutral states and determining the status of aliens.

The promulgation of the *Lieber Code*[68] in 1863 by President Lincoln marks the first official statement on the laws relating to the conduct of hostilities. The Code, although originally adopted by the President for application during the American Civil War, continued to govern United States practice for some 50 years, as well as influencing the conduct of other states. The Code served as a blueprint for the Brussels Conference when considering the law of land warfare. The Declaration emanating from that Conference in 1874 was never ratified, but its importance is evident in its contribution to the 1899 International Convention with respect to the Laws and Customs of War on Land[69] and the subsequent 1907

---

[67] S.C.O.R., 21st year, *Resolutions and Decisions*, p.5; 5 I.L.M. 534 (1966).
[68] Called after its principal author, Professor Francis Lieber.
[69] The Hague, July 29, 1899; T.S. 11 (1901); Cd.800.

Convention concerning the Laws and Customs of War on Land[70] and the regulations attached thereto. These constitute the core rules on the conduct of armed conflict in contemporary international law, and are recognised as customary international law.[71]

Essentially, the law restricts the ways of injuring the enemy by prohibiting unnecessary calculated suffering by the employment of arms, projectiles, or materials.

The Hague Conference of 1899 adopted two Conventions relating directly to the conduct of war and forbidden weapons,[72] and a number of Declarations outlawing the discharge of projectiles and explosives from balloons, the use of asphyxiating gases and expanding bullets.

A further 13 Conventions were adopted at the 1907 Hague Conference. These related, *inter alia*, to the opening of hostilities, the rights and duties of neutral powers, the conversion of merchant ships into warships, the laying of automatic submarine contact mines and bombardments by naval forces in time of war.[73] The only Convention which was not ratified was the 12th, on the establishment of an International Prize Court.

In addition to the foregoing, subsequent attempts at international regulation include a Protocol (Geneva)[74] in 1925, forbidding the employment of asphyxiating, poisonous or other gases as well as bacteriological methods of warfare; a 1972 Convention,[75] prohibiting the development, production and stockpiling thereof; a 1980 Convention, prohibiting and restricting the use of certain conventional weapons deemed to be "Excessively Injurious or to have Indiscriminate Effects",[76] and a 1993 Convention on the Prohibition of the Development, Production, Stockpiling and Use of Chemical Weapons and On Their Destruction.[77] The Chemical Weapons Convention is the first disarmament agreement negotiated within a multilateral framework which provides for the elimination of chemical weapons under the control of an international agency.[78]

---

[70] The Hague, October 18, 1907; T.S. 9 (1910); Cd.5030.
[71] For a synopsis of the laws of war, see, Jochnick and Normand, "The Legitimisation of Violence: A Critical History of the Laws of War" (1994) 35 *Harvard International Law Journal* 1.
[72] Hague Conventions I and II.
[73] Hague Conventions III, V, VII, VIII and IX.
[74] Geneva, June 17, 1925; T.S. 24 (1930) Cmd.3604.
[75] London, Moscow and Washington, April 10, 1972; T.S. 11 (1976) Cmnd.6397.
[76] Geneva, October 10, 1980; 19 I.L.M. 1523 (1980); Misc. 23 (1981) Cmnd.8370.
[77] January 13, 1993, 32 I.L.M. 800 (1993). In force as of April 29, 1997.
[78] The Convention establishes a permanent agency, the Organisation for the Prohibition of Chemical Weapons, which will have its seat in the Hague.

In autumn of 2001, the second meeting of the Review Conference to look at ways of strengthening the 1975 Biological Weapons Convention took place.[79] A major problem in respect of this convention is the absence of monitoring compliance, and indeed what compliance mechanisms should be established.

International efforts have concentrated on tackling the devastating effects of landmines.[80] It is estimated that 25,000 people are maimed or killed by a landmine each year; most are civilian women and children working and playing in fields. Some 100 million mines lie buried or hidden in over 62 countries and remain virtually undetectable because they contain no metal. The United Nations has estimated that present landmine areas would take 1,000 years to clear, which does not take into account areas currently being mined. An inter-governmental review conference was convened in May 1996 in Geneva to amend the landmines protocol to the 1980 UN Convention on Prohibition on the Use of Certain Conventional Weapons Which May Be Deemed to be Excessively Injurious or to Have Indiscriminate Effects, known more simply as the UN Inhumane Weapons Convention.[81]

Intergovernmental negotiations culminated in the 1997 Convention on the Prohibition on the Use, Stockpiling, Production and Transfer of anti-personal (AP) mines and on their destruction (the OTTAWA Convention). The Ottawa Convention prohibits the use of AP landmines and the gradual destruction of stockpiles and mines already in the ground. The Treaty entered into force on March 1, 1999. All types of conflict are covered, civil war and international, this is in recognition of the increasing use of land mines in civil wars (amendment to Protocol II of the 1980 Convention).[82]

---

[79] The Conference was adjourned on December 7, 2001.

[80] In 1993, the UN GA unanimously adopted a resolution calling for a moratorium on the export of landmines A/Res/48/75K, November 1993. Other resolutions passed by the UN in 1993 were, *inter alia*—strengthening of UN assistance to mine clearance efforts (A/Res/48/7) and additional protection of children against the effects of mines (A/Res/48/157).

[81] There are four Protocols to the Convention. Protocol II, which deals with Prohibitions or Restrictions on the Use of Mines, Booby Traps and Other Devices, was reviewed at the conference in 1996 and amended on May 3, 1996.

[82] The Organisation of American States (OAS) also adopted a resolution which provides for the establishment of a continent-wide zone free of all landmines at its 26th General Assembly in Panama City in June 1996. The resolution asks states to declare a moratorium on the production, use and transfer of all anti-personnel mines and to ratify the 1980 UN Convention on Certain Conventional Weapons and the amended Protocol. It further provides for the opening of a register at the organisation's General Secretariat to record information on existing stocks and the mine-clearing situation.

NUCLEAR WEAPONS

The advent of nuclear weapons added a new dimension to the use of force, and for some 20 years, international relations, especially between the United States and the USSR, were dominated, albeit with varying emphasis, by arms limitation talks. The breakup of the Soviet Union and the emergence of other powers with a nuclear potential, for example India and Pakistan, highlights the need for a new multilateral arms control agenda.

Major agreements on nuclear weapons

Multilateral

Limited Test Ban Treaty (LTBT) 1963.[83] This treaty prohibits nuclear tests in the atmosphere, in outer space and underwater. Also prohibited is any such explosion by a state in any other environment if that would result in the presence of radioactive debris outside its territory.

Treaty on the Non Proliferation of Nuclear Weapons (Non Proliferation Treaty) 1968.[84] Under this treaty the "nuclear weapons parties" undertake not to transfer to any recipient nuclear weapons or devices, or to assist any "non-nuclear weapon State" to manufacture, acquire or control such weapons or devices. "Non-nuclear weapon parties" undertake corollary obligations.

Treaty for the Prohibition of Nuclear Weapons in Latin America 1967 and Additional Protocols I and II.[85] The treaty establishes Latin America as a deneutralised region. Protocol I requires states from outside the region to apply the treaty to territories within the region for whose international rules they are responsible and Protocol II requires states with nuclear weapons to respect the deneutralised status of the region.

Strategic Arms Limitation Talks (SALT I). The Strategic Arms Limitation Talks held between 1969 and 1972 produced a number of agreements, namely the 1971 Agreement on Measures to Reduce the Risk of Outbreak of Nuclear War (the Accidents Agreement), the 1971 Agreement on Measures to Improve the Direct Communications Link (the Hot-Line Upgrade Agreement), and the 1972 Treaty on the Limitation of Anti-Ballistic Missile Systems (ABM). The SALT II negotiations did not prove so

[83] 480 U.N.T.S. 43; U.K.T.S. 3 (1964) Cmnd.2245; 14 U.S.T. 1313.
[84] 729 U.N.T.S. 161; U.K.T.S. 88 (1970) Cmnd.4474; U.S.T. 483; 7 I.L.M. 809 (1968).
[85] U.K.T.S. 54 (1970) Cmnd.4409; 6 I.L.M. 533–534 (1967).

fruitful. Only one treaty was produced, namely the 1979 Treaty on the Limitation of Strategic Offensive Arms and this was never ratified by the United States.

The 1980s witnessed the initiation of new talks—the Strategic Arms Reduction Talks (START) and Reduction of Intermediate-Range Nuclear Forces (INF) and treaties were signed respectively in 1987 by Presidents Reagan and Gorbachev and in July, 1991 by Presidents Bush and Gorbachev. The emphasis is now more on reduction than elimination. On May 24, 2002, the US President, George Bush, and the Russian President, Vladimir Putin, signed a Nuclear Arms Reduction Treaty (the Moscow Treaty). The Treaty is designed to substantially reduce deployed, strategic, nuclear warhead arsenals by December 31, 2012.

A problem the international community has agreed to tackle is the illicit trafficking in small arms and light weapons. What essentially, has been agreed is an action plan following an International Conference, held under the auspices of the United Nations, in July, 2001. The plan envisages the strengthening of export controls and embargo enforcement, and the criminalisation of the illegal manufacture, possession and trade of these weapons.

A comprehensive Nuclear Test Ban Treaty was opened for signature in September, 1996 after it received majority support in the General Assembly. The Treaty seeks to impose an international ban on all nuclear testing. It remains doubtful, however, if this treaty will ever become international law, due to India and Pakistan's refusal to sign. It is a condition of the treaty that all 44 states known to possess nuclear reactors sign before it can become law.[86] The International Court of Justice considered the legality of the use of nuclear weapons in 1996. In an Advisory Opinion on the Legality of the Threat or Use of Weapons, the Court expressed the view that "[T]here is in neither customary nor conventional international law any specific authorisation of the threat or use of nuclear weapons."[87] The court could not reach a definitive conclusion on the use of nuclear weapons in self-defence but observed that the requirements of a lawful self-defence would have to be met, for example proportionality. Nor could the Court conclude, definitively that the use or threat of nuclear weapons could be legitimately used in the extreme circumstances of self-defence if the very survival of the state were at stake. However, it found, unanimously, that an obligation did exist to negotiate, in good faith, and also bring to a conclusion those negotiatins that would lead to nuclear disarmament under strict and effective international control.

---

[86] Annex 2; for full text, see 35 I.L.M. 1439 (1996).
[87] Re UN General Assembly Res. 49/75K. See 35 I.L.M. 809 (1996).

HUMANITARIAN LAW

The first expression of protection for the individual involved in armed conflict was the 1864 Geneva Convention for the Amelioration of the Condition of the Wounded and Sick of Armed Forces in the Field.[88] However, contemporary humanitarian law is contained in the four 1949 Geneva Conventions and the two 1977 Protocols,[89] thereto which are now regarded as customary international law. Sick, wounded and shipwrecked military personnel are afforded protection by Conventions I and II, the third Convention sets out the minimum treatment to be afforded to prisoners of war, while the fourth articulates the protection of civilian persons (this represented an advance, in that earlier protection to civilians had been relatively limited, being contained in the Hague Regulations and customary international law). The Geneva Conventions originally applied only to all international armed-conflict situations, but this definition was extended in 1977 to include wars of "self-determination" (Protocol I) and victims of "non-international armed conflicts" (Protocol II). The latter builds on Art.3, which is common to all four Conventions, and provides that certain minimum provisions apply in "armed conflict not of an international character." Specifically excluded are instances of "internal disturbances and tensions, such as riots, isolated and sporadic acts of violence and other acts of a similar nature."[90]

Mention should also be made of the Convention for the Protection of Cultural Property in the event of Armed Conflict, adopted in 1954,[91] which aims at protecting cultural objects and religious places, as well as objects designated vital to the survival of the civilian population—drinking-water supplies, foodstuffs, agricultural areas for production thereof, and irrigation works (provided they are not used exclusively by the armed forces or in furtherance of military action).

Spies and mercenaries are denied the general protection which is enjoyed by either prisoners of war or combatants. Mercenaries are those who sell their fighting services for personal gain, and their recruitment is deemed to be contrary to international law—see, for example the Declaration on Principles of International Law Concerning Friendly Relations and Co-operation Among States in Accordance with the Charter of the United Nations 1970, and Art.18 of the International Law Commission's Draft Code of Crimes against the Peace and Security of Mankind 1990.

---

[88] Geneva, August 22, 1864; 129 C.T.S. 361; 55 B.F.S.P. 43.
[89] 75 U.N.T.S. 31; U.K.T.S. 39 (1958) Cmnd.550; 16 I.L.M. 1391 (1977).
[90] *ibid.*, Art.1(2).
[91] The Hague, May 14, 1954; 249 U.N.T.S. 215; Misc.6 (1956) Cmd.9837.

Contracting Parties to the Four Geneva Conventions and the additional Protocols are under a duty "to respect and to ensure respect" for the provisions contained therein "in all circumstances." Art.8 of the International Criminal Court Statute defines a grave breach of the Geneva Convention of "12 August 1949" as a war crime over which the court has no jurisdiction. Committing rape, sexual slavery, enforced prostitution and forced pregnancy, or any other forms of sexual violence, is now also characterised as a grave breach of the Geneva Conventions.[92]

International Red Cross

Any survey of humanitarian law would be incomplete without a mention of the International Red Cross. The International Red Cross is made up of the International Red Cross Committee (ICRC) national Red Cross Societies and a co-ordinating body, the League of the Red Cross. The ICRC, which each of the Geneva Conventions recognise as "an impartial humanitarian body" has been responsible for developing much of the substantive humanitarian law. The ICRC still has a role in contemporary international society. Principles of humanitarian law in armed conflict are often violated, for example the crisis in the former Yugoslavia.[93] The depth of civilian suffering in recent conflicts has highlighted the need for greater protection of individuals caught up in armed conflict. An international conference was convened in Geneva in September, 1993, specifically to discuss ways to protect war victims caught up in armed conflicts.[94] The Declaration adopted at the conference condemned, *inter alia*, violations of international humanitarian law and called for the establishment of an intergovernmental group of experts to "study practical means of promoting full respect for and compliance with that law . . .".[95]

---

[92] Art.8(2)xxii.
[93] One prominent member of the ICRC concluded that "in this conflict (the former Yugoslavia) international humanitarian law is a dead letter. Unacceptable practices are going on, including mass expulsion and the concentration of people in camps based on their ethnic origin." Pierre-Andre Conod, Chief Delegate of the International Committee of the Red Cross.
[94] International Conference for the Protection of War Victims: Declaration for the Protection of War Victims 33 I.L.M. 297 (1994).
[95] *ibid.* at 302. The Vienna Declaration on Human Rights (1993) also confirmed that "effective international measures to guarantee and monitor the implementation of human rights standards should be taken in respect of people under foreign occupation, and effective legal protection against the violation of their human rights should be provided, in accordance with human rights norms and international law." 32 I.L.M. 1661 (1993) at para.3 for the text of the declaration.

73

CONCLUSION

Force, save in the accepted exceptions acknowledged by international law, is prohibited by contemporary international law. A resort to force in other circumstances is to turn from law to an alternative, which, if states are to co-exist and to continue to meet, is untenable.

12. ARBITRATION AND JUDICIAL SETTLEMENT OF INTERNATIONAL DISPUTES

States are under an obligation to "settle their international disputes by peaceful means in such a manner that international peace and security, and justice, are not endangered".[1] However, states are always reticent to submit disputes to independent, impartial adjudication and have always been particularly reticent to agree *in advance* to the compulsory jurisdiction of an independent judicial body. The majority of inter-state disputes—that is, "a disagreement on a point of law or fact, a conflict of legal views or of interests between two persons" (that is, international persons)[2]—are settled by direct negotiation. Negotiation is the primary vehicle for attaining settlement on the international scene, as peaceful co-existence and conciliation are seen as being more important than the characterisation of one state as "guilty"

---

[1] Art.2(3) of the UN Charter—also recognised as a rule of customary international law. See also Art.33 of the UN Charter; 1982 Manila Declaration on the Peaceful Settlement of International Disputes; 21 I.L.M. 449 (1982).

[2] *Mavrommatis Palestine Concessions Case* P.C.I.J. Ser.A, No.2 at 11–12 (1924).

and another as "innocent". The obligation to enter into negotiation received judicial support in the *North Sea Continental Shelf
Case*,[3] when the International Court of Justice declared that:

> "... parties are under an obligation to enter into negotiations
> with a view to arriving at an agreement . . .; they are under
> an obligation so to conduct themselves that the negotiations
> are meaningful, which will not be the case when either of
> them insists upon its own position without contemplating
> any modification of it."[4]

However, negotiations "do not of necessity always presuppose a
more or less lengthy series of notes and dispatches; it may suffice
that a discussion has been commenced, and . . . a deadlock is
reached, or if finally a point is reached at which one of the Parties
definitely declares himself unable, or refuses, to give way."[5]

Negotiation may be required by international agreements
before other settlement procedures may be attempted. Other
methods involving the participation of a third party, that is a
state, a group of states or an individual, may be utilised if the
states in dispute consent. Such methods include good offices, conciliation, mediation and commissions of inquiry.[6]

Good offices

A third party may bring the disputing states to the negotiating
table and may suggest the general framework for producing a
settlement.

Mediation

The mediator may be active in attempting to reconcile the positions and claims of the respective interested parties. Mediation
has been employed in a number of instances, including the dispute between Chile and Argentina with regard to the Beagle
Channel; in former Yugoslavia, leading ultimately to the conclusion of the Drayton/Paris agreement; and in respect of Kosovo.
Suggestions of the third party do not have binding effect.

Conciliation

The task of a conciliation Commission is to examine the claims of
the parties and make proposals to them for a friendly solution. If

[3] I.C.J.Rep. 1969 3.
[4] *ibid*. at 47.
[5] *Mavrommatis Palestine Concessions Case*, above, n.2 at 13.
[6] All such methods are identified in Art.33, of the UN Charter.

agreement is not reached, the Commission produces a report containing observations, conclusions and recommendations. The Commission's findings or proposals are not binding upon the parties.

Commission of Inquiry

The primary function of a Commission of Inquiry is to establish the facts pertaining to the dispute, for example by the hearing of witnesses or visiting the area where the alleged breach of international law is said to have occurred. Dispute settlement may also be initiated either or in or by international organisations, for example as the Security Council of the United Nations did in 1982, when a fact-finding commission was established following an attempted coup in the Seychelles. Specialised agencies of the United Nations, such as the International Labour Organisation (ILO)[7] and the International Civil Organisation (ICAO)[8] have also initiated inquiries. A Commission of Inquiry refers to a type of international tribunal introduced by the Hague Convention.[9]

Although the success of these methods cannot be denied, it is only with arbitration and judicial settlement that adjudication is done in accordance with legal principles and an award made which is accepted as binding on the contesting parties.

ARBITRATION

The International Law Commission defined arbitration as "a procedure for the settlement of disputes between States by a binding award on the basis of law and as a result of an undertaking voluntarily accepted."[10]

The essential difference between arbitration and judicial settlement is that arbitration parties are more active in deciding, for instance, the law to be applied and the composition of the tribunal, whereas parties submitting to judicial settlement must accept an already constituted tribunal with its jurisdictional competence and procedure laid down in statute. Arbitration allows parties a degree of flexibility which is denied to them in judicial settlement.

---

[7] In respect of labour conventions.

[8] *e.g.* in respect of the shooting down of a South Korean aircraft over Soviet territory, KE007 incident 1093.

[9] See the Hague Convention for the Pacific Settlement of Disputes (1899), Arts 9–14; U.K.T.S. 9 (1901) Cd.798; see also the 1907 Hague Convention for the Pacific Settlement of Disputes 54 L.N.T.S. 435; U.K.T.S. 6 (1971) Cmnd.4575.

[10] Y.B.I.L.C. 1953 11 at 202.

The idea of entrusting an impartial authority with finding a legally based solution to international disputes is an old one and examples of arbitration settlement were evident in ancient Greece, China and amongst Arabian tribes. However, the modern history of arbitration and the revitalisation of an interest in arbitration as a mode of settlement is traced from the 1794 Jay Treaty between the United States and Great Britain. That Treaty provided for the establishment of three mixed Commissions to which both states nominated an equal number of members, presided over by an umpire. Although, strictly speaking, the Commissions were not organs of third party adjudication, they were intended to function to some extent as tribunals, for example the Commissions were to decide for themselves whether a claim fell within their jurisdictional competence. Throughout the nineteenth century, arbitration was frequently utilised, with each party to the dispute nominating two representatives to serve on the tribunal. In 1871, under the Treaty of Washington, whereby the United States and Britain agreed to submit to arbitration alleged breaches of neutrality by Britain during the American Civil War, it was provided that, while the United States and Britain were to nominate a member of the tribunal of five, so also were Brazil, Italy and Switzerland. The nomination and involvement of three independent states was an innovation and the *Alabama Claims Arbitration*[11] heralded an increasing utilisation of arbitration, as many treaties provided for recourse to arbitration in the event of a dispute.

The 1899 Convention on the Pacific Settlement of International Disputes[12] adopted by the First Hague Peace Conference, marked a new era in arbitration settlement with the Convention providing for the creation of a Permanent Court of Arbitration. In 1907 following a Second Hague Conference, a further Convention was adopted revising its predecessor, but maintaining the Court.[13]

The Permanent Court of Arbitration, established in 1900, began functioning in 1902. It is still in existence, but it is *neither* a court *nor* a permanent institution. It is rather a panel of some 300 persons (four nominated by each Contracting Party to the 1899 and 1907 Conventions) from whom states may select one or more arbitrators to constitute a tribunal for the settlement of a particular dispute. Only the Bureau of the Court, which acts as a registry, is permanent. What was established in 1899 was

---

[11] Moore, 1 Int.Arb. 495 (1872).
[12] U.K.T.S. 9 (1901) Cd.798.
[13] U.K.T.S. 6 (1971) Cmnd.4575.

essentially a machinery to call tribunals into being. Since its inception, the Court has provided the mechanism for the hearing of over 25 cases, including some of considerable importance, for example the *Island of Palmas Case*.[14]

Arbitration presupposes and depends upon the willingness of the states involved to submit to adjudication and their desire to reach a settlement. A state is not required to submit a dispute to arbitration. Consent is a prerequisite. Consent can be on an ad hoc basis, as in the *Canada/France Maritime Delimitation Case*[15] and the *Guinea/Bissau Maritime Delimitation Case*.[16] The identity of the arbitrators, the formulation of the question to be submitted to the tribunal, the rules of law to be applied and the time limit within which an award must be made must also be mutually agreed upon by the states concerned. Such issues are spelt out in a special agreement between the parties, known as the *Compromis*. The functioning of the Permanent Court therefore presupposes that the states not only have a desire to reach a settlement, but that they reach agreement on the issues which are the content of the *Compromis*.

Model rules on arbitration procedure, which were adopted by the 1899 Convention, were considerably revised in 1907. Arbitration agreements may refer to these, while others may refer to the General Act on the Pacific Settlement of International Disputes adopted under the auspices of the League of Nations in 1928 and revised by the United Nations in 1949.[17] "Model Rules on Arbitral procedures" were submitted by the International Law Commission to the General Assembly and adopted in 1958. Normally awards of arbitration tribunals are binding and the *Compromis* will expressly provide for this.[18]

Compliance with the arbitration awards has been high. Rejection of an award has only occurred when the tribunal has allegedly exceeded its jurisdiction or has been guilty of a manifest procedural error.

---

[14] 2 R.I.A.A. 829 (1928). An example of dispute settlement via the Permanent Court of Arbitration, is that between Eritrea and the Yemen on questions of territorial sovereignty and delimination of maritime boundaries; see Permanent Court of Arbitration (PCA): Eritrea–Yemen Arbitration (first stage: territorial sovereignty and scope of dispute) [October 9, 1998] 40 I.L.M. 900 (2001) Permanent Court of Arbitration (PCA): Eritrea–Yemen arbitration (second stage: maritime delimitation) [December 17, 1999] 40 I.L.M. 983 (2001).

[15] 31 I.L.M. 1145 (1992).

[16] 77 I.L.R. 636.

[17] 71 U.N.T.S. 101.

[18] A dispute may be referred to arbitration for an advisory report, in which case the parties to the dispute will normally be charged with putting that report into effect.

The use of arbitration as a medium of dispute settlement declined, especially as disputes between states and treatment of aliens were increasingly solved by a "lump sum settlement agreement".[19] Arbitration has continued to be employed,[20] for example the Convention on the Settlement of Investment Disputes between States and Nationals of Other States 1965[21] makes available conciliation and arbitration procedures for the settlement of cases between Contracting Parties and companies of the nationality of a Contracting Party when both sides consent, see also the Iran/United States Claims tribunal, established in 1981.[22] In 1996, the UN Compensation Commission (the UNCC) delivered its first decision concerning the corporate–governmental claims in the Iraq–Kuwait conflict. The UNCC specifically dealt with the costs to Kuwait of extinguishing the fires started by Iraqi troops in Kuwait's oilfields during the Gulf crisis.[23]

Representatives from a third of the world's countries have sat on the UNCC's governing Council and all decisions have been adopted by consensus.[24]

Only with the establishment of a judicial organ by and through the League of Nations[25] was there created a permanent international judicial institution, that is, a court in the real sense of the term, ready to function at any time. There was established an international tribunal of a corporate character before which a state could, by unilateral application, bring a dispute against another state calling upon it to appear before the Court, without the need for prior agreement to be reached on the composition of a tribunal and the questions to be submitted to it, provided, that is, the other state had accepted the jurisdiction of the Court.

The Permanent Court of International Justice was the forerunner of the International Court of Justice.[26] The Permanent Court

---

[19] Discussed in Ch.8: State Responsibility.

[20] See, for instance, the decision of the Iran–US claims Tribunal: Partial Award Containing Settlement Agreements on the Iranian Bank Claims Against the United States and the International Court of Justice Case Concerning the Aerial Incident of July 3, 1988—35 I.L.M. 553 (1996).

[21] U.K.T.S. 25 (1967) Cmnd.3255; 575 U.N.T.S. 159; 4 I.L.M. 532 (1965).

[22] 20 I.L.M. 223 (1981). For background information on these claims, see, David Caron, "The Nature of the Iran–United States Claims Tribunal and the Evolving Structure of International Dispute" Resolution A.J.I.L. 1990 Vol. 84, p.104.

[23] The UNCC was established on April 3, 1991 by UN SC Res. 687 as a subsidiary organ of the UN SC, 30 I.L.M. 846 (1991).

[24] Kuwait was awarded $610,048,547 in December 1996.

[25] The Court was never an integral part of the League of Nations. There was close association between the two bodies, *e.g.* the League Council and Assembly elected the members of the Court and both the Council and the Assembly were competent to request an advisory opinion from the Court.

[26] Both Courts are frequently referred to as the World Court.

of International Justice (PCIJ) sat for the first time at the Peace Palace in The Hague on February 15, 1922. The Court's activities were interrupted by the outbreak of the Second World War and the Court was dissolved in 1946 on the dissolution of the League of Nations.

THE INTERNATIONAL COURT OF JUSTICE

The International Court of Justice is the principal judicial organ of the United Nations and, as such, is an integral part of the organisation[27] with its Statute annexed to the UN Charter. Although favouring the creation of a new Court, the delegates at the San Francisco Conference wished to maintain continuity with the Permanent Court of International Justice and the Statute of the International Court is essentially that of its predecessor. The International Court adopted, without any substantial amendment, the Rules of Court of its predecessor.[28] At the last meeting of the Permanent Court, it was decided to take the necessary steps to ensure the transfer of the archives and effects to the then new International Court of Justice. The judges of the Permanent Court resigned on January 31, 1946, and, at the first meeting of the UN General Assembly the judges to the International Court were elected. The Permanent Court was formally dissolved in April, 1946.

Composition of the International Court

The International Court is composed of 15 judges. The judges, of whom no two may be nationals of the same state, are elected by an absolute majority at separately and, in theory, simultaneously held meetings of the Security Council and the General Assembly.

---

[27] Art.92 of the UN Charter.
[28] The Rules of Court have since been substantially amended and new rules entered into force in September, 1972 and July, 1978. However, the Court in recent years has been looking at ways of improving its working methods and accelerating its procedures. In October, 2001, the Court adopted Practice Directions for use by states appearing before it. This was an innovative step for the Court. It does not involve any amendment to the rules of Court but is designed to address the problem of a growing case load within increasing budgetary constraints. Further measures to streamline procedures have been introduced by way of an amendment to Art.45 para.1 regarding pleadings. A single round of pleadings is to be considered the norm unless necessary in the circumstances of the case (ICJ Press Release 2002/12, April 4, 2002.) Earlier measures include that of April, 1998 and the issuing of a "Note containing recommendations to the parties to new cases" and December 2000 – change to Art.79 regarding preliminary objections and Art.80 relating to counterclaims. These amendments came into effect on February 1, 2001.

In practice, the frequent disagreement and political bargaining over the appointment of judges means the Security Council is aware of what the General Assembly is doing and vice versa. Candidates for election are nominated by the national groups in the Permanent Court of Arbitration or by specially constituted groups for those UN Members who are not represented in the Permanent Court of Arbitration. Persons eligible for election are those "of high moral character, who possess the qualifications required in their respective countries for appointment to the highest judicial offices, or are jurisconsults of recognised competence in international law."[29] Under the Court's Statute, judges are to be elected without regard to nationality and there is no entitlement on the part of any one state to membership. In practice, an equitable geographical distribution is sought and the five permanent members of the Security Council, save China, have always been represented.[30] Judges are appointed for a 9-year term and may be re-elected. To ensure continuity elections are staggered with five judges being elected every three years. A judge who is elected to fill a sudden vacancy holds office only for the remainder of his predecessor's term. The judges elect from amongst their number a President and Vice-president for three years and both may be re-elected.[31] The first woman judge was elected to the Court by the General Assembly and the Security Council in accordance with Art.10 of the Court's Statute. Professor Rosalyn Higgins Q.C. succeeded the previous UK judge, Sir Robert Jennings on July 12, 1995.[32]

A judge may only be dismissed from office when he/she is considered no longer fit to discharge his/her function, and, only then on the unanimous vote of the other judges. This has never happened. During his/her term in office, a judge may not perform any political or administrative function, nor may he/she act as counsel, agent, or advocate in any suit or participate in the decision of a case in which he has represented one of the parties involved. Nevertheless, a judge is not barred from sitting on the bench, even if he/she has previously participated in an international forum when what is essentially the subject-matter of the case was being discussed, for example *Legal Consequences for States of the Continued Presence of South Africa in Namibia (South West Africa) (1971) Notwithstanding Security Council Resolution* 276)[33]—members of the

---

[29] Art.2 of the I.C.J. Statute.
[30] China was not represented from 1967 to 1984, when no candidate was put forward. On November 7, 1984, Ni Zhangyu J. was elected, and currently Shi Jiuyong has been Vice President since February, 2000.
[31] In February, 2000, Gilbert Guillaume (France) was elected president of the Court.
[32] She was re-elected on February 6, 2000.
[33] I.C.J.Rep. 1971 at 16.

bench, including the President, had been members of the Security Council when it had condemned South Africa's continued presence in Namibia. In spite of South African representations, the Court refused to withdraw those concerned.

A judge is not prohibited from sitting in a case in which the state of his/her nationality is a party. The Rules of Court do specify that if the President is a national of one of the parties to a case before the Court, then he/she will refrain from exercising his/her functions as President for that particular case. If a state to a dispute does not have a representing judge, an ad hoc (for that purpose only) judge may be appointed. If the bench includes no judge of the nationality of the parties involved, each of the parties may select an ad hoc judge. An ad hoc judge need not be of the same nationality as the nominating state. Cases which are conducted in either of the Court's two official languages, English and French,[34] are decided by a majority of the judges present. In the event of a tie, the President has the casting vote, which may be different from his/her initial vote. Dissenting judgments and separate opinions are published in full. Cases may be heard by either a full Court (a quorum of nine being sufficient) or by a Chamber of three or more judges constituted for handling a particular case or a particular category of case. The Court's Statute makes provision for the establishment of Chambers.[35] In January, 1982, the Court approved, for the first time, the creation of a Chamber to deal specifically with the dispute between Canada and the United States over the Gulf of Maine area.[36] This procedure has been repeated in the *Frontier Dispute Case (Burkina Faso v Mali)*,[37] the *Land, Island and Maritime Frontier Dispute (El Salvador v Honduras)*[38] and *the Elettronica Sicula S.p.A. (ELSI) (U.S. v Italy)*.[39] The Court has created Chambers specifically to deal with environmental issues. On August 6, 1993 the Court established a Chamber for Environmental Matters pursuant to Art.26(1) of the Statute. The agreement of all parties involved is required before a matter may be brought before the Chambers rather than the plenary court. The Chambers is constituted by seven judges, elected by secret ballot.

Jurisdiction of the court

The Court can hear contentious cases and deliver advisory opinions.

---

[34] A Party may be authorised by the Court to use another language.
[35] Art.34 of the ICJ Statute.
[36] I.C.J.Rep. 1984 at 246.
[37] I.C.J.Rep. 1985 at 6.
[38] I.C.J.Rep. 1987 at 10.
[39] I.C.J.Rep. 1989 at 15.

Contentious cases

Ratione personae (locus standi before the court). Only states have *locus standi* and may be party to a contentious case before the court.[40] In the *Case concerning the Application of the Convention on the Prevention and Punishment of the Crime of Genocide (Bosnia and Herzegovina v Yugoslavia Serbia and Montenegro) (Indication of Provisional Measures in 1993)*,[41] the Court had to consider whether either state had *locus standi* in the action, as the statehood of both countries was in dispute at that time. The court ultimately decided that both were competent under Art.35(2) of the Statute because they were parties to the Genocide Convention, which provides for a reference to the International Court of Justice on disputes arising from the Convention.

All members of the United Nations are *ipso facto* parties to the Court's Statute. A non-UN Member may become a party to the Court's Statute on conditions determined by the UN General Assembly pursuant to a Security Council recommendation. These conditions are (i) an acceptance of the provisions of the Court's Statute; (ii) an agreement to accept and enforce the Court's judgments (that is, an acceptance of Art.94, UN Charter); and (iii) an undertaking to contribute to the Court's expenses as may be assessed by the General Assembly. Nauru and Switzerland are two States which have lodged such instruments of acceptance. (N.B. Switzerland, in a referendun held, in March, 2002, has voted to join the United Nations.)

Access to the Court may also be available to a state which is neither a member of the United Nations nor a party to the Court's Statute, if that state lodges a special declaration with the Court's registry accepting the obligations of the Court's Statute and Art.94 of the UN Charter. A declaration may be either particular or general. A particular declaration accepts the Court's jurisdiction in respect of a particular dispute or disputes which have already arisen. A general declaration accepts the Court's jurisdiction in respect of all disputes, or of a particular class or classes of dispute(s) which have already arisen or which may arise in the future.

A state may be entitled to appear before the International Court of Justice, but no state, unless it has expressed its consent, is required to appear in proceedings before the Court. This was affirmed in the *Case Concerning East Timor (Portugal v Australia)*[42]

---

[40] Art.34 of the ICJ Statute.
[41] I.C.J.Rep. 1993 at 325.
[42] 34 I.L.M. 1581 (1995).

in which Portugal objected to a treaty between Australia and Indonesia. The Court was unable to exercise jurisdiction to adjudicate upon the dispute because Indonesia had not accepted the jurisdiction of the Court.[43] The Security Council can recommend, but only recommend, that disputing states refer to the Court.[44] Such a recommendation does not confer jurisdiction on the Court independently of the wishes of the parties to the dispute. A state must have agreed that the dispute or the class of dispute should be dealt with by the Court.

Acceptance of the Court's jurisdiction may be expressed in different ways.

Article 36(1). Art.36(1) of the Court's Statute provides that the Court has jurisdiction in all cases "which States in a dispute may agree to refer to it and all matters specially provided for in the Charter of the United Nations or in treaties and conventions in force." States need not express consent to the Court's jurisdiction in advance or in any particular form.[45] States may agree by special agreement ("*compromis*") to submit an already existing dispute to the Court and thereby recognise the Court's jurisdiction over that particular case. The Court may entertain the case once the special agreement has been lodged with the Court. Examples of cases which have come before the Court via a special agreement are the *Asylum Case*,[46] *Minquiers and Ecrehos Case*,[47] *Continental Shelf (Tunisia v Libya) Case*,[48] The *Danube Dam Case*[49] and *Kasikili/Sedudu island (Botswana/Namibia)*.[49a]

Forum prorogatum. Occasionally the Court has prorogated jurisdiction. This arises when, at the initiation of proceedings, only one state has expressly consented to the Court's jurisdiction for that particular dispute. The absence of express consent by one party has not acted as an obstacle to the Court being seised of the case, as consent can be implied. A letter from the Albanian Deputy Minister for Foreign Affairs was taken by the Court in the *Corfu Channel (Preliminary Objection) Case*[50] as expressing

---

[43] To do so would have meant the Court's deciding on whether or not the treaty between Indonesia and Australia was lawfully concluded. It was unable to do so given that Indonesia was not a party to the case.

[44] Art.36 of the UN Charter.

[45] *Corfu Channel Case* I.C.J.Rep. 1948 15 at 27.

[46] I.C.J.Rep. 1950 at 266.

[47] I.C.J.Rep. 1953 at 47.

[48] I.C.J.Rep. 1982 at 18.

[49] *Gabcikovo-Nagymaros Project (Hungary v Slovikia)* (1997) I.C.J. 7; 38 I.L.M. 162.

[49a] I.C.J. 1, October 13, 1999.

[50] Above, n.38.

Albania's consent, whilst consent to submit to the Court has been inferred through the acts of a state.[51] Jurisdiction may not be implied, however, from a consistent denial of the Court's jurisdiction.[52]

Prorogatum jurisdiction is rare as states not wishing to submit to the Court's jurisdiction will refrain from behaviour from which consent could be deduced.

Attempts by one state to bring unilateral application proceedings against another state, when the former acknowledges that the latter has not recognised the Court's jurisdiction, have proved unsuccessful. The applicant state, relying on the doctrine of *forum prorogatum*, invites a positive reaction from the respondent state, that is a subsequent acceptance of the Court's jurisdiction.[53]

Jurisdiction is also conferred on the Court by treaties which states have negotiated. Many bipartite and multipartite treaties contain compromissory clauses providing for recourse to the Court in the event of a dispute.[54] Compromissory clauses are found in treaties which are of two types: (i) those designed specifically to promote the pacific settlement of disputes between two or more states and which frequently provide, not only for judicial settlement, but for the employment of conciliation and arbitration, for example, Revised 1928 General Act for the Pacific Settlement of International Disputes 1949[55] and the European Convention for the Pacific Settlement of Disputes 1957[56]; and (ii) those on a particular subject which contain a provision for recourse to the Court in the event of a dispute arising over the interpretation or application of the treaty, for example the Convention for the Suppression of Unlawful Acts Against the Safety of Civil Aviation (the "Montreal Convention") 1971[57] and the UN Convention on the Law of the Sea 1982.[58] For an example of the Court establishing jurisdiction on such a basis, see the *Nicaragua*

---

[51] See *e.g. the Rights of Minorities in Polish Upper Silesia*, P.C.I.J.Rep., ser.A, No.15 (1928); *the Monetary Gold Case*, I.C.J.Rep. 1954 at 19.

[52] See *Anglo–Iranian Oil Co. Case* I.C.J.Rep. 1952 93 at 114.

[53] *e.g. Treatment in Hungary of Aircraft of the U.S.A. Cases* I.C.J.Rep. 1954 at 99, 103; the *Antarctica Cases*, I.C.J.Rep. 1956 at 12, 15.

[54] *e.g.* The *Territorial Dispute Case (Libya v Chad)* 1994 I.C.J.Rep. 6 was referred to the Court under a jurisdictional clause in a bipartite treaty whereas the Prevention of Genocide Case, above, n.41 was brought before the Court under the multipartite Genocide Convention.

[55] 71 U.N.T.S. 101.

[56] 320 U.N.T.S. 243; U.K.T.S. 10 (1961) Cmnd.1298.

[57] U.K.T.S. 10 (1974) Cmnd.5524; 10 I.L.M. 1151 (1971).

[58] 21 I.L.M. 1261 (1982).

Case.[59] Treaties with such compromising clauses are registered with the UN Secretariat, while the Yearbook of the International Court publishes the text of the compromissory clauses.[60]

Article 36(2)—The optional clause. States may accept the Court's jurisdiction by way of a declaration under Art.36(2):

> "The States Parties to the present Statute may at any time declare that they recognize as compulsory *ipso facto* and without special agreement, in relation to any other State accepting the same obligation, the jurisdiction of the Court in all legal disputes concerning:
>
> (a) the legal interpretation of a treaty;
> (b) any question of international law;
> (c) the existence of any fact which, if established, would constitute a breach of an international obligation;
> (d) the nature or extent of the reparation to be made for the breach of an international obligation."

States are not required to make a declaration under Art.36(2).[61] Declarations under Art.36(2) are optional, but once the Court's jurisdiction has been accepted, reference to the Court is compulsory. Such declarations, being unilateral acts, obviate the need for agreement. The effectiveness of Art.36(2) depends on the participation of many states. States have been reluctant to make declarations 64 states have currently made a declaration under Art.36(2). Declarations must be lodged with the UN Secretary-General and copies transmitted to parties to the Statute and the Registrar of the Court. States which have made a declaration accepting the Court's jurisdiction, in principle, possess the right to bring before the Court another state accepting the same obligation, while conversely it has by its declaration undertaken

---

[59] *Case Concerning Military and Paramilitary Activities in and against Nicaragua* I.C.J.Rep. 1984 392 at 429 in respect of the 1956 Treaty of Friendship, Commerce and Navigation. Libya's application to the Court in March was based on Art.14(1) of the Montreal Convention which provides for submission to the Court of a dispute between two or more Contracting Parties which cannot be settled through negotiation. See *Questions of Interpretation and Application of the 1971 Montreal Convention Arising from the Aerial Incident at Lockerbie.* (Jurisdiction and admissability) (1998) I.C.J. 3.

[60] Art.37 of the ICJ's Statute stipulates that in respect of compromissory clauses which conferred jurisdiction on the PCIJ, the ICJ is to be substituted, thus preventing such clauses from losing their effectiveness.

[61] In the *Jan Meyen Case (Denmark v Norway)*, Denmark invoked Art.36(2), the first time compulsory jurisdiction has been exercised in a maritime delimitation case.

to appear before the Court should proceedings be initiated against it. The subject-matter of the dispute must fall within the terms of the acceptance lodged by both parties, as the Court only has jurisdiction to the extent that the declarations coincide. Common ground is not always easy to find, as Art.36(3) provides that declarations may be made "unconditionally or on condition of reciprocity on the part of several or certain states or for a certain time." Reservations are found in most declarations and the Court's jurisdiction over a case is restricted to those disputes that states have not excluded from its jurisdiction.[62] If, for example, State A has accepted the compulsory jurisdiction of the Court as of April 2 and State B accepts the Court's jurisdiction but excludes all disputes relating to incidents arising before May 14, the Court will only have jurisdiction to hear a case arising after May 14. This would be the case regardless of which state was the applicant— that is, if State B in spite of its reservation attempted to bring before the Court a dispute relating to an incident on April 30, State A could rely on State B's reservation to prevent the Court being seised of the case. A reservation of this type is a reservation *ratione temporis*. In the case of *Military and Paramilitary Activities in and against Nicaragua*,[63] the Court held that Nicaragua (whose declaration contains no reservation) was entitled to invoke against the United States the six-month time proviso, contained in the latter's 1946 declaration, stating that the declaration could be terminated, but that termination would only be effective six months after notice of such intention had been intimated. The undertaking to give six months' notice formed an integral part of the declaration, and, accordingly, the 1984 notification providing for immediate effect could not "override the obligation of the United States to submit to the compulsory jurisdiction of the Court *vis-à-vis* Nicaragua."[64] In this context, the Court held that the most important question was whether the United States "was free to disregard the clause of six months' notice which, freely and by its own choice, it had appended to its 1946 Declaration. In doing so the United States entered into an obligation which is binding upon it *vis-à-vis* other States parties to the Optional-Clause system."[65]

The Court refuted the argument advanced by the United States that Nicaragua had not accepted the same obligation for the

---

[62] Hence, the Court found it had no jurisdiction to adjudicate in the dispute between Spain and Canada, because the said dispute came within the terms of the reservation contained in para.2(d) of the Canadian Declaration of May 10, 1994—*Fisheries Jurisdiction Case (Spain v Canada)* I.C.J.Rep. 1998.

[63] Above, n.59.

[64] Above, n.61 at 421.

[65] Above, n.61 at 419.

purposes of Art.36(2)[66] and stated that the notion of reciprocity is one "concerned with the scope and substance of the commitments entered into, including reservations, . . ." and that "reciprocity cannot be invoked to excuse departure from the terms of a State's own declaration, whatever its scope, limitations or conditions." The Court then reiterated the position it had adopted with respect to the effect of reciprocity in the *Interhandel Case*[67]:

"Reciprocity enables the State which has made the wider acceptance of the jurisdiction of the Court to rely upon the reservations to the acceptance laid down by the other party. There the effect of reciprocity ends."[68]

A State may, in other words, invoke a reservation to an acceptance which it has not expressed in its own declaration, but which the other party has expressed in its own declaration.[69]

Reservations most frequently exclude disputes for which another means of peaceful settlement is provided; which arose before a specific date or which relate to a situation prior to that date, normally the date of the state's initial declaration; which arose during or because of hostilities; which arise between certain states, for example as between Commonwealth countries[70]; or which relate to matters falling within the domestic jurisdiction of the declaratory state, as determined by international law[71] or by the declaratory state itself as, for example, expressed in United States' 1946 declaration.[72] Such automatic or self-judging reservations particularly undermine the idea of compulsory jurisdiction. It is possible for a government, relying upon such a reservation, to declare that a question in relation to the subject-matter of the proceedings initiated against it falls within its domestic jurisdiction and thereby seek to deprive the International Court of Jurisdiction. Such a reservation was successfully invoked in the *Certain Norwegian Loans Case*,[73] when the International Court of Justice discussed the French claim and allowed Norway to invoke, on the basis of reciprocity, the automatic/self-judging

---

[66] The US argument was based on the undefined duration of the Nicaraguan Declaration.
[67] I.J.C.Rep 1959 6.
[68] *ibid.* at 23, quoted in the *Nicaragua Case* at 419.
[69] See decision in *Norwegian Loans Case*, I.C.J.Rep. 1957 9; and judgment in *Interhandel Case*, above, n.67.
[70] As in the UK Declaration.
[71] *e.g.* as in Canadian Declaration 1985.
[72] US Declaration, August 26, 1946, 61 Stat.1218; 1 U.N.T.S. 9.
[73] Above, n.69.

reservation contained in the French declaration.[74] Although the Court itself has not pronounced on the validity of such reservations, judges in both the *Norwegian Loans Case* (Lauterpacht and Guerrero JJ.) and the *Interhandel Case* (Lauterpacht, Spender and Klaestad JJ.) have questioned their validity, the principal objection being that they are contrary to Art.36(6) of the Court's Statute, which provides that "in the event of a dispute as to whether the Court has jurisdiction, the matter shall be settled by the decision of the Court." The Court is also prohibited, as an organ of the United Nations, from intervening in matters "which are essentially within the jurisdiction of any State . . ."[75]

Declarations are generally made for a specific period, normally five years, with tacit renewal. Declarations can generally be terminated on notice, taking effect after a specified time or immediately and may also be subject to modification. Ideally, at least from the Court's standpoint, declarations should be for a definite period as a declaration which can be unilaterally terminated at any time provides a state, anticipating a dispute, with the opportunity of denying the Court jurisdiction.[76] Thus, in 1954, Australia withdrew its existing declaration and issued a new one excluding from the Court's jurisdiction any disputes relating to pearl fishing off the Australian coast, the possibility of Japan raising a dispute on such a matter under Art.36(2) having prompted this move, while the United Kingdom narrowed the scope of its declaration so as to exclude an application to the Court in its dispute with Saudi Arabia over the Buraimi Oasis (after the breakdown of the attempted arbitration).[77] A temporal reservation relating to the termination of acceptance cannot operate retroactively so as to disseise the Court's jurisdiction by reserving to themselves the right to remove on notice certain classes of disputes from the Court's competence, for example on April 6, 1984, the United States withdrew from the Court's jurisdiction "disputes with any Central American State or any dispute arising out of or related to

[74] It was also invoked in the *Interhandel Case*, but was not dealt with by the Court, as the case was dismissed on grounds of the non-exhaustion of local remedies; see also *Aerial Incident of July 27, 1955 Case*, I.C.J.Rep. 1960 146. Note American statement in the *Nicaragua Case* that the US did not intend to invoke such a reservation before the Court but that this did not prejudice its right to do so in any subsequent pleadings, proceedings or cases before the Court, above, n.59 at 422.

[75] Art.2(7) of the UN Charter.

[76] See Separate Opinion of Jennings J. in the *Nicaragua Case*, above, at 551 in which he considered the "most striking examples".

[77] See Jennings J. above, n.76; on effect of Reservation 1(b) contained in UK's declaration excluding a dispute which has already been submitted to arbitration by agreement with any States which had not at the time of submission accepted the compulsory jurisdiction of the I.C.J.

events in Central America over a period of two years." The International Court, as already mentioned, found it had jurisdiction as, *inter alia*, the United States could not validly derogate from the time-limit proviso included in its 1946 declaration, namely "this declaration shall remain in force for a period of five years and thereafter until the expiration of six months after notice may be given to terminate this declaration."[78] The UK Government, in its acceptance, reserves:

> "the right at any time, by means of notification addressed to the Secretary-General of the United Nations, and with effect as from the moment of such notification, either to add to, amend or withdraw any of the foregoing reservations, or any that may hereafter be added . . .".

There also exists what is known as a multilateral treaty reservation, the effect of which is to exclude disputes "arising under a multilateral treaty", and require that "all parties to the treaty affected by the decision "be parties to the case before the Court." The US 1946 Declaration accepting Art.36(2) contained such a reservation which the United States invoked before the Court in an attempt to exclude the Court's jurisdiction in the *Nicaragua Case*. The United States accordingly maintained that the Court would only enjoy jurisdiction if all treaty parties (that is, to those treaties being submitted to the Court by Nicaragua—including, *inter alia*, the UN Charter) affected by a prospective decision of the Court were also parties to the case.[79] The Court observed that all the "affected" treaty parties were not only free to invoke Art.36(2) (all having made a declaration) but could avail themselves of the incidental procedures offered by the Court's Statute. The affected states were not left defenceless against any consequences that may arise out of adjudication by the Court, or their needing the protection of the multilateral reservation of the United States.[80] As to the question of which states may be affected by the decision, the Court concluded that this itself was not a jurisdictional problem and that this particular objection of the United States did not constitute an obstacle to the Court's exercise of jurisdiction.

Declarations must be valid at the time of application for proceedings to be initiated. However, the modification or expiry of a declaration once the Court has been validly seised of a case will not deny the Court jurisdiction.[81]

---

[78] The US on October 7, 1985 terminated its acceptance of the Court's jurisdiction under Art.36(2), 24 I.L.M. 1742 (1985).

[79] The affected parties in this instance were El Salvador, Honduras and Costa Rica.

[80] Above, n.59 at 425.

[81] *Nottebohm Case (Preliminary Objection)*, I.C.J.Rep. 1953 111 at 122.

Art.36(5) of the Statute of the International Court of Justice provides that declarations made under the optional clause of the Statute of the Permanent Court of International Justice and still in force are "deemed, as between the parties to the present Statute, to be acceptances of the compulsory jurisdiction of the International Court of Justice for the period which they still have to run and in accordance with their terms." This provision's applicability was discussed at considerable length in the *Nicaragua Case*,[82] as a consequence[83] of the United States' allegation that the International Court of Justice was not competent to hear the case brought by Nicaragua, as the latter had never become a party to the Statute of the Permanent Court of International Justice and, although Nicaragua had made a declaration in 1929 accepting the Court's jurisdiction, no instrument of ratification was received by the League of Nations in Geneva. Accordingly, the American argument was that Nicaragua could not and did not make an effective acceptance of the compulsory jurisdiction of the Permanent Court of Justice, and that the 1929 acceptance could not be said to be "still in force" for the purposes of Art.36(2).[84] The Court responded by acknowledging that although Nicaragua's Declaration "had not acquired binding force prior to such effect as Art.36 paragraph 5, of the Statute of the Court of Justice might produce", the Declaration "could have done so." The Court continued by articulating the nature of the Nicaraguan's Declaration as having a "potential effect which could be maintained indefinitely" because of the fact that it had been made "unconditionally" and was valid for an unlimited period.[85]

The Court, on the basis of the potential effect argument was able to conclude that "Nicaragua's 1929 Declaration was valid at the moment when Nicaragua became a party to the Statute of the new Court; ...".[86]

---

[82] Above, n.59 at 392.

[83] And considered here in some length because, in the Court's words, of the "novelty" of the problem.

[84] Above, n.59 at 400.

[85] The Court illustrated this point by stating that if the declaration had contained a time limitation provision of five years then the potential effect would have disappeared in 1934.

[86] Above, n.59 at 404. Nicaragua ratified the ICJ Statute in 1945 and the Court cited in favour of its conclusion official publications of the Court identifying Nicaragua as having made a declaration under Art.36(2) by virtue of Art.36(5), and the non-registration of any objection by any State to this being the position (pp.411–415). *cf. the Aerial Incident Case (Israel v Bulgaria)* I.C.J.Rep. 1959 at 127 where the issue was whether a declaration that was binding under the Permanent Court of International Justice could be transposed to the ICJ when the state making the declaration was neither present at the San Francisco Conference nor had become a Party to the ICJ Statute of the ICJ until long after the extinction of the PCIJ. The Court concluded that in these circumstances the Bulgarian declaration was not valid.

Reservations apply only to the Court's jurisdiction under Art.36(2). The Court may have jurisdiction over the subject-matter in question by some other means, for example a treaty. The majority of cases come before the Court by means other than Art.36(2). However, two cases in which Art.36(2) formed the basis of jurisdiction were the *Temple Case* (1962)[87] and *Military and Para-military Activities in and against Nicaragua*.[88] The importance of Art.36(2) lies in the fact that it is the only provision which seeks to establish universal compulsory jurisdiction by an international legal body over disputes which arise between states.

Incidental jurisdiction. The Court may be called upon to exercise an incidental jurisdiction, that is, independently of the main proceedings, of preliminary objections; an application to intervene; and interim measures.

Preliminary objections. A party may challenge the Court's jurisdiction. The most common instance is that of preliminary objections raised by the respondent state in an attempt to prevent the Court from delivering a judgment on the merits. The filing of objections suspends the proceedings on the merits (and obviously delays any decision on the merits) and gives rise to independent proceedings pursuant to which the Court will either uphold or reject each objection.

Intervention. A state which is party to a convention, the construction of which is before the Court, but is not a party to the main proceedings, has the right to intervene.[89] Under Art.62 of the Court's Statute, a state which considers it has an interest of a legal nature, which may be affected by the decision in the case, may submit a request to the Court for permission to intervene. It is for the Court to decide upon a request to intervene, for example in 1981, Malta's request to intervene in the case between *Tunisia v Libyan Arab Jamahiriya* was rejected by the Court. The Court considered that the interest invoked by Malta would not be affected by the decision in the case.[90] However, in 1990, Nicaragua was granted permission to intervene with respect to the *Land, Island and Maritime Frontier Dispute* between El Salvador and Honduras,[91] establishing new principles of intervention by third parties. Third parties are in any event, protected by Art.59 of the

[87] I.C.J.Rep. 1961 17—Judgment on Preliminary Objections.
[88] Above, n.59.
[89] Art.63 of the ICJ Statute.
[90] I.C.J.Rep. 1981 3.
[91] *Case Concerning Land, Island and Maritime Frontier Dispute Case (El Salvador v Honduras (Nicaragua Intervention)* I.C.J.Rep. 1992 92.

Statute, which states that "the decision of the Court has no binding force except between the parties and in respect of that particular case." Provided the immediate dispute before the Court does not form the "very subject-matter" of a dispute involving an unrepresented state, the interests of a third state which is not a party to the case are protected by Art.59. This was applied in the *Certain Phosphate Lands in Nauru Case* (*Nauru v Australia, Preliminary Objections*).[92]

Interim measures. Art.41 of the Court's Statute provides that the Court "has the power to indicate, if it considers that circumstances so require, any provisional measures which ought to be taken to preserve the respective rights of either party." The Court can, on the basis of Art.41, indicate interim measures of protection for the purpose of protecting "rights which are the subject of dispute in judicial proceedings."[93] If appropriate, the Court then may call upon the parties to refrain from any acts that might jeopardise the effectiveness of any decision which the Court may make on the request. A request for interim protection is given priority and a decision is reached quickly. Not all requests are granted. The Court will indicate provisional measures if "there is urgency in the sense that action prejudicial to the rights of either party is likely to be taken before a final decision is given."[94] Interim orders may request parties not to take any action that may aggravate the tension between the parties or increase the difficulty of resolving the dispute, for example the *Case Concerning United States Diplomatic and Consular Staff in Tehran*.[95] Interim measures may be indicated to prevent "irreparable prejudice" to the rights which are in dispute as, for example, in the *Nuclear Tests Cases*[96] where the possible effect on Australian and New Zealand territory of radioactive fall-out as a consequence of the French tests, was considered irreparable.[97]

---

[92] 1993, 32 I.L.M. 46.

[93] *Aegean Sea Continental Shelf* I.C.J.Rep. 1976 3 at 9; *Diplomatic and Consular Staff in Tehran* I.C.J.Rep. 1979 7 at 19. *cf. Passage Through the Great Belt Case* (*Finland v Denmark*) *Provisional Measures*, n.94, below, in which the Court was asked by Denmark to adjudicate not on whether there was a basis of jurisdiction but whether or not Finland possessed any *rights* which required protection.

[94] *Passage through the Great Belt* (*Finland v Denmark*) (*Provisional Measures*) I.C.J.Rep. 1991 12 at 17. Although the Court refused to indicate provisional measures the refusal was issued with an assurance to reach a decision on the merits with all possible expedition, *ibid.* at 20.

[95] Above, n.93.

[96] I.C.J.Rep. 1973 99, 135.

[97] Libya on March 3, 1992 requested that the Court indicate provisional measures in order "to preserve the rights of Libya." The Court found by 11 votes to 5 on April 14, 1992 that the circumstances of the case(s) did not warrant indicating provisional measures.

The principal difficulty confronting the Court in respect of interim measures has been that of identifying the conditions in which measures should be indicated before the Court's jurisdiction has been established. Accordingly, the Court will be satisfied that there is at least *prima facie* a good basis for jurisdiction. Interim measures will only be indicated if the Court is of the opinion that it does not manifestly lack jurisdiction. However, such measures are "indicated" only and are not required or ordered. For instance, the Court declined to exercise certain aspects of its jurisdiction in the case of *Libya v U.K.* (the *"Lockerbie"* case) as the Security Council was seized of the dispute at that time and had adopted substantive measures under Chapter VII of the UN Charter.[98] Interim measures were however, indicated in the *Prevention of Genocide Case*, possibly due to the gravity of the Case.[99] Requests for interim measures have to date come only from an applicant state, though they may be requested by the respondent state or by a motion of the Court itself. The granting of interim measures was not a guarantee that the respondent state would comply, for example as in the Tehran Hostages Incident. That was the position until the International Court of Justice made it unequivocally clear, in 2001, that "orders on provisional measure under Article 41 have binding effect."[1] The Court continued that the Order issued on March 3, 1999 "was not a mere exhortation. It had been adopted pursuant to Article 41 of the statute. This Order was consequently binding in character and created a legal obligation for the United States."[2]

The law applied by the court. The function of the International Court of Justice is "to decide in accordance with international law such disputes as are submitted to it"[3] and, in furtherance of its task, the Court applies:

"(a) international conventions, whether general or particular, establishing rules expressly recognized by the contesting States;

---

[98] The Court specifically declined to indicate interim measures of protection. See I.C.J.Rep. (1992) at para.22. It also refused to order interim measures in the *Guinea-Bissau v Senegal Case* in I.C.J.Rep. 64 (1990).

[99] *Case Concerning the Application of the Convention on the Prevention and Punishment of Genocide (Bosnia and Herzegovina v Yugoslavia Serbia and Montenegro) (Indication of Provisional Measures)*, above, n.41.

[1] *LaGrand Case (Germany v United States)* June 27, 2001 (2001) 40 I.L.M. 1069 at para.109.

[2] *ibid.* at para.110.

[3] Art.38(1) of the ICJ Statute.

(b) international custom, as evidence of a general practice accepted as law;

(c) the general principles of law recognized by civilized nations;

(d) subject to the provisions of Art.59, judicial decisions and the teachings of the most highly qualified publicists of the various nations, as subsidiary means for the determination of rules of law."[4]

The Court may also decide a case *ex aequo et bono*—according to the principles of equity—should the parties agree thereto.[5]

The decision. A case may be brought to a conclusion in one of three ways:

(a) at any stage in the proceedings the parties concerned may inform the Court that they have reached a settlement. On receipt of this information, the Court will issue an Order for the removal of the case from its list— as in the *Border and Transborder Armed Actions* (*Nicaragua v Honduras*) *Case*, May 11, 1992;

(b) the applicant state may decide to withdraw and not proceed any further with the case. An Order for the case to be removed from the Court's list will then be made. If the Court is not sitting, the President will issue the Order;

(c) the Court delivers a judgment.

Effect of judgment. "The decision of the Court has no binding force except between the parties and in respect of that particular case."[6] In spite of the absence of *stare decisis* the Court does in fact have regard to previous decisions to substantiate its reasoning for arriving at a judgment. There would have to be good reason, for example the subsequent development of international law, for the Court to depart from an earlier decision if confronted with a similar case.

The Court's decision is binding, final and without appeal.[7] The Court will, however, interpret at the request of either party, a

---

[4] See Ch.2 in which Art.38 is fully discussed.
[5] This provision has never been applied.
[6] Art.69 of the ICJ Statute.
[7] A number of treaties provide that appeal may be made to the Court following a decision, *e.g.* from an organ of an international organisation, *e.g.* Art.84 of the Convention on International Civil Aviation (the Chicago Convention) Cmd.8742 provides for appeal to the ICJ from decisions of the Council of the International Civil Aviation Association.

judgment where there is uncertainty or disagreement as to the meaning and ambit of the Court's judgment. A revision of the Court's judgment may be requested if there should come to light material of a decisive nature previously unknown to both the Court and the party requesting a revised judgment.[8] A revision of the judgment must be requested within six months of the new fact emerging and within 10 years of the delivery of the judgment.

In 1985, the Tunisian Government requested a revision and interpretation of the judgment of February 24, 1982 in the *Continental Shelf (Tunisia v Libya) Case*. This was the first time that the International Court had received a request to revise one of its judgments and only the second time it had been requested to interpret a judgment.[9] The Tunisian request was also the first combined request for a revision and an interpretation.

Compliance with the court's decision. The majority of the Court's judgments have been complied with by the parties. There have been exceptions, for example Albania did not adhere to the Court's order to pay compensation to the United Kingdom for the damage inflicted on the latter's warships whilst passing through the Corfu Channel in 1946,[10] and Iran failed to comply with the Court's decision in the *Case Concerning United States Diplomatic and Consular Staff in Tehran*.[11]

Non-appearance however, presents a problem. There have been a number of cases, particularly in which the respondent state has failed to appear, absenting itself from either certain parts of the proceedings or from the entire case—as did the United States in the *Nicaragua Case*.[12] The Court will proceed with the case if it is satisfied that it has jurisdiction and will eventually issue judgment, though it is likely to be disregarded by the respondent state, as in the *Fisheries Jurisdiction Case*.[13]

---

[8] Art.61 of the ICJ Statute.

[9] The first application for an interpretation was in respect of the judgment given by the Court in the *Asylum Case*, November, 1950. The Court ruled unanimously on December 10, 1985 that the request for a revision of the 1982 judgment was inadmissible and that although the request for an interpretation was admissible the 1982 judgment should be implemented.

[10] *Corfu Channel Case (Assessment of Compensation)* I.C.J.Rep. 1949 244. Compensation was fully paid in 1996.

[11] I.C.J.Rep. 1980 3.

[12] *Nicaragua (Merits) Case*, I.C.J.Rep. 1986 14. Note Security Resol. (UN Docs S/18250 (1986); 25 I.L.M. 1352–65 (1986) and GA Res. calling for "full and immediate compliance" with the Court's judgment. see also *Case Concerning the Maritime Delimitation and Territorial Questions (Qatar v Bahrain)* I.C.J.Rep. 6 1995, in which Bahrain failed to appear, although it did indicate this in advance and submit written pleadings.

[13] I.C.J.Rep. 1974 3.

Advisory opinions

In addition to its jurisdiction in contentious cases, the International Court of Justice is also competent to give an advisory opinion[14] on any legal question at the request of the General Assembly of the United Nations, the Security Council[15] and other bodies so authorised. States are excluded from seeking an advisory opinion, but they may participate in proceedings before the Court.[16] Advisory opinions are not legally binding on the requesting body, though an international organisation may undertake to recognise such an opinion as binding; as such, an advisory opinion is, in theory, a weaker statement of law than a judgment. In practice, however, advisory opinions have been accepted by the requesting body and any other party so affected, and certain advisory opinions have undoubtedly contributed to the development of international law, for example *Advisory Opinion on Reparation for Injuries Suffered in the Service of the United Nations 1949*[17] (legal personality of United Nations), *Advisory Opinion on Certain Expenses of the United Nations*[18] (legitimate expenses of the organisation), and *Advisory Opinion on Western Sahara*[19] (decolonisation) and, more recently, the *Advisory Opinion on the Legality of the Threat or Use of Nuclear Weapons*, which specifically dealt with the issue raised in UN General Assembly Resolution 49/75 K as to whether the threat or use of nuclear weapons is, in any circumstance, permitted under international law.[20] On the other hand, others have been concerned with more specific issues raised by the requesting body. *Applicability of Art.VI, Section 22, of the Convention on the Privileges and Immunities of the United Nations*[21] (first request by the Economic and Social Council of the United Nations), and *Application for Review of Judgment No. 333 of the U.N*,[22] and *Difference Relating to Immunity from Legal Process of a Special Rapporteur of the Commission of Human Rights*. The system of advisory opinions has been comparatively seldom employed, with the International Court of Justice delivering fewer opinions than the Permanent Court of International Justice. It has been suggested that the reason for the relatively low number of advisory opinions is because the

---

[14] Art.65 of the ICJ Statute.
[15] Art.96 of the UN Charter.
[16] Art.66 of the ICJ Statute.
[17] I.C.J.Rep. 1949 174.
[18] I.C.J.Rep. 1962 151.
[19] I.C.J.Rep. 1975 12.
[20] 35 I.L.M. 809 (1996).
[21] I.C.J.Rep. 1989 177.
[22] I.C.J.Rep. 1987 18.

organisations eligible to seek such opinions all employ highly qualified legal advisors.[23]

Role and future of the court

The impact of the Court has been somewhat ad hoc. This is understandable, given that the Court has to wait until it is seised of a case or requested to give an opinion. To encourage states, and in particular, developing states, to seek a solution to their legal disputes through the Court is the declared purpose of the UN Secretary-General's Trust Fund, established in 1989. The Trust Fund makes available limited financial assistance to help defray the cost involved in employing the Court procedures.

The Court's jurisdiction is restricted to legal disputes and Art.36(2) specifically limits the jurisdiction of the Court to "legal disputes", but Art.38(1) of the International Court of Justice's Statute instructs the Court to "decide in accordance with international law such disputes as are submitted to it." However, although the Court has acknowledged that there are limitations on the exercise of its judicial function,[24] no dispute has ever been rejected because it involved non-legal issues. The Court has maintained that to dismiss a case because the legal aspect is only one element of a political dispute would be to impose a "far-reaching and unwarranted restriction upon the role of the Court in the peaceful settlement of international disputes."[25] The Court's decision in finding jurisdiction in the *Nicaragua Case* precipitated the termination of the United States' acceptance of Art.36(2), as that decision represented "an over-reaching of the Court's limits, a departure from its tradition of judicial restraint, and a risky venture into treacherous political waters."[26] In international relations political and legal issues are intertwined and it must be acknowledged that the decision to seek judicial settlement is itself often a political one. The Court refused to deliver an opinion in the *Eastern Carelia Case*[27] which the Permanent Court felt would be tantamount to giving a decision in a dispute.

However, the Court, as a permanent institution, has served as a constant reminder to states that judicial channels do exist through which the peaceful settlement of international disputes may be sought, the Court's procedures and jurisdiction are known to the international community, and the growth in different

---

[23] O'Brien, J. International Law, p.667.
[24] *Northern Cameroons Case* I.C.J.Rep. 1963 15 at 29.
[25] *Case Concerning United States Diplomatic and Consular Staff in Tehran* I.C.J.Rep. 1980 3 at 19 indorsed in the *Nicaragua (Jurisdiction) Case* at 439–440.
[26] Department of State File No.P85, 0009–2151, reproduced in 79 A.J.I.L. 441 (1985).
[27] P.C.I.J.Rep. ser.B, No.5 (1923).

mechanisms which states can employ to settle their disputes is testament to the impact of the Court. However, the International Court of Justice is no longer the only player in the field and there has been a marked growth in the number of permanent and ad hoc international courts and tribunals. These bodies have been established to deal with disputes in specific subject matter frequently limited geographically and temporally, for example the European Court of Human Rights, the Inter American Court of human rights, the ad hoc tribunals on Yugoslavia (ICTY) and Rwanda (ICTR), the Tribunal on the Law of Sea, the dispute settlement procedure within the World Trade Organisation (WTO) and the Permanent International Criminal Court. In the final analysis, the future role of judicial settlement does not lie with the Court but with the states. States must be willing to submit their disputes to independent adjudication and demonstrate a willingness to comply with the Court's decision.

13. CONCLUSION

Students are often disconcerted when confronted with international law. Why? Its character is intrinsically different from municipal law, yet the law student and the trained lawyer are guilty of approaching international law with the prejudices of the lawyer trained to deal with a mature municipal legal system.

Law is most commonly associated with authoritative institutions, possessing the competence to lay down the necessary legal rights and duties for the community. International law does not fit into such a mould. Consequently, to the legally trained, international law may, in character, be confusing and, in effect, disappointing.

The rules of international law are not as readily identifiable and established as those of the municipal legal system. Art.38 of the Statute of the International Court of Justice is only a direction to the Court on how disputes confronting the Court should be tackled. It is not an exhaustive statement on the sources of international law. Furthermore, with respect to one established source, international agreements (international law's nearest equivalent to legislation) the student is confronted with the provision for states to opt out by way of "reservations". The student deals with a legal system which is essentially voluntary in character rather than mandatory. International law is not imposed on states, but has evolved through the concerns of states and is adhered to because of the need for states to co-exist.

In examining international personality, students find that the concept of personality is not static and that any definition must be sufficiently flexible and open-ended to accommodate new entities which may be required to participate on the international plane. In looking at the recognition of states, the student is brought face to face with politics in inter-state relations. The role of politics is something which lawyers must appreciate. Lawyers, however, are guilty of over-emphasising rules of law in interstate relations, and consequently fail to appreciate that states are primarily motivated by politics and that, in international relations, there is, as a norm, more than one acceptable course of action. Lawyers, therefore, must not be blinkered in their approach to international law, but rather must attempt to perceive problems from a standpoint other than that of the lawyer, and try to see, for example, how international law is interpreted by the politician. International law may be utilised by politicians to identify and accomplish goals and is accordingly their "box of tools"[1] which may be used to further a state's national interests. If law will not further a state's interest, then law may be denied any influence. It will not be flouted blatantly, but the state may articulate the issue as exclusively political and thus allegedly incapable of settlement by the application of legal principles. Lawyers must therefore recognise that a decision to initiate legal procedures or legal principles for the settlement of a dispute will be a political decision.

The absence of mandatory sanctions distinguishes international law from municipal law. This should not be seen as a fault or weakness in the international legal system, but rather as a consequence of the intrinsically different character of international law. The overriding aim of international law is to achieve international peace and security not through the characterisation of an alleged offending state as "guilty", but through the promotion of conciliation. Hence, low key negotiations are the principal channels initially utilised in efforts to settle a dispute between states.

Lawyers must appreciate that, although all states on the international scene are in theory equally sovereign, such states do not today share common interests. The number of states is constantly increasing, and a noticeable effect of this consequence has been a questioning and challenging of some of the traditional established rules of international law. International law is not confined to regulating the relations of a homogeneous grouping

---

[1] R. Fisher, "International Law: A Toolbox for the Statesman" (1979) 9 C.W.I.C.J. 3.

of states, but rather is attempting to bring within its ambit a heterogeneous grouping of states which differ politically, economically, ideologically and socially from each other.

The subject-matter of international law is not exhaustively defined and its boundaries are not firmly established. International law is still a young and developing system which is constantly embracing subject-matter which once was considered exclusively domestic.

Why is it that the expectations of international law are higher than the expectations of the municipal law? Why should it be anticipated that international law can prevent all violations of international law when it is accepted, for example, that the domestic criminal law does not prevent all crimes and that the existence of contract law does not prevent contracts from being broken? Lawyers and laymen seem to forget that the municipal law is disregarded every day and yet they base their criticism and scepticism of international law on the fact that international law is broken. They forget that international law itself cannot exert influence independently, but only primarily through the organ of states. It is also forgotten by critics that international law functions very efficiently over a wide range of subject-matter every day and that when violations of international law occur, it is in politically sensitive issues which, consequently, are newsworthy and receive extensive media coverage. Critics of the international legal system *must* see violations of international law in perspective.

To obtain the optimum advantage from a study of international law, students must rid themselves of their preconceived notions about "law". They must refrain from attempting to fit international law into the character of municipal law. If they do not, international law will most definitely be seen to be deficient. Students must also guard against having too high an expectation of international law. International law can only be utilised to the extent that states will allow it to be used: it is dependent upon and not independent of states.

International law can mould behaviour; it should also be dynamic, adapting to, accommodating and responding to different conditions and sets of circumstances. International law should be conceived not only as a system but as a language—a language which may not necessarily solve all international problems but which will rather facilitate the resolution of the issues which confront and concern the contemporary global community —a language which will address the needs, the circumstances and the expectations of all members—men, women and children. Members of the international community need to speak to each other, that is accepted, but to do this there must be a medium of communication—a common language which in its vocabulary includes respect for the rule of law, democracy, justice, and, above all, respect for the human dignity of all individuals, without distinction. The language which is readily translated is international law. What is required is an increasing fluency in international law so that it may be employed to educate and mould the behaviour of those responsible for the policies of states, and those other actors which now feature on the international stage. This is essential if the role, present and potential, of international law in the contemporary global community is to be realised to its maximum.

BIBLIOGRAPHY

General texts

Brownlie, I., *Basic Documents in International Law* (5th ed., Clarendon Press, Oxford, 2002).

Cassesse, A., *International Law* (Oxford University Press, Oxford, 2001)

Evans, M., *International Law Documents* (5th ed., Blackstone Press, 2001).

Harris, D.J., *International Law* (5th ed., Sweet & Maxwell, 1991). (Fifth edition due 1998.)

Henkin, L., Pugh, R., Schachter, O. and Smit, *International Law: Cases & Materials* (West Publishing Co., 1993).

Kindred, Hugh et al., *International Law Chiefly as Interpreted and Applied in Canada* (6th ed., Emond Montgomery Publications Limited, 2000).

McCorquodale, R., and Dixon, M., *Cases and Materials on International Law* (3rd ed., Blackstone Press, 2000).

Merrils, J.G., *International Dispute Settlement*, (3rd ed., Cambridge University Press, Cambridge, 1998)

O'Brien, J., *International Law* (Cavendish Publishing, London, 2001)

Shaw, Malcolm N., *International Law* (4th ed., Cambridge University Press, 1997).

Reference

Encyclopaedia of Public International Law (Max Planck Insitute for Comparative Public and International Law 5 Vol. Consolidated Ed).

Specialised texts

The list of texts identified below should not be treated as exhaustive.

Alston, P. (ed.), *The United Nations and Human Rights: A Critical Appraisal* (Oxford University Press, 1992).

Aust, A., Modern Treaty Law in Practice, (Cambridge University Press, 2000).

Birnie, P.W., and Boyle, A., *International Law and the Environment* (Oxford University Press, 2nd ed., 2002).

Churchill, R. and Lowe, V., *The Law of the Sea* (3rd ed., Manchester University Press, 1999).

Crawford, J., *The International Law Commission's Articles on State Responsibility*, (Cambridge University Press, 2002).

Goodwin-Gill, G., *The Refugee in International Law* (2nd ed., Clarendon Press, Oxford, 1995).

Gray, C., *Judicial Remedies in International Law* (Clarendon Press, Oxford, 1990).

Gray, C., *International Law and the Use of Force*, (Oxford University Press, 2001).

Hargrove, J.L. and Henkin, L. (eds), *Human Rights: An Agenda for the Next Century* (1994).

Higgins, R., *Problems and Process, International Law and How to Use It* (Clarendon Press, Oxford, 1994).

Leigh, M. and Blakeslee, M.R. (eds), *National Treaty Law and Practice* (ASIL, 1995).

Roberts, A. and Kingsbury, B. (eds), *United Nations, Divided World* (Clarendon Press, Oxford, 1995).

Schwebel, S.M., *Justice in International Law. Selected Writings of Judge Stephen M. Schwebel* (Cambridge University Press, 1994).

Steiner, H.J. and Alston, P., *International Human Rights in Context, Law, Politics and Morals* (Clarendon Press, Oxford, 2nd ed., 2000).

Wallace, R.M.M. *International Human Rights, Text and Materials* (Sweet & Maxwell, 2nd ed., 2001).

Journals

There is an increasing number of law journals which focus on specialised topics of international law in addition to those which provide a more general coverage. The following are particularly recommended:

Human rights

Human Rights Law Journal
International Journal of Refugee Law

Use of force

International Affairs
International Peacekeeping
Journal of Armed Conflict
International Environmental Law
Colorado Journal of International Environmental Law and Policy
Harvard Environmental Law Review
Yearbook of International Environmental Law

Journals featuring articles on general issues of contemporary international law

American Journal of International Law
America University Journal of International Law and Policy
Australian Yearbook of International Law
British Yearbook of International Law
Canadian Yearbook of International Law
Common Market Law Review
Cornell International Law Journal
Denver Journal of International Law and Policy
European Journal of International Law
Georgia Journal of International Comparative Law
German Yearbook of International Law
Harvard International Law Journal
International Comparative Law Quarterly
Melbourne Journal of International Law
Netherlands International Law Review
Recueil Des Coeurs
Stanford Journal of International Law
Virginia Journal of International Law
Yale Journal of International Law

Reference materials

International Legal Materials

USING THE INTERNET

International law is particularly well served by the Internet. There is an increasing number of world web sites which a student of international law would be well advised to consult so as to keep abreast of developments in contemporary international society. The sites identified below are merely starting points for further research, and because of this the list has been kept to a minimum, rather than extended. The Kent University web page is a good starting point; as is the United Nations web page, see both below.

WORLD WEB SITES (*N.B.* SITE LOCATIONS ARE SUBJECT TO CHANGE).

Human Rights

http://www.umn.edu/humanrts/index.html

European Court of Human Rights

http://www.echr.coe.int.

United Nations High Commissioner for Refugees

http://www.unhcr.ch/

International Red Cross

http://www.icrc.org/eng

U.K. Foreign and Commonwealth Office

http://www.fco.gov.uk/

United Nations

http://www.un.org

International Court of Justice

http://www.icj.org

Law of the Sea

http://www.un.org/Depts/los/index.html

General international law

http://www.asil.org
http://library.ukc.ac.uk/library/lawlinks/default.htm

INDEX

prohibition, 254–257
regions, 266–268
reprisals, 254, 268
resolutions, 255
retorsions, 268–269
self-defence, 254, 257–260
  anticipatory, 260
  collective, 265–266
Somalia, 264
sovereignty, 264
states, 62
territory, 96
threats, 257
United Kingdom, 257
United Nations, 252, 254–256,
  258–260
United States, 258, 264, 267
veto, use of, 273–274
Yugoslavia, 263, 275

VIENNA CONVENTION, 37,
  230–231, 244–245, 250–251
**VIENNA CONVENTION ON
  CONSULAR RELATIONS**,
  133
VOTING,
  resolutions, 29, 30
  United Nations, 29, 30

WAIVER,
  diplomatic immunity, 130, 134
WAR, 2, 4
  See also HOSTILITIES; USE OF
    FORCE; WAR CRIMES;
    YUGOSLAVIA
  civil, 262–264
  Cold War, 262
  cultural property, 283
  customary international law,
    283
  Geneva Conventions, 283–284

Gulf War, 96, 152, 193, 291
individuals, 283–285
intention, 96
Iran-Iraq war, 262–263
mercenaries, 283
prisoners of war, 283
Red Cross, 284
rules of, 4
self-determination, 283
ships, 153
spies, 283
territory, 96
treaties and conventions,
  283–285
WAR CRIMES,
  Charter of the Nuremberg
    Military Tribunal, 114
  human rights, 225–229
  individuals, 71
  International Tribunal for
    Yugoslavia, 114–116,
    225–229
  jurisdiction, 114
  Rwanda, 227
WRITERS,
  Grotius, 28
  McNair, 28
  sources of law, 27–28
  state practice, 28

YEMEN, 76
YUGOSLAVIA,
  European Union, 79
  human rights, 225–229
  International Tribunal for
    Yugoslavia, 114–116,
    225–229
  peace-keeping forces, 275
  recognition, 79
  Red Cross, 284
  use of force, 263, 275